CONSTITUTIONAL REVOLUTION

GARY JEFFREY JACOBSOHN
AND YANIV ROZNAI

Constitutional Revolution

Yale
UNIVERSITY PRESS

NEW HAVEN AND LONDON

Published with assistance from the Mary Cady Tew Memorial Fund.

Yale University Press books may be purchased in quantity for educational, business, or promotional use. For information, please e-mail sales.press@yale.edu (U.S. office) or sales@yaleup.co.uk (U.K. office).

Set in Scala type by IDS Infotech Limited, Chandigarh, India.
Printed in the United States of America.

ISBN 978-0-300-23102-1 (hardcover : alk. paper)
Library of Congress Control Number: 2019949104
A catalogue record for this book is available from the British Library.

This paper meets the requirements of ANSI/NISO Z39.48-1992 (Permanence of Paper).

10 9 8 7 6 5 4 3 2 1

For Nayeli and Tavo (G.J.)
For my parents—Talia and Zvi (Y.R.)

CONTENTS

ACKNOWLEDGMENTS

THE JOINT WORK ON THIS BOOK BEGAN roughly four years ago, in 2015, at the Law and Society Association Annual Meeting in Seattle. Since then, many professional encounters and conversations with colleagues have challenged our thinking and shaped this book; we owe them all our gratitude.

In particular, we are greatly indebted to Andrew Arato, Joel Colón-Rios, Zach Elkins, Anna Fruhstorfer, Gábor Halmai, András Jakab, David Law, Suzie Navot, Monika Polzin, Zoltán Pozsár-Szentmiklósy, Kim Lane Scheppele, Joshua Segev, and Hillel Sommer, all of whom provided extremely valuable comments on earlier drafts of specific chapters.

Thank you also to Dor Paska for his excellent research assistance and to Ruvik Danieli, who helped with careful editing. Special thanks to Richard McNulty for carefully reading the entire manuscript (numerous times!) and providing very useful feedback.

Parts of the book were presented at academic conferences and seminars. We thank the participants at the University of Milan's "Israel's Constitutional Revolution and Counter-Revolution" lecture (December 5, 2018); the 2018 International Society of Public Law Annual Conference at Hong Kong University (June 25, 2018); and the 2017 International Society of Public Law Annual Conference at the University of Copenhagen (July 7, 2017).

A revised version of some of the material in chapter 2 appeared in "Theorizing the Constitutional Revolution," *Journal of Law and Courts* 5, no. 2 (2014), and in "Making Sense of the Constitutional Revolution," *Constellations* 5, no. 19 (2012). Permission to incorporate this material is gratefully acknowledged.

Above all, we thank our families, for everything.

CONSTITUTIONAL REVOLUTION

1
Introduction

> Revolutions are the only political events which confront us directly and inevitably with the problem of beginning.
>
> Hannah Arendt

ON JUNE 26, 1857, ABRAHAM LINCOLN delivered a speech in Springfield, Illinois, in which he gave voice to themes he would reprise the following year in his famous debates with Stephen Douglas. The speech may be considered the preliminary for that event, since Douglas had spoken in the same place two weeks earlier, laying down rhetorical challenges to which Lincoln felt compelled to respond. One of those concerned the meaning of the Declaration of Independence.

Douglas had aligned himself with Chief Justice Roger Taney in affirming that the founding document was intended only to apply to white people. For both of them, "the authors of that instrument did not intend to include negroes, by the fact that they did not at once, actually place them on an equality with the whites."[1] Lincoln strenuously disagreed, and in his categorical rejection of the idea that an existing state of inequality could be taken to mean that the enjoyment of "certain inalienable rights" did not extend to all men, said of the Declaration's authors, "They meant simply to declare the *right*, so that the *enforcement* of it might follow as fast as circumstances should permit."[2]

That we now must sadly acknowledge the slowness that accompanied the arrival of these circumstances does not diminish the revolutionary significance of the Declaration. The 1776 proclamation did, after all, detail the particulars that served to justify the illegal creation of a new regime. Momentous as this development was, that a political entity's declaration of independence from a governing power culminated in a revolutionary rupture of historic consequence is in itself conceptually unremarkable. Lincoln, however, went on to say: "The assertion that 'all men are created equal' was of no practical use in effecting our separation from Great Britain; and it was placed in the Declaration, not for that, but for future use."[3] It was not needed to substantiate the case for armed revolution; the document's lengthy catalogue of imperial abuses served that purpose very well. With respect to the Declaration's immediate "practical use," paramount were the ending of colonial rule and the commencing of a newly formed polity, both of which arguably required a decisive break with the past in order to confer legitimacy on the constitutional order of the future. Or as the maxim of the ancient Stoic philosopher Seneca put it: "Every new beginning comes from some other beginning's end."

Lincoln's invocation of the Declaration's signature words had as its purpose the same objective that inspired the writing of this book, the enlargement of our understanding of what a revolutionary beginning might entail, specifically the type that involves major constitutional transformation. In Lincoln's rendering, the affirmation of the self-evident truth about human equality may have been unrelated to the illegalities and violence attendant on the colonies' severance from British rule, but its revolutionary significance was nonetheless implicit in the text of the document's opening paragraphs. Thus, the "future use" to which these words would be put was clearly a reference to the efforts succeeding generations would be morally bound to undertake in order to fulfill the promise of the constitutional experiment that had been made possible by violent revolution. Understood in this way, a revolutionary constitutional departure could be conceptualized in a way that did not require for its authentication a blatantly illegal break with a prior regime. It could simply portend the eventual attainment of a substantially different political or social reality, one made possible by the displacement of one constitutional orientation by another.

But American independence *was* achieved through blatantly illegal actions. The illegitimacy of the transference of power from one political entity to another arguably provided a measure of authenticity—actual legitimacy—to the nascent constitutional order, whose framers and defenders could confidently assert that their creation possessed an indigenous identity that would otherwise have been difficult to maintain had their efforts been encumbered by the legalities of colonial authorization. Indeed, imagining an indigenously generated identity that assumes lasting constitutive significance has a distinctly American ring to it, as when in a Fourth of July oration John Quincy Adams proclaimed, "A nation was born in a day."[4] America, he said, "spoke herself into existence as a nation," which for Adams meant that the document signed in Philadelphia in 1787 signified the *legal codification* into existence of the nation.[5]

In the ungainly vernacular of modern legal theorizing, it might be said that the Americans had arrived at a state of constitutional autochthony, a condition in which the authority to rule is ultimately a matter of pedigree, specifically the absence of external agency in determining the arrangements by which a new polity is henceforth to be governed.[6] In this way of thinking about revolutionary transformation, the substance of these arrangements is clearly subordinate to the interruption in legal continuity that preceded the establishment of the constitutional order. Thus, if the principles that for Lincoln figured decisively in shaping the revolutionary significance of the American constitutional experiment had been filtered through a process not ordained by "We the People" but rather by the prior colonial power, their content would not have mattered nearly so much, certainly not in the decisive way Lincoln had imagined.

Such a counterfactual is easy to envision given the more recent real-life examples of a nation's constituent power being exercised under the express authorization of the antecedent regime. Where independence is obtained in accordance with a legally prescribed scenario that culminates in the convening of a constituent assembly whose charge is to draft a constitution for the newly sovereign nation, a question naturally arises about the status of the resulting document: Does it embody an indigenous identity expressive of a revolutionary departure in constitutional development? In Ireland and India, for example, severance from British rule did not follow the eighteenth-century American precedent, in that it came about legally, with the enactment of statutes of independence detailing the path to constitutional autonomy.[7]

In both countries, however, the dominant extant legal theory was, as we shall see, clear in distinguishing autonomy from autochthony. As has been astutely noted, the very legality of the transformations necessitated the contriving of a "benign constitutional revolution."[8] And so we find in the final article of what became the world's longest governing charter that the framers of the Indian Constitution renounced the source of their constituent power. This they did by repealing both the Government of India Act of 1935 and the Indian Independence Act of 1947, the two enactments that had established a lawful framework for composing a constitution for a newly sovereign India. In addition, they violated the terms of the 1947 statute by not submitting the Constitution to the governor-general for his approval. Easy it is, then, to infer that the document's opening words—"We, the people of India"—would likely have invited mockery without Article 395's repudiation of the real immediate inspiration for what transpired in the Constituent Assembly: a statutory grant from an imperial power in a faraway land.

While it can be argued that "there was an extensive debate . . . in the Constituent Assembly, resulting in the Indian Constitution . . . [and] provid[ing] the clearest statement of the country's self-given identity" consistent with orthodox legal theorizing, it was the post hoc removal of these markers of legal continuity that effectively bestowed on this fresh identity whatever revolutionary meaning it had.[9] Thus, to the extent that a constitutional revolution occurred in India, by the logic of this account the evidence for its existence was to be found not so much in the substance of the newly adopted document as in the carefully concocted arrangement through which a break in legal continuity could serve to validate a claim to revolutionary origins. "Since there was no 'revolution,' one had to be deliberately made up in order to secure an autochthonous Constitution."[10] It then follows that the appropriate nomenclature for describing the new constitutional departure that succeeds a revolutionary transition is captured by the term "constitutional revolution."[11]

Our aim is to challenge this sort of thinking about radical constitutional change. We proceed by way of comparative inquiry and reflection to illuminate the concept of constitutional revolution, an idea for which no canonical meaning exists. We offer a clarifying lens for comprehending the type of change that results in substantial departures from constitutional practice and identity. Through this lens, we will see that to confine the meaning of such revolutions to the specific occasion of a constitution-producing political revolution conceals from view the richer possibilities that inhere in a more capacious rendering of the concept. Thus, we question the well-known test for affirming continuity over revolutionary change, according to which "it does not matter how fundamental changes in the substance of the legal norms are if they are performed in conformity with the provisions of the constitution."[12] Much as Lincoln's invocation of the Declaration's famous paragraphs asks us to focus on the profoundly transformative philosophical commitments that defined the revolutionary significance of the American founding, we argue for a broader conceptual understanding of constitutional revolution, one that shifts attention from category-defining questions of process to ones of substance.

Why should this matter? As we begin to elaborate in the next chapter, conventional modes of thinking about revolutionary change have obscured the diverse ways in which fundamental constitutional change occurs. A narrow focus on the activity that culminates in a break in legal continuity leaves us with insufficient analytical resources for recognizing and appreciating the results of this activity, especially since, in this account, the only such activity that carries revolutionary significance is that which occurs outside the parameters of legality. If a certain constitutional change is revolutionary, it must be unconstitutional. If it is a constitutional change, how can it be revolutionary? Seen in this light, connecting the terms "constitutional" and "revolution" leaves us with a curious oddity whose oxymoronic features can easily preclude the kind of serious scholarly engagement that a proper understanding of its meaning should summon.

In this book, we present detailed accounts of some notable examples of major constitutional changes in which conventional expectations about what qualifies as "revolutionary" provide an inadequate basis for accurately describing the transformational significance of what occurred. It is not that those conventional explanations are inapplicable to the phenomenon with which we are concerned, for they do account for a subset of constitutional transformations in which the appearance of a radical separation from past experience may result in the sort of substantial change in constitutional identity that is the hallmark of the thing we are trying to illuminate. In chapter 2, however, we offer a more capacious way of understanding what occurs when the trail of constitutional development diverges from the well-trod path on which a polity's governors and governed are accustomed to traveling. Imagine that the path suddenly veers off in a new direction without any obvious fissure separating the new way forward from the familiar course of the past. Imagine, too, that in finding oneself at this juncture there is nothing particularly jarring to immediately confront the senses; in fact, what lies ahead looks different only if one can anticipate discovering it by continuing down what could very well be a long and winding road. This is the path we follow in this book.

Besides trying to make sense of constitutional revolution as something other than the incongruity that results from conventional thinking about what exactly it is, we hope to demonstrate that the substance of constitutionally inspired change may require an extended period of time for its revolutionary meaning to be realized and certified. The "constitutional moment" has acquired a justifiably accepted place on the time line of groundbreaking change, but to the extent that it may encourage us to expect that a paradigm-altering transformation will be evident in that moment or shortly thereafter, we argue that a realistic accounting may require a more incremental approach that incorporates sensitivity to the ways in which radical change can occur through constitutional channels. As has been wisely noted: "Not only is incrementalism not in tension with transformative constitutionalism, it may even be the most efficient way of securing it. Indeed, the larger the scale of the transformation sought, the larger is the gap between the status quo and the end goal. The sheer impossibility of bridging this gap immediately would give reasons even to the staunchest advocates of the transformation to accept some deferral."[13]

To be clear, Bruce Ackerman, the scholar whose influential work is most closely identified with the constitutional moment, is not wrong when he says, "The moment to begin is when the promise of revolutionary renewal remains alive."[14] What is more, there could be, as he argues, "long-term costs of a short-term failure to act at the moment of revolutionary triumph."[15]

Still, some instances in the diverse pathways of revolutionary constitutional change are unaccompanied by triumphal moments even though they lead to places where momentous change is evident in the transformed landscape of fundamental law. Whether this puts a polity in a better place depends on the substance of the changes wrought.

Our emphasis on substance over process should not, however, detract from the importance of the latter. While not decisive for determining the genuineness of a constitutional revolution, the manner in which such change is brought about can in decisive ways influence the legitimacy and long-term prospects of the substantive transformation. For example, the revolutionary promise that Lincoln saw in the Declaration of Independence was affirmed in the language of the Fourteenth Amendment; as Thaddeus Stevens said in introducing the measure, "I can hardly believe that any person can be found who will not admit that every one of these provisions is just. They are all asserted in some form or other, in our Declaration of organic law."[16] We need not resolve here the much-debated question whether, consistent with Stevens's comment, the amendment's revolutionary bona fides should be questioned, or rather, whether the fact of newly constituting the federal government as the primary guardian of the Declaration's promised rights is reason enough to find in the amended constitutional document a revolutionary transformation.[17] Nor need we weigh in on the contentious matter of whether the irregularities attendant on the adoption of the postwar amendments rendered them constitutionally illegitimate.[18] That they were so held by a large fraction of the people whose behavior they were designed to change doubtless exacerbated the problem of achieving compliance with the directives of amendments whose substance alone provided this population with sufficient justification for sabotage and obstruction. What seems clear, as Sanford Levinson has said, is that "there can be little doubt that the so-called Civil War Amendments . . . partake of at least a limited constitutional revolution."[19]

Changing the substance of a constitutional trajectory through the amendment process may arouse legitimacy issues even in the absence of the irregularities often alleged in connection with the texts adopted in the aftermath of the Civil War. In chapter 3 we show how formal constitutional amendments, implemented in full compliance with prescribed procedure, can at once be profoundly transformative and potentially destabilizing. To illustrate this, we focus on Hungary, where the transformation from communism to democracy was achieved by way of constitutional amendments to that nation's constitution of 1949, or what a leading actor during this time designated a "revolution under the rule of law."[20] After first briefly describing several prominent examples of amendment-induced constitutional transformation—in Chile, Taiwan, Japan, and South Korea—we turn to the Hungarian case as the archetype of a constitutional revolution occurring without the invocation of an extraconstitutional constituent power. Paradigmatic constitutional change enveloped within a facade of legality offers several potential benefits. It allows for constitutional transformation through legal mechanisms while avoiding the risks of a permanent extraconstitutional revolution. It can also enhance the stability and legality of the new order.

Or not. The Hungarian constitutional revolution of 1988–89 suffered from serious legitimacy problems. Within a span of less than thirty years, the country experienced a second constitutional revolution, this time culminating in the entrenchment of a decidedly illiberal and authoritarian regime. It too was brought about through the exercise of the extant amendment process and the preservation of legal continuity, which is to say, a 1949 constitutional document endured two radical transformations before its formal replacement in 2011. This new Fundamental Law was itself subsequently amended several times, the cumulative purpose of which was to extend the reach of the constitutional revolution so as to, in effect, diminish the likelihood of a third such makeover. The path connecting the first of these revolutionary alterations to the second provides historians with much to ponder and debate, including the possibility that, as we surmise in this chapter, the distinctive feature of the first constitutional revolution—its thread of legal continuity—ironically did much to undermine the stability of the constitutional order it produced.

The disturbing developments in Hungary, in which the 1989 "revolution under the rule of law" and its promise of constitutionalism sadly mutated into the lived experience of "constitutionism" (or, as it came to be known, illiberal democracy), have left us with a sobering reminder that constitutional revolutions can take very different paths, not all of which terminate at a better place. If the change that occurs in the sometimes-extended course of these makeovers has the potential to culminate in an altered constitutional identity that represents a troubling deterioration of legal and moral standards, one might hope for a counterrevolutionary force to forestall its realization. In chapter 4 we show what such a force might look like as we consider the resolve of the German Constitutional Court to defend the Constitution's identity against threats—real or imagined—emanating from sources inside and outside the nation's borders.

As is the case in other polities, German constitutional identity is infused with revolutionary meaning, and the country's history provides ample justification for viewing identity as the cornerstone of the ensuing jurisprudential enterprise. This explains why, as one German constitutional scholar has observed, key framers of the Basic Law intended "to deny potential future revolutions their legitimacy (in accordance with the [document's] standards)."[21] The principal instrument for achieving this denial was the eternity clause, which was promoted by some at the Constitutional Convention as essential for "destroy[ing] a revolution's mask of legitimacy."[22] At the time of their adoption, these clauses were clearly designed to preclude the use of constitutional means to extinguish constitutional order. But it was not only painful memories of an earlier national nightmare that eventually set the boundaries for the defense of constitutional identity. The European Union was formed in part to ensure that this nightmare would not reappear on European soil, yet the project of European integration became the focal point for the German Constitutional Court's most intensive exploration of the defensive properties of national constitutional identity. It is also the object of our interest in this chapter; we consider the concept of constitutional revolution through the lens of the landmark *Lisbon* decision in 2009, in which the Court confronted the potentially transformative constitutional effects of elevated submissiveness to the rule-making authority of European institutions.

Our attention to the German Court's *Lisbon* jurisprudence—that part of it that features the guardianship of constitutional identity—leads to a quite mixed assessment. To the extent that the Court's defense of identity recognizes that a fundamental reorientation in constitutional essentials can have revolutionary consequences, and further that these may come about through an incrementally fashioned pathway, it rightly underscores a critical—and we think correct—interpretative strand in the conceptualization of a constitutional revolution. To the degree, however, that this preoccupation with identity is rendered in a manner that is impervious to the dynamic aspect of constitutional identity and that ignores its adaptive potential and hence its significance to the salutary process of nonrevolutionary regime redefinition, the German Court delimits the reach of its extraordinary contribution to constitutional theory and practice.

One place where the dynamic features of constitutional identity have proved important in the narrative of revolutionary constitutional development is India. We use the Indian experience to demonstrate not only that revolutionary action is possible within the constraints of the constitutional order, but also that in certain circumstances, namely, where a formal constitutional change holds out the promise of fundamental societal transformation, it may be indispensable. Consistent with the emphasis on substance over process in our conceptualization of constitutional revolution, the determination of a constitutional amendment's standing as a legitimate or illegitimate exercise of the formal amendment-adopting mechanism depends less on whether it is a genuine expression of the constituent power than on whether it advances or impedes the fulfillment of what Jawaharlal Nehru, in speaking to the Constituent Assembly of the new document's revolutionary objectives, described as "the purpose behind the Constitution."[23] Difficult as it is to disentangle the procedural and substantive strands of fundamental constitutional change, the Indian case suggests that an emphasis on the aspirational commitments embedded in the document will ultimately prove more instructive than a preoccupation with the specific character of the power that framed it.

Chapter 5 touches on several other themes in our understanding of constitutional revolution. As one Indian constitutional scholar put it: "The Indian Constitution was perceived by many in the post-colonial world to be a revolutionary document."[24] Emerging from the lengthy debates of a carefully chosen deliberative body, that document endorsed a socially reconstructive agenda that initiated a "long democratic revolution," or in Nehru's words, a "step by step" progression toward validation of the Constitution's identity. This protracted revolutionary unfolding was not simply a manifestation of the cautious incrementalism that can be expected to accompany the societal implementation of massive reconstructive work. Rather, it was the inevitable consequence of the disharmony inherent in the constitutional condition. Indeed, the political moves Nehru took in the early years of his newly independent nation implicitly acknowledged that his modestly formulated, goal-oriented constitutional understanding entailed taking steps backward and forward as conflicting interests and constituencies struggled for ascendancy in light of divergent readings of the Constitution.

During and after Nehru's dominance of the political scene, constitutional amendments occupied a large space in the meandering path of Indian constitutional development. In our account of India's signature contribution to constitutional jurisprudence—the Basic Structure doctrine—we see in its evolution from a defensive canon of extraordinary politics to an affirmative dictate of ordinary politics that a constitutional amendment can become a redemptive instrument for the fulfillment of transformative change. The German experience with the amendment issue may not have left one primed for an identity-reinforcing exertion of judicial power in support of paradigmatic constitutional change. The consideration of just such an amendment in this chapter—concerning the vexed issue of reservations policy (affirmative action)—focuses attention on the judiciary's less well-known role as enforcer of the dynamic imperatives of the constitutional revolution.

In chapter 6, the judiciary's role in constitutional revolution assumes pivotal importance. While the Supreme Court in India has played an enabling and facilitative role in nurturing the constitutional revolution projected in the document framed at the Constituent Assembly, in Israel the Supreme Court has performed the lead role in making the constitutional revolution in that nation a reality. How this came to pass is discussed at length, but in detailing the idiosyncratic path of Israeli constitutional development, we highlight several aspects of the story that underscore the broader thematic content of our conceptualization of constitutional revolution.

The absence of a formal comprehensive document is what is most distinctive about Israeli constitutionalism.[25] That absence reflects the conscious decision to allow the achievement of independent statehood to proceed unaccompanied by a "constitutional moment." Thus, with the termination of the British mandate, it was widely assumed that a constitution would be adopted by a Constituent Assembly. Instead, the constitution-writing assignment was never undertaken. The presumptive framers opted for a compromise formula by which the drafting process would evolve by increments in the shape of a series of Basic Laws that would at some unspecified point culminate in a comprehensive constitutional document. That time never arrived, and even with the passage of two Basic Laws on human rights in the final decade of the last century, the Israeli constitutional order remained a parliamentary-sovereignty archetype.

We argue that this all changed through an interpretative exercise by the Supreme Court that resulted in a fundamentally transformed constitutional order. As in Hungary, the Israeli "revolutionary" experience proceeded without an extraconstitutional invocation of constituent power. The difference was that in the latter instance, the transformation was directly traceable to the actions of the branch of the government furthest removed from public accountability. While a case can be made that it was the Knesset's enactment of human rights legislation in 1992 that triggered the constitutional revolution, we submit that without the landmark *Mizrahi Bank* ruling in 1995, the transition from parliamentary sovereignty to constitutional democracy would not have occurred.

Thus, in deciding that the Basic Laws carry a supreme constitutional status, that the Knesset has only limited legislative powers, and that the judiciary possesses the authority to conduct judicial review of legislation, the justices of the Supreme Court reconstituted the Israeli political system. As one noted commentator observed, the Court was "the instigator of the constitutional revolution, and not merely . . . [charged with] implementing it."[26] And in line with our general theory, it was the disharmonies of constitutional politics—involving in Israel the dual commitments to democracy and Jewish identity—that created the conditions out of which fundamental change occurred.

We also show how in the opposing opinions of the Court's two foremost legal thinkers, the very legitimacy of the constitutional revolution would likely remain highly contestable in light of the controversial process by which this turning point in Israeli constitutional law was brought about. In the words of the most vocal opponent of the process, Justice Mishael Cheshin, "I cannot agree to it that we adopt a constitution without the people's input."[27] Cheshin echoed a basic principle in constitutional theory: all governmental powers should derive from the constituent power of the people.

Accordingly, chapter 7 examines the doctrine of constituent power, which is generally conceived as "the capacity to enact a constitution, by revolutionary means or otherwise, thereby giving rise to a novel legal order."[28] It is accepted that in a democracy, this capacity belongs to the people. Nonetheless, such a vague expression conceals many complexities: Who are the people? How do we recognize them? Through which mechanisms can the people speak with one voice? Perhaps this is the reason why "jurists throughout history have always been fascinated by the constituent power and its theory."[29]

The concept of constituent power runs throughout this book. In chapters 4 and 5, we demonstrate how the exercise of constituent power in Germany and in India gave birth to new constitutions whose formal amendments were expected to be exercised within the constitutional framework in a way that preserved the constitution's core identity. This protection of the constitutional core from possible internal or external encroachments also guards constituent power from what is regarded as an ultra vires (authority-exceeding) exercise of constituted powers created by the constitution. But as we show in chapter 3, it is precisely through formal constitutional powers, such as amending procedures, that the constitution can be revolutionized. It was the use of the amendment formula that allowed the Hungarian Parliament to twice bring about a constitutional revolution. Furthermore, as we argue in chapter 6, the exercise of constituent power often requires retrospective recognition by constituted organs, most notably by an authoritative court. Consequently, revolutionary transformations may not only be brought about through legal mechanisms but also be identified by judicial organs.

Constitutional revolutions thus challenge some of the basic premises of constitutional theory as shaped in the French revolutionary era by Abbé Emmanuel Joseph Sieyès. In justifying the revolutionary destruction of the ancien régime, Sieyès developed the notion that a constitution is produced not by constituted powers but by a constituent power. He thereby created a distinction between the extraordinary power to form a constitution, which is prior and external to the constitutional order, independent of any constitutional forms or restrictions, and constituted powers, which are limited institutions created by the constituent power. According to this traditional understanding of constitutional ordering, constituent power cannot, conceptually and logically, be constrained by existing rules, institutions, and procedures. It cannot be brought "within the four corners of the constitution."[30] But as we demonstrate, the dividing line between the powers is much blurrier than often portrayed. There is interdependency, a relational account between "the people" and constituted political and legal institutions, since the revolution is often created precisely "within the four corners of the constitution."

Thus, "the people" may not necessarily be the "authors" or "creators" of the new constitution, yet they remain the originators of the ultimate source of legitimacy. In the modern era, the constitution of a nation is regarded as receiving its normative and universal status from the political will of the people to act as a constitutional authority, through which the entity "the people" manifests itself as a political and legal unity.[31] The notion that all power originates from the people is now explicitly expressed in many constitutions.[32] And so, although in reality the constitution is created through a variety of processes that regularly involve a number of authors, negotiations, and—very often—imposition, we still hold to a romantic notion of constitution-making enacted by "we the people."[33] It is for this reason that intraconstitutional revolutionary change can make a claim for enhanced legitimacy if created through mechanisms and institutions that mirror a "popular sovereignty" constitution-making process, at least in our imagination of constituent power. Hence, the constitutional revolution may be brought about by constituted powers; yet to claim a mantle of legitimacy, the process that culminates in transformative constitutional change should aspire to approximate the people's constituent power.

When constituted organs exercise constituent power, a constitutional revolution results. Such at least is one metric for acknowledging fundamental changes in constitutional development that warrant recognition as revolutionary. In embarking, in the next chapter, on our journey in search of conceptual clarification, we set out to explore other attributes of transformations within the constitutional domain that justify application of a term whose familiar connotation seems at first a curious fit with the discourse of revolution. The core fundamentals of our conceptual claims are introduced and then pursued in several case studies. By the end, we hope to have demonstrated the truth of the following propositions:

1. The distinction between legal and illegal transformations is not determinative in establishing the existence of a constitutional revolution, although it can help differentiate among its types.
2. A constitutional revolution is accompanied by critical changes in constitutional identity. How much change in identity is necessary to merit the designation "revolutionary" is one of the interpretative discussions we welcome.
3. A constitutional moment may or may not attend the arrival of a constitutional revolution. A substantial reorientation in constitutional practice and understanding often proceeds incrementally, without a decisive rupture or violent usurpation.
4. Constitutionally driven change often occurs during an extended period when revolutionary aspirations are solidified.
5. The characteristic of constitutions prevalent in all forms of constitutionalism is a condition of disharmony that functions as the engine for change, sometimes culminating in the radical displacement of constitutional norms and practices. This disharmonic condition remains a continuing source of potential counterrevolution, which may follow a constitutional revolution encumbered by a legitimacy deficit.
6. To an extent that varies from case to case, the novelty of constitutional transformation draws on resources well entrenched in the historical past.

In that Springfield speech in 1857, Lincoln conceded that if the *Dred Scott* ruling, decided earlier that year, had been affirmed and reaffirmed over the years, to not acquiesce in it as a precedent "would be, factious, nay, even revolutionary."[34] But in his estimation, it was clearly unsettled law and, moreover, had been "based on assumed historical facts which are not really true."[35] And so Lincoln counseled resistance to it as a controlling precedent.

In doing so, he was in essence proclaiming that the Supreme Court's alarming decision was a veritable counterrevolutionary act, a calculated effort to undermine progress toward fulfillment of the radical aspirations embodied in the Declaration. Without sustained resistance, the decision would eventually be reaffirmed and legitimated, thus subverting the revolutionary principles of that founding document. As would become evident in the near future, Lincoln considered some constitutional revolutions worth fighting for.

2

Theorizing Constitutional Revolution

> We must reassess the very idea of revolution before we can define its future.
>
> Bruce Ackerman

RARELY IN THE DOMAIN OF PUBLIC LAW has an analytical construct experienced such ubiquitous yet undertheorized application as the term "constitutional revolution." It is an idea that has been generously applied to all manner of things that are dissimilar in significant respects. And just as "there is no general agreement on the necessary and sufficient characteristics of revolution," there is no broadly accepted understanding of the concept's specific constitutional derivative.[1] What is more, the association of revolution with a modifier that at first glance provokes more confusion than illumination poses an additional challenge for users of the term: demonstrating the utility of a seemingly oxymoronic terminological linkage.

The larger challenge, however, and the focus of this chapter, is to sharpen conceptual clarity in the way we depict constitutional change, specifically that species of change that entails significant breaks or departures in the workings of the constitutional order. Such discontinuities can take varied forms, ranging from the embrace of wholly new constitutional arrangements to the textual or interpretative displacement of long-standing expectations about how matters of constitutive import are to be resolved. While change is the common variable in all instances commonly referred to as constitutional revolutions, much of the controversy surrounding the use of the term has to do with disagreement about the nature of that change: most importantly, how much of it is required to convincingly attach the label "revolution" to an altered state of constitutional affairs, and how quickly must such change come about?

The task, a formidable one, is well known to students of revolution, constitutional or otherwise. As the historian Crane Brinton observed, "The social scientist cannot measure change by [an] exact thermometer, and say exactly when ordinary change boils over into revolutionary change."[2] Yet if exactitude in ascertaining the precise moment when one form of change becomes another is elusive, conceptual assumptions regarding revolutionary transitions are less indeterminate: they presume a rupture in continuity that is stark and decisive. Without a clear determination that such a break has occurred, we might as well, in accordance with this understanding, describe what has transpired as evolutionary. But first we might take heed of Bruce Ackerman's sound advice: "A systematic comparison of evolutionary and revolutionary exercises in constitutionalism should be high on the agenda of future researchers."[3]

Ackerman has weighed in famously in connection with the constitutional revolution conundrum. His theory of constitutional change is well known for the capaciousness of its revolutionary understanding: the successful repudiation of the past, conjoined with the higher-law transformation of a nation's political identity, need not be tethered to just those moments when repudiation and renewal display the formal attributes of conventional revolutionary activity. The punctuation of American history by "successful exercises in *revolutionary reform*" is for Ackerman both a refutation of Burkean incrementalism and an occasion for celebrating the transformative potential of acts of collective and self-conscious mobilization that may decisively redirect a nation's governing principles and practices.[4] Borrowing selectively from Hannah Arendt's celebrated work *On Revolution* (1963), Ackerman accepts most of the normative and empirical implications of the finding commonly linked to the Arendtian understanding: "A Constitution is a natural culmination of a successful revolution."[5]

Ackerman's theory of constitutional transformation centers on the "constitutional moment," a now-iconic demarcation in American constitutional literature that, particularly in his comparative work, provides only a short window of opportunity for achieving revolutionary change.[6] In Ackerman's words: "The long-term costs of a short-term failure to act at the moment of revolutionary triumph are easy to underestimate."[7] Such is the influence of Ackerman's contribution that it is now "conventional wisdom to expect a revolution—'thunder and lightning . . . [and] fire' [Exodus 19:16]—as prerequisites to achieving a constitutional transformation, especially one of the magnitude necessary to transform a political system."[8] In this chapter, we question this assumption and argue that with respect to transformations of the constitutional variety, the standard criteria for revolutionary certification are inadequate and deficient. In our account, a constitutional revolution can be said to exist when we are confronted with a paradigmatic displacement, however achieved, in the conceptual prism through which constitutionalism is experienced in a given polity. In some cases, this achievement unfolds incrementally and without the benefit of the sort of dramatic rupture and follow-up usually associated with generic revolutionary activity. This shifting of focus from the process through which change occurs to the substance of the change wrought should lead to more sensitive and accurate assessments of the historic meaning of constitutional change. Our shift in emphasis accommodates more examples of revolutionary constitutional change than a reliance on one's intuition or conventional opinion might provide, although in each purported instance of such transformation, the claim that it occurred requires persuasive argument about the extent of substantive constitutional displacement in order realistically to secure a high measure of scholarly agreement and certification. The effort, however, is worth pursuing if only to avoid obscuring the radical nature of constitutional change, which could otherwise result from a focus on the evolutionary manner of its attainment.

In table 1, types (a) and (c) lack the substantial, paradigm-shifting displacement that indicates the presence of a constitutional revolution, even if in type (a) the occurrence of a new constitution after a successful social or political revolution could easily lead one to conclude otherwise. In fact, a dramatic rupture in political continuity that produces minimal change in the constitutional experience of the polity achieves a constitutional revolution in name only. By contrast, when major constitutional transformation follows a radical break, type (b), applying the constitutional

Table 1. Types of constitutional revolution

	Substantive change	
Process	Minimal	Major
Sudden break	(a) nominal	(b) classic
Evolution	(c) [none]	(d) quiet

revolution label to the occasion appears to be an obvious move. More controversial, however, are those instances in which a polity undergoes a substantial reorientation in constitutional practice and understanding without the revolutionary political moment that is present in the classic variant; this combination is seen in type (d). While more open to interpretative contestation, these constitutional transformations are no less revolutionary for the incremental aspect that marks their arrival.

In the first section of this chapter, we discuss several of the standard criteria for establishing the existence of a revolutionary event in the context for which it is in least need of adjectival modification. Thus, when the word "revolution" stands alone, we may infer that the reference is to the overthrow of an established government or political system. It is only when the word appears alongside another (for example, sexual, industrial, or intellectual) that we are asked to contemplate a revolutionary situation at some distance from the standard, politically freighted instance. In these cases, the meaning of the dual construction takes on a metaphorical representation, connoting a sudden or marked change in the circumstances attendant on the designated subject matter. A strikingly new pattern of sexual interaction, a restructuring of the production of material goods, or a novel way of viewing the world may or may not be accompanied by those attributes we ascribe to a stand-alone revolution; what makes them arguably revolutionary is the magnitude of the changes occurring within their particular contextual settings.[9]

A constitutional revolution is a more complicated case, one whose meaning is not discernible in exclusively metaphorical terms. A revolution of this type might, after all, culminate in the displacement of an existing government or political system, which is only to say that constitutional change is a genus of political transformation and cannot therefore easily be abstracted from the original conceptual formulation. But some constitutional revolutions have transformative impacts that appear negligible—or at least not obvious—and that is reason enough to pursue the idea in its various permutations, thus enabling us to retain the descriptive nomenclature of revolution while attempting to enhance the analytical bite of the concept.[10]

In the second section, we discuss types of change that might be considered revolutionary in their constitutional import. Constitutional revolutions can occur as a governing set of rules and principles establishing a constitutional order based on a political revolution that overturned a previous regime, or as a major change in the constitutional order emerging within the parameters of an extant constitutional setting and without any, or at least without significant, violence or illegality. In either case, their impact will be experienced through political and social avenues of expression, sometimes decidedly so in one direction or another. The distinctions between legal and illegal constitutional transformations and between the subsequent political and social changes are by no means unambiguous, but a close familiarity with specific cases enables one to account for changes that might be sufficiently far-reaching to be plausibly recognized as revolutionary. This ambiguity—inevitable, it should be said, in what is an essentially interpretative presentation—may be disturbing to some, who may, however, appreciate it as a provocation to further reflection (that is, the following account may raise as many questions as it answers).

We go on to argue that approaching the analytical task as a specific articulation of the more general account of how constitutional orders change their identities best advances this aspiration. We give special attention to the engine driving such change: constitutional disharmony. Within the dissonance inherent in the constitutional condition, what may appear to fall short of revolutionary execution often comes across very differently. Indeed, the disharmonies of constitutional politics ensure that a nation's constitution will over time come to mean quite different things. This discord bestows a divided legacy that provides ample resources for those engaged in the pursuit of major course corrections in constitutional direction and commitment. Through the creative interaction between divergent strands within an extant constitutional tradition, the specific components of an identity evolve as these elements play off against one another within the national historical narrative. Thus, constitutional identity is not a static or fixed essence. Its dynamic quality results from the interplay of forces seeking either to introduce greater harmony into the constitutional equation or to create further disharmony. One could imagine the latter development culminating in a rupture of constitutional continuity, thereby setting in motion a process whose goal is the reconstituting of the polity. A possible outcome of all of this is a constitutional revolution.

The third section presents two notable instances of constitutional transformation that were paradigm shifting with respect to how constitutional development thereafter unfolded within their polities. The accustomed rendering of revolutionary transitions conjures up images of speedy replacement of the old with the new, but we need to recognize that a more deliberate, incremental pace comports with the changes produced by some constitutional revolutions. The cases to be considered—the United States and Ireland—involve a major reorientation in constitutional commitment that illustrates the conceptual importance of this recognition. What happened in these two constitutional locales supports the argument that when constitutional development assumes a radical departure from previous experience, the transformative significance of what has transpired ought not to be minimized or negated by the extended period accompanying the consolidation of revolutionary aspirations. Exceptional in many respects as was the unfolding of the Irish and American constitution-making experiences, in their progressions through rupture, aspiration, and consolidation they were very much exemplars of a more familiar story line associated with the constitutional revolution.

In the fourth section we suggest that the Irish and American examples highlight the workings of a political dynamic present in all regimes. The playing-out of this dynamic will vary considerably in accordance with the intensity and configuration of disharmonic constitutional politics in particular places, but this variation ought not to obscure a ubiquitous, fundamental characteristic of the unfolding of constitutional development.

Basic Meanings

After listening to a brief explication of our ideas on the subject of revolution, a scholar at the institution with which one of us is affiliated responded critically: "Certain words have basic meanings that can be bent, but should not be broken. 'Revolution' means a large change in a short period of time. How large? You can define that. How short? You can define that. But what you should not do—in my opinion—is say that a change can be revolutionary regardless of its size or regardless of the length of time over which it occurs. Because to do so would eviscerate any distinction between 'revolution' and 'evolution.'"[11]

The scholar's objection was well founded, based as it was on an extensive literature that is generally supportive of the point he was making. How then to respond? A satisfactory rejoinder could do worse than begin with Giovanni Sartori's simple truth: "In a natural language almost no word is . . . endowed with only one meaning."[12] While his insight ought not to function as a license for tendentiously conjuring up any meaning at will, it should serve a useful enough purpose if it directs our attention to the elasticity of concept formation, particularly as this recognition relates to a context-specific application of the basic idea in question.[13] First, however, we should briefly highlight some of the important benchmarks commonly held for ascertaining the presence of a revolution.

The Standard Instance

The predominant view in the social science literature concerning the generic concept is rather straightforward. Thus, "there is a general consensus that a minimally necessary characteristic of revolution is some wholesale and unconstitutional replacement of the governing body."[14] Accordingly, for a revolution to be associated with constitutional change, we would expect to encounter a governing set of rules and principles establishing a constitutional order based on a political revolution that had unlawfully overturned a previous order. For example, Article 2 of the amended Turkish Constitution of 1937 states, "The Turkish State is republican, nationalist, democratic, State-controlled, laic and revolutionary."[15] All the affirmations leading up to the final assertion detail a cohort of commitments flowing directly from the Kemalist ascendance following the revolutionary overthrow of Ottoman rule in Turkey. In a number of late-twentieth-century constitutions under the sway of Soviet influence, one finds more specific references to revolutionary inspiration. In Yugoslavia, it stemmed from the "the People's Liberation War and Socialist Revolution";[16] in Bulgaria, from "the historic victory of the Ninth of September Socialist Revolution of 1944";[17] and in Czechoslovakia, the Constitution of 1948 declares on behalf of the Czechoslovak people, "We are determined to defend with all our strength the achievements of our national and democratic revolution."[18]

The end of Soviet domination did not signal the disappearance of such revolutionary invocations. In Romania, for example, "the ideals of the Revolution of December 1989" were inscribed in that nation's new document as a repudiation of an earlier revolutionary legacy.[19] While this rejection was confined to the European continent, other socialist constitutions maintained their earlier perfervid commitments; see, for instance, China's amended charter's reverential gesture to its "glorious revolutionary tradition" (from both 1911 and 1949).[20] Cuba too continues to see its Fundamental Law as "mak[ing] possible the realization of the Revolution";[21] as does Vietnam's recommitment in 1991 "to safeguard the socialist regime and the fruits of the revolution."[22]

Similar allusions to specific revolutionary moments with aspirational significance are also present in constitutions with political orientations quite different from the ones just cited. Nepal's Interim Constitution of 2007 has a preamble that promises a permanent constitution that will "institutionalize the achievements of the revolution."[23] The preamble of the Panamanian Constitution of 1972 decrees a document in which are consecrated "the social, political, economic and moral principles that inspired the Panamanian Revolution."[24] The preamble to the Constitution of the Islamic Republic of Iran points out that the new regime's core identity embodies the meaning of "the great Islamic Revolution of Iran."[25] The document then discusses what it claims is a distinctive "feature of this revolution," namely, that it is "ideological and Islamic."[26] In doing so, it raises questions that lurk in the background of all these textual inclusions. Does the codification of revolutionary ideology produce a constitutionally legitimate result independent of the substance of the ideology?[27]

Indeed, one might be tempted to conclude that the textual invocation of revolutionary language may itself signify the absence of a genuinely constitutional revolution. Since many, perhaps most, of the revolutions accorded exalted status in the texts of constitutions—others besides the above include documents from Syria, Egypt, Libya, Guinea-Bissau, Algeria, Angola, Congo (Zaire), and Liberia—were not harbingers of freedom, the documents to which they gave rise might be viewed as tainted by the association.[28] Thus, when a new constitutional document explicitly proclaims its revolutionary credentials, the cautious reader would do well to deflect any sudden urge to celebrate the achievement.

In addition, for most theorists of revolution, illegitimate nullification and displacement of the political order must be accompanied by violence.[29] In her classic work on the subject, Hannah Arendt, although idiosyncratic in many of her reflections on revolution, was fully supportive of this orientation. It then followed for Arendt that the idea of the constitutional revolution made sense only as a descriptive term to refer to what happens when a violent rupture in political continuity liberates a people from oppression and then leads to the adoption of a freedom-enhancing constitution.[30] In the nexus between a specific revolutionary event and an ensuing constitution, the reality of a constitutional revolution ultimately depends on whether the meaning of the first has any substantive constitutive significance. Unreal would be any depiction of a revolution that somehow was directly traceable to an existing constitution without seeking that charter's destruction and replacement.

Accordingly, the American Revolution was both a revolution and a constitutional revolution, but the "New Deal Revolution" of a century and a half later has, unless one is speaking metaphorically, no coherent meaning.[31] The same incomprehension would be the response to events in Israel, South Africa, the United Kingdom, and Hungary that, whatever their differences, have been characterized as constitutional revolutions despite displaying little of the decisive rupture and repudiation that is often viewed as the necessary predicate for recognition as such. Here, then, we have our first critical conceptual distinction, and it speaks less to the substance of constitutional change than to its originating source. Consistent with conventional accounts, we note that for political change to be revolutionary, it requires contra-constitutional action; as we shall see, however, to have that activity (or other activity that may not be so obviously illegal) identified as revolutionary in a constitutional sense, the focus must shift from the process to the result produced by that process, namely, constitutive arrangements of substantially different orientation from what preceded them. In the familiar telling, we are left with a rather straightforward definition of a constitutional revolution: the establishment of a new constitutional order after the illegal overturning of a previous order.[32] The sequential, linear aspect of this rendering avoids the oxymoronic difficulty subsumed in the joining of seemingly contradictory terms.[33] A political revolution occurs, and then, as Arendt (and Ackerman) stipulated, a constitution is framed to consolidate the achievements of the revolution.[34] Importantly as well, the consolidation culminates in the rapid ascendancy of novel governing arrangements.

The most influential articulation of the familiar view is to be found in the writings of the Austrian legal theorist Hans Kelsen. For Kelsen, the norms of every legal system are interconnected by a chain of validity in which lower norms derive their validity from higher norms.[35] Since positive law derives its validity from another norm, a constitutional norm derives its validity from its "creation" according to the formal amendment rule established in the constitution (the current or previous one).[36] A revolution, according to Kelsen, occurs "whenever the legal order of a community is nullified and replaced by a new order in an illegitimate way . . . not prescribed by the first legal order."[37] While his account places strict limits on what counts as a revolutionary transition, it is much less constrained in attaching the "constitutional" label to whatever governing arrangement emerges in the wake of a radical changeover. Thus, significantly, the constitutional legitimacy of the new order is not contingent on its capacity to weather the challenge of rigorous moral examination; for as Kelsen famously pointed out, "The validity of a legal order cannot be questioned on the ground that its contents are incompatible with some moral or political value."[38] In Joel Colón-Ríos's aptly formulated assessment, "If one is looking for something more than a descriptive theory of constitutional transitions, one must go beyond Kelsen."[39]

Another significant and related understanding pertains to the substance of the change associated with the idea of revolution. There is broad agreement that however the variable of change is conceptualized, it must fit within the account just elaborated, namely, that the transformation be decisive and nonincremental. Here again the literature on the generic term helps in thinking about the more restricted concept. It reveals that the deepest fault line among theorists lies at the social-political divide, with conceptual outcomes hinging on whether the term "revolution" is to be more closely aligned with class conflict and social change or with political breakdown and structural change. These are not mutually exclusive categories; as Christopher Kotowski correctly points out, "Everyone would agree that the French Revolution was a true revolution; however, different authors will characterize the event as either the birth of a new order or as the 'breakdown' of a system."[40] Yet consensus is lacking on the extent of the change necessary for revolutionary success and certification: political change may be a necessary condition, but is it in at least some circumstances a sufficient condition?[41]

For some, the answer is most assuredly not. So, for example, Barrington Moore says of the American Revolution that, since it "did not result in any fundamental changes in the structure of society, then there are no grounds for asking whether it deserves to be called a revolution at all."[42] But in Charles Tilly's rendering, "A revolutionary outcome is the displacement of one set of power holders by another."[43] Yet unless this minimalist view of political breakdown and displacement is linked with a more substantive reorientation in political aspiration and commitment, it offers a somewhat hollow conceptual alternative to the expansive transformation imagined by Moore and the others in the societal-reconfiguration school. Perhaps the most prominent—albeit controversial—substantive counter is Hannah Arendt's insistence that the goal of political liberty define the revolutionary project: "Only . . . where the liberation from oppression aims at least at the constitution of freedom can we speak of revolution."[44] The power of the people to bind the future through the entrenchment of principles that constituted the people as the legitimate source of sovereign authority was for Arendt the essence of the revolutionary achievement.[45] In accordance with the perspective advanced in this chapter, Moore is wrong in denying revolutionary meaning to the constitutional achievement of 1787 because of its insufficiently social significance; Tilly is correct in acknowledging its revolutionary importance, albeit for the wrong reasons (that is, the displacement of power holders must be accompanied by displacement in constitutional orientation and experience); and Arendt is justified in finding in the redirection of constitutional aspiration to the achievement of political liberty a sufficient basis for affirming 1787 as a constitutional revolution but mistaken in limiting such an affirmation to only one type of historic displacement.

At the constitutional level, this debate expresses itself in several ways. The most explicit manifestation is the text itself. In the American case, for example, Moore's questioning of the revolutionary bona fides of the American Revolution is arguably supported by the inattention of the 1787 document to social transformation. That same document, with its opening invocation of the people as the source of governing power—commonplace today but strikingly original at the time of its writing—presents equally compelling evidence for Arendt's celebration of the American achievement as the purest form of revolutionary accomplishment. In contrast, many constitutions—Cuba's, for example—not only proclaim their revolutionary agenda as the culmination of a successful (and violent) overthrow of an unjust regime but also do so without concealing the goal of societal upheaval they are designed to facilitate.[46] Starting from Moore's premises, Cuba's was a successful revolution (in the empirical sense); from Arendt's, the absence of a freedom agenda negates its—and the Cuba Constitution's—revolutionary pretensions.

Both of these examples fall under the heading of illegal ruptures, in which a new constitution follows the forced ending of the previous order.[47] Additional contrasts may be drawn from instances of constitutional displacement occurring within the parameters of arguable legality. These are cases of paradigmatic change unrelated to the overthrow of a prior constitutional order, but nonetheless involving activities whose irregular or extraordinary character have the potential for being strongly challenged over their questionable legitimacy.

The American experience is illustrative. Thus, the adoption of the Fourteenth Amendment, undoubtedly the most consequential formal change in American constitutional development, "would never have been ratified if the Republicans had followed the rules laid down by Article Five of the original Constitution."[48] Yet however dubious the legality of the process by which the Constitution was altered, even more interesting are the competing interpretations of the resulting substantive changes in constitutional understanding and meaning. First, the illegality of the incorporation is consistent with the transgressive nature of the changes included in the amendment, which, in their radical reconfiguration of governing principles, were the culmination of a violent campaign to uproot the original constitutional design.[49] Also, the irregularities of the ratification process are not so different from those accompanying the adoption of the 1787 document, and in both instances the extraordinary efforts were driven by a desire to redeem the original promise of the revolution through major course corrections in constitutional direction. Thus, Michael McConnell writes, "Far from reflecting the revolutionary developments of a new regime, these key provisions deploy the very language of the documents of the Founding."[50] This second understanding can further mean either or both of the following statements: by its major displacement of power to the national level, the amendment sought to break down the structure of exclusiveness that had confined the practice of political freedom to ascriptively privileged groups; and by its major displacement of power to the national level, the amendment created the potential for a substantial adjustment in the relative social standing of previously marginalized groups and the eradication of entrenched societal inequalities.

A range of similar interpretative possibilities presents itself for other countries—for example, South Africa, India, Ireland, and Hungary—where the intra-systemic path to fundamental change has engendered controversy with respect to the procedures implemented to pursue it and to the nature of the change to which it led. Whether those transformations are portrayed as mainly political or social, the revolutionary rhetoric that accompanied them often did not match the incrementalism that followed the constitutional break. It was for this reason that in her study of constitutional design in deeply divided societies, Hanna Lerner asks us to look closely at "the relationship between constitution-making and time: whether the constitution represents a revolutionary moment or rather marks a beginning of an evolutionary process linked to gradual social and political change."[51] Yet as we shall see, a constitution can be both a revolutionary moment and the commencement of measured and continuing change. Particularly in the case of constitutional revolutions not connected with certifiable revolutionary upheavals, their aspirational character necessarily entails a high degree of uncertainty in establishing their ultimate transformative impact.[52] To be sure, it is also true that what contemporaneous political actors insist is a revolutionary moment in constitutional development will sometimes later be confirmed as an event of decidedly lesser significance.

Another View

How do we account for a constitutional revolution occurring within an intact constitutional setting? In what sense would such a construction embody conceptual coherence?

Again, the generic concept should be our point of departure. Sartori's discussion of the "semantic field" may help enhance the appeal of a seemingly defiant conundrum. In essence, it asks us to consider a concept's elasticity by situating it in relation to neighboring terms; for the case at hand, types of violence represent a semantic field with which revolution finds easy affinity, but so too do types of illegal political change.[53] These semantic fields are compatible with the above articulation of constitutional revolution, but they fall short of legitimating any claim of authenticity for the alternative meaning. For that to happen, we would need some connection with a more inclusive terminological neighborhood, the most obvious candidate being types of radical political or social transformation. One type that qualifies for incorporation within the field would be intraconstitutional changes that arguably leave the document with such a significantly altered identity that it might lead someone to question whether such "legal" changes were indeed legitimate. Such questioning has occasionally—and increasingly—arisen in the face of constitutional amendments deemed unconstitutional for substantive reasons.[54] Therefore, a constitutional change may be deemed revolutionary, even if accepted according to the prescribed constitutional procedures, if it conflicts with unamendable constitutional provisions or collapses the existing order and its basic principles and replaces them with new ones, thereby changing its identity.[55]

Instead, then, of Kelsen's emphasis on process—specifically, on a break in the chain of legality as a decisive marker for determining whether a constitutional revolution occurred—a theory of unamendability, in which a governing document's foundational principles and deepest structural commitments establish limits to constitutional change, directs us to a search for more substantive benchmarks for ascertaining whether a legal or illegal transition should be construed as revolutionary. Rather, it is in Carl Schmitt's writings that we find an early voice for the articulation of this more substantively oriented alternative. Ironically, given his work in the Nazi regime, it provided theoretical ballast for the postwar German Constitutional Court's legal embrace of the concept of an unconstitutional constitutional amendment. As Schmitt stated in 1928: "The boundaries of the authority for constitutional amendments result from the properly understood concept of constitutional change."[56] Thus, for Schmitt, change was justifiable "only under the presupposition that the identity and continuity of the constitution . . . is preserved."[57] As Joel Colón-Ríos notes, "Under [Schmitt's] approach, a constitutional transition occurs when one of the fundamental political decisions that comprise 'the constitution' is altered regardless of how that alteration takes place."[58]

An emphasis on far-reaching constitutional transformation is all the more compelling if we consider that it is sometimes the case that this kind of change is notably absent from those transitions that are both violent and illegal. Take, for example, the Egyptian Revolution of 2011. As things unfolded, it quickly became evident that the revolutionaries of Tahrir Square, diverse in their goals and aspirations, confronted a disturbing reality of frustrated hopes and unfulfilled expectations. For some, the symbol of their disappointment came swiftly in the guise of a new constitution whose construction seemed designed to maintain the power and privileges of the prerevolutionary regime. For others, this same document shifted power ominously to groups within the society long identified with hostility toward liberal democratic precepts, a view vindicated when the new president, who embodied the agenda of these groups, wasted little time in governing illiberally. His removal left Egyptians anticipating the drafting of yet another constitution. But since the next round of constitution making was to be directed and administered by the ruling military, confidence in the quality of the resulting product was never very high. To be sure, the result was not the same constitution as its predecessor, differing in substantial respects from it. Nevertheless, a pervasive sense that not much had changed as a consequence of its adoption was keenly felt, even as the events associated with the dislocations of the revolution and its extended aftermath were prematurely credited at the time with changing the political landscape and dynamic of the Middle East.

By the measure of the standard instance, Egypt experienced both a revolution and a constitutional revolution.[59] But was it anything more than a nominal constitutional revolution? That a revolution occurred in 2011 was not in doubt, and the revolutionaries decidedly had as one of their principal goals the replacement of the old regime's constitution. As Antoni Abat i Ninet and Mark Tushnet pointed out, "The revolutionary transition . . . [put] the creation of a new constitutional identity on the political agenda."[60] Still, did a constitutional revolution take place? The link between revolution and constitution was noted in the preamble of the first replacement constitution, which declared that the Egyptian people were "determined to achieve the objectives of their peaceful revolution." The body of the document, consisting of 236 articles, established the framework and guiding principles through which these revolutionary objectives were presumably to be achieved. But as the deep divisions over the drafting process had glaringly revealed, there were substantial disagreements concerning the substance of the objectives to which the people were committed. In addition to a deficiency of common purpose about matters central to constitutional identity, striking resemblances between the new constitution and its 1971 predecessor were difficult to miss—notably Article 2, which affirmed that the "Principles of Islamic Sharia are the principal source of legislation." So if constitutional continuity was extensive with respect both to critical provisions in the document and to the weaknesses attributed to it by long-standing rivals embracing contrasting understandings of the revolution's meaning, what basis is there for viewing these constitutional developments as revolutionary?

The revolutionary repudiation of the constitutional order of the immediate past, followed by the drafting of a new constitution by a constituent assembly, may satisfy the minimal conceptual criteria associated with such transitional sequences of events, but the absence of a clearly defined and profoundly felt directional shift in constitutional orientation fails to meet the more rigorous requirements of the substantive model of constitutional revolution. As one student of constitutionalism and revolutions wrote,

"Egypt had all the hallmarks of revolutionary constitutionalism but has so far failed to achieve the revolution's goal of constitutionalism."[61] That model, however, presumes the tentativeness of any initial judgments, since the confirmation of a paradigmatic displacement requires a retrospective judgment at a distance from the initial rupture in constitutional continuity.[62] Had, for example, the Muslim Brotherhood and President Muhammad Morsi succeeded in establishing a constitutional theocracy based on "credible sources accepted in Sunni doctrines" (Article 219), then it would have been easier to affirm the achievement of a genuine constitutional revolution. The paradigmatic change in Egypt's constitutionalism would have been decisive—if for many also deeply disheartening—for rendering a judgment on the nature of the transformation.

The overreaching of Morsi and the Muslim Brotherhood and the subsequent assertion of authoritarian military rule prevented that from happening. The revolutionary moment initiated a new round of contestation amid the surroundings of a fundamentally altered political and legal environment. A theorist of theocracy noted: "Modern Egypt has long been torn between multiple and at times even contradictory identities; . . . above all [tensions between] secularism and religiosity have characterized the country for at least forty years."[63] The freshly minted constitutional text offered one side of this contested terrain a briefly held advantage in translating the political revolution into a constitutional revolution of a certain stripe. With the ascendance of President Abdul Fattah el-Sisi's authoritarian regime, the latter transformation did not occur, but the same interests that disputed the legitimacy of the first constitution-making process can be expected to pursue their preferred constitutional vision, however dim their prospects look at the moment.[64] Were they eventually to succeed, then nominal revolution will be seen as a very early stage in the achievement of an authentic constitutional revolution.[65]

Typically, extended periods of time are required to assess the fallout from major ruptures in political continuity. As we will see, the abruptness of a break in political continuity is not incompatible with subsequent incremental change. But now consider a very different case: South Africa, which experienced a "revolution . . . but one achieved constitutionally, in the sense that the previous constitutional disposition was turned on its head, and . . . the content of the new dispensation differed radically from the previous one."[66] It was, as Heinz Klug argued, "a dramatic, substantive revolution . . . represented by the triumph of constitutionalism over parliamentary sovereignty."[67] Here too, questions remain about just how much the lives of South Africans have changed as a result of this new dispensation; yet that the Constitution, often referred to as the "birth certificate of a nation," has fundamentally elevated prospects for significant and far-reaching change is not seriously contested. As was proudly asserted by one of the justices in an early and important case before the new South African Supreme Court, "Viewed in context, textually and historically, the fundamental rights and freedoms have a poignancy and depth of meaning not echoed in any other national constitution."[68]

How better to capture the essence of this momentous development than by recognizing it as a constitutional revolution? But we can do so only with a modification of the first definition, a revision that requires distancing the concept from the semantic fields that had earlier figured prominently in its derivation. As Andreas Kalyvas asks, "Why do radical political changes need to be associated with ruptures, disruptions, and discontinuity?"[69] With the assistance of a clearer distinction between the general concept of revolution and its more particular constitutional variant, we can derive a more inclusive definition that will incorporate some constitutional narratives that fit the standard revolutionary criteria, along with some that would otherwise be excluded (for example, South Africa). Accordingly, a constitutional revolution can be said to exist when we are confronted with a paradigmatic displacement, however achieved, of the conceptual prism through which constitutionalism is experienced in a given polity.[70] This leaves open the possibility that a revolutionary displacement could develop within the constraints of legality, though establishing whether those constraints were respected will almost certainly be contested. The innovation of a constitutional revolution lies as much in how a polity refocuses its constitutional vision as in how it repudiated its past.

(R)evolutionary Constitutional Change

Once the conditions for a constitutional revolution are divested of their blatantly extralegal character, the types of changes that can be accommodated under this second heading include the following: new constitutional arrangements sanctioned by the authority of the previous constitutional order (as in Hungary, South Africa, Chile); new constitutional arrangements imposed by an external power (for example, Japan, Iraq); major constitutional departures legislatively enacted (such as Canada, Great Britain); major constitutional departures secured through the use of the amendment power (the United States, Norway, for instance); major constitutional departures engineered through the interpretative power and reach of a court of law (as in Israel, the United States, Colombia, South Africa). Since the terminology of revolution is used to describe significant changes in the constitutional condition of polities in widely different circumstances, one should expect considerable disagreement regarding application of the concept to these varied transitions. Indeed, experience shows that the legitimacy of the results flowing from actions associated with each of the aforementioned types will, with varying intensity, be called into question. The first two in particular, entailing as they do clear separations from immediately antecedent constitutional practice, will appear to many as not having been divested of their patently illegal character. The status of a new constitutional beginning launched in the highly irregular manner involved in these situations possesses an inherently ambiguous quality that cannot help affecting the perceived legality of the transitions. The last three have the potential as well to engender skepticism concerning the appropriateness of the methods employed. More than that, however, their connection with revolutionary, as opposed to evolutionary, change will be doubted. Evolution is a process of developing in detail what is implicit in an idea or principle. Revolution involves significant change or alteration of a particular condition or state of affairs. If what is developed in detail through evolution culminates in radical change, we might call it a revolution. But not all such evolutionary processes end up there—probably not many, in fact. The types of (constitutional) revolutions that are the focus of this book often entail an evolutionary progression that is headed toward a significant alteration in an extant state of affairs. If that is the case, then it is clear that the terminology of constitutional evolution would not, in most cases, capture the paradigmatic shifts we are highlighting.

Precisely because the shifts in constitutional direction emerging from these sorts of political activities are initiated and driven by constitutionally sanctioned institutions wielding procedurally correct power, it may be difficult to appreciate the paradigm-altering potential inherent within them. Evolutionary constitutional development occurs without the realization of such potential, which is why we reserve the term "revolution" for incremental change that portends the promise of major transformation.

When, for example, we encounter constitutional displacement resulting from ordinary legislation, which proceeds in so routine and deliberate a manner as easily to avoid early recognition as a potentially pivotal moment in a polity's constitutional narrative, the revolutionary implications of the effort will likely not be widely apparent. Indeed, in Bruce Ackerman's familiar distinction between lower and higher lawmaking, in which revolutionary change can be certified as such only by "meeting the obstacles prescribed by the higher law making system," a manipulation of the "ordinary way of parliamentary democracy" cannot culminate in transformations of revolutionary consequence.[71] Yet consider that the "constitutional revolution" in Israel stemmed from the Knesset's passage of two Basic Laws in 1992 that led a prominent member of the Supreme Court to question "whether the Knesset members themselves were aware of the 'revolution' they were generating."[72] Justice Aharon Barak, the revolution's principal proponent and defender, said of the legislators who adopted the laws, "They didn't know what it meant, or at least they didn't think they were doing something special."[73] For Barak, however, it was very special, since it enabled the Court over which he presided to legitimize judicial review and establish the "normative superiority" of rights. This in itself was a revolutionary achievement, even if it stemmed from the workings of the lawmaking system.

Similarly, the "quiet" transformation currently under way in Great Britain is in full compliance with legal norms; how transformative it will become is very uncertain, as are the revolutionary objectives of its proponents. Both the ongoing devolution of power away from the British Parliament and the adoption of the Human Rights Act in 1997 may very well "cause a 'paradigm shift' in the foundations of British Constitutional Law," but as with developments in Israel, considerable time may have to pass before their revolutionary authenticity and significance can be assessed and, then, possibly confirmed.[74] For example, with the benefit of hindsight, the English Reform Acts of 1867 and 1884, both of which represented extraordinary regime-defining expansions of the franchise, are strong candidates for inclusion under the rubric of constitutional revolutions. As one careful student of those developments noted, "Britain has proved that a new beginning may be possible through an evolutionary process rather than a mega-moment."[75] The Brexit crisis, which looks very much like a sudden break, can similarly be regarded as the concluding act in a progression of cumulative events. As Felicity Matthews argues, "Whilst the crisis wrought by Brexit may appear sudden, it should instead be regarded as the culmination of decades of constitutional drift. The ratcheting of the devolution settlement, the half-reform of the Lords, the establishment of a separate Supreme Court, the extension of direct democracy, the entrenchment of parliamentary terms. Taken together these reforms are suggestive of a constitutional revolution."[76]

These sorts of developments are difficult to reconcile with the "revolutionary" presumption of a radical, sudden break or rupture that culminates in the rapid ascendance of novel governing arrangements. As applied to those revolutions we have designated as constitutional, the presumption needs to be modified in order to fit the conditions associated with this specific categorical type. Before we elaborate, it is worth reiterating that for a constitutional revolution to be properly designated as such, there must be, at a minimum, a discernible transformation in the substance of a polity's constitutional identity. It would be erroneous to describe a transition in a nation's constitutional experience as revolutionary if it could be shown that the change in question, however noteworthy, was less than paradigm shifting in meaning and consequence. Such a shift could result from the adoption of a new text or from the reinterpretation of an old one.[77] Did the doctrinally innovative achievements of the New Deal "constitutional revolution," even if amounting to a "paradigm shift" in constitutional law, qualify as genuinely revolutionary, given the arguably narrow spectrum of jurisprudential choice available to actors in the United States?[78] Was Justice Barak's self-described "constitutional revolution" properly labeled in the face of criticism that the important innovations it provided the Israeli constitutional order were consistent with a natural progression in democratic political development?[79] Questions of this sort can also be raised in connection with other purported constitutional revolutions; no doubt the predictably varied responses to them would reflect the inherently interpretative nature of the process by which such determinations are made.[80]

Disharmony and Constitutional Change

If considered, however, within the context of the disharmony inherent in the constitutional condition, we may perceive the conceptual issues quite differently. Such dissonance fuels the development of constitutional identity along two dimensions: the first, internal to the document (assuming one exists), includes alternative visions or aspirations that may embody different strands within a common historical tradition; the second entails a confrontational relationship between the constitution and the social order within which it operates.[81] While not likely to hasten the sort of disequilibrium that precedes a dramatic revolutionary upheaval of the generic type, circumstances may arise that trigger a revolutionary dynamic from within the environs of a preexisting constitutional disharmony.

The ubiquity of conflict and constitutional change is an old story, and it extends both horizontally across national boundaries and vertically across generations. Vicki Jackson encapsulated the story smartly: "All societies have conflicts, and ongoing conflict within society often motivates constitutional change. . . . Whether constitutions emerge in the wake of fundamental regime change . . . or from within an ongoing democratic polity, whether they are regarded as 'clean breaks' or as incrementalist change, constitutions provide links to a particular past—perhaps imagined and mythic, and certainly partial."[82] Jackson's insight underscores a prominent theme in this chapter: change that results in profound modification of constitutional practice and vision—whether the result of a political rupture in regime stability or the outgrowth of an existing set of political arrangements—has a restorative dimension to it that typically entails the galvanizing of latent, but not entirely quiescent, sources within a conflicted tradition having deep roots in a nation's history.

The dissonance of constitutional politics guarantees that a polity's constitution will possess different meanings over the course of its history. Such disharmony creates a splintered bequest that culminates in a readily available deposit of ideas for those involved in the pursuit of historic constitutional course corrections. In the American case, the argument for constitutional revision was, as we shall see, a redemptive effort to revive the animating spirit of founding principles that the Federalists interpreted as requiring a powerful central authority to fulfill a promise to anchor sovereign authority in popularly accountable governing institutions. What is more, the original break with colonial governance had appealed to an older legal tradition—rooted not in popular sovereignty but in the imperfect accountability of the common law—that had itself known its share of adversarial friction within the larger political tradition of British imperial rule. As Jack P. Greene has argued, "The American Revolution had derived out of a disagreement over the nature of the constitution of the British Empire."[83] And if we project ahead through the struggle to save the Union, which culminated in the adoption of game-changing amendments, through the next century's extended and heatedly contested effort to nationalize policy-making authority, to the recent Tea Party–inspired campaign to innovate and transform by returning to a pre-Federalist understanding of constitutional meaning, one cannot help being struck by the recurring pattern of generational linkage. Throughout this progression, arguably revolutionary intentions were advanced through the invocation of one side of a divided past.[84]

A similar pattern presents itself in the constitutional politics of other countries. The adoption of the postwar Japanese Constitution can be seen as a chapter in a larger story of constitution making in which the Japanese and American collaborators drew on the incongruities in the Meiji Constitution of the previous century to extend the logic of the nonauthoritarian strand of that "incomplete" revolution to infuse the new constitutional identity with a strong commitment to popular governance. The Constitution of 1889 was a bundle of contradictions, capable of justifying both liberal-democratic rule and authoritarian governance. A culmination of the Meiji Revolution—a restoration, actually—it embodied competing visions of the state and the individual, imperial rule and Western reforms. Among other factors, this has led some scholars to discredit the depiction of the Japanese Constitution of 1946 as some kind of alien transplant; rather, it represented the emergence of a new constitutional identity from the cauldron of disharmony embodied in the incomplete constitutional revolution of the previous century.[85] In Chaihark Hahm and Sung Ho Kim's trenchant analysis of the Japanese case: "In order to establish a new democratic polity, the Constitution had to be seen as somehow connected to, and drawing from, certain principles, if not precedents, in the nation's history." And so "the whole Meiji era was . . . recast as an inspiration for a new democratic constitution."[86]

Given the resilience of entrenched principled contestation, incompleteness may well be an inherent feature of constitutional revolutions, no matter the regime type. So, to cite another example, students of the Iranian constitutional revolution of 1906 have emphasized the "dynamic intermixture of the old and the new, the renewed and the invented," in their accounts of that historic turning point in the nation's constitutional progression.[87] As Fakhreddin Azimi notes, "a novel understanding of governance" emerged from this transformation, featuring the radical idea of "citizens as bearers of equal political and civil rights."[88] Yet along with this new awareness there remained an older understanding of where sovereignty was to be situated, and the contradiction embodied in these antithetical constitutive assumptions became an enduring part of the legacy of a constitutional revolution defined as much by what it did not resolve as by what it did.[89] Indeed, in Nader Hashemi's account, "The present conflict in Iran . . . is rooted in this legacy of the unresolved ideological dispute over the proper location of political sovereignty in the early twentieth century."[90] In contrast with Iran, Japan's ultimate resolution has been in favor of a citizen-driven principle of constitutional legitimacy, even as old tensions and contradictions remain to further refine the results of the postwar constitutional revolution.

India presents a prominent example of the disharmonic balance between temporal and spiritual commitments. The constitutional project had a distinctly subversive aspect to it: the framers targeted religion as an impediment to be overcome in the interest of creating a more hospitable environment for a just society (see chapter 5).[91] The revolutionary paradigm resonates with an enduring theme in Indian history, one captured well in a little-known observation by Alexis de Tocqueville: "India cannot be civilized as long as she conserves her religion and her religion is so intermingled with the structure of its social state, of its customs and of its laws."[92] Indigenous versions of this insight were prominently represented at the Constituent Assembly, as reflected in delegate K. M. Panikar's comment, "If the State considers that certain religious practices require modification by the will of the people, then there must be power for the State to do it."[93] So deep was religion's penetration into the fabric of Indian life, and so historically entwined was it in the configuration of a social structure that was by any reasonable standard manifestly unjust, that the framers' hopes for a democratic polity meant that state intervention in the spiritual domain could not be constitutionally foreclosed.

The prevailing social structure, while deeply rooted in centuries of religious and cultural practice, was contestable in accordance with sources from within the Indian tradition. History revealed disharmony within established traditions and between the dominant strand and the existing social order. The Constituent Assembly's excavations of the ancient Ashokan example, as well as invocations of nonconforming Hindu voices from the nineteenth century, show how continuity in the construction of a constitutional identity can draw on alternative (and even dissenting) sources within one tradition and then reconstitute them to serve as a reproach to other strands (and their societal projections) within the same tradition.[94] In examining this construction, the indication that a constitutional revolution occurred is to be found in the displacement of a dominant strand or commitment by its dissenting counterweight. The construction is manifest in the Constitution of India; how fully realized the displacement has proved to be remains contestable.

Novelty and Restoration

Revolutions represent new beginnings, which means that they also involve closure. As Paul Kahn notes, "Revolution has the dual meaning of ending and beginning."[95] But closure does not entail a clean and definitive separation between the novelty that builds upon it and the conditions and practices that preceded it. In this regard, we might consider an older rendering of revolution that evokes the astronomical imagery associated with a cyclical return to a previous condition. The momentous events of 1789 in France severed the connection with this earlier meaning, and thereafter the designation "revolutionary," at least as applied to political happenings, would come to signify a decisive and final rupture with the past. These conceptual changes in what the phenomenon of revolution connotes are entrenched and doubtless irreversible. But the specific concept of constitutional revolution can still benefit from reflection on the older view. While of particular importance for our understanding of constitutional revolution, it is also applicable to the concept of revolution more generally. Its analytical bite can be sharpened if a modified version of the astronomical perspective is grafted onto the modern perspective, revealing additional attributes of those revolutions we think of as constitutional. Such revolutions come in several types, but in many of their permutations, novelty and innovation are accompanied by an important rotational aspect that attests to the continuity embedded in their constitutional transformations.

In Hannah Arendt's account of the French and American Revolutions, revolutionary intentions were not always evident, at least not in the early stages of the upheavals: "The French and American Revolutions were played in their initial stages by men who were firmly convinced that they would do no more than restore an old order that had been disturbed and violated by the despotism of absolute monarchy and the abuses of colonial government. They pleaded in all sincerity that they wanted to revolve back to old times when things had been as they ought to be."[96] Arendt earlier noted that "the element of novelty is inherent in all revolutions," so her take on the incipient period of these revolutions invites us to consider how an older, pre-1789 restorative understanding of revolution might illuminate our conception of constitutional revolution.[97] Specifically, it could enable us to see that the absence of "an entirely new story, a story never told before," need not require abandonment of the concept.[98]

There is much that is controversial in Arendt's reflections on revolution, not least her assessments of the two late-eighteenth-century cataclysmic events that gave fresh meaning to the subject. What is not controversial is her emphasis on novelty. It fits comfortably within the familiar depiction of "radical change initiated and implemented by militant political actors sworn to a nurtured and internally coherent doctrine of innovation and not of cyclic recurrence."[99] Just as innovation is essential to a positive recitation of revolutionary attributes, cyclic recurrence is negatively associated with such an enumeration. On this point, Arendt's thinking about revolution was surely mainstream, since she found the astronomical model, wherein "the few known forms of government revolve around the mortals in eternal recurrence and with the same irresistible force which makes the stars follow their prescribed paths in the skies," of no analytical value in making sense of revolutions in the post-Enlightenment era.[100]

But might it not retain some purchase in making sense of constitutional revolutions? As Arendt herself acknowledged, "Even the 18th-century revolutions cannot be understood without realizing that revolutions first broke out when restoration had been their aim, and that the content of such restoration was freedom."[101] In Arendt's telling, until they embraced the idea that their struggle for national independence meant independence from the political and legal ideas of the past, the Americans had been engaged in a restorative campaign—"how dear the idea of revolving back, of restoration, was to the hearts and minds of the revolutionaries"[102]—whose model, the Glorious Revolution, would become a paradoxically fraught misnomer in the cold light of Arendtian retrospective reevaluation. One might describe it as a coup d'état, or even perhaps as a Dutch invasion, but to the extent that novelty had become the benchmark for revolutionary certification, the English people's collective effort to reaffirm ancient constitutional rights rather than to affirm new ones could acquire its revolutionary bona fides only through the generosity of interpretative license.

But what if the distinction between old rights and new ones, between restoration and novelty, presents a false dichotomy that undercuts our effort at conceptual understanding? What if, instead, the reassertion of constitutional rights, the attempt to innovate by coming back around more or less circularly to an earlier state—or at least claiming to do so—is important in theorizing a key aspect of what often occurs in constitutional revolutions? In this regard, the Glorious Revolution, which brought about an enduring change in power relations within the English Constitution, offers a useful template for making sense of the concept in a way that illuminates a familiar component in the seemingly very different circumstances to which the term is applied.[103]

To see how, we need to account for the adjective, or why the revolution became glorious. One explanation is that it represented the vindication of the ancient constitution, a restoration of the rule of law after the transgressions of James II. Thus, that idea supports the older view of revolution, or as a scholar of the upheaval put it, it was revolutionary in the manner "of a wheel turning round to a former state."[104] This account is essentially the Whig revolution narrative—Arendt is hardly alone in embracing it—in which the deletion of novelty from the story line renders it difficult to construe the glory of the transition as particularly revolutionary. Rather, it represented a redemptive achievement, a fulfillment of the implicit promise of the English constitutional order. As J. G. A. Pocock noted, "Those who called the Revolution 'glorious' in the centuries of Whig supremacy and Whig interpretation meant to suggest that it had preserved the constitution by constitutional means; even those like Burke, who insisted on the element of extraconstitutional necessity, did not deny the major premise of the assertion."[105] Burke's interpretation of the revolution as preservative of the constitution rather than subversive of it not only was a reflection of his Whig political identity but also fit comfortably within his extensively elaborated theory of constitutional identity.[106]

But there is another side to the Whig interpretation of the revolution, one in which "its glory consisted in the final triumph of parliament over the Crown."[107] The revolution's outcome may seem inconsequential if the measuring rod is John Locke's *Second Treatise of Civil Government.* That yardstick would, however, be an entirely unreasonable standard to apply to events contemporaneous with its publication. As a touchstone for measuring significance, its time came nearly a century later in distant colonies. As Jack Greene noted, "For the development of the British Empire as a whole . . . the most important results of the Glorious Revolution were the localization of power and the growth of parliamentary institutions, not just within Britain but also in Ireland and the American colonies."[108] Yet even if one confines an assessment of the revolution's achievements to its immediate aftermath, it is hard to minimize the significance of replacing absolute with limited monarchical rule. It is also hard to deny that exchanging one king for another corresponded to, and was ultimately of less importance than, the ascendance of one type of kingship over another. Destroyed was "the theory of divine-right monarchy, the idea of direct heredity successor, the prerogatives of the king over law, the military, taxation, and judicial procedures that were to the detriment of the individual."[109] The Glorious Revolution was, by this and many other accounts, a turning point in English and European history. Left to be decided, however, was this question: was it a turning point—indeed revolutionary—in the astronomical sense or in the novelty of its constitutional innovation?

The ambiguity surrounding this question bears directly on how one might think about a constitutional revolution. Pocock said of Burke that he "was obliged to represent the Revolution as . . . constitutional," and the same may be said of many who participated in and had a stake in its outcome.[110] An exhaustive study of the revolution's lasting, tangible legacies—the Declaration of Rights and the Bill of Rights—reveals that the "Whig myth of an ancient constitution" is a mostly fair characterization of the familiar version of events, but that in certain particulars the wheel metaphor captures a good deal of what transpired in the politics of late-seventeenth-century England.[111] It captures it both as a depiction of the political strategy by which conservative garb was used to obscure and hence facilitate the underlying reality of constitutional change, and as a representation of the actual recovery of ancient rights of the realm. As the historian W. A. Speck noted of the constitutional revolution (without using that term): "The spirit of a constitution is not confined to its documents. While the letter of the law might not have changed greatly, the whole attitude of and towards government altered drastically."[112] What is more, consistent with our argument, the revolutionary significance of what changed drastically was not, as Jennifer Carter has pointed out, a "foregone conclusion" at the time of the Glorious Revolution, but required at least a half century to become manifest, once Parliament matured into the supreme sovereign entity it came to be.[113]

Confirmation of a paradigmatic displacement in the conceptual prism through which constitutionalism was experienced after 1689 need not depend on a definitive answer to the novelty conundrum. Indeed, uncertainty about this question is a natural condition of constitutional revolutions; in this sense, the Glorious Revolution is a model case.[114] The reason lies not simply in the perceptual screens through which important changes inevitably are seen, but in the nature of what is changed—a constitution. Its identity, even when undergoing a significant transformation, will remain tethered to past conflicts that do not dissipate with the implementation of novel constitutional arrangements. As Hanna Pitkin observed, "How we are able to constitute ourselves is profoundly tied to how we are already constituted by our own distinctive history."[115] Thus, much of the novelty of constitutional innovation has an aspect rooted in the past—at least to an imagined past that allows one to affirm as constitutional that which may be achieved through questionable or even extraconstitutional action.

Two Cases

United States, 1787

The extent to which innovations in constitutional practice and orientation will ultimately be seen as having vindicated the wishes of their most visionary advocates may be decisively affected by their very ordinariness. Thus, a presumption of radical change does not readily attach to those shifts that stem from the regularity of prescribed process. Rather, when things go off constitutional course, we are more likely to judge the results as potentially far-reaching and pathbreaking, for better or worse. People rely on constitutions to order change. Such reliance can mean one of two things—or both. In the first meaning, the rules and principles that make up a constitution's content are used to influence the character of the changes that occur within a society committed to the rule of law. If the constitution is working well, then changes that flow from the choices made by individuals, groups, and institutions will be orderly, which is to say, in conformity with the procedures set out in the governing document. In the second meaning, the constitution is committed to ensuring not only that changes occur in an orderly, legal manner, but also that the substance of the changes is compatible with the document's essential commitments. Thus, constitutions may be viewed as instruments to order change in the sense of prescribing both the type and the degree of transformation in accordance with directives enshrined in key textual provisions.

The change that resulted in the adoption of the Constitution of 1787 was famously not achieved in compliance with the text of the Articles of Confederation: "The very convening of the convention may be considered as a 'de-constituent' step, on the verge of a legal revolution."[116] That the Constitutional Convention was acting illegally in effectively replacing the Articles with a new charter is less interesting, however, than the question of exactly what was wrought by the change. It is a question most intriguingly raised by James Madison in his defense of the convention's dubiously sanctioned transformative undertaking. In *Federalist* 40, he posed the question in a way that speaks directly to our concern in this chapter. He focused on "the boundary between authorized and usurped innovations; between that degree of change which lies within the compass of *alterations and further pro-*

visions, and that which amounts to a *transmutation* of government."[117] One might then ask, did a constitutional revolution occur?

Madison's response is revealing when set against the conceptual distinctions set out earlier. While conceding that the alterations made in Philadelphia were "irregular," and that they were "instituted by some *informal and unauthorized propositions,*" he maintains that the changes, "substantial" though they were, amounted to an "expansion of principles which are found in the articles of confederation."[118] Still, we are quickly informed that such faithful adherence to the core commitments of the earlier document is perhaps more consequential than this purported exercise in continuity might suggest: "The misfortune under the [articles] has been, that these principles are so feeble as to justify all the charges of inefficiency which have been urged against it, and to require a degree of enlargement which gives to the new system the aspect of an entire transformation of the old."[119] Had the Constitution emerged more in line with Anti-Federalist thinking, it too would have been seen as falling within the constitutional tradition of the colonial period. But it would not have bequeathed to Americans a constitutional solution that, in its contribution to political science, was truly original in concept and scope.

What are we to make of this "degree of enlargement" that has an "aspect of an entire transformation of the old"? If it is simply a course correction ("correcting the errors" of the Articles), then in what sense, if at all, can the move from the document drafted by the Continental Congress to the one later framed by the Constitutional Convention be construed as revolutionary? If the "*fundamental principles* of the Confederation" were, as Madison took pains to point out, "not within the purview of the convention," then how can one describe the work of that body as anything other than, well, conventional?[120]

Reflecting further on the second meaning of constitutionally ordered change best addresses the conundrum. Whereas the first connotation assumes a well-functioning constitution that contemplates rigid compliance with the legal forms—including procedures for amendment—prescribed in the document, the second envisions the possibility of malfunction, a condition that exists when constitutional forms fail to advance the substance of the constitution's animating principles. When this occurs, we might say that the disjuncture between form and substance is evidence for the absence of constitutional order, which Madison sanctioned as justification for "*informal and unauthorized*" actions to secure the harmony between form and substance, as our aspirations for a just constitutional settlement requires. Indeed, that is exactly what he does in arguing, with specific reference to the most revolutionary of passages in the Declaration of Independence, "that in all great changes of established governments, form ought to give way to substance."[121]

The mention of that revolutionary document is critically important. Recall the two definitions of constitutional revolution presented earlier, the first of which—any illegally established postrevolutionary constitutional order—is surely applicable to the ratification of America's first charter in 1781. The second, more inclusive construction focused on the substance and outcome of a constitutional displacement—however achieved—that leaves the practice of constitutional governance in a very different place from where it had previously been. In this account, rupture and discontinuity are not defining criteria for establishing the presence of a constitutional revolution. The sort of revolutionary displacement involved under this second heading originates and develops within the domain of legality, although it may reach its destination only after a controversial passage through questionable extralegal terrain. Madison's insistence on the principled continuity of the Articles and their 1787 replacement provides both efforts with a common source of revolutionary inspiration. His defense of the irregularity of the movement from one to the other does not contradict his belief that only with the proposed changes could the revolutionary promise of the rupture from British rule effectively be realized.

Indeed, Madison's emphasis on continuity speaks to a larger point. In a discussion of Arendt's views on revolution, Andreas Kalyvas notes, in connection with the break with colonial governance, that "the American revolutionaries were able to avoid the language and practice of absolute ruptures," relying "on a pre-existing legal layer . . . which remained intact during the entire period of political foundation." Also, "by refusing to eliminate them, the American revolutionaries remained within the law even during such exceptional moments."[122] If we take the entire period of foundation to include both constitutional framings, then Madison's argument in *Federalist* 40 may be seen to contain a deeper significance for theorizing constitutional revolution. Thus, the "course correction" of 1787 represents a familiar example of constitutional identity formation in which a divided legacy serves as a continuing resource for those seeking major change in the workings of the constitutional order.[123] A fundamental, even radical departure in a nation's constitutional way of doing things may be presented as an effort to revive a superior approach, one previously displaced in the vortex of political contestation. Or put another way, Madison was engaged in an activity essential to the success of constitutional revolutions, particularly of the second type: enhancement of the outcome's legitimacy by insisting on its restorative intent.[124]

Ireland, 1937

Now consider Ireland, which has a story that, in its two-stage developmental progression (spanning fifteen years), recalls the American case (spanning eleven years), and that, in its entanglement with an intrusive foreign power, evokes the Japanese experience. It is instructive briefly to reflect on European developments from about the time of the first stage in the Irish constitutional saga. Thus, Article I of Germany's Weimar Constitution reads: "The German Reich is a republic. State authority derives from the people." The numerous flaws in the ill-fated Weimar Constitution should not diminish the significance of this revolutionary affirmation. As the first German constitution to embody the principle of popular sovereignty, the document occupies a unique place in the history of constitutionalism. As a constitutional revolution, however, there was nothing unique in the manner of the new republic's emergence: the 1918 overthrow of the imperial structures of the Bismarckian state was a direct by-product of the outcome of a war.

Yet its significance has been famously diminished. Thus, another by-product of the 1918 German revolution was the "jurisprudence of crisis," and it has provided legal scholars of the twentieth century with a treasure trove of philosophical reflection on law and the state.[125] At the center of this jurisprudential effusion was Carl Schmitt, whose critique of Weimar constitutionalism is also worth considering in connection with the Irish constitutional transformation that was an outgrowth of the same war. Seen in the light of Schmitt's critique, the Irish case can help address one of the more vexing conceptual challenges of constitutional-revolution theorizing: the problem of rupture and continuity.

Schmitt called into question the revolutionary importance of the 1918 revolution: "The new German Reich is a constitutional democracy. It has a constitution, just as it had a constitution under the monarchy; here, in the 'constitutional,' lies an essential continuity linking today's Reich with the old Reich of 1871. . . . There is no break, no revolution in the strict legal sense between the old and the new form of state. A constitutional democracy replaced a constitutional monarchy. The German Reich is not simply a democracy but a *constitutional* democracy."[126] What is more, the integrity of the nation had been badly compromised by the Versailles Treaty, rendering what the regime's champions trumpeted as their crowning accomplishment—popular sovereignty—a hollow achievement. "The Reich has not gained complete sovereignty, and this lack of political substance would relativize the importance of any constitution."[127]

Schmitt's argument serves as a skeptical rejoinder to the classical model of constitutional revolution, which was easily identifiable as a new constitutional order succeeding the forceful removal of a previous order. What, however, was presented as straightforward is, in Schmitt's account, subject to two objections: revolutionary political change (that is, illegal, violent upheaval that produces a substitution of one form of government for another) is not a prelude to constitutional revolution without a break in continuity that culminates in an authentic expression of popular sovereignty; and to the extent that internal constitutional transformation is shaped by the exertion of political power external to the sovereign will of the nation, it diminishes the constitutional significance of even postrevolutionary new beginnings.

The Constitution of the Irish Free State was adopted in 1922 after a sequence of events that included a bloody conflict with Great Britain culminating in the Anglo-Irish Treaty. That agreement gave Dominion status to the newly independent state. A division among Irish political leaders over acceptance of the treaty led to a civil war, the conclusion of which, in 1923, failed to end the debate over the legitimacy of the new constitutional creation. Despite passage of a number of amendments in the following years to reduce the formal dependency of the Irish on the British, a government formed in 1932 under the leadership of Eamon de Valera was determined to replace the Free State Constitution with a new document that would officially end all ties under the treaty and establish a constitutional republic. This goal was achieved in 1937 after a draft constitution was adopted by a referendum, a development described by one of Ireland's leading constitutional commentators as "a break in legal continuity; . . . a supplementing of one *Grundnorm* (albeit a disputed one) by another; and thus, legally speaking . . . a revolution."[128] (*Grundnorm* is Hans Kelsen's conceptual term for establishing the legitimacy of law through its connection with an originating legal source.)

There are two ways in which the Irish developments of 1937 can be depicted as a constitutional revolution, and both display conceptually significant similarities to the American case. Recall Madison's claim that the changes wrought by the Constitutional Convention represented an "expansion of principles which are found in the articles of confederation." The new constitution was not so much a rejection of the old as its fulfillment or completion, an occasion for correcting the earlier failure to align the form and substance of the effort's animating principles. It was an exercise in continuity that was revolutionary in a constitutional sense because it provided closure to the regime reordering initiated previously.[129] Also, the irregularity of the major course correction—its questionable legality—provided the second constitutional moment with a measure of radical separation that one expects to see in a revolutionary scenario. The coupling of rupture and continuity may seem paradoxical, but it is a familiar conceptual association for the sort of constitutional change with which we are concerned.

An important assessment of the Irish Free State constitution published ten years after its adoption described the achievement as an "essentially republican constitution" that embodied the "theoretical postulates of a revolutionary upheaval" more than the "legislative crystallization of an organic development."[130] More recently, it was said of the 1922 constitution that it "followed the rituals of a new beginning, but there was no constitutional moment." There was no "radical change, instead, the Free State's constitutional order was gradually reduced to the basic structure of the Westminster system."[131] That same analysis identified the 1937 developments as a "constitutional revolution," one, however, manifesting "substantial continuity" with important commitments from 1922, namely, to "personal rights, religious freedom, and an independent judiciary."[132] Notably, it did not include as a continuing commitment what the earlier account had emphasized: "the principle of the sovereignty of the people as the fundamental and the exclusive source of all political authority."[133]

As in the American case, the question raised by these differing perspectives is one of form and substance played out in an extended transformational progression spanning two major ruptures in constitutional continuity. In each instance, the first break followed a violent struggle to secure independence from Great Britain, resulting in complete success for the Americans and partial success for the Irish, the latter being unable to obtain autonomy over the framing and adoption of their new constitution. In each instance, too, the initial effort was the occasion for deep partisan division over the direction of the new constitutional undertaking, leading eventually to a second break, which in turn enabled a subsequent group of framers to attempt to redeem the revolutionary promise of their predecessors. "The American Constitution," Hannah Arendt wrote, "finally consolidated the power of the Revolution."[134] Similarly, "the purpose [behind the Irish Constitution of 1937] was to consolidate rather than to experiment and start anew."[135]

If the redemptive effort by the second transformational moment is successful—as it was in both countries—then it becomes necessary to belabor the point that a revolution is a process, not an event or a "moment." The extended Irish development underscores a reality that can easily be obscured in the more concentrated form in which constitutional revolutions often present themselves. This in turn should inform the rejoinder to Schmitt's argument, which, insistent on a radical break in constitutional continuity as the basis for revolutionary validation, can easily, through a too narrowly focused appraisal of the initial displacement, lead to a misreading of the resulting protracted rollout of change. The transition to popular will as the legitimate source of sovereign authority is not likely to occur abruptly, and in some cases it may require an extended conversion period. To the extent that such is required, it will also diminish the force and appeal of Schmitt's second objection, since the presence of external sovereign intervention in the substitution of one title to rule for another may now be viewed as a necessary stage in the changeover culminating in genuine transformation just as easily as it can be seen as a fatal subversion of a people's aspiration for a more just, popular regime.

Depicting the adoption through a plebiscite of the Constitution of 1937 as a constitutional revolution relies on the commonly held view of its illegal framing, which lay outside the scope of extant authority, and on the severance of the remaining Free State impediments to the expression of an authentic popular sovereign will. These achievements are themselves not severable, since the Constituent Assembly that enacted the Free State Constitution expressly denied to the legislature the power to amend the document in ways that would be contrary to the Anglo-Irish Treaty. De Valera, the prime mover behind the new constitution, in fact bypassed the legislature (which was relegated to a pro forma role in the process) and the Constituent Assembly; in light of the existing constitution's provisions, the irregularity of the process was blatant—and deliberately so. Still, an alternative understanding holds that "the authority of the Constituent Assembly which enacted the Constitution of 1922 itself derived from the people . . . and so the enactment by the people of the Constitution of 1937, whilst in breach of the Constituent Act, maintained the same legitimation as that Act."[136]

The effort to salvage a legally sanctioned constitutional rewrite, though surely strained, nevertheless helps clarify the question of constitutional revolution in Ireland and more generally. According to this view, a "legal revolution" occurred in 1937, as had also happened in 1922, which saw "a legal revolution based on popular sovereignty."[137] However important the dispute among Irish historians regarding the legalities of the 1937 Constitution, more important here is the eminently plausible characterization—also of course in dispute (a civil war was fought over it)—of the earlier source of constitutional authority as having been popularly grounded. As pointed out previously, agreement on whether a revolutionary displacement occurred within the constraints of legality will typically be difficult to achieve. Critical, though, is whether the displacement, however achieved, was of paradigmatic significance for the way constitutionalism was thereafter experienced. Undoubtedly, the incorporation of the Anglo-Irish Treaty within the terms of the 1922 Constitution compromised the sovereign integrity of the new venture.[138] Still, to deny that both the securing of independence from a regime famously known for its institutionally based locus of sovereign authority, and the subsequent adoption by a Constituent Assembly of a document explicitly committed to the principle of popular sovereignty, was a signal achievement in radical constitutional transformation is a difficult argument to sustain.

As more material has become available concerning the drafting of the 1937 Constitution, we learn that de Valera's purpose in submitting the document for approval in a plebiscite was to highlight the new republic's fresh start. Doing so in this manner would vividly represent its principal and long-delayed substantive achievement: popular sovereignty. But we also learn that the de Valera–led group that wrote the constitution was a rather small, secretive cohort of political and religious activists whose efforts in popular constitution making arguably are less notable in this regard than the earlier labors of members of the Constituent Assembly (in concert with the British), which framed the Free State Constitution. Much like the Weimar Constitution, also a Constituent Assembly creation, the 1922 charter was not presented for a popular referendum. Because of the problems of legitimacy associated with constituent assemblies and their ex nihilo creations, over the course of the century referrals to the people increasingly came to be seen as critical for achieving credibility and support among affected populations. Looking, then, at the fifteen-year Irish progression from constitution to constitution as a cumulative constitutional revolution, the plebiscitary end point represents symbolic closure on a process that commenced with a substantially compromised expression of a nation's *pouvoir constituant* (constituent power).

The Bunreacht Na hEireann (the Constitution of 1937) concluded the extended revolutionary progression that anchored Irish constitutionalism in a fundamentally transformed state. It also consolidated another defining commitment that ensured a continuing struggle for the meaning of the post-rupture settlement. Natural law, exceedingly muted in the Free State Constitution, is boldly featured in the replacement document as a principle limiting the expression of the popular will.[139] It has been correctly said that everything "worthwhile in the Irish Free State Constitution of 1922 received renewed expression in *Bunreacht Na hEireann*, 1937";[140] in invoking as prominently as it does some signal precepts from Catholic natural-law theology, the republican constitution invested in an act of recovery from a tradition that long antedated the much more recent celebration of popular sovereignty. As de Valera explained, "Since the coming of St. Patrick, fifteen hundred years ago, Ireland has been a Christian and Catholic nation. . . . She remains a Catholic nation."[141]

A constitutional identity is an evolving phenomenon rooted in a disharmony often manifest in the tension between commitments expressive of a nation's past (for example, Ireland's Catholic tradition) and the determination of those who seek to transcend or modify it—in Ireland through the trumping power of popular sovereign authority. When it happens, a constitutional revolution is a hinge moment in the development of this identity. The elevation of Thomistic natural law to a position of constitutional prominence not only is a distinctive part of Ireland's constitutional revolution, but also, in its restorative aspect, speaks to a thread of historical continuity that is a staple of such occurrences. Together and to varying degrees, rupture and continuity are the yin and yang of constitutional revolutions. Those, like Schmitt, who insist only on a decisive break with the past to authenticate the presence of a revolutionary passage may be asking for more than the constitutional variant of such change can bear. Or perhaps they are implicitly, but mistakenly, making another point: that there is no such thing as a constitutional revolution.[142]

It has become a common practice of constitution writers to include in the preambles to their documents statements that capture some aspect of the national experience deemed relevant to the task at hand. As we have seen, a number of these constitutions refer specifically to the revolutionary moment without which the occasion for constitution writing would not exist (for example, the constitutions of Romania, China, Cuba, Vietnam, Panama, Iran, and Nepal). This moment, even when unmentioned—as, for example, in the American case—has loomed large not just for those who compose constitutions but also for those who study them. Thus, for Bruce Ackerman, "*revolution* and *constitution* describe the two faces of liberal political transformation,"[143] a generally hopeful nexus in which "a people might plausibly break with its past, and construct a new political identity for itself."[144]

It does not always work out that way. During debate in the First Israeli Knesset, a member of the ruling Mapai party said: "One does not create a constitution at the beginning of a revolution, but when it is completed. All constitutions are an attempt to 'freeze' certain principles, to preserve them, inasmuch as it is possible to preserve any particular thing in the life of a nation."[145] His purpose was to delay codification of a new constitution for the newly independent State of Israel. That effort succeeded, and to this day there is no fully realized, comprehensive constitutional document. The member's point was more Israel-specific than he perhaps let on, since it was meant to reinforce David Ben-Gurion's argument that the drafting of a constitution should not precede the "Ingathering of the Exiles."[146] Only then could there be a determination of the nature of the regime, whether it was to be a Western state, a state of the Jewish people, a Jewish state, or all of the above. Still, the line of reasoning conforms to a familiar claim that has been urged in connection with constitutional revolution; or in Ackerman's framing, "a Constitution is a natural culmination of a successful revolution." In this account, a revolutionary displacement of one regime by another is followed by a codification of the fruits of victory, which is to say, the principles and commitments that came to define the transformational moment. In Israel, this did not happen, and unfortunately, "the constitutional moment passed into history."[147]

In this chapter, we have argued that this account needs refinement. In the American case, for example, the Articles of Confederation did indeed provide constitutional legitimacy to the revolutionary severance, but the more successful framing venture in 1787 was not attributable to any massive infusion of new members into the ranks of the citizenry. Rather, it resulted from specific lessons learned from actual experience under the earlier constitutional structure. In fact, the document was eventually sold as an improvement over its predecessor not because it had discovered the true meaning of the revolution, but because it represented a better prospect for realizing its aspirations. This second document, with its tragic internal contradictions, most glaringly evident in its concessions to officially sanctioned human inequality, was itself only a partial and incomplete congealing of principles set out in the nation's revolutionary manifesto.[148] In a strictly legal sense, those principles became constitutionally "frozen" only after the addition of the Civil War amendments—in the spirit of the Knesset member's comment, only after the true completion of the American Revolution.[149]

What occurred in the United States can be viewed as a process common to constitution making in deeply divided societies: "The constitutional arrangements in these societies [are] designed to prevent potentially explosive conflict essentially by not addressing contentious issues head on, and leaving foundational aspects of the constitution to be decided in the future."[150] Accordingly, radical change is deferred to a distant time, breaking the link between constitution and revolution. Alternatively, we might say that the constitutional disharmony present in the most intensely divided societies—where vehement dissonance complicates the establishment and ascertainment of a constitutional identity—only highlights the workings of a political dynamic that is present in all regimes. The actual playing-out of this dynamic varies considerably in accordance with the intensity and configuration of disharmonic constitutional politics in different places, but this variation ought not to obscure a fundamental ubiquity in the unfolding of constitutional development in regimes of disparate character.

When the development assumes a radical departure from previous experience, the transformative significance of what has transpired ought not to be minimized or negated by the extended period that accompanies the consolidation of revolutionary aspirations.[151] The progression of Irish constitutionalism from the rupture codified in 1922 to the more fully realized achievement of that moment's defining commitment in 1937 was "part of a gradual process of constitutional development through which the Irish state became sovereign."[152] Conceivably, it might have occurred within the framework of the 1922 Constitution, but circumstances dictated that the attainment of popular sovereignty be presented as a novel departure rather than as the culmination of a process whose beginnings were blemished by the stigma of colonial entanglement and insinuation. Exceptional in many respects as was the unfolding of the Irish constitution-making experience, in its progression through rupture, aspiration, and consolidation, it was very much an exemplar of a familiar story line associated with constitutional revolution.

Michael Collins, the Irish political leader and champion of the Free State Constitution whose life was taken because of his close identification with that blemish, was correct in believing that constitutions "could be crafted over time, and did not require a dramatic, revolutionary moment for their creation."[153] In this regard, he might have been understandably wary of the

Ackermanian notion of a "constitutional moment," to the extent at least of its suggestion that a new constitutional order is in any meaningful sense perceptible in the immediate aftermath of a revolutionary break. The constitutional moment passes very quickly, and it is a time to exploit the opportunity to validate a clean start with a governing document affirming a new constitutional reality. The adoption of the Indian Constitution, with its serious attention to issues that were of little official concern before independence, is another case in point, although it is reasonable to ask how the reality to which such affirmations are attached conveys anything more than a collection of rules, principles, and aspirations whose meaning and reach are as yet only the expressed will of framers of varied mind-sets and purposes. There may be a dominant view on these matters—arguably, in India it had to do with a commitment to dismantle entrenched structures of injustice—but invariably there are also powerful dissenting voices whose influence does not end with the signing of a document.[154] All constitutions are crafted over time in the sense that their meanings and identities evolve gradually in ways determined by a dynamic fueled by their internal tensions and contradictions and by their confrontations with a social order over which they have limited influence. In time, a constitutional order is constructed and shaped, and the ambitions inscribed in, or attributed to, the constitution are realized or not—or more likely, approximated to a greater or lesser degree. And that is the moment for assessment of the constitutional revolution.

3

Revolutionary Constitutional Amendments: Hungary Between Rupture and Continuity

> If someone who desires or who wishes to reform a state in a city wishes it to be accepted and capable of being maintained to the satisfaction of everyone, he is under the necessity of retaining at least the shadow of its ancient modes so that it may not appear to the peoples to have changed its order even if in fact the new orders are altogether alien to the past ones.
>
> Niccolò Machiavelli, *Discourses on Livy*

IN JULY 1940, THE FRENCH PARLIAMENT transformed democratic France into a dictatorship, destroying the foundations of the Third Republic in a way that complied with the Third Republic's legal procedure for constitutional revision as prescribed by the Constitution of 1875. The initial law amending the constitution, adopted July 10, 1940, by a vote of 569 to 80, gave Marshal Pétain the power to create a new constitution and in fact transferred to him *pouvoir constituant:* "The National Assembly grants all the powers of the government of the Republic, under the authority and signature of Marshal Pétain, to promulgate by one or more acts a new constitution of the French state." In the first constitutional act issued by Pétain, on July 11, 1940, he proclaimed himself the "Chief of the French State"; the second constitutional act, enacted the same day, defined the powers of the chief of state, granting Pétain all governmental and legislative power.[1] When speaking in Parliament in favor of Pétain, M. Jean Taurines reminded his colleagues in the National Assembly of Pétain's words: "I do not wish to be either a dictator or a Caesar."[2] Ironically, even within the historical institution of dictatorship—when, during times of crisis, an eminent citizen was called by officials and temporarily granted almost absolute powers in order to overcome the crisis and defend the republic—the dictator could not alter the constitutional order, as occurred in France. As Machiavelli noted, the dictator "could not do anything that might diminish the state, as taking away authority from the Senate or from the people, undoing the old orders of the city and making new ones, would have been."[3] In other words, the dictator could not subvert or alter the republic. He could not use his powers in order to change the basic character of the state or its institutional framework. A Roman dictator could not have replaced the constitution with a new one.[4] But this is precisely what happened in the case of Pétain. In July 1940, France, with large sectors of its territory under German and Italian occupation, inaugurated a new constitutional order.[5]

Noteworthy in these events is that even under extreme conditions, the constitutional undoing and replacement followed correct procedure for adopting a constitutional amendment (or revision, as it is called in France). Reflecting on the legality of the 1940 transformation, Karl Loewenstein wrote:

> It is axiomatic in French constitutional jurisprudence that a revolution is a legally recognized procedure for abrogating an existing constitution. As a matter of fact, almost all preceding French constitutions were terminated by revolutionary process. It is of record that not a single one of the nine constitutions since 1789 has been abrogated or replaced in the manner prescribed by the instrument itself. The constitution of 1875 is the first of its kind to be terminated in full conformity with the constitutional procedure intended when enacted. This is perhaps the most perplexing phenomenon of the "revolution" of 1940.[6]

The procedures employed in the 1940 constitutional reform, Loewenstein concluded, "were carried out with a full, and even excessive, sense of legality, and in complete accordance with the requirements of the constitution which they destroyed. It was the most orderly 'revolution' that ever occurred in France."[7] Was it, then, a constitutional amendment—after all, the formal rules of amendments were followed—or was it a constitutional replacement, since the Third Republic was effectively destroyed and replaced by a new regime? In this chapter, we explore the possibility of constitutional revolution through formal constitutional amendment, without a break in legal continuity. We focus on Hungary, a country that experienced two dramatic constitutional transformations in less than thirty years, both of which occurred without the invocation of an extraconstitutional constituent power.

Specifically, we explore a particular type of constitutional change: formal constitutional amendments adopted in accordance with existing procedures. Yet not every constitutional change—indeed, perhaps not even every constitutional replacement—counts as a constitutional revolution. As we emphasized in the previous chapter, a constitutional revolution represents constitutional change on a certain substantive scale, regardless of the form assumed by that change. It is a change that amounts to a paradigm shift in the basic principles or features of the constitutional order. After such alteration, the constitutional order is no longer the same; it has been drastically transformed and effectively replaced.[8]

And herein lies a puzzle. It is possible formally to replace a constitution with something so similar in substance that we are left with no real transformation of the constitutional order.[9] Conversely, it is possible to revolutionize a constitutional order—through amendment or interpretation—without replacing the existing constitution. Thus, the text of constitutions can be formally modified through constitutional amendments enacted in accordance with procedures stipulated within them, resulting in fundamental change in the constitutional order. With this in mind, Richard Albert contrasts constitutional amendment with "constitutional dismemberment": whereas, consistent with its existing design, a constitutional amendment "is an adjustment made to better achieve the purpose of the existing constitution," constitutional dismemberment aims to repudiate the essential characteristics of a constitution by destroying its foundations and transforming its identity, fundamental values, and architecture while leaving its formal legal continuity intact. Albert's core claim is that "some constitutional amendments are not amendments at all"; rather, they are "self-conscious efforts to repudiate the essential characteristics of the constitution and to destroy its foundations." Such constitutional changes "dismantle the basic structure of the constitution" and are therefore to be distinguished from the traditional conception of a constitutional amendment. They should, he argues, be identified as moments of "dismemberment" rather than amendment.[10]

To be sure, some constitutional "amendments" do not amend at all. They seek to transform the constitution, to replace it with a new one, and to revolutionize the constitutional order.[11] Although the term "dismemberment" seems apt, it does not accurately describe the phenomenon at hand. It emphasizes the constitution's destruction. But destruction represents only one aspect of fundamental constitutional change. "Dismemberment" fails to encompass the element of reconstruction. Accordingly, we prefer the term "revolution" to describe such constitutional transformations. Also, dismemberment is the act of cutting, tearing, pulling, or otherwise removing the limbs of a living thing. It has been practiced upon human beings as a form of capital punishment. It thus carries a misleading negative normative connotation. In contrast, constitutional revolution is a descriptive—not a normative—concept. It can describe constitutional transformation that either generates or destroys a liberal democratic constitutional order. As is shown in this chapter, Hungary offers examples of both types of revolution: in the 1980s, a successful transition from communism to a liberal democracy and a capitalist market, and a second, backlash transformation in 2011, culminating in an increasingly illiberal constitutional order.

Formal Constitutional Replacement and Constitution Making

A constitution can be replaced with a new constitution following a formal constitution-making process. By one estimate, about four or five constitutions are replaced with new ones every year.[12] The Arab Spring, which wrought significant social and political changes across North Africa and the Middle East, brought about a recent wave of constitutional revolutions.[13] Over the course of the nineteenth and twentieth centuries, from 1816 to 2003, there were over 500 transitions to democracy and over 360 changeovers in the opposite direction, to authoritarian rule.[14] Each of these regime conversions was necessarily accompanied by some type of a constitutional revolution.

Indeed, constitution making occurs more frequently than many people realize. As Zachary Elkins, Tom Ginsburg, and James Melton demonstrate, "the median survival time (the age at which one-half of constitutions are expected to have died) is nineteen years."[15] How are constitutions replaced? Constitution making takes many different forms. Some constitutions are formed in the aftermath of a revolution or in the process of state building. In such a revolutionary setting, the constitution-making body acts without preexisting constitution-making rules or simply ignores them. Famously, and as discussed in the previous chapter, the establishment of the U.S. Constitution was a constitutional replacement rather than an amendment of the Articles of the Confederation, since its framers exceeded their original mandate and failed to comply with the required procedure for amending the Articles.[16] Likewise, following the French Revolution and the proclamation of the French National Assembly of 1789 as a Constituent Assembly, many states, especially in Latin America, used constituent assemblies as instruments of what is termed ex nihilo creation, a type of constitution making in a legal void or in disregard of constitutional boundaries.[17]

Not all constitutions are created in such a manner. Recent examples demonstrate that the constitution-making process may be exercised in accordance with certain predetermined procedural and substantive rules. The South African constitution-making process is the exemplar. For the purpose of clarifying and ensuring the direction of the constitution-making process, the interim Constitution of 1994 stipulated that the constitution-making process would take place within a framework of thirty-four principles. To guarantee conformity with these principles, the Constitutional Court of South Africa was given explicit authority to review the draft Constitution and examine its compliance with those principles. In the famous *Certification Case,* the Court declared that the Constitution, although establishing democratic institutions and protecting human rights, failed to comply with some of the agreed-on principles. Only after the draft Constitution had been amended in light of the Court's decision did the tribunal declare that the Constitution conformed to the principles.[18] To be sure, this constitution-making in stages, with a court being asked to take the extraordinary task of scrutinizing the constituent power of the people, raises thorny questions about the concept of constituent power and the role of courts.[19] If a new constitution is created on the basis of existing constitutional procedures, was constituent power reduced in fact to a constituted power? Or was the initial decision concerning the guiding principles perhaps the "real" constitution-making moment?[20] We return to these questions in chapter 7.

Formal constitutional replacement presumes the exercise of the constituent power, or constitution-making power, of the people, which cannot be limited by the existing constitution's forms or procedures and can rightfully abrogate the constitution. As is elaborated in chapter 7, the ability of the constituent power to act free from legal constraints is consistent with one line of thought in constitutional theory from Joseph Sieyès to Carl Schmitt.[21] Accordingly, most constitutions do not establish a procedure for their own replacement. Yet some constitutions do attempt to establish rules even for their own replacement, thus regulating the exercise of the constituent power.[22] For instance, the Constitution of Venezuela of 1999 states in Article 347: "The original constituent power rests with the people of Venezuela. This power may be exercised by calling a National Constituent Assembly for the purpose of transforming the State, creating a new juridical order and drawing up a new Constitution." (Articles 348–49 further regulate this process.) Other constitutions prescribe a procedure for their "total reform," "complete revision," or "adopting a new constitution."[23] The Venice Commission, an advisory body of the Council of Europe composed of independent experts in the field of constitutional law, "strongly endorse[s]" the use of legal procedures for the adoption of "new constitutions," since such procedures "strengthen the stability, legality and legitimacy of the new system."[24]

Apart from formal replacements, can a constitution be replaced by amending the original constitution? A growing number of constitutions restrict the possibility of transformation by amendment by limiting the substantive scope of permissible amendments. In many cases, so-called eternity clauses purport to shield the constitution's core value and identity from alteration or destruction via amendments.[25] Such clauses raise the difficult question of how one is to determine whether a formal amendment is significant or fundamental enough to count as a potentially impermissible transformation rather than a legal reform of the constitutional order. As Elkins, Ginsburg, and Melton observe, there is a "fuzzy line between amendment and replacement," and that ambiguity creates classification challenges for scholars seeking to study such questions as the longevity of constitutions. Those authors' solution is to adopt a highly formal definition of amendment that turns entirely on whether amendment procedures set forth under the existing constitution were followed. Their approach has the advantage of being simple and yielding clear-cut answers that are amenable to empirical analysis, but as they acknowledge, it does not capture the magnitude of the actual change to the constitutional order.[26]

Constitutional Revolution by Formal Constitutional Amendment: Preliminary Examples

Whereas most constitutions do not provide a process for their formal replacement, about 96 percent of world constitutions include provisions for their formal amendment. Such provisions are a useful mechanism allowing constitutions to be sufficiently responsive to political, economic, and social changes.[27] A degree of responsiveness and flexibility may help a constitution to endure. For example, the Norwegian Constitution has been in operation since 1814, making it the second-oldest constitution still functioning (after only the U.S. Constitution), but it has undergone significant amendments. The Austrian Constitution dates to 1920, and since its reinstatement in 1945 after the end of the Austro-Fascist regime (1933–38), has been amended over eight hundred times.[28]

Some countries are so attached to their "historical" constitutions that they allow constitutional amendments that clearly modify even their basic structure or identity. For example, in Norway the Constitution of 1814 has been amended more than two hundred times and undergone major reforms, notwithstanding the explicit provision of Article 112 that expressly protects the "spirit" of the Constitution and its fundamental principles from constitutional amendment.[29] Similarly, in Belgium the unitary structure of the state, guaranteed under the Constitution of 1831, was later replaced with a federal system.[30]

The fact that a constitution has never been formally replaced may paint a misleading picture of its stability. As Claude Klein and András Sajó observe: "It is possible that through amendments the constitution becomes fundamentally different from the one which remains in formal existence, raising the issue of fundamental change of the constitution without making a formally new constitution."[31] In Chile, for example, the Pinochet Constitution of 1980 included antidemocratic features such as political veto power for the military, appointed senators, and overrepresentation of right-wing interests in the political system.[32] After Pinochet lost the 1988 presidential plebiscite, negotiations between the opposition coalition (Concertación de Partidos por la Democracia, CPD) and the right-wing supporters of the military regime led to an agreed-on regime transition in 1989 to democratic rule. The mechanism chosen for this transformation was a constitutional reform that modified several articles of the Constitution of 1980, essentially removing most authoritarian elements from it and enhancing its principles of representation, separation of powers, and popular sovereignty. Additional reforms between 1990 and 2003, and most notably in 2005, continued this transformation as the constitutional amenders eliminated or modified most of the remaining authoritarian "enclaves."[33] According to Fredrik Uggla, who analyzed the 1989 negotiation process:

> The very constitution itself, was a crucial element in the negotiations. In contrast to the situation during most transitions, the regime's constitution was not simply a dead letter. Instead . . . both government and opposition at this time were playing strictly by the rules laid down in the constitution . . . [which] formed the basis for all discussion. Although this arrangement primarily favored the regime—whose creation it was—certain elements also benefited the CPD [the opposition coalition], primarily the low quorum required to reform the process of amendment. . . . This point . . . shows how a previously created institution serves as a master frame that later participants find impossible to escape from. . . . Reform, whether it came from the regime or the opposition, would have to be done by the book, and the relevant text in this regard was the constitution itself.[34]

Thus, constitutional revolution in Chile, transforming the regime from authoritarian to democratic, took place gradually (the second major reform, in 2005, occurred fifteen years after the initial transition), and did so by using the amendment procedures of the old authoritarian Constitution.[35] What transpired was a revolution under the rule of law. As discussed later, a similar revolution disguised within the forms of legal continuity occurred in Eastern Europe, most conspicuously in Hungary.[36]

A comparable story of legal continuity and substantive rupture emerged in South Korea and Taiwan, transforming these countries via constitutional amendment from authoritarian regimes to democratic orders. The Taiwanese (Republic of China) Constitution was enacted in 1946 by Chinese Nationalists after their loss in the civil war. The Nationalist authorities initially adopted a policy of "no revision," yet as it became clear that changes were necessary, "temporary provisions" were added to the constitution, leaving the body of the text intact. These "temporary provisions" facilitated the consolidation of President Chiang Kai-shek's power, legitimating authoritarian measures and making formal constitutional revisions unnecessary. Within this framework, martial law was declared in 1949.[37] In 1987, after nearly forty years of a "soft-authoritarian" state, Taiwan entered a period of political transformation to a liberal democracy. This transformation, however, "took place within the constitutional processes and institutional framework, which have shown how a constitution could function in a transitional moment."[38]

President Chiang Ching-kuo lifted the martial law that had been in place since 1949 and announced a plan for parliamentary reform. The abandonment of martial law removed the bar on organizing new political parties. After Chiang's death in 1988, his successor, Lee Teng-hui, pledged to carry out his policies of reform and democratization. Very cautiously, President Lee started a gradual process of democratization, pushing for constitutional reforms within the extant constitutional framework. He organized an ad hoc National Affairs Conference to which representatives were invited from political, business, and academic circles, in some respects resembling the roundtable talks held during Eastern European transitions. Some conference delegates suggested the drafting of a completely new constitution, while the majority favored amendments to the Constitution of 1947. The ruling authorities rejected the idea of a new constitution and opted for incremental constitutional change through amendments. But the only formal institution possessing the legal authority to amend the constitution was the National Assembly, whose members had not been reelected since 1948 and who therefore lacked the democratic legitimacy to proceed accordingly. And so President Lee adopted a "two-stages" doctrine, in which a legitimate institution that would represent the Taiwanese through popular election would be created in the first stage, and in the second stage the legitimate body would develop a program of substantive amendments to the Constitution. In April 1991, the National Assembly passed constitutional amendments providing for new elections for all parliamentary branches—the National Assembly, the Legislative Yuan, and the Control Yuan. By the end of April, President Lee annulled the "temporary provisions" and announced the termination of the civil war status with the mainland. This invalidation paved the way for a new constitutional process. But to keep the continuity of the existing legal system, the constitutional changes took place in phases through a series of constitutional amendments, enacted in 1991, 1992, 1994, 1997, and 2000, that fundamentally altered the governmental structure and character.[39]

Taiwan's constitutional order thus experienced a remarkable change. In ten years, an authoritarian regime was radically transformed in a democratic direction. This constitutional revolution was achieved gradually and under the legal parameters of the existing constitutional framework. As in Chile, this measured revolutionary transformation proceeded with minimal social disorder and violence; the continuity with the past and the avoidance of a sudden break in authority maintained remnants of the former regime. As we will see, such maintenance is a recurring theme in constitutional revolutions brought about by constitutional amendments to standing constitutions.

The bloodless and legal transformation in Taiwan is often regarded as a "quiet revolution." "The celebrated 'quiet revolution' in Taiwan," Jiunn-rongn Yeh wrote, "was carried out and codified into the existing constitution that used to be considered as externally imposed."[40] Of course, the best example of an externally imposed constitution achieved through the use of constitutional amendment is the Japanese Constitution.

The Japanese constitution-making process is a fascinating example of the use of the constitutional mechanisms of an old constitutional order, even under the extreme conditions of an external occupying power, to address the tension between continuity and discontinuity. The initial policy goal of the postwar occupation, besides dismantling the war-making powers of the state and the institutional apparatuses that had allowed militarism to take over, was to repudiate the past: to transform the political culture and the allegedly authoritarian mind-set of the Japanese people. For the occupying power, the past was not merely an object of rejection or repudiation. Its repudiation was linked with another goal: maintaining a certain continuity with the past. The construction of a new democratic polity was to draw from the nation's history and values.[41]

This notion of continuity was shared by General Douglas MacArthur, who insisted on "complete legal continuity" in the constitution-making process. The Far Eastern Commission (FEC), the supervisory institution created under the auspices of the State Department, expressed a similar view, issuing a mandatory policy decision titled "Criteria for the Adoption of a New Japanese Constitution." One of the criteria was that "complete legal continuity from the [Meiji] Constitution of 1889 to the new Constitution should be assured."[42] The initiation of "a new constitution" by maintaining legal continuity was deemed necessary to forestall any future claims about the illegality of the constitution and, hence, its invalidity.[43] The new constitution was adopted following the amendment procedures of the Meiji Constitution. Consistent with Article 73, the emperor had to initiate the constitutional amendment process, after which the Imperial Diet, formed under the old constitution, would ratify it. This sense of continuity not only contributed to the legal legitimacy of the document but also allowed for the maintenance of deep respect for the imperial institution.[44] These decisions, Chaihark Hahm and Sung Ho Kim noted, "facilitated the process of producing a revolution while maintaining continuity with the past."[45]

Still, this revolutionary rupture through legal continuity caused some strange inconsistencies. Corresponding with the Preamble's celebrated opening—"We, the Japanese people," who "proclaim" and "establish" the Constitution—the new constitution declares in Article 1 that sovereignty resides with the people. Yet contrary to this affirmation of popular sovereignty, in the preface to the Constitution it is the emperor who "sanctions and promulgates" the "amendments" to the Meiji Constitution. This seems prima facie contradictory: does sovereignty rest with the emperor or with the people? If "the people" are sovereign, why was the emperor's assertion required? In other words, the reference to the authorization of the emperor points to ongoing imperial sovereignty rather than popular sovereignty. What is more, according to the Preamble, the Japanese people were "acting through [their] duly elected representatives in the National Diet [Kokkai]."

The National Diet, however, had not been created at the time, and it was the Imperial Diet (Teikoku Gikai) that actually passed the new constitution. Emphasizing the tension between continuity and rupture, Hahm and Kim remarked that "popular sovereignty was enshrined for the first time in Japanese constitutional history by following the old formalities and procedures that the new Constitution was designed to displace."[46]

The continuity-discontinuity tension generated an intellectual debate in Japan between two schools of thought. Linkage with the past was emphasized by Tomoo Otaka, who argued for a certain continuity of the "sovereignty of nomos" (law or justice), which bridges the old and new constitutions. The alternative and more popular view was that the new constitutional order represented a profound rupture in Japanese history. The notion of a radical departure from the previous constitutional order—indeed revolutionary change—was evident in Toshiyoshi Miyazawa's famous "August Revolution" theory (*hachigatsu kakumeisetsu*). For Miyazawa, changing the fundamental principles of the Meiji Constitution should be regarded as legally impossible, since it would result in using the amendment procedure for the destruction of the Constitution itself. Thus, using Article 73 to modify the idea that sovereignty resided with the emperor and divine will would exceed the limits of the amendment power. For Miyazawa, acceptance of the terms of the Potsdam Declaration in 1945 had brought about a bloodless revolution of Japan's constitutional order. The transformation from imperial sovereignty to popular sovereignty, from militarism to pacifism, and from theocracy to democracy altered the basic premise (*konpon tateme*) of the Meiji Constitution, effectively terminating it. In this account, the Japanese Constitution should be referred to as a new constitution, not an amended constitution.[47]

From a purely legal-positivist perspective, in abiding by the required procedure for formal constitutional change, the transformation from imperial sovereignty to popular sovereignty was legally legitimized. Legality is one thing; substantively, a fundamental divergence exists between the two constitutions, which in our account makes what was accomplished a constitutional revolution.[48]

The Japanese Constitution, promulgated in 1946, has never been amended.[49] This stable trajectory of Japanese constitutional history can be sharply contrasted with the volatility of what has occurred on the southern side of the Korean Peninsula. From the end of the Korean War to the implementation of the current democratic constitution in October 1987, the Constitution of 1948 was amended several times as six republics were established during that period. It was through a series of constitutional amendments that South Korea was incrementally transformed from authoritarian rule to a functioning democracy.[50]

The 1948 Constitution established a system whereby the president was elected by the National Assembly. The first constitutional amendment, in 1952, introduced direct election of both the president and a bicameral legislature, followed two years later by a contentiously enacted second amendment. President Syngman Rhee needed a constitutional amendment in order to run for a third term, and on September 8, 1954, such an amendment was proposed and then controversially adopted. In April 1960, vast popular student-led demonstrations culminated in the resignation of the president. Following the fall of the Rhee government, the Constitution was amended again to introduce a parliamentary system of government, thus launching the Second Republic. This Third Amendment represented a first step in the direction of Korea's democratization.

Although the amendment brought a dramatic change to Korea's system of government, it was implemented according to the provisions of the Constitution. Dae-Kyu Yoon notes that because "the new government was rushing the amendment through the National Assembly, the existing constitution was used as the basis."[51] Succumbing to the pressure of popular opinion, in that same year the Fourth Amendment was enacted, allowing for retroactive punishment of those guilty of election irregularities, corruption, and appropriation of public property. In 1961, the military seized governmental power through a coup d'état. The military junta then dissolved the National Assembly and under martial law established the Supreme Council for National Reconstruction, which took over state authority and instituted a series of constitutional reforms. The revolutionary regime formed an ad hoc committee to draft a new constitution, which was to be approved in a plebiscite. The "new constitution" was in fact another constitutional amendment, the Fifth Amendment, which gave rise to the Third Republic, marked by a strong presidential system. In 1969, the constitution was amended for the sixth time to authorize a third term for President Park Chung-Lee.

The Fourth Republic was established at the end of 1972 after President Park, then in his third term, invoked martial law in anticipation of a North Korean–South Korean dialogue. By emergency decrees, the Constitution was suspended and the National Assembly dissolved. Soon thereafter, the State Council enacted a new constitution, using the amendment procedure, which was approved in a referendum. The "new constitution" brought about the so-called *Yusin* ("restoration order"), under which the president was vested with nearly unlimited power to override the three branches of government. He was free to serve as many terms as the National Congress for Reunification might determine; he could name one-third of the National Assembly and dissolve the legislature; he could appoint judges; and he was authorized to issue extraordinary measures to suspend constitutional provisions. The Constitution of 1972 removed the power of judicial review from the ordinary courts and explicitly stated that emergency decrees were not subject to constitutional review.[52]

After seven years of ruling through emergency powers, President Park was assassinated in October 1979. One year later, the Fifth Republic was established through passage of the Eighth Amendment. The amendment launched a "new Constitution" that abolished many of the undesirable provisions in the *Yusin* document. In this new constitutional order, the president would serve only one seven-year term, yet he still possessed vast authority. Indeed, authoritarian rule continued until 1987, when it gave way to popular demands for democracy.

In that same year, millions of South Koreans participated in nationwide protests against the regime. In response to the popular support for democratic reform, the military government decided to negotiate with opposition leaders about major revisions to the Constitution. This cooperative government-opposition effort led to landmark constitutional amendments—in essence a new liberal democratic constitution, still in force today, that provides for direct election of a president, a single five-year presidential term, enhanced powers for the legislature, and protection of individual rights.[53] The currently functioning South Korean Constitution establishing the Sixth Republic is thus, formally, the Ninth Amendment to the Constitution of 1948.

We have sketched this period in Korean constitutional history because it offers an intriguing case study of a constitutional revolution realized through formal constitutional amendments. In this account, the military and authoritarian rulers were careful to maintain a facade of legality by observing the amending formula, even as the amendments brought about new constitutional orders. As Yoon put it: "The procedures pursued in these constitutional amendments clearly show how authoritarian government can commit unjust acts by mobilizing all the resources at its disposal to put a mask of lawfulness on them."[54] In short, there was no constitutional break accompanied by a new constitution-making process outside the formal legal rules of the amendment procedure. And significantly, the amendments led to radical transformations in the constitutional order, most recently with the democratization of the state.

Taiwan, Japan, South Korea, and Chile are examples of regimes that fundamentally transformed themselves via ordinary procedures of constitutional transformation without having to resort to formal replacement. But this method of transforming the constitution has its drawbacks. Amaya Alvez Marin, for example, suggests that the Chilean reliance on amendments "created an element of continuity with the previous authoritarian regime, which hindered the democratization and liberalization process."[55] Notwithstanding the extensive and significant amendments to the Constitution of 1980, mainly in 1989 and 2005, the Constitution's authoritarian origins and its remaining authoritarian features raise questions as to whether the use of the amendment power to bring about a constitutional revolution could realistically culminate in a democratic outcome. The constitutional reforms, in which the 1980 Pinochet Constitution with its authoritarian elements was simply amended, "whitewashed" the former regime's constitution.[56] While transformation by amendment has the advantage of preserving formal continuity with the old regime, it does so at the potential cost of calling into question the legitimacy of the new regime. We will confront this problem later in Hungary, where a lack of legitimacy can be causally related to the remnants of the old communist Constitution of 1949, a preservation that arguably contributed significantly to constitutional backlash, expressed in the campaign to counter a constitutional revolution that had seemingly transformed the country into a liberal democracy.

Indeed, as Georg Jellinek noted more than a century ago, constitutional changes that, "without any sudden disruption of the state itself, completely destroy the existing state system and have as their ultimate result the complete rebuilding of the state" raise the most difficult questions of legitimacy.[57] Transformation by amendment rather than replacement may represent a missed opportunity to signal a fresh start or new beginning.[58] For this reason, it is arguably preferable to have a formal replacement of a constitution in order to signal a "clean break" or new beginning, whether or not the substance of the constitution has been meaningfully altered. Bruce Ackerman, for example, contends that postcommunist countries should not rely on mere amendments to transform their constitutions: "The old texts were more propaganda symbols than serious operational realities. If the aim is to transform the very character of constitutional norms, a clean break seems desirable."[59] This path was not followed in transitions in Eastern Europe, notably in Poland and Hungary.

In Poland, the collapse of communist rule was carried out incrementally in a series of amendments to the Constitution of 1952 that rewrote the constitutional foundations of the Soviet-style system. The first amendments, in April 1989, marked the end of the communist system of autocratic, centralized authority in Poland by reestablishing bicameralism in the Polish Parliament, restoring the office of the president, and providing for an "equilibrium" of state power between governmental branches. After free national elections in June 1989, additional amendments enacted in December 1989 made fundamental changes to the constitutional order. They abolished the constitutional clause describing the economy of Poland as based on "socialized means of production," replaced Article 1's description of Poland as "a Socialist State" with a provision describing the Republic of Poland as "a democratic state ruled by law," replaced the provision proclaiming the "leading role of the Communist Party" in Polish governance, guaranteed political pluralism and freedom of political parties, removed the provisions regarding Polish ties to the Soviet Union, and vested "Supreme Authority" in "the People" and not "the working people," for whom the 1952 Constitution was framed. In short, by democratizing the 1952 Constitution, the amendments of June and December 1989 can be regarded as examples of constitutional amendments destroying the basic structure of the existing constitutional order.[60] The nation's aspirations for a full democracy were later fulfilled by a new constitution fashioned in 1997.

In Hungary, two major constitutional amendments, enacted in 1989 and 1990, changed the constitution almost in its entirety, leaving the old constitution just an empty vessel filled with the two additions. The amended constitution remained in force for almost twenty years, until a new constitution was adopted in 2011. Unlike the 1997 Polish Constitution, which was ordained as the concluding piece of the transition process, the Hungarian Constitution of 2011 and subsequent amendments entrenched the authoritarian revision of the post-1989 order. Constitutional amendments in Poland and Hungary (as well as in Chile, Japan, Taiwan, and South Korea) eviscerated the identity of the existing constitutional orders. Hungary is particularly apposite for our scrutiny of constitutional revolutions through amendment, since in the space of less than thirty years it experienced such a revolution twice: first in the transition from communism to liberal democracy, and then in the conversion from liberal democracy to illiberal and increasingly authoritarian rule. As explored below, in both cases constitutional changes formally styled as amendments had in reality the effect of destroying the existing constitutional order and replacing it with a new one.

A Tale of Two Constitutional Revolutions: Revolutionary Amendments in Hungary

After the Austro-Hungarian Compromise (1867) and until the end of World War I, the Habsburg emperor reigned as the king of Hungary. With the collapse of the Austro-Hungarian monarchy on November 16, 1918, Hungary was proclaimed a republic, and on March 21, 1919, a coalition of the Hungarian Social Democratic Party and communists established the Hungarian Soviet Republic. On April 2, 1919, a temporary constitution was adopted by the revolutionary council, and on June 2, 1919, the national Soviets proclaimed a comprehensive constitution. Romanian forces, however, soon occupied Budapest, and the Hungarian Soviet Republic ceased to exist. On February 1, 1920, a Constitutional Statute restored a monarchical system, but Hungary remained a kingdom without a king, since the functions of head of state were vested in a regent, who enjoyed similar royal privileges. Legislative powers were vested in the national assembly, with a suspensive veto power given to the regent. The regent and ministers (who were nominated and recalled by the regent) were granted executive power. When Germany attacked Poland in 1939, Hungary declared itself nonbelligerent and refused to allow the German army to pass through its territory. But after heavy German pressure, Hungary joined forces with Hitler to invade the Soviet Union in 1941. After suffering severe losses, Hungary fell under German occupation until the Nazis were driven out by Allied forces. The country was nominally placed under the control of an Allied commission, but in fact a Soviet official was in total command. On January 31, 1946, a provisional constitutional statute introduced a republican form of government.[61] The Social Democratic Party and the Hungarian Communist Party then merged into the Hungarian Working People's Party, and a modern constitution for the Hungarian People's Republic was installed on August 20, 1949.

Reflecting postwar geopolitical circumstances, the Constitution of 1949 was modeled after the 1936 Constitution of the Soviet Union in its nationalization of all major industries and its institutionalization of single-party rule. It was described as "a slavish imitation of the Soviet-type constitutions, with some variations resulting from the historical and political differences between the Soviet Union and Hungary."[62] In accordance with its terms, Hungary became a people's republic, "the state of the workers and working peasants." While the Presidential Council, elected by Parliament, was to be a collective head of state, true power rested with the Working People's Party. The National Assembly, which is described in the Constitution as the "supreme representative organ of the people," actually convened for about ten days each year, with most rules taking the form of presidential and ministerial decrees. The Constitution guaranteed a variety of fundamental rights, but they were only for working people or had to be in harmony with their interests. Moreover, no means existed for ensuring these rights' obligatory enforcement. Church and state were separated.[63]

A popular uprising against the regime was crushed in 1956, and this event still plays a decisive role in Hungarian political culture. The post-1956 regime, under Hungarian Socialist Workers' Party[64] secretary János Kádár, gradually softened its totalitarian grip, and from 1968 onward introduced an economic policy that harmonized state planning and market development.[65] While the Constitution's basic features remained intact until

1989, the regime adopted important amendments in 1950, 1953, 1954, 1972, and 1983.

Notably, Act I of April 26, 1972, broadly rewrote parts of the Constitution. The Preamble continued to praise the country's Soviet "liberators" but added a longer historical perspective, referring to the Marxist-Leninist regime as a product of a "millennium" of the people's struggle. It also further acknowledged the role of mass movements, trade unions, and the party in the building of socialism, thereby describing the achievements of the regime under Secretary Kádár. Private producers were recognized as long as they did not "violate collective interests." Article 2 was revised to state that "the Hungarian People's Republic is a socialist state." While the social, economic, and political order remained as before, fundamental rights were now guaranteed for all citizens instead of only for workers. Nonetheless, certain rights, such as freedom of speech, press, or assembly, still had to conform to the interests of socialism and the people.[66] These constitutional changes were in fact window dressing for foreign policy purposes and had no real practical influence; the 1949 Constitution was widely viewed as a sham.[67]

The 1972 amendments marked the beginning of a degree of liberalization that continued with the 1983 and 1987 amendments. The Act of 1983 amended the Constitution and established the Constitutional Law Council, a parliamentary committee with the authority to consider the constitutionality of legal rules. The council, however, had no power to annul unconstitutional statutes, and individual citizens lacked direct access to it.[68] The Act of 1987 amended the Constitution by defining certain issues that would be exclusively under the legislative competence of Parliament, thereby weakening the legislative power of the Presidential Council, which, until then, could issue decrees having the force of law.[69] These amendments reflected the strengthening of democratic trends in Hungary.

The erosion of the Soviet Union's influence and the decline of the ruling party between 1956 and 1989 advanced a constitutional transformation featuring constitutional amendments.[70] As detailed below, over the course of 1989 and 1990, the 1949 Constitution was thoroughly transformed by a series of constitutional amendments aimed explicitly at a "peaceful political transition to a constitutional state, . . . a multi-party system, parliamentary democracy and a social market economy," as described in the Preamble of the amended constitution. The new constitutional order was democratic rather than communist and based on principles of the rule of law, the separation of powers, and rights protection. In its transition from communism to democracy, Hungary experienced a constitutional revolution—but only the first of two such transformations.

From Communism to Democracy: The First Constitutional Revolution

The progression in Hungary's transition from communism to liberal democracy began in late 1988 and early 1989 when, in response to public demands, Parliament enacted several important laws, notably the Freedom of Association Act and the Freedom of Assembly Act, which, in formally recognizing political freedoms and legalizing political opposition, paved the way for the establishment of political parties. In 1988, several new democratic parties (Fidesz, the Alliance of Young Democrats; MDF, the Hungarian Democratic Forum; and SZDSZ, the Alliance of Free Democrats) had joined with other organizations to form what has come to be known as the Opposition Round Table (ORT) in an attempt to bring about a constitutional transition. By not succumbing to governmental pressure to negotiate separately as individual parties, the opposition parties gathered under the collective ORT umbrella became a decisive factor in the success of the negotiations and ultimately procured meaningful change.[71]

Conditions for a peaceful transition were negotiated by a conference comprising ORT, the Hungarian Socialist Workers' Party (still in power), and representatives of civil society, mostly linked with the Hungarian Socialist Workers' Party. The conference evolved into a sort of constituent assembly, known as the National Round Table (NRT), for creating a new constitution. The NRT delegated the writing of a document to drafting committees, suborgans of the NRT, which originally were composed of experts, scholars, and communist politicians. But the center of constitution making eventually shifted from the committees to the roundtable conference, where representatives of the groups discussed the crucial issues of a peaceful regime transition. The use of roundtable negotiations not only avoided civil conflict and violence but also provided an alternative to the familiar bottom-up (revolutionary) or top-down (old regime) impositions of constitutional arrangements. In the interests of time, instead of waiting for the completion and adoption of a new constitution, the groups reached agreements to pass necessary constitutional amendments.[72] After political negotiations, the NRT's proposed amendments to the 1949 Constitution were formally codified by the communist Parliament on October 18, 1989 (Statute 31 of 1989), by a two-thirds majority. The constitutional amendments, which had the effect of transforming the country into a liberal democracy, were promulgated on October 23, 1989 (the day of the "promulgation of the Republic"), paving the way for free parliamentary elections in March 1990.

As in Germany, where the Basic Law of 1949 was enacted as a temporary instrument (yet eventually remained after reunification), what was crafted in Hungary was intended to be a temporarily amended version of a constitution that would later be finalized as a formal constitution.[73] The Parliament that enacted the amendments to the constitution was considered democratically illegitimate for purposes of adopting a new constitution. In the face of this legitimacy problem, the aim was to achieve constitution making in stages. Much as in South Africa, an interim constitution paved the way for a full transition to democracy. The appeal of the multistage constitution-making process was that it permitted a revocation of the constituent power without resorting to extraconstitutional or forcible means. Constitution-making power exercised this way would thus receive its authority from its legality. In Andrew Arato's conceptualization, what results is best described as "post-sovereign" constitution making, a process that does not vest constituent power in a single individual or institution, but rather, in emphasizing the role of interim legal instruments, is based on values such as pluralism, inclusion, publicity, compromise, and legality. Besides its enhanced legal legitimacy, constitution making in stages allows for, as seen in the South African certification cases, possibilities for learning and correction at each stage.[74] But whereas in South Africa the interim constitution included precise rules for the activity of making the final constitution, this important component was unfortunately omitted in the Hungarian transitional constitution-making process. And while the South African process brought about a final new constitution in continuity with the interim constitution, Hungary failed to produce a permanent constitution until the more recent counterrevolution.

In the absence of a freely elected parliament, the constitution-making process proceeded without active popular participation. Still, it did not entirely exclude the people. In November 1989, four significant constitutional questions were approved by popular referendum: Should party activity in the workplace be banned? Should the workers' militia be dissolved? Should party property be liquidated? Should presidential elections be postponed until after the general elections? Involvement of the people in the constitution-making process, however limited, was unprecedented in the country's history.[75] Yet aside from this restricted popular involvement, what occurred was purely an elite affair.[76] Thus, for the sake of enhanced democratic legitimacy, it might have been more efficacious, as we elaborate in chapter 7, for the entire new constitutional document to have received popular approval through an inclusive process.[77] After the free parliamentary elections, the Hungarian Democratic Forum formed a moderate right-wing coalition with the Christian Democratic Party and the Independent Smallholders' Party. To amend the constitution, the coalition needed a two-thirds majority, so it made a pact with the Alliance of Free Democrats, which agreed on constitutional amendments in exchange for receiving the position of the president of the republic. Accordingly, in 1990, Parliament enacted an amendment (Statute 29 of 1990) that aimed to stabilize Hungary's parliamentary system and improve governance. It specified that the president would be elected by Parliament, adopted the German model of a "constructive vote of no confidence" in order to make the executive branch more stable, and reduced the number of policy areas in which it was necessary to have a two-thirds majority of all MPs in order to legislate, as previously required.[78] The two constitutional amendments of 1989 and 1990 were brought about under the rule of law while legal continuity was maintained.

As in Poland, legal continuity should not obscure the revolutionary character of the amendments. As Gábor Halmai notes:

> One of the peculiarities of the Hungarian transition that has been going on since 1989 is that the institutions that have been defined in the Constitution have been developed by formally amending the old Constitution . . . in serial fashion. And from the old Constitution almost only one sentence remains—that the capital of the country is Budapest. . . . There was no revolution in Hungary which would have swept out the Constitution of the

> *ancien régime*. . . . The reforms . . . that are of revolutionary importance have disconnected the continuity of the legitimacy of the previous regime, through (for example) declaring that Hungary is a republic and guaranteeing a state that operates under the rule of law.[79]

The Hungarian story thus presents a signature case of formal legal continuity conjoined with a substantive constitutional rupture. Rejection of the communist regime was achieved in the context of a formal reliance on its legal legitimacy for transitioning toward a new order.

Indeed, this was a revolution within legal boundaries. Under the 1989 amendment, the 1949 Constitution was stripped of its socialist trappings (although, as we shall see, some remnants of the socialist legacy remained), with the intention of distancing it from the past forty years of history. Under communism there had been minimal commitment to the rule of law or respect for human rights, and only a unitary or monolithic concept of power. The first reaction to the fall of communism was a total rejection of the regime's basic structures. András Sajó noted that the 1989 amendment amounted for all practical purposes to a new constitution based on principles of checks and balances, the rule of law, and protection of fundamental rights.[80] The new Preamble of the amended constitution stated that the revision was needed "in order to facilitate a peaceful political transition to a state under the rule of law, realizing a multi-party system, a parliamentary democracy and a social market economy." In addition to a revision of the Preamble, references to "socialism" were carefully deleted. Article 1 declared that "the State of Hungary is a republic"; Article 2(1) replaced the original text stating that Hungary was a socialist state with "The Hungarian Republic is an independent, democratic state governed by the rule of law." And whereas the previous Constitution declared, "In the Hungarian People's Republic all power belongs to the working people," Article 2(2) now affirmed, "In the Republic of Hungary all power shall belong to the people exercising its sovereignty through its elected representatives as well as directly."

Under the 1949 Constitution, as amended in 1989, the Hungarian Parliament—elected every four years—is the supreme organ of state. Thus, Parliament is responsible for the constitutional structure of the country (Article 19(2)). Also, since the 1989 amended constitution was meant to be temporary, Parliament was granted the authority to adopt a new constitution (Article 19(3)(a)). Constituting Parliament as the supreme body of the state is a remnant of the socialist concept of the state, in which Parliament is at the apex of the state hierarchy, exercising state power without restriction. It appears that during the comprehensive constitutional reform of 1989, this passage was overlooked and remained in the text of the Constitution.[81] As in Chile and Taiwan, retaining remnants of the old regime's characteristics, values, or institutions was a largely unavoidable consequence of the attempt to realize a constitutional revolution by amending the old constitution. Another critical remaining structural feature was the constitutional amendment formula: constitutional amendments could be initiated by any relevant source (president, Parliament member, or parliamentary committee), and as in the original 1949 Constitution, the only restrictive requirement was that there be a two-thirds vote in a single-chamber parliament. As we shall see, this combination—Parliament's supreme authority and the relatively flexible amendment formula—paved the way for the more recent revolutionary displacement toward an illiberal regime.

Another source of intellectual resistance to communism embodied in the constitutional transformation was a return to a "glorious past." For example, the legal status of the president was restored. Much like the Japanese transformation, in which links to a national past or heritage were emphasized, as Sajó pointed out: "During the Hungarian round table talks of 1989, the 1946 system of 'weak' presidency was used as a model and as a compelling argument. The 1946 model represented both national tradition and sufficient return to the denied past. This was compelling enough to make it legitimate for Communist government and opposition groups alike."[82] As discussed in chapter 2, this emphasis on a return to a glorious past conforms to the rotational aspect of constitutional revolutions, in which a revolution, besides representing a new beginning, often evokes the astronomical imagery associated with a cyclical return to a previous or older condition and the practices associated with it. Describing the need for a new constitution instead of relying on the amended 1949 Constitution, József Szájer, a prominent member of the Fidesz party, argued that in fact constitutional continuity had been disrupted by communism: "Hungary had a constitutional system that had been functional for centuries, and in fact, was one of the most advanced of its time. . . . In this sense, we had an existing and functional constitution, which provided a clear framework for Hungarian society and jurisprudence. By adopting a constitution in 1949, the Communist Parliament intended to throw away the preceding 950 years in the spirit of 'wiping the slate of the past clean,' in a legal sense as well as symbolically."[83] The idea expressed here is that the effort to break from the more recent past was best viewed as a successful reconnection with a greater past imaginary.

A main focus of the transition was the judicial branch, specifically the creation of a new institution, the Hungarian Constitutional Court (HCC), entrusted with judicial review authority. Foreign to the Hungarian constitutional tradition, the HCC contained eleven members, elected by a two-thirds majority of Parliament.[84] During its first term under the presidency of László Sólyom, the HCC was a strongly "activist" and powerful institution,[85] which satisfied the expectations of both parties to the NRT—the communists, who hoped that judicial independence would ensure their interests in a future when they anticipated no longer being the leading party, and the opposition, which sought the opportunity to create a truly independent court with its attendant benefits.[86]

The most important components of the HCC's jurisdiction were judicial review of legislation and the constitutional-complaint mechanism for handling violations of personal constitutional rights. The Court's decisions were deemed final, binding upon everyone, and it possessed the power to declare an unconstitutional legal act as wholly or partly null and void. Also, the HCC's perceived strength was tied to the standing system of *actio popularis,* according to which anybody could raise ex post facto constitutional challenges to promulgated legal provisions. The logic behind this system—the desire to accord protection of minorities—resulted in an extremely wide expanse of judicial review authority.[87]

The HCC played a substantial role in the post-transformation period by maintaining constitutional stability through the adoption of a new constitution in 2011.[88] Since the post-1989 Constitution was a rewrite of the communist-era Constitution, it included internal inconsistencies and was filled with gaps. Without a rule-of-law tradition or knowledge of the techniques by which human rights could effectively be protected, the Court borrowed heavily from Western constitutional law, developing principles and methodology that came to be known as the theory of the "invisible constitution." In accordance with this theory, the Constitution was to be regarded as a holistic unity of principles and rules; the invisible constitution was viewed as embracing all the underlying principles necessary for rendering coherent the written document and its constitutional law.[89] The theory was strikingly on display in the HCC's recognition of rights that were only implicit in the Constitution, and in its dramatic invalidation of capital punishment.[90] The jurisprudence's implementation led some to claim that the "invisible constitution" had actually rendered unnecessary the completion of the new constitution anticipated by the 1989 amendments.[91] But the HCC's commitment to the transition to constitutional democracy, and the inevitable entanglement in political controversies that followed, contributed to a widely held view that the Court had become one of the world's most powerful and polarizing judiciaries, a perception often accompanied by severe criticism.[92]

An emphasis on fundamental rights was at the heart of the Court's transition role. The revised 1989 Constitution guaranteed the nondiscriminatory enjoyment of rights, including a long list of civil and political rights such as human dignity, personal security, equality, property, freedom of expression, freedom of conscience and religion, and the right of assembly and association.[93] With these guarantees, new institutions and mechanisms for enforcing rights, such as an ombudsman for civil rights, an ombudsman for the rights of national and ethnic minorities, and an ombudsman for data protection, were established and charged with investigating violations of constitutional rights.

Importantly, the HCC proved willing to impose affirmative obligations on the state to secure certain constitutional rights, including a minimal social system based on human dignity.[94] It also imposed affirmative obligations on the state to act in furtherance of so-called negative rights traditionally understood as limiting what could be done by the state. For example, the HCC stipulated that "in addition to the right of the individual to the freedom of expression . . . the Constitution imposes the duty on the State to secure the conditions for the creation and maintenance of a democratic public opinion."[95] In putting a positive gloss on supposedly negative rights, the HCC relied on Article 8(1) of the Constitution, which describes the protection of "fundamental human rights" as a "primary obligation of the State." Civil duties such as defending the country and contributing to national expenditure were also included in the Constitution; however, of utmost importance when reflecting on the 1989 revised Constitution is the separation of rights from duties, the latter no longer being a condition for enjoyment of rights, as had been the case in previous socialist bills of rights.[96]

We see, then, in this review of the amended Constitution a divergence between the constitutional order of the 1949 Constitution and that of the same Constitution as modified after 1989. The constitutional order was essentially revolutionized in the transition from communism to a liberal democracy. The transformation was conducted within the parameters of established legality, in that it was based on the existing constitution, and with a peaceful process that did not involve civil war, mass state or popular violence, or any other extraconstitutional means. In Andrew Arato and Zoltán Miklósi's apt summary, "As one political regime, a Soviet-type dictatorship, was fully replaced by another, liberal democracy, the destructive logic of friend and enemy well known from the history of revolutions—purges, proscription, massive denial of rights, and terror—was avoided."[97] In substantive terms, there was a clear rupture, since the amended text resulted in a fundamentally new constitutional order rooted in parliamentary democracy: "In the legal-formal sense the constitution is still the original one with drastic changes, but regarding its social-political content it is a genuinely new document."[98] Technically, then, the old legal order remained valid. The legal continuity with the former legal system signified that "the new power accepts the legality of the legal system, namely the formal lawfulness and validity of the legal rules enacted during the Communist regime."[99] Since the constitutional reform maintained legal continuity while bringing about a substantive constitutional revolution, some have suggested a middle concept between reform and revolution: "refolution" or "coordinated transition."[100] As János Kis rightly notes, a coordinated transition raises dilemmas regarding the legitimacy of old versus new constitutional orders: "The new regime draws its legitimacy from the establishment of the rule of law, and of institutions protecting the rights of individuals. It claims a radical break with the old, communist regime, where human rights have been systematically violated and the perpetrators were generally not prosecuted. . . . If the new regime refuses to face the problem of rendering justice, its legitimacy, again, might be tainted. But it might also be tainted if it makes attempts to attack the problem, because there are tremendous constitutional obstacles to putting the past perpetrators on trial."[101]

This dilemma was precisely what was in play in the famous and controversial lustration case.[102] On November 4, 1991, the legislature passed a law on the "prosecutability of serious crimes committed between 21 December 1944 and 2 May 1990 and left unpunished for political reasons." The law would have lifted the statute of limitations on treason, murder, and grievous crimes conducted by the previous regime. The president of the republic refused to sign and promulgate it, and asked the HCC to examine its constitutionality. In its ruling, the Court found that the bill conflicted with the current penal-law provision defining the statute of limitations for crimes committed under the laws in effect at the time. Lifting the statute of limitations was therefore deemed unconstitutional, since it created ex post facto legislation, in conflict with the Constitution.

The Court explained its view concerning legal continuity in Hungary: "There is no substantive distinction between legal rules enacted under the Communist regime and since the promulgation of the new Constitution. Consequently, there is no double standard in adjudicating the constitutionality of the legal norms. . . . The Constitution and the basic laws that introduced revolutionary changes from a political point of view were enacted without formal defects according to the rules of lawmaking of the old regime and deriving their binding force from them."[103] Therefore, the new constitutional state was shaped according to principles of legality and legal continuity. The regime change took place legally, and the principle of legality requires the constitutional state to give absolute effect to the rules governing that legal system. Even the revolutionary changes to the Constitution, the Court maintained, observed the rules of lawmaking of the old regime and accordingly derived their binding force from them:

> The change of system has been carried out on the basis of legality. The principle of legality imposes on the state under the rule of law the requirement that legal regulations regarding the legal system itself should be abided by unconditionally. The politically revolutionary changes adopted by the Constitution

> and all the new fundamental laws were enacted in full compliance with the old legal system's procedural laws on legislation, thereby gaining their binding force. The old law retains its validity. With respect to its validity there is no distinction between "pre-Constitutional" and "post-Constitutional" law.[104]

The HCC also held that the fundamental guarantees of the rule of law could not be put aside by invoking considerations of substantive justice: "Legal certainty based on objective and formal principles takes precedence over justice, which is generally partial and subjective."[105] The Court, in essence, interpreted the legal changes in Hungary as being regulated by the existing legal framework. As noted by Jiří Přibáň, the Court refused to compromise its formal reading of the "rule of law" principle by taking into account historical injustices and particular circumstances that might require a different, more flexible approach.[106] "Can the revolutionary momentum continue," Bruce Ackerman asked, "if no steps are taken to right the wrongs of the past?"[107] And looking ahead to the second constitutional revolution, did the 1989 regime suffer from a legitimacy deficit precisely because transitional justice was not done properly?[108] Did the binding of the new constitutional order to an earlier one widely perceived as unjust render the case for rejection of the 1989 institutional solution more plausible and appealing?

Contrasting this decision with the Czech case that confronted the same problem of transitional justice is instructive. On July 9, 1993, the Czech Parliament passed the Law on the Illegitimacy of and Resistance to the Communist Regime, declaring the former Communist Party "illegitimate" and "criminal," and honoring those persons who "on the basis of democratic, moral or religious conviction" fought against the Communist Party. In a decision handed down in December 1993, the Czech Constitutional Court ruled that the law should be upheld.[109] According to the Court:

> The Czech Constitution accepts and respects the principle of legality as a part of the overall basic outline of a law-based state; positive law does not, however, bind it merely to formal legality, rather the interpretation and application of legal norms are subordinated to their substantive purpose, law is qualified by respect for the basic enacted values of a democratic society and also measures the application of legal norms by these values. This means that even while there is continuity of "old laws" there is a discontinuity in values from the "old regime." This conception of the constitutional state

> rejects the formal-rational legitimacy of a regime and the formal law-based state. Whatever the laws of a state are, in a state which is designated as democratic and which proclaims the principle of the sovereignty of the people, no regime other than a democratic regime may be considered as legitimate.[110]

Thus, in marked contrast with the HCC emphasis on formal legality and its reasoning that legal continuity is the cornerstone of a democratic constitution, the Czech Constitutional Court focused on substantive justice. The rejection of legal formalism and the accentuation of substance facilitated the delegitimation of the old communist regime. This contrast between the Czech and Hungarian approaches to legal continuity is so sharp "that one wonders whether it was in part written with an eye to the Hungarian case which had been decided a year earlier."[111] The Hungarian separation of law and justice raises a serious question about a constitutional revolution that occurs within the boundaries of the existing order but whose execution lacks significant popular input: will it yield the requisite level of legitimacy to enable it to shield its achievement against the anticipated pushback and backlash it will face?

The wholesale transformation of the state in Hungary by constitutional amendments rather than constitutional replacement struck most observers as unproblematic and consistent with the established rules for constitutional amending. Indeed, in the years afterward, as Arato observed, "the method of coping with radical political change through legal continuity (characteristic of the whole Hungarian transformation) was not only continued but was raised to a norm."[112] In 2010, with the sweeping election victory of the right-wing Fidesz party, the Hungarian constitutional order underwent another drastic change in direction. The 1949/89 Constitution experienced a slew of further amendments beginning in 2010, ultimately to be replaced in 2011 by the "Fundamental Law" (entered into force in 2012). From 1989 until the eventual adoption of a new constitution in 2011, the 1949 constitution was revised more than thirty times.[113] These changes transformed Hungary from a liberal constitutional state, characterized by the vigorous enforcement of rights and other limits on state power, into a regime exhibiting increasingly illiberal tendencies and "grounded on absolute parliamentary sovereignty and the practical weakening of all counterweights to it."[114]

From Liberalism to Illiberalism: The Second Constitutional Revolution

As we have seen, the amended 1949 Constitution was designed and intended to be temporary. The Preamble explicitly contemplated "the adoption of the new Constitution," and article 19(3)(a) specifically assigned Parliament this task. The Constitution, however, was silent about the rules or procedures for a constitution-making process. The only existing rule relevant to changing the Constitution was the two-thirds-approval requirement of a single chamber of Parliament for a constitutional amendment.[115] In 1994, the Hungarian Socialist Party (formally, the successor to the Hungarian Socialist Workers' Party) joined forces with the Alliance of Free Democrats, allowing the combined group to obtain the two-thirds majority necessary for constitutional amendments. This coalition government adopted a constitutional amendment requiring a majority of four-fifths for implementing a new constitution, thereby creating multitrack procedures, one for amending and one for new constitution making.[116] The purpose of the supermajority was to gain public trust for the process by showing that at least a part of the opposition would be included in the preparation of the new constitution.[117] That amendment, however, was only temporary and was designed to lose its effect by the end of the sitting Parliament, which had been elected in 1994.[118] Disagreements led to the collapse of the talks in the constitution-making process in 1997, and so the attempt to finalize the constitutional revolution with a comprehensive new document failed, a failure that may well have been one of the reasons for the backsliding that soon followed.

The year 2010 brought a tectonic shift in the political landscape. A government led by Prime Minister Viktor Orbán was elected with the support of a two-thirds majority in Parliament and thus with the ability to amend the constitution. Orbán's goal was nothing less than to build a new political, economic, and social system. Within nineteen months of the election, the 1989 Constitution would be amended twelve times.

What were these changes? Some were aimed at restricting the independence and power of the HCC. The composition of the parliamentary committee responsible for nominating HCC justices shifted to one of proportional representation, contrary to the former regulation, which had required parity. This change, in conjunction with the government's two-thirds majority, allowed the government effectively to control HCC candidate nominations. Another amendment increased the number of justices from eleven to fifteen, which ensured that the government could immediately appoint at least four justices of its choosing. Judicial review was also limited so that the HCC could review budgets, tax laws, and statutes regulating local government taxation only if those laws violated certain listed rights, thereby making it nearly impossible for the Court to second-guess budget and tax policy.[119] The amendments also sought to debilitate the government's critics and opponents by restricting liberal freedoms and undermining opposition parties. One amendment modified provisions guaranteeing freedom of press, speech, and opinion, and the right of free access to information, and permitted the establishment of an authority that would oversee the media and possess wide regulatory and sanctioning powers. A set of amendments enacted in August 2010 restricted the ability of police and other armed-forces officials to join political parties. One applied a tax on revenues in the public sector that were "acquired immorally," which was retroactively applied to members of past socialist and socialist-liberal governments.[120]

These developments were only the first step in the second constitutional revolution. Orbán conferred upon the new Parliament the status of "constitutional convention," with the clear intention that it produce a new constitution. And indeed, a special constitutional committee was established in Parliament to propose the general framework for such a document—a new Fundamental Law.[121] Nevertheless, the draft version of the Fundamental Law was not prepared in this committee, but rather by József Szájer, the prominent leader of the Fidesz party. And as Szájer stated, the desire to have a new governing charter was directly linked with the first constitutional revolution and the amendments to the 1949 Constitution:

> In Hungary . . . by amending the Soviet-style pseudo-constitution we failed to create a fully legitimate Western-style fundamental law that would have been acceptable in every respect. The transition failed to do this, which is why we continue to have an ongoing dispute today about why the new Fundamental Law refers to the historic constitution. In a legal sense, and the sense of legal theory and social philosophy, the new Fundamental Law had to define its position with respect to the thousand-year tradition that had always secured for Hungary a position at the forefront of Europe. It had to

> come up with a response as to how to integrate this tradition as well as what kind of foreign models it would adopt. This also explains why we needed a new constitution. Maybe we did not need one in a legal sense: you can sip wine from a plain drinking glass, as it is perfectly suitable for the purpose of drinking, but for this to be more than just an act of becoming inebriated, you have to do it in proper style. It is a totally different feeling to sip the same wine from a nice crystal wine glass. A constitution defines a country's identity—it condenses what we think of our history, achievements and attainments. . . . Hungary's previous Constitution did not fulfil this function of defining the nation's identity. It functioned as a plain "water glass," one which was even chipped here and there, so it perpetuated many problems and unresolved issues.[122]

Thus, the need to break with the communist constitutional legacy contributed to the making of the new Constitution. What is more, the previous Constitution's failure in "defining the nation's identity" can in this account be connected with the legitimacy problem associated with the legality of the 1989 transition. So, for example, the HCC's effort to tie the validity of the new constitutional order to that of the 1949 Constitution enabled its political opponents to call into question the legitimacy of the 1989 alterations on the grounds of the broadly perceived illegitimacy of the earlier arrangement. The Court's emphatic commitment to continuity and the rule of law was widely admired for its attention to a core principle of constitutionalism, but that very commitment also had an abstract quality to it that nourished a countervailing critique that saw in this effort a neglect of what was specific to Hungarian constitutional identity. To a degree, the assertion of identity entails the negation of something else, which meant that in the understandable effort to uphold the rule of law through the establishment of legal continuity, an opportunity was lost to advance a positive articulation of constitutional identity. "There was no regime change" was the appropriate motto for the proponents of the identitarian critique.[123] Orbán could in essence deny the reality of the first constitutional revolution for its alleged failure to establish a clear identity for the Hungarian nation; his "revolution of the voting booth" could then be defended as satisfying the people's hunger for the constitutional revolution that had, in his supporters' view, yet to be achieved.[124]

To be sure, the process of formulating the new Fundamental Law was highly problematic. It was characterized by a lack of transparency, exclusion of legal scholars, and the nonparticipation of the opposition parties, which, believing that the constitutional drafting committee was only a charade, eventually left the committee. The procedure used to adopt the new Constitution was the same one that applied to the adoption of amendments—passage by a two-thirds majority of Parliament. Although the requirement of approval by a four-fifths supermajority for the adoption of a new constitution had by then expired, the government's failure to follow a special consensual constitution-making procedure nevertheless created great distrust.[125]

The Fundamental Law was signed by the president of Hungary on April 25, 2011, and was implemented on January 1, 2012, after receiving two-thirds approval in Parliament (over a boycott by the opposition). Aside from changing the name of the country (from the "Republic of Hungary" to "Hungary"), the 2011 Fundamental Law did little to alter the basic organizational structure of the state or the catalogue of constitutionally protected rights. It did, however, weaken institutions capable of exercising independent oversight, such as the ombudsmen and the HCC.[126] The HCC's broad jurisdiction and authority had rested in large part on the effectively universal availability of standing to bring suit, and on the availability of abstract judicial review, even in the absence of a specific complaint. The Fundamental Law, and the new Law on the Constitutional Court, passed shortly thereafter, restricted access to the Court to those who could demonstrate personal harm.[127]

With all of these developments, should we conclude that the 2011 Fundamental Law was in fact a constitutional revolution? Procedurally, Gábor Halmai observes, "it wasn't a revolutionary act, since it was enacted on the basis of the constitution-making rules of the 1949/1989 constitution"; substantively, however, "the new Fundamental Law of Hungary can be treated as revolutionary, as it introduced a new, illiberal type of constitutional system, instead of the liberal constitution of 1989."[128] The transformation in constitutional identity brought about by Órban's efforts embodied "an unprecedented shift in the characteristics of Hungarian constitutionalism."[129] To fully appreciate what this means, however, the ongoing nature of what has been and is occurring in Hungary must be recognized, a cognizance of the incremental properties of its constitutional revolution.

Since its adoption, the Fundamental Law has been amended several times. The first of these amendments arose from the controversy surrounding Parliament's enactment of "Transitional Provisions" in December 2011. These provisions imposed responsibility for the Communist Party's past actions while in power, and also held its successor, the Hungarian Socialist Party (and the opposition to Fidesz, the governing party) accountable for the crimes of its predecessor, while concurrently voiding the statute of limitations applicable to said crimes. This marked a sharp contrast with the lustration decision of 1992 and provided further gloss to its significance—symbolic or real—for the events that followed. Additionally, the Transitional Provisions removed the president of the Supreme Court from office, enabled Parliament to enact regulations that effectively stripped the courts of jurisdiction over matters concerning the legal status of religious communities, prohibited the HCC from ever reviewing fiscal laws enacted when public debt is more than 50 percent of the GDP, and roused public sentiment against the HCC and the European Court of Human Rights by enabling the government to levy specifically earmarked direct taxes upon citizens for the express purpose of covering the costs imposed by judgments of these courts.[130]

The ombudsman for fundamental rights, Máté Szabó, filed a complaint to the HCC against the Transitional Provisions, arguing that they were not of a transitional or temporary nature, thus violating the conditions set forth in the Fundamental Law. In response, and apparently in order to shield them from judicial review, the government secured the enactment of the first amendment to the Fundamental Law. This amendment clarified the constitutional status of the Transitional Provisions by stating that they were part of the Fundamental Law. In November 2012, Parliament enacted the second amendment by amending the Transitional Provisions of the Fundamental Law and requiring individual registration at a governmental database as a precondition for voting, thus in fact infringing the right to vote.[131]

In the next month, a 10–5 decision of the HCC found key articles in the Transitional Provisions of the Fundamental Law unconstitutional for being enacted ultra vires of the constitutional delegation of power to enact transitional provisions to the new Fundamental Law.[132] Reacting to the decision, the government adopted the Fourth Amendment, which went into effect in April 2013. This massive, fifteen-page amendment was one-third as long as the Fundamental Law itself. Among other things, it incorporated the contents of the Transitional Provisions into the constitutional text, restricted HCC review to matters specifically raised by a claimant in a case before it, restricted judicial review of the Fundamental Law and constitutional amendments to procedural objections, and prohibited reliance in any HCC case on law decided before the effective date of the Fundamental Law.[133]

Certain provisions of the Fourth Amendment were challenged before the HCC. In its 2013 decision, the Court ruled that it was beyond its competence to conduct substantive judicial review of constitutional amendments in light of the explicit constitutional provision adopted as part of the Fourth Amendment, which limited its jurisdiction to review amendments only to a formal procedure-based assessment.[134] The ruling presents a revealing contrast with what happened in similar circumstances in India. After a series of cases in which the Indian Supreme Court declared that Parliament's constituent power does not include the authority to amend the basic structure of the Constitution in a manner that would change its identity, Parliament enacted the Forty-Second Amendment to the Constitution, affirming that there are no limitations on Parliament's constituent power when amending the Constitution. When, however, this provision was subsequently challenged before the Indian Supreme Court, the justices decided that Parliament had only limited legislative powers, and these limitations extended to the adoption of amendments. Since a limited organ cannot turn itself into an unlimited organ, the contested provision was deemed unconstitutional.[135] Whereas in India it was the judiciary that had the final word, in Hungary the political branches possessed ultimate authority. While in itself the denial by the HCC of its power to declare an amendment unconstitutional on substantive grounds is not, by the standards of comparative jurisprudence, an especially controversial or noteworthy development, in the context of the ongoing constitutional revolution in Hungary, the judicial outcome is perhaps best seen as an indication of the Court's tacit acceptance of the impact of that revolution on the constitutional order.

Extensive criticism of the Fourth Amendment from scholars and the international community, including the Venice Commission,[136] prompted passage of the Fifth Amendment on September 16, 2013, which eased some of the aforementioned restrictions.[137] But subsequent amendments expanded the constitutional scope of the second constitutional revolution. On June 7, 2016, the Sixth Amendment to the Fundamental Law was adopted, authorizing the National Assembly to declare a "state of terrorism threat" and allowing the government to suspend laws and to take other "extraordinary measures" departing from existing laws during such a declared terrorism state of emergency.[138] The Seventh Amendment to the Fundamental Law, adopted on June 20, 2018, provides that "alien peoples cannot be settled in Hungary" and that "the protection of Hungary's constitutional self-identity and Christian culture is the obligation of all organs of the state." It also prohibits homelessness, with reference to the protection of the public use of public space, and restricts freedom of assembly by stating that "practicing the right to assembly cannot involve the violation of others' private and family life or home."

What is this "self-identity" that all organs of the state must protect? In its decision from 2016 concerning the EU's relocation program for asylum seekers, the now-packed HCC provided an abstract interpretation of the new Fundamental Law and its "identity" provisions, and it defined the role of constitutional identity in matters related to Hungary's participation in the EU as achievements of Hungary's historical constitution: "The Constitutional Court of Hungary interprets the concept of constitutional identity as Hungary's self-identity and it unfolds the content of this concept from case to case, on the basis of the whole Fundamental Law and certain provisions thereof, in accordance with the National Avowal and the achievements of our historical constitution."[139] According to the HCC: "The constitutional self-identity of Hungary is a fundamental value not created by the Fundamental Law—it is merely acknowledged by the Fundamental Law. Consequently, constitutional identity cannot be waived by way of an international treaty," and thus "the protection of constitutional identity shall remain the duty of the Constitutional Court as long as Hungary is a sovereign State."[140] Regarding the HCC's role in guarding the nation's constitutional identity, Judge Dr. István Stumpf emphasized in his concurring opinion that "in establishing the constitutional principles and values worth[y] of actual constitutional protection, a special emphasis should be put on the historical dimension,

Hungary's constitutional tradition, and the achievements of the historical constitution."[141] Setting aside the fact that the nature of Hungary's historical constitution is highly ambiguous and contentious, the reasoning of the HCC, which emphasized a duty to preserve a glorious past, corresponds with the rotational aspect of constitutional revolutions—in this case the counterrevolution—manifested in the desire to return to an ideal historical order.[142] Because the jurisprudence of the post-1989 HCC did not rely on "traditional Hungarian constitutional law," this historical record was used as a valuable tool in the counterrevolutionary movement,[143] as in József Szájer's previously noted explanation regarding his desire to return to Hungary's early "constitutional system that had been functional for centuries."[144]

If, then, the amendment-driven progression from a communist legal system to a liberal democratic order to an increasingly illiberal constitutional polity had been not unambiguously clear in its trajectory, these most recent amendments to the Constitution of 2011 brought a clarifying perspective to the generation-long constitutional narrative in Hungary. The illiberal transformation of the post-1989 order—what we have referred to as the second constitutional revolution—has been roundly criticized for turning Hungary into an illiberal state and generally failing "to comply with minimum standards of constitutionalism."[145] This state of affairs brought the European Parliament to launch proceedings against Hungary's government based on concerns that the functioning of the constitutional system violates the values incorporated in Article 2 of the Lisbon Treaty ("respect for human dignity, freedom, democracy, equality, the rule of law and respect for human rights, including the rights of persons belonging to minorities").[146] This failure was hardly accidental, since the revolution had been engineered for precisely this purpose. As Prime Minister Viktor Orbán stated in a public speech: "The new state that we are constructing in Hungary is an illiberal state, a non-liberal state. It does not reject the fundamental principles of liberalism such as freedom . . . but instead includes a different, special, national approach."[147]

In institutional terms, what made this revolution possible was the Fidesz party's possession of a two-thirds majority in Parliament, which it abused to unilaterally amend and replace the Constitution in pursuit of its partisan goals. Hungary is thus a prime example of how the tools and procedures found in a constitution can be turned against the Constitution itself, resulting in the self-destruction of the constitutional order and its replacement with something very different.[148] From a broader perspective, however, this paradigmatic displacement in the way constitutionalism has been experienced in Hungary is attributable to the shortcomings of the first constitutional revolution in securing and entrenching its liberal democratic aspirations in the broader political culture.

In hindsight, some commentators claim that the perceived strength of the HCC under the 1989 revised Constitution, in which the HCC practically ran Hungary and became what Kim Lane Scheppele called a "courtocracy,"[149] was a contributing factor in this "Constitutional Backlash."[150] It is an argument very familiar to students of American constitutional politics; as Gerald Rosenberg put it, "When judges make unpopular decisions, people may feel that their lives are being reordered without their input. Thus, the judiciary may be institutionally structured to be susceptible to backlash."[151] A similar argument can be made regarding other jurisdictions with strong courts that exhibit judicial activism. As we explain in chapter 6, in Israel, where an activist court advanced a constitutional revolution through interpretation by expanding its powers vis-à-vis other governmental branches, the constitutional order has been experiencing a counterrevolution in a clear attempt to weaken the Court. In both Hungary and Israel, it is the governing political parties that aim to shift the fundamental principles of the constitutional order away from the constitutional revolutions the two states experienced in the 1990s. And both states are attempting to strengthen their particular national identity at the expenses of universal-liberal characteristics of the legal order: Hungary by its effort to strengthen its self-identity and Christian culture (for example, through the Seventh Amendment), and Israel by its nation-state law (entitled "Basic Law: Israel—The Nation-State of the Jewish People"), which aims to prioritize Jewish values over democratic ones. The constitutional revolutions in Hungary and Israel suffered from legitimacy problems that were followed by powerful reactions aimed at leading the countries in an illiberal direction.

The use of the French Third Republic's legal devices to form the pro-Nazi Vichy regime was described by Georges Liet-Veaux as a "fraud upon the constitution" (*fraude à la constitution*). A fraud upon the constitution occurs when political actors mask their intent to undermine the content or spirit of a constitution by adhering to its text: "*Respect de la forme pour combattre le fond, c'est la fraude à la constitution, ou plus exactement, le cas le plus intéressant de fraude à la constitution.*"[152] For the French theorist, to destroy the existing state under the guise of maintaining or reforming it, in accordance with the legal requirements of the existing constitution, is to perpetrate a fraud upon the constitution.

This understanding prioritizes the substance of a constitution over its form. It contrasts sharply with the Kelsenian approach discussed in the previous chapter. For Kelsen, the use of a constitution's amendment formula to drastically change the constitution—even to completely replace it with a new one—upholds the same constitution. Kelsen understood "revolution" as a changing or replacing of the constitution in a way that is incompatible with a constitution's existing amendment procedure.[153] His understanding, widely shared in the early to mid-twentieth century, reflected the revolutionary constitution-making model of the American and French Revolutions, in which the idea of an extralegal constituent power that can create or destroy entire constitutional orders at will assumes a central place. This notion, we believe, should be rejected. As the examples discussed in this chapter show, in the material sense, that of substance and not merely of form, using the amendment procedure to replace the constitution substantively means that the constitution has been replaced with a new one. A constitutional revolution has occurred, notwithstanding the legal tools used in the process: "A constitution, or at least an ultimate rule of succession of rules, cannot be wholly replaced in accordance with its own stipulations; purported replacements are really 'legal camouflage' for a 'peaceful revolution' in which the replacement is a break with the past."[154]

Indeed, it is clear by now that revolutions can come in different shapes and sizes. Legal continuity must not be confused with regime continuity. As we argue in this chapter, constitutional transformations of revolutionary magnitude can occur through formal amendments. There is no necessary correlation between the process and the substantive scope of constitutional change, a truth that the recent history of Hungary illustrates twice. Its post-Soviet transformation into a liberal constitutional democracy took the form of sweeping amendments to the 1949 Constitution. The Orbán government, elected in 2010, adopted still more amendments, and it used the prescribed constitution-making procedure, which was then similar to the amendment formula, to adopt an entirely new constitution (that contains the very same amendment rule) in order to bring about a democratic but illiberal regime lacking in constitutional checks and balances.

Why do some countries opt for a transformation through amendments rather than engage openly and explicitly in constitution making? One reason may be as simple as a lack of established procedures. Constitutions invariably address how they may be amended, but with the exception of temporary or interim constitutions, it is much rarer for them to provide for their own replacement or demise. In the absence of an existing formal mechanism for creating a new constitution, the most obvious way to pursue constitutional transformation may be through the mechanism of amendment.

Other possible explanations offer strategic or political considerations. Adherence to existing amendment procedures allows political leaders to cloak their desired changes in legality and continuity, thus framing their actions in the norms of formal legitimacy. A strategy of transformation through amendment may allow political actors to avoid the heightened risk of failure associated with the making of an entirely new constitution. The initiation of a constitution-making process might be risky, since it opens the entire constitution for renegotiation, increases costs, and invites strategic behavior of greater magnitude and scale.[155]

An incremental approach to constitutional replacement that relies on amendments is likely to entail lower political costs, especially if the amendment process is relatively undemanding, as in Hungary. It may also be less time-consuming and thus advantageous in urgent times.

It is also the case that the path of negotiated constitutional amendments controlled by the government may explain why regimes agree in the first place to consider constitutional change. For example, in the 1989 Chilean constitutional revolution, "the regime wanted to rule out the possibility of the constitution being dismantled in the future, and a referendum on a limited set of reforms backed by a broad consensus might actually preclude that possibility."[156] In other words, by being able to preserve some key institutions, such as military autonomy and designated senators, the regime was ready to consider amendments to the Constitution.

Therefore, in a constitutional transition to democracy, as examples such as Hungary and Chile demonstrate, the allure of a peaceful transfer of power may lead reformers to preserve some legal continuity. Likewise within existing democratic regimes, there are strong incentives for using the existing constitution to regulate the transformation process. It might secure more inclusion and consensus at the elite level, and also prevent particular actors (such as a powerful or charismatic leader) from (mis)using citizen participation by following in the Napoleonic "I am the constituent power" tradition.[157]

There are, however, grave potential costs associated with revolutionary amendments. Maintaining constitutional continuity with the previous regime can be, as we have seen, a double-edged sword: while it may lend the revolution formal legality, it also represents a missed opportunity to make a clean break with the past. Failure to make a fresh start with a new constitution can hinder democratization processes by saddling the new regime with undemocratic vestiges of the old regime, in addition to painful symbols and reminders of the past, as in Chile.

Revolution by amendment may also be procedurally deficient and thus fail to generate the social legitimacy that constitutions need (in contrast with legal legitimacy).[158] Compared to procedures for wholesale constitution making, regular amendment procedures may offer too few opportunities for popular participation and may rely too heavily on existing institutions (such as regular legislatures) not designed or intended to engage in constitution writing. Lacking the legitimacy for performing this task, such a process may yield results that struggle to reach the necessary level of acceptability for regime success. This was arguably the case in Hungary, where the changes in the constitutional document brought by the transitional Parliament did not include public participation and therefore lacked democratic legitimacy. The poor levels of popular participation in the early-1990 regime in Hungary doubtless contributed to a legitimation deficit.[159] Indeed, we believe that there is a strong link between the legal continuity of the 1989 constitutional revolution and the events that led to the subsequent transformative iteration.

Apropos the question of the legitimacy of the constitutional order, János Kis has argued that "the 1989 Constitution, bearing the stigma of consisting, technically, in an amended version of the 1949 Constitution and lacking democratic confirmation by a freely elected parliament, proved insufficiently resistant to the disruptive forces generated by the social, economic, and political transition."[160] A comprehensive, newly crafted democratic constitution, produced by an elected constitutional assembly under stricter consensual and participatory rules, and approved by the people in a referendum, perhaps would have generated additional democratic legitimacy for the document, thereby making it more difficult to subvert. We will return in chapter 7 to the legitimacy question as it relates to the exercise of constituent power in bringing about a constitutional revolution.

Aside from possible normative lessons attendant on the use of revolutionary amendments, the Hungarian case has important implications for the conceptualization of constitutional revolution, which, as shown in this chapter, need not be a violation of the constitutional order's formal rules. It may well be achieved under the rule of law while maintaining legal continuity. And this formal legal continuity may be consistent with the dramatic displacement of the constitutional order's foundational values and premises. Further, a constitutional revolution may lack finality and find itself in a constant struggle with counterrevolutionary forces. In turning to Germany in the next chapter, we show how a constitutional identity, rooted in revolutionary aspirations for a new constitutional ordering, has found institutional protection against counterrevolutionary threats.

4
Revolution, Counterrevolution, and the Question of German Constitutional Identity

> All constitutions are overthrown either from within or without; the latter, when there is some government close at hand having an opposite interest, or at a distance, but powerful.
>
> Aristotle

IN HIS KEYNOTE ADDRESS AT THE STATE ceremony celebrating the fiftieth anniversary of the German Federal Constitutional Court (FCC), the legal scholar and former Stanford University president Gerhard Casper spoke of "the continuity of the new Germany that has been developing, by way of an evolutionary revolution, since 1949."[1] He contrasted American and German constitutional history, pointing out that during the two hundred years of the former's existence, Germany had experienced numerous regime transformations, from the end of the Holy Roman Empire, through several federations, the Bismarck and Weimar constitutions, and, following the nightmare of the Third Reich and the subsequent foreign occupation, a Basic Law that was to become a constitutional-design archetype. That last transformation, whose stability and widely heralded success were being commemorated in 1999, was also notable for having seamlessly absorbed the extraordinary shock to the system that arrived in the form of national reunification.

The numerous discontinuities that distinguish this fascinating political history are more than sufficient to supply the necessary backdrop for a consideration of German constitutional identity, yet it is the prospect of further regime transformation—the country's acceptance of European integration—that has given rise to an invigorated interest in the identity question. Indeed, it is in connection with the nature of the relationship being forged between Germany and the European Union that the elusive subject of constitutional identity has explicitly entered the jurisprudential equation. Thus, as the FCC has adjudicated a series of vexing questions pertaining to German participation in the expanding and increasingly intrusive regime of European governance, it has developed criteria to determine the permissible reach of that regime, and among them the nation's constitutional identity has emerged as a benchmark of signal importance.

To understand its significance, in the German case and more broadly, we want to link it with a phenomenon of similarly subtle meaning—constitutional revolution—which, as stated in chapter 2, is a paradigmatic displacement, however achieved, in the conceptual prism through which constitutionalism is experienced in a given polity. As noted by Casper, the adoption in 1949 of a new constitution (Basic Law) represented a transition of revolutionary consequence; however, unlike the earlier prominent such occasion in 1918, this radical postwar transformation was a constitutional success story, in no small part because of the lessons learned from that ill-fated Weimar experiment. What the German-born and German-educated Casper proudly referred to as "the continuity of the new Germany" obtained its poignancy from recollections of tragic constitutional failure and from the fact that the "evolutionary" stability of the nation's governing document could plausibly be associated with the related inclusion of explicitly preservative entrenchment provisions.[2] Designed as a hedge against any retreat from the "new" Germany to the old, the invocation of these provisions came to be regarded as a defining assertion of constitutional identity, an expression of how, at its highest legal competence, a postrevolutionary German nation conceived of itself and how it expected to be perceived by others.

While a nation's constitutional identity may be imbued with revolutionary significance, once established it quite naturally mutates into the focal point for resistance to radical change. Occasionally, this leads to some absorbing constitutional politics and jurisprudence, and in this chapter we consider the German case as perhaps the most prominent such instance.

Specifically, we examine the question of constitutional identity in the context of what Casper astutely describes as "the third regime transformation that the Federal Constitutional Court has had to address."[3] Since this was at stake in its landmark *Lisbon* decision in 2009, it could not escape notice that in assessing and delineating the terms of German engagement with the European Union, the Court mentioned the term "constitutional identity" over thirty times. One aspect of this arrangement—the relationship between national courts and the European Court of Justice—has for years preoccupied the justices of the Karlsruhe Court. Intrinsic to the attention directed toward the issue have been the potentially transformative governing implications of enhanced deference to the decision-making authority of European institutions. Constitutional transformations, as we argued earlier, are no less revolutionary for the incremental aspect that sometimes marks their arrival, which is why Germany's legal ties to the European Union bear close watching. By some accounts, the projected realization of this transformative potential would indeed be tantamount to a constitutional revolution, and to the extent that this has been viewed as an unwelcome outcome, reliance on constitutional identity becomes essential to preventing it.

We argue that such reliance on the defensive properties of constitutional identity can function very well as a strategic counter to revolutionary ambitions; yet as is illustrated by the German case, a conceptual and practical price must be paid if, through these efforts, identity is rendered synonymous with or confined to preservative status quo goals and aspirations. The formulation adopted by Gerhard Casper—evolutionary revolution—underscores the main theoretical points of this chapter: constitutional identity embodies a dynamic dimension that enables it to facilitate as well as hinder dramatic changes in systemic legal configuration; and the process by which such change occurs may have revolutionary implications even if the specific shape and structure of the resulting settlement emerge, in seemingly unrevolutionary fashion, as an incremental constitutional accession.[4]

As for why Germany, the reasons speak directly to these issues. Perhaps in no other polity does the question of constitutional identity loom so large in legal and political discourse. This makes perfect sense in light of a history that might lead one to imagine a person whose character at some point had so clearly changed radically for the worse as to invite sustained and disturbing inquiry into the mysteries of individual identity.[5] So too with the nation. Surely it is no coincidence that the doctrine of the unconstitutional constitutional amendment originated in German jurisprudence, which had in the immediate postwar period come to accept the idea that there were implied and enforceable limits to constitutional change, particularly to changes going to the very essence of what it means to be governed constitutionally.[6] For the German people, having experienced the horrors of what it means to be governed unconstitutionally, and having entrenched limits to paradigm-shifting change within provisions whose inviolability encouraged their straightforward recognition as the German constitutional identity, to see the textual guarantees as anything other than fixed and immutable would require overcoming the historically appealing, logical implication that preventing things from getting radically better was a price worth paying to ensure that they would not again become radically worse. And since we know what radically worse looks like, and that the vision of a state of affairs deemed radically better will always be contestable, we may expect that under these circumstances the notion of an evolving constitutional identity will get very little traction.

In the next sections, we will see how this has played out in the constitutional debate over European integration. By one account, the FCC's rulings on the extent of German participation in extraterritorial governance in Europe convey a very conservative message, in which constitutional identity and national sovereignty are closely aligned; to defend one is in essence to defend the other: "The waning of sovereignty . . . prepares the field for the rise and blooming of constitutional identity."[7] Accordingly, much of the pointed criticism the Court received for its protective efforts has focused on the alleged Euro-skepticism of the decisions, which are arguably also insufficiently open to the evolutionary possibilities in the nation's constitutional identity. Thus, whether or not one agrees with how the substance of constitutional identity has come to be understood, to claim that such an understanding may have assumed an unalterable, unyielding status in the course of judicial scrutiny betrays a fundamental misconception about the nature of the concept in question. Alternatively, the Court's cautious approach to

European integration does not foreclose a dialogical process of judicial and political interaction that presumes the inherent mutability of constitutional identity. In this account, it is illusory to isolate a specific identity (Germany's) from the larger historical narrative of which it is a part (Europe's) and believe that the former will remain unaffected by the connection. Instead, the identity challenge "calls for judicial dialogue to settle a balance between centripetal and centrifugal dynamics."[8] Thus, it is disputable that an identity—in this case, the German constitutional identity—once discovered, simply is what it is and must be preserved as such. It develops over time, which is to say, it is not an entity inhabiting a constitutional text, there to be found and maintained as is by those to whom it applies.

In adopting the latter position on constitutional identity, specifically in relation to the German predicament, we do not wish to understate the risks associated with the presumption of mutability. As the Court clearly recognized, and as Gerhard Casper's remarks suggest, an evolving identity is one that could culminate in revolutionary transformation. Whether such risks are worth undertaking depends on one's view of the desirability of the transformative possibility. While exceedingly remote, if something like a federal European state were to emerge out of the legal and political activity on the Continent, it would constitute a radical development whose revolutionary significance would be celebrated by some and deplored by others. Our intent is not to weigh in on this or other reconstitutive prospects. Rather, it is to consider the German case for what it can reveal about the intriguing association between identity and revolution.

Identity, Integration, and Revolution

Constitutions are strange places to find revolutionary launching pads.[9] To be sure, their very existence is often the direct result of a successful revolution, but once adopted, they are meant to endure.[10] So one reads with interest Article 24(1) of the German Basic Law, which provides that "the federation may by law transfer sovereign powers to international organizations."[11] This provision was never intended as a clarion call for revolution, but to the extent that it was incorporated in the document to facilitate integration into the developing supranational European order, its language has become at least a potential source for radical constitutional transformation. That potential is implicit in scholarly references to "a 'silent constitutional revolution'" and "a quiet revolution," which, though not conjuring up images of storming the Bastille, allow us to envision, through the "transfer[ence] of sovereign powers," a substantial displacement in the way constitutional governance is practiced.[12]

Such a paradigm shift is by no means assured, and there is certainly nothing inherently revolutionary about advocating for European integration. As Dieter Grimm, a German legal scholar and former member of the FCC, noted, "We are neither witnessing the foundation of the European project nor a new beginning after a radical historical break. On the contrary, European integration is a process of gradual expansion and consolidation."[13] Consistent with the orthodox view of the subject, Grimm's emphasis on gradualism in the absence of an abrupt—and no doubt violent—rupture in historical continuity is an implicit denial that the process occurring in Europe has any revolutionary meaning or significance.[14] Should legal and political developments in this process reach a point where Grimm found in the substance of Germany's participation in the union a dramatic modification of constitutional meaning and practice, he might or might not consider such a transformation constitutionally revolutionary. At some point, however, perhaps if expansion and consolidation were directly implicated in a discernible and troubling revision of German constitutional identity, it would prove difficult for him not to acknowledge the revolutionary import of such a development.

Indeed, after the *Lisbon* decision, Grimm indicated as much, insisting that "German state institutions may not permit a transfer of powers by which the identity of the German Basic Law would be affected."[15] A year later, this concern expressed itself in connection with some reflections on the disharmonic character of two regimes of law in Europe. In contrast with the more dominant view, which holds that European constitutional identity draws upon a reservoir of general principles present in the experience of the EU's member states, Grimm commented, "The consequences for domestic constitutions would be less grave if EU law and national constitutional law were guided by the same values and principles."[16] Against the backdrop of twentieth-century German history, the concern for the constitution's identity extended to the identity of the nation itself. While there may be no evading the past, the Basic Law, while not unique among constitutions, is the most conspicuous example of a document that performs a critical redemptive role by essentially repudiating an identity that had, over an extended period, provided ignoble distinctiveness to the nation.[17] As noted by one commentator, "The very nature of the new Basic Law . . . was . . . an identity-building exercise."[18] Hence, it is understandable that those charged with interpreting the constitution would be vigilant regarding the features of the document seen as denoting Germany's transcendence of its past.[19]

Lisbon is only the most recent venue for the expression of such vigilance. Judicial engagement with German constitutional identity in the context of European integration commenced in 1974. It was then that the FCC called attention to deficiencies in democratic legitimacy and in protection for fundamental rights in the existing state of European governance, stipulating that "so long as" this was the case, the Court would require enforceable limits to the transfer of sovereign authority to the European Community.[20] Thus, in *Solange I* it declared, "[Article 24] does not open the way to amending the basic structure of the Basic Law, which forms the basis of its identity, without a formal amendment to the Basic Law."[21] Fundamental rights were integral to this basic structure, which therefore obliged the Court to defend them—and also by implication German constitutional identity—against any infringements imposed by an external tribunal. "Only the Federal Constitutional Court is entitled, within the framework of the powers granted to it in the Basic Law, to protect the fundamental rights guaranteed in the Basic Law. No other court can deprive it of this duty imposed by constitutional law."[22] The ruling, it has been said, "opened an amicable rivalry . . . between the Constitutional Court and the European Court of Justice."[23]

For those eager to hasten the process of integration, it became a source of consternation. Thus, the "infamous" decision was seen as an invitation to member states "to declare all kinds of issues to be part of their national identity in order to shield them from European law."[24] Twelve years later, in *Solange II*, the Court backed off, certifying that the European Economic Community had made notable progress in democratic governance and the protection of fundamental rights, to the extent that the FCC could now exercise its option to decline to rule on the constitutionality of EEC law affecting these matters. The ruling was seen as "the highest point of harmony and convergence between the German federal Constitutional Court and the European Court of Justice."[25] Still, the Court reaffirmed its earlier take on Article 24(1): "The provision does not confer the authority to surrender, by way of ceding sovereign powers to international institutions, the identity of the prevailing constitutional order of the Federal Republic. This identity consists of the Basic Law's framework, that is, its very structure."[26] So while the pronounced skepticism and caution of the 1974 decision were replaced by a much greater openness to the idea of European integration, the identity-based parameters for the sovereign transfer of authority remained in place. What is more, it did not require a vivid imagination to anticipate heated disagreements in the future over whether those constraints were being breached.

But where exactly are these parameters to be drawn? Or as one commentator asked, "What is the German constitutional identity and where does it come from? Is it a defining feature of Germany as a community or of the German constitution as a legal text?"[27] Would it make sense to say of two nations—for example, Germany and Italy—that the incorporation in their constitutions of similar core principles meant that their respective constitutional identities were the same? Does the absence of a comprehensive text, as in Great Britain and Israel, mean that constitutional identity does not exist in such places, or rather that we need to understand the concept of identity as comprehending more than the specific passages in a document? In the United States, codification by the post–Civil War amendments of the principle of equal treatment was a signal moment in the development of American constitutional identity, marking the official ascendance of the universalist strand in the nation's conflicted constitutional tradition. Textually at least, the change was of a magnitude that would make difficult a denial of its revolutionary significance. But the system's highly fragmented distribution of political power guaranteed that the other, more particularistic strand in that tradition would not lack for institutional muscle as its advocates fought to undermine the constitutive implications of the changes wrought through the amendment process. The constitutional identity of the text may have changed, but the constitutional identity of the American people (citizens and public officials) was only beginning its transformation.

Ultimately, stability in the identity of the constitutional order depended on a convergence of the two.[28]

To invoke the structure of the constitution, as was done in the *Solange* cases, does not, then, provide much guidance for imposing limits. In 1992, the Treaty on European Union—better known as the Maastricht Treaty—was signed, resulting in an extraordinary expansion in the array of subjects placed under the governing authority of the union. In conjunction with German ratification of the treaty, the Bundestag and Bundesrat amended the Basic Law; in a new Article 23, on the European Union, a more specific answer to the identity question was provided in the form of a requirement that any delegation of sovereign power would have to respect the unalterable principles contained in Article 79(2) and Article 79(3). Among these are the unamendable guarantees of human dignity, democracy, and federalism included in Articles 1 and 20, which together impart somewhat more definition to the elusive subject of constitutional identity.

It was also a concern of the FCC in the *Maastricht Treaty Case,* in which the agreement was challenged for "virtually transform[ing] the European Union into a supranational federal state capable of eroding Germany's constitutional order."[29] This contention was rejected as the Court asserted, "There is no intention at the moment to establish a 'United States of Europe' comparable in structure to the United States of America."[30] While German participation in a more formidable European Union was upheld, the sovereignty and identity-based apprehensions that generated the objections to the treaty were not left unaddressed by the Court. In blunt terms, the justices excluded from legitimacy "any act amending the constitution which affects the core of the Basic Law that is exempt from amendment."[31] Indeed, it was the terms of the treaty that enabled the Court to secure its own future monitoring role in blocking any radical departure from adherence to constitutional essentials. It did so by "elevat[ing] the principle of subsidiarity to the level of a binding legal principle for the European Union and the European Community."[32] The FCC's assurance that union affiliation would not culminate in an evisceration of sovereign primacy in matters fundamental to the existing constitutional order was based on its reading of the intent underlying the subsidiarity commitment: "to protect the national identity of the Member States and to preserve their powers."[33]

National identity, however, is not, in principle, coterminous with constitutional identity. For example, where a constitution is designed to function in effect as a subversive instrument seeking the transformation of a distinctive and entrenched social order that is central to the nation's identity, care must be taken not to mistake one identity for the other. India and South Africa are examples of transformative constitutions whose success or failure can be measured by their ability to facilitate the restructuring of their respective societies. Hence, progress in these places has been marked by the degree of achieved convergence between national and constitutional identities. In theory, maximum success would mean they had become indistinguishable. There is a transformative aspect to the German constitution as well, in the sense that its adoption signals the moment when the foundation for achieving a new identity in that country was established.[34] "To a great extent," Juliane Kokott argued, "the national identity of post-war Germany is founded on and shaped by the Constitution. . . . Respect for the Constitution is indispensable and has to be ensured to prevent even the appearance of a relapse to the past."[35]

There is an additional side to indispensability, and it illuminates not only the identity question but also our related concern—revolution. It is captured by the German constitutional theorist Ulrich Preuss: "No constitution can contain rules which allow its abolishment altogether; this would permit revolution, whereas it is the very meaning of constitutions to avoid revolutions; and to make them dispensable."[36] But even if constitutions do not explicitly contain rules for their own eradication, most do not provide insurance against the possibility of this happening. Germany is the most notable exception; its eternity clauses are, in Preuss's terms, intended to render revolutions dispensable. Stated differently, its document is structured to prevent a transformation of such principled magnitude that its constitutional identity would become something very different from what it is. Or as Kokott's formulation would have it, such prevention is essential in order to preclude any possibility that the substance of German national identity would be permitted to look anything like it did before the constitutional revolution that produced the Basic Law.

Placed in a comparative context, her point is sharper. The U.S. Constitution is perhaps the most frequently cited example of identity equivalence, the paradigmatic case of a nation constituted by its constitution. The ideas upon which the polity was established formed the identity of the nation, even while ascriptive realities—notably, race—gave to that identity an aspirational significance that is often underappreciated in standard accounts of American constitutionalism.[37] Yet critical as the Constitution is to the national identity of the United States, the *Maastricht Case* points to a more obvious centrality for the German document in the life of that nation. Thus, there is no comparable statement in American constitutional jurisprudence to this assertion by the FCC: "Article 79, para. 3 of the GG [Grundgesetz; Basic Law] links the development of the State in Germany to that core of the constitutional order which it itself describes, and thus seeks to secure the prevailing constitution against any development which endeavors to establish a new constitution."[38] What is more, important as constitutional principles are to American identity, in addition to not standing as a bar to radical amendments, they do not apply uniformly across different levels of government, and they do not, as they do in Germany, possess a jurisprudentially delineated objective quality that extends their application from the public domain to the private.[39]

In exempting the core of the Basic Law from amendment, the Court was not breaking new ground, having declared as much in the earlier integration cases and as far back as the *Klass Case* in 1970. The famous distinction in Abraham Lincoln's First Inaugural Address between the right to amend and the right to overthrow is actually more clear-cut in German jurisprudence than in its American counterpart. "This country," Lincoln said, "belongs to the people who inhabit it. Whenever they should grow weary of the existing government, they can exercise their CONSTITUTIONAL right of amending it, or their REVOLUTIONARY right to dismember or overthrow it."[40] But the U.S. Supreme Court, to say nothing of the preponderance of opinion among American constitutional theorists, has never embraced the idea that a duly enacted amendment could be successfully challenged on the ground that in substance it was so radical as to effectively "permit revolution" through the constitutional process. In Germany, however, disenchantment with the functioning of government may properly trigger the amendment process so long as the result is not a revolutionary one. If such were the outcome, one could easily imagine a case in which the FCC executed what it has long accepted as a conceptual possibility (though never to this day implemented), namely, the invalidation of an "unconstitutional" constitutional amendment.

Significantly, the jurisprudential assumptions underlying the amendment issue are the same as those invoked by the FCC in connection with European integration. They both assume the existence and importance of a constitutional identity whose defense is a principal responsibility of the Court. One reason the identity question has attracted much less attention in the United States than in Germany is that an external political entity does not present itself as a threat to the continued existence of the U.S. Constitution's distinctive personality. In the period between Maastricht and Lisbon, the discussion of constitutional identity was extended to a wider constituency of interest, since the high-stakes debate over the adoption of a constitution for Europe centered on just this point. To be sure, the contestation largely focused not so much on how extranational precepts and principles could be integrated into the jurisprudence of nations possessing unique histories and ways of doing things, but how—or whether—the distinctive political and legal cultures of a diverse group of nations could be incorporated within an overarching framework of international governance so as to create a constitutional identity for the new entity as a whole.[41] Yet in much the way that the adoption of a federal state in 1787 presented political units at the local level with challenging questions about their identities in relation to the larger American whole—what is it that makes Virginia what it is?—the prospect of a European federal state inevitably fueled concerns in Germany and other countries about the status of their own self-understandings, particularly if, as was widely believed, "constitutional identity is an inalienable element to the democratic self-determination of a people."[42]

The European Constitution never came to fruition, but for the many Euro-skeptics in Germany and elsewhere, the Treaty of Lisbon of 2007 made the earlier failed effort a reality in all but name. Even before its adoption, it could be argued that "from a functionalist point of view, there is no doubt that the EU, which is neither a state nor a state in the making, has a constitution."[43] The treaty alleviated some concerns traceable to *Solange I;* for example, by giving formal recognition to the Charter of Fundamental Rights, it made it more difficult to question Europe's commitment to a robust regime of individual liberty. But with the treaty's expansion of union competences and enhancement of central democratic institutions, the sovereignty apprehensions and anxieties that had accumulated during the battles over the proposed constitution did not dissipate after Lisbon; additionally, they ensured that the ensuing debate would not lack either passion or reasoned contestation.[44] As we will see, the judicial spotlight became fixed on the question of constitutional identity, as if all previous considerations of the idea in the earlier European integration cases had been just a prelude to the Court's climactic featuring of it in its *Lisbon Treaty* ruling. What we need to examine closely is the Court's understanding of the concept and its implications for the radical displacements in constitutional development that we think of as revolutionary. Critical to this inquiry are at least two key questions: Is constitutional identity to be conceived of as rigidly composed, with the result that to defend it is to preserve its fixed meaning? If instead it is best seen as an evolving phenomenon, how does it change and should there be boundaries to constrain the reach and direction of the transformation?

Courting Revolution

Berlin on the last day of June 2009 saw the opening of a new exhibition documenting the fall of the Berlin Wall and commemorating the twentieth anniversary of the "Peaceful Revolution." As it turned out, that early summer date soon acquired a less celebratory branding: "30 June 2009 will be remembered as a black day in the history of Europe."[45]

For a continent all too well known for its share of dark days, singling out the midpoint of 2009 for ignominious recognition provoked a chill and a pause. Its appearance in a German law review no doubt limited its readership, but within the circle of legal scholars, its note of despair over a landmark FCC ruling in Karlsruhe reflected the sentiment in a substantial segment of that elite community. If the comment represented the rhetorical outer limit of displeasure with the Court's decision in the *Lisbon Treaty Case,* its gloomy projection was echoed in a cohort of critiques that lambasted the constitutional tribunal for what struck many as a decidedly sovereigntist, anti-Europe jeremiad. On the other side were those who found such reactions wildly excessive in the face of a judgment that in fact approved the substance of the treaty with only a modest disclaimer about an easily remedied flaw in the legislative process by which it was ratified.[46] Included in this number were sympathetic voices that found in the Court's lengthy accompanying dicta a sensible and welcome counterweight to an uncritical acceptance of a potentially dangerous project of supranational commitment.

So what was it that so blackened an otherwise festive day in Germany? The following are some examples of the negative reactions to the judicial decision, out of which we want to underscore a common theme that connects the FCC's emphasis on constitutional identity and the largely dormant idea of constitutional revolution that is contained within the movement toward greater integration into the regime of European governance.

> "The Court is ideologically opposed to the course of European unity because it sees that cause as a threat to national homogeneity which one assumes it takes to be the basis of justified legality."[47]
>
> "All in all, the revolutionary act of constitution-making is downsized to an ordinary act that is henceforth under review of the Court. According to the decision, the people who want a democratic revolution must petition the Court."[48]
>
> "For the first time, [the FCC] affirms that the Basic Law prohibits Germany from participating in the founding of a European federal state."[49]
>
> "The tenor of the Court's judgment . . . is that 'identity trumps integration.' "[50]
>
> "The Union is presented as a foreign entity, not as part of Germany's identity. Hence, the main task of the Court seems to be the defense of Germany against intrusions by this entity."[51]

These observations are taken from critiques of the *Lisbon* decision that, while not supportive of one another on all major points of contention, are convergent on at least one important thematic strand: Germany's apex Constitutional Court has arrogated to itself the responsibility of verifying the legitimacy of the country's formal engagement with the European community. In exercising that responsibility in the momentous 2009 case concerning Germany's acceptance of the terms of the Lisbon Treaty, the FCC used the occasion to articulate its collective mind-set on the merits of enhanced integration and to establish a jurisprudential framework for determining the constitutionality of any subsequent initiatives to delegate sovereign powers to Europe. The burden of this critical account of the Court's massive opinion is that first and lamentably, the justices aligned themselves with the legion of Euro-skeptics in Germany and elsewhere, and by virtue of the authority they presently wield over treaty-related issues, the Court is well poised to impede the progress of further European integration. Second, the methodology for doing so involved a protective invocation of German constitutional identity that can (will?) lead to the creation of a false dichotomy between the values and principles of the nation and those of the larger political community. Finally, to the extent that a constitutional revolution would be an appropriate designation for the achievement of a European federal state—in the sense that "it [would] brea[k] with traditional conceptions of the political organization of societies"—the FCC has disturbingly positioned itself to become the designated instrument of German counterrevolution.[52]

To be sure, the critics who endorsed the thrust of the above "indictment" would likely concede that their worries were not traceable to the specific holding in the case. With respect to the fundamental issue raised in the constitutional complaint, the FCC found no incongruity between the Lisbon Treaty and Basic Law obligations.[53] A focus only on the statements in the judgment having direct bearing on the constitutional issues before the Court might even suggest that the outcome was unequivocally "pro-European." For example, "The Act Approving the Treaty of Lisbon is compatible with the requirements of the Basic Law, in particular with the principle of democracy."[54] Although it was argued in the legal challenge that "a 'sellout of the state's very own competences' [had] taken place," the Court rejected this claim, insisting that the augmentation of European competences contained in the agreement was consistent with the sovereign integrity of the German state.[55] Indeed, "There are no doubts concerning the continued existence of the German state and people."[56] Moreover, to the degree that the Court discerned some merit in the complaint, its secondary finding, that the treaty's accompanying legislation had not achieved the level of democratic legitimacy necessary to pass constitutional muster, could hardly form the basis of a convincing denunciation of the Court's motives or agenda.[57] Was this the evidence for a black day in European history?

Perhaps not, but why did the FCC adopt such a mistakenly myopic view, the critics might well ask. Much like the joy of those who cheered the U.S. Supreme Court's upholding of most provisions of the Affordable Care Act ("Obamacare"), satisfaction with the decision upholding the law (treaty) should be tempered by the prominent inclusion of an ominous line of constitutional reasoning in which a majority of the justices established a doctrinal predicate that could easily subvert similar, and possibly more ambitious, efforts in the future. Thus, while the Supreme Court upheld the health care law, American conservatives had their disappointment with the specific result mitigated by the realization that a majority had struck such a devastating blow against the Commerce Clause that it will doubtless render constitutionally suspect subsequent exertions by the national government to pursue large-scale societal undertakings. And nothing suggested that the FCC's commitment to its ill-conceived jurisprudential agenda, unlike the Supreme Court's in *National Federation of Independent Business v. Sebelius,* rested precariously on the strength of a bare majority of jurists. If that suspicion proves correct, and if the inferences drawn about the potential significance of the opinion's extended discourse on the principles governing Germany's participation in the EU are similarly perspicacious, then European integrationists have ample reason to experience a bout of *Lisbon* pessimism.

To evaluate whether this pessimism is warranted or misplaced is to enter the conversation about German constitutional identity, the hub of the FCC's controversial extended dicta in the *Lisbon Treaty Case.* The difficulty in going there is that the judicial end of the conversation speaks in a voice that can be heard saying quite different things, a problem exacerbated by a long-standing institutional decision-making norm of consensus that may in some instances work to reduce the clarity and precision of the judicial message.[58] Whether *Lisbon* is one such instance may never be definitively known, but it would not be surprising if it were. The uncertainty surrounding the conceptual reach of constitutional identity, to say nothing of its vexed content in a country where the issue is famously fraught, might suggest not only that the decision's meaning and implications will be long debated, but also that the debate most likely originated on the Court itself.[59]

It is apparent from a reading of the Basic Law that the identity issue and its significance for the course of European constitutional development are tied to a tension between openness and sovereignty built into the text of the document.[60] It is an inscribed disharmony less stark than, say, the Israeli requirement that the state be both Jewish and democratic, but in its own way it is constitutionally challenging in comparable ways. Unlike Israel, where competition between seemingly irreconcilable visions of national identity has shaped the course of that nation's unconventional constitutional development, Germany exemplifies a more familiar example of a polity in which a tension or inconsistency in the constitutional order may lie largely dormant, occasionally emerging to establish the contours within which a difficult issue gets addressed, and receding from prominence after it passes from scrutiny. In Israel, the contradiction lives as a lurking omnipresence that dominates the discourse of ordinary politics, intermittently threatening to undermine the societal equilibrium that makes such politics possible. The conflicting though not quite so incompatible commitments in Germany may play a similarly substantial role in facilitating—or forestalling—major constitutional transformation.

Foreign and Domestic: Framing the Response to an Ambiguous Invitation

Our account of constitutional revolution has a more substantive than procedural focus, yet the relationship of national constitutional courts to a supranational entity such as the European Union suggests that the line separating the two is not always easy to draw. For example, the voicing of domestic trepidation in Ireland about heavily intrusive EU policy making had a procedural aspect to it—a constitutional revolution, it was argued, would occur when external power supersedes the only rightful authority to determine the essentials of constitutional identity—but also a substantive dimension: when something as critical to Irish constitutional identity as abortion policy is targeted from whatever source, there is the possibility of a paradigmatic, and hence revolutionary, displacement in the constitutional order.[61] This leaves open the question of just how much of the shift would satisfy the criterion for revolution; for example, only if it represented a clear repudiation of basic Thomistic natural law theory? In the German case, the numerous judicial expressions of concern about constitutional identity incorporate comparable apprehensions that speak both to the substantive competences affected by the terms of the treaty and to the methods by which governing authority has been exerted in their derivation. For example, the *Lisbon* Court concluded: "From the perspective of the principle of democracy, the violation of the constitutional identity codified in Article 79.3 of the Basic Law *is at the same time* an encroachment upon the power of the people. In this respect the constituent power has not granted the representatives and bodies of the people a mandate to depose of the identity of the constitution."[62]

How, then, are we to make sense of the Treaty's importance for thinking systematically about constitutional revolution? Although the Lisbon opinion is replete with references to constitutional identity, it never explicitly mentions a constitutional revolution. Since the treaty's much-discussed Article 4(2) in effect invites national courts to address the identity question, this in itself is not surprising. It says in part: "The Union shall respect the equality of Member States before the Treaties as well as their national identities, inherent in their fundamental structures, political and constitutional, inclusive of regional and local self-government." As has been rightly pointed out, the provision "not only demands the respect for national constitutional identity, but can be understood as permitting domestic constitutional courts to invoke, under certain limited circumstances, constitutional limits to the primacy of EU law."[63] Just how far such respect should be permitted to extend is of course a large unresolved question, although considerable support exists for setting clear limits. Accordingly, "Article 4(2) was *not* designed as a shield or a sword in the hands of the Member States, which their national (constitutional) courts can raise in order to fence off or challenge European law: it does not give them a trump card."[64]

To seriously engage with the limit problem, we should underscore the germaneness of the constitutional revolution to that question. Indeed, a close reading of the Court's opinion suggests that the absence of an explicit invocation of the term is not indicative of its insignificance to the issue. Thus, the following are instances in which the Court's identity-related concerns implicitly relate to the type of constitutional change that should be recognized as revolutionary.

> "Through what is known as the eternity guarantee, the Basic Law reacts on the one hand to the historical experience of a creeping or abrupt erosion of the substance of a democratic fundamental order. However, it makes clear on the other hand that the Constitution of Germans, in accordance with the international development which has taken place in particular since the existence of the United Nations, has a universal foundation which cannot be amended by positive law."[65]
>
> "The principle of democracy may not be balanced against other legal interests; it is inviolable. The constituent power of the Germans which gave itself the Basic Law wanted to set an insurmountable boundary to any future development. Amendments to the Basic Law affecting the principles laid down in Article 1 and Article 20 of the Basic Law shall be inadmissible (Article 79.3). The so-called eternity guarantee even prevents a constitution-amending legislature from disposing of the identity of the free constitutional order. The Basic Law thus not only presumes sovereign statehood for Germany but guarantees it."[66]
>
> "The Basic Law strives to integrate Germany into the legal community of peaceful and free states, but does not waive the sovereignty contained in the last instance in the German constitution as a right of the people to take constitutive decisions concerning fundamental questions as its own identity."[67]

What is clear in each of these statements from the *Lisbon* case is the Court's preoccupation with constitutional identity. Although they are not straightforwardly articulated, only minimum exertion is required to find in each of the judicial assertions a corresponding point that speaks to a specific aspect of constitutional revolution. Thus, in the first excerpt's allusion to "historical experience" is an explicit awareness by the Court that while the "substance of a democratic fundamental order" may be transformed abruptly, the possibility of "creeping" erosion needs also to be guarded against. As discussed in chapter 2, rupture and discontinuity are not defining criteria for establishing the presence of a constitutional revolution. Such transformations are no less revolutionary when brought about incrementally.[68] It might be a revelation in some quarters that a revolutionary displacement in constitutional orientation could occur within the parameters of legality, and that its realization might stem from the workings of what Bruce Ackerman calls "the lower lawmaking system."[69] As *Lisbon* makes very clear, the Federal Constitutional Court is not likely to be such a place.[70]

The incrementalist scenario is mirrored by developments at the other end of the supraconstitutional relationship: "The 'European constitution-in-the-making' (Wandelverfassung) as a whole is the product of an evolutionary process without revolutionary backing, or any functional equivalent for a revolutionary constitution that constitutes a new political and social regime by the will of the people."[71] Or put differently, "The incremental evolution in quantitative and qualitative terms has raised the problem of 'silent constitutional revision.'"[72] Consistent with the argument in the Court's opinion, one pathway to a constitutional revolution is through consolidation from above and compliance from below with respect to substantive changes that leave the constitutional playing field in a fundamentally altered state. To the degree that such changes culminate in a new landscape on which the high mound of objectively ordered values no longer remained a fixed and readily identifiable extension of the local constitutional scenery, one could expect an effort to either contest the new reality or accommodate to it.

The absence of accommodationist language explains much of the scholarly resistance to the decision. According to the Court, eternity clauses are the Basic Law's preferred solution to the challenge posed by the "creeping" erosion of constitutional essentials. Surely, then, a constitutional revolution unaccompanied by a formal exercise of the constituent power is at all costs to be avoided.[73] Yet notice that in the Court's view, these clauses draw their special status as unamendable provisions from principles external to the local context. This presents an intriguing conundrum. If the fixed and unalterable substance of German constitutional identity is directly linked with universal principles embedded in international law, and if the Court were to arrogate to itself the responsibility of defending the core meaning of that identity, then its assigned preservative task would require for its fulfillment an active engagement with sources outside the indigenous scope of sovereign authority. As Juliane Kokott astutely observed, "The special openness for integration is also a part of the constitutional identity of the Basic Law."[74] So it matters that in *Lisbon* the Court became the officially designated instrument of identity review, thereby ensuring that the problem would not remain unaddressed. As its opinion declared, "The obligation under European law to respect the Constituent power of the Member States as the masters of the Treaties corresponds to the non-transferable identity of the constitution (Article 79.3 of the Basic Law), which is not open to integration in this respect. Within the boundaries of its competences, the Federal Constitutional Court must review, where necessary, whether these principles are adhered to."[75]

The second excerpt above deepens the difficulty while manifesting additional judicial cognizance of the characteristics that distinguish the specific constitutional variant of revolution from its standard instance. In it we see clearly that the "general consensus that a minimally necessary characteristic of revolution is some wholesale and unconstitutional replacement of the governing body" does not extend to the radically transformative displacement that can occur directly through the deployment of legitimate constitutionally prescribed measures.[76] "Deposing of the identity of the free constitutional order" does not require as a distinguishing feature of its revolutionary authenticity that there be, in Kelsenian terms, an illegitimate nullification of the existing legal order. So resistant must this order be to the threat of elimination and replacement—legally or illegally executed—that the constituent power itself must be rendered, in accordance with its own presumed wishes, impervious to any identity-altering action of the higher lawmaking authority. What is more, in the next paragraph of its opinion, the Court leaves unresolved the further and graver question of whether the constituent power can, through a subsequent exercise of that very power, destroy the free constitutional order: "It may remain open whether, due to the universal nature of dignity, freedom, and equality alone, this commitment even applies to the constituent power, i.e., to the case that the German people, in free self-determination, but in a continuity of legality to the rule of the Basic Law, gives itself a new constitution."[77]

Again, we see the outlines of the aforementioned problem, which perhaps is best expressed paradoxically. Thus, the second excerpt concludes with an explicit linkage of identity and sovereignty, with the Court affirming the purported presumption in the Basic Law that a guarantee of national self-governing autonomy is entrenched in the same provisions that codify and preserve German constitutional identity. Yet in reasserting the "universal nature" from which the essentials of that identity are derived, the Court is confronted by the quandary of having to appeal to extra-sovereign standards in order to defend the inviolability of sovereign authority.[78] As we argue below, a much less paradoxical predicament follows if sovereignty and identity are kept distinct; indeed, the EU Treaty by design avoided using the term "sovereignty." Rather, it "emphasi[zes] instead the joint responsibility for the 'national identities' of the member states."[79] The terminological conflation by the Court—through which, in essence, constitutional identity acquires the expressive attributes of sovereignty—has implications that extend well beyond the specifics of the *Lisbon* case. Thus, the Court's self-delegated task to exercise the function of identity review with respect to initiatives of the EU that arguably go too far in encroaching on legitimate national prerogatives will in practice be difficult to distinguish from a traditional defense of sovereign entitlements.

The third excerpt provides a telling perspective on the Court's operational view of German autonomy, and at the same time it revealingly—yet inadvertently—illuminates why there should be a conceptual separation of sovereignty from identity. The judges stipulate that the Basic Law's goal of European integration must be achieved without any surrender of the nation's sovereignty, which is here defined as the "right of the people" to undertake constitutive decisions concerning the substance of identity. That collective right—elsewhere described as "the right to free and equal participation in public authority"—is inviolable and immune from balancing because it is "enshrined in human dignity."[80] But as we have seen, this collective right cannot be absolute; otherwise, the lessons of history would have minimal instructive value. The Court's well-established strictures against the legitimacy of any revolutionary modification of extant German constitutional identity suggest that sovereignty, if it is to be understood in this popular way, must have clear limits.[81] In keeping with the Lincolnian distinction between a "constitutional right" and a "revolutionary right," it follows that only when "constitutive decisions" about identity culminate in something short of paradigm-shifting change may they be considered rightful exercises of democratic authority.[82] What is more, the problem here extends beyond the issue of incoherence. Unless sovereignty and identity are kept analytically distinct, the constitutionally prescribed goal of European integration risks failure through judicial insistence on a gratuitous "'them and us' perspective."[83] Thus, ironically, the protection of identity from encroachment by a foreign entity saps the vitality of a process critical to the long-term well-being of that very identity. Of course, this presumes an understanding of constitutional identity that is absent from the Court's numerous invocations of the concept, namely, that it embodies a dynamic dimension that is fueled in part by the dialogical interaction of commensurate commitments in the Basic Law and the law of the European Union.

Bounded Fluidity

We are now in a position to articulate more precisely what is at stake in the *Lisbon* constitutional conundrum. The treaty affirms the union's respect for the constitutional identities of the member states and in doing so implicitly invites national constitutional courts to weigh in on what this means in their immediate settings.[84] At the same time, its reaffirmation of the primacy of European law ensures that there will be future conflict over the extent of the EU's deference to local determinations. On the German side, the FCC acknowledges the Basic Law's commitment to European integration and concurrently maintains that the obligations flowing from it do not include compromising the inviolability of constitutional identity. By designating itself the instrument of identity review, and by embracing a fundamentally static interpretation of constitutional identity, Europe's most powerful national court has become the institutional epicenter for assessing the precise character of supranational "respect" for indigenous constitutional essentials.

Little in these developments has escaped the notice of the many informed continental commentators who have examined the cohort of constitutional issues related to European integration. Some of them have targeted the missed opportunity in the Court's accentuating of constitutional identity, arguing that collectively the judges should "be an important critical interlocutor of the integration process."[85] As part of "a composite system of constitutional adjudication," the FCC should "interact closely" with the European Court of Justice to find "an appropriate balance between national constitutional identity and primacy of EU law."[86] Working within a context of "constitutional pluralism," there ought to be a strong reliance on "judicial dialogue to settle a balance between centripetal and centrifugal dynamics."[87] When functioning optimally, the Court is accordingly an instrument of "multilevel constitutionalism," engaged in "an interactive process of establishing, organizing, sharing, and limiting powers."[88] And so it follows that constitutional identity "is a dynamic notion, that evolves and changes through and along constant and continuous social spontaneous processes."[89] Consequently, "it has to develop over time, which means that it *can* in fact develop over time."[90]

These commentators succeeded in capturing an essential attribute of constitutional identity, one glaringly absent from the Court's heavy reliance on the concept. Their concerns were alarmingly highlighted in a subsequent "identity review" case, in which the majority opinion claimed that such "review is not to be assessed according to Union law but exclusively according to German constitutional law."[91] They appear to recognize that a theory of constitutional identity that cannot account for its prospective mutability is an incomplete theory. They rightly understand identity as an interactive process whereby a constitution, much like a person, develops its distinctive character or individuality through engagement with its environment, within the broader context of its being. They might agree with the philosopher Charles Taylor's insight, "My own identity crucially depends on my dialogical relation with others."[92]

But there are competing considerations. In addition to these normal adaptive progressions, there are exceptional instances when a person's identity undergoes a transformation that leaves the party in a fundamentally different existential state, the result of some sudden, radically induced alteration, or of an evolving makeover that may be discernible only when the process has culminated in an arguably novel identity. Experience suggests the latter possibility happens infrequently. The evolution more often than not entails changes within an extant identity, in response to which observers might voice gratification or concern once enough time has elapsed to make a qualitative assessment of what has transpired. Critics of the *Lisbon* opinion's static or defensive invocation of constitutional identity seemed to have this bounded understanding of identity in mind when they disparaged the Court for its failure to appreciate the more fluid and dynamic aspect of the phenomenon. They quite properly emphasized the salience of dialogue for fulfilling the constitutional identity requirements of European integration. Yet given the critics' presumption of a harmonious center-periphery interaction purportedly inherent in the process of European integration, largely missing from their accounts was any serious engagement with constitutional revolution. After all: "As long as the European Union . . . operate[s] according to its established institutional mechanisms, no encroachments on Germany's constitutional identity can be expected. The loss of national identity through the European integration process is a chimera."[93]

For the Court, on the other hand, such a prospect is anything but chimerical, which is to say, in its account, the terrain of European integration occasionally comes across as a potential minefield of constitutional revolution. If "the perspective of the German Constitutional Court" can be styled "very German," reflecting a "'them'-versus-'us' logic," perhaps it is because the vision of a fixed identity to which the Court subscribes inflates the threat to national constitutional identity implicit in the very openness of the Basic Law to European law.[94] The difficulty here is aptly clarified by Franz Mayer, who portrays the Court's protectiveness of German sovereign interests as paradoxical in light of the Basic Law's incorporation of the idea that these interests are well served by the perception that Germany is committed to the advancement of European interests.[95]

Between these two interpretative approaches on the German-EU constitutional relationship—one seeing a congruence with respect to the things that matter most, the other embracing a much more skeptical take on this—is an outlook that, unlike the second view, dissociates identity from sovereignty yet finds greater revolutionary potential than the first in the dynamic properties of constitutional identity.[96] Without a clear separation of identity and sovereignty, the EU's foreignness will remain an obstacle to accepting the union's importance in the development of German constitutional identity.[97] Indeed, the issue here is reminiscent of debates over the constitutional migration of ideas, in which critics of the application of foreign legal materials to domestic disputes occasionally express their misgivings as distress over the loss of sovereignty. In Justice Antonin Scalia's words, "We must never forget that it is a Constitution for the United States of America that we are expounding."[98] To trifle with indigenous constitutional sources by exposing them to contact with transnational materials is potentially to compromise the integrity of the national constitutional identity and the sovereign political process through which it is expressed. On the other hand, engagements with sources external to the domestic constitutional environment may have, as Sujit Choudhry has argued, the salutary effect of deepening appreciation for the local identity as well as providing its overseers with a model to guide and enhance its evolutionary prospects.[99]

Still, a dispassionate appraisal of the constitutional migration debate would have to concede that a too credulous appropriation of foreign ideas is potentially problematic, leading in the extreme case to a situation in which core elements of the local constitutional identity were rendered vulnerable to erosion. When, for example, in its landmark privacy decision, *McGee v. Attorney General,* the Irish Supreme Court eschewed using the constitutional logic of the famous American privacy case *Griswold v. Connecticut* and instead adopted an approach compatible with the nation's prevailing Catholic constitutional identity, it deflected any paradigmatic shift away from the Thomistic natural-law tradition of Irish constitutionalism.[100] To be sure, Justice Brian Walsh's decision in that case to proceed in this way involved considerations different from those confronting a national court in its legal relations with a supranational entity. The Irish ruling, after all, was not complicated by the presence of external treaty obligations. If anything, however, this more volitional aspect contrastingly established the basis for a greater concern about a possible threat to constitutional identity on the part of judges immersed in the fraught activity of "foreign relations." And so even if the FCC in *Lisbon* betrayed an excessive fixation with the problem of identity displacement, it was arguably not remiss in calling it to our attention.

A Brief Heuristic Detour to Ireland

But is it a reality-based apprehension? Is the quandary faced by member states in relation to supranational integration genuinely difficult? A quick look at one of those states—Ireland—may clarify what is at stake in the *Lisbon* case, since the revolutionary implications of conflicting national and supranational commitments were there set in much bolder relief than in the more nuanced German setting. Consider, for example, how the issue of disharmony between the two legal jurisdictions was delineated by an Irish legal scholar: "What if, in any conflict where Irish law does not accommodate the claims of European Community Law . . ., the Supreme Court nevertheless upholds European Community Law in breach of Irish constitutional law? This would be to cause a constitutional revolution—a discontinuity in the validation of laws—and by implication to seek to establish a new Irish constitutional law legitimation."[101]

Irish worries about the possibility of such discontinuities occurring had a significance extending well beyond whatever theoretical importance one might be able to discern in them. Indeed, arguably there would have been no *Lisbon* case—for that matter, no Lisbon Treaty—had these concerns not been addressed in the extended ratification process that culminated in the adoption of the accord. Unlike the other members of the European Union, Ireland required submission of the treaty to a popular referendum for approval, and in 2008 the implementation of this judicially mandated procedure led to the treaty's defeat in that nation, which was also effectively a veto of the treaty for the broader European community.[102] One year later, a second referendum resulted in a landslide acceptance of the treaty that saw a popular swing of just over twenty percentage points from the voting in the previous year.

Any comprehensive explanation of the different outcomes would have to feature the global economic crisis and its exceptionally severe impact in Ireland. Yet as important as that crisis was in incentivizing the Irish people to achieve greater integration with Europe, the identity-revolution question was clearly in play as well, inscribed in the legally extended guarantees that the Lisbon Treaty would not impinge on certain provisions in the Irish Constitution, including the right to life.[103] These concessions were deemed essential in order to bring the Irish people to a second referendum vote: "In demanding a guarantee that the Irish stance on abortion would not be altered as a key issue to be resolved before Ireland would hold its second referendum, Ireland effectively managed to bargain on a human rights related issue. Regardless of the role abortion played in the first Irish No, it does raise some questions regarding the homogeneous nature of European human rights."[104]

Until the referendum in 2018 that dramatically changed constitutional policy, Ireland's strict policies on abortion implicated multiple human rights questions; it is in these policies' broader symbolic importance in the protracted revolutionary struggle to acquire sovereign republican identity status that they help illuminate the constitutional identity challenge embedded in the *Lisbon* case. Thus: "The question of identity is central to [the abortion question]. Irish abortion law is . . . the product of an Irish context and the result of a specific Irish experience. What we can see in Europe today . . . is a conflict between these old identities based on nation-state, and a new identity based on membership in a larger European community."[105] In this familiar account, context and experience refer specifically to the historic nexus between Catholic identity and the Irish national struggle, with the abortion issue emblematic of the former and tangentially instrumental in advancing the latter. Seen in this light, its political significance transcends its religious meaning; while the spiritual aspect has been an enduring component of personal affiliation with the Catholic Church, the associated nationalist subtext figures prominently in the Irish narrative of resistance to colonial subjugation. However accustomed we are to placing the opposition to abortion within a religiously and culturally conservative popular mindset, we need also to recognize it as a signifier of Catholic identity in an extended collective exertion of revolutionary defiance.

The injection of the abortion issue into the Irish referendum debate anticipated certain themes related to European integration later to emerge, most prominently in Germany, in the Continent's *Lisbon* judicial rulings. To the extent, for example, that the FCC's decision envisioned the mandates of the European Union as potentially antagonistic to German constitutional identity, this particular genre of tension between two legal entities was more explicitly imagined in the protocol arrangements that preceded the eventual Irish acceptance of the treaty. In effect, these guarantees seemed to affirm for Ireland what was left ambiguous in the treaty and later at Karlsruhe, the potent idea of identity trumping integration. Thus, among the revolutionary purposes served by Catholic identity was the definitive avowal that a republican Ireland was not England. Moreover, should there have been any lingering doubt about the nature of the relationship between the two unhappily paired nations, the explicitly Catholic Constitution of

1937 resolved such uncertainty in favor of two countries instantly recognizable as foreign to each other. Looking to the future, this assertion of revolutionary self-awareness would serve equally well in mitigating, but not eliminating, any potential European intrusions into the constitutive domain of Irish identity.[106]

Still, the Irish story is not a simple one of explicit resistance to revolutionary constitutional transformation accompanied by an implicit reassertion of revolutionary constitutional achievement. It is also a story of dialogical engagement between local and external legal systems. Consider what occurred in the years leading up to the Lisbon Treaty. Committed though Ireland had been to the distinctiveness of its cultural identity—particularly in regard to the abortion question—its integration into the European community (beginning with its entry into the EEC in 1973) did not leave its constitutional identity untouched. To be sure, the securing of a protocol in the Maastricht Treaty in 1992 exempting the Irish constitutional ban on abortion from any decision affecting its application may be simply portrayed as successfully isolating from external threat an area of domestic law expressive of constitutional identity. Indeed, it is a textbook example of what has been referred to as "differentiated integration," the nonjudicial protective exclusion of specific subject areas that implicate the identity-related concerns of member states.[107] Preceding this achievement, however, were a series of judicial decisions in Europe that reversed Supreme Court rulings in Ireland upholding antiabortion policies based on the 1983 constitutional amendment protecting "the right to life of the unborn."[108] In effect, supranational legal restrictions had left the domestic status of Irish abortion law in considerable doubt. Although the 1992 protocol might have removed much of this doubt, the fact that this treaty-based accommodation was followed later that year in Ireland by a referendum approving a new amendment loosening abortion restrictions on the right to travel and receive information meant that even with the protocol in place, the gap between Irish law and European supranational obligations had been significantly narrowed. These developments can be viewed as the culmination of an ongoing interjurisdictional contestation over the evolution of constitutional policy.[109] In the end, the resulting policy represented a modest adjustment—in this case, in the practice and availability of abortion—that more closely aligned Irish constitutional jurisprudence with prevailing norms in many Western democracies, without abandoning the distinctive character of the local constitutional culture. At the same time, it points to a similar adjustment in the evolution of constitutional identity.

It is true that what appears as a plausible and very real concern in Ireland—that a constitutional revolution could result from accession to the antagonistic orientation of a foreign political entity—is on its face a less pressing issue in Germany. Quite different are the abortion–Catholic natural law traditions in Ireland and the core "human dignity shall be inviolable" commitment of the German Basic Law. The first, expressive of a very particular understanding of dignity, was respected by the constitutional politics of differentiated integration, and the second, expressive of the more universal version of the same principle—hence common to the aspirations of the broader European community—is a fitting object for undifferentiated integration. But what seems evident may conceal real complexity. The German constitutional affirmation of "inviolable and inalienable human rights as the basis of every community, of peace and of justice in the world" does not remove all disharmonic possibilities from the jurisprudential calculation. Are these inalienable rights, for example, best understood as rights possessed by individuals against a governing power, or rather as rights claimed by individuals in their collective capacity as agents of governance?

Initially, the question presents what looks like a false dichotomy, since the two constructions can readily be viewed as together being necessary for the attainment of the common goal of achieving political liberty. Nevertheless, given the tensions inherent in balancing the rights of persons and the right of the people, a commitment to rights grounded in popular sovereignty is destined to produce occasions of serious conflict or disharmony in the arena of constitutional politics. As the *Lisbon* case makes clear, this arena includes the dominion of European constitutionalism. Persons do indeed have a guaranteed set of rights—some of them, as stipulated in the Basic Law, may be understood as inalienable, and others as the creation of those with the power to bestow them—but the people acting in their collective capacity have the authority as a matter of right, legislatively or through the amendment process, to determine the scope and substance of these and other rights. As Christoph Möllers has noted, "The Grundgesetz is . . . a constitution that adheres to normative individualism. It starts with the person, not with the people, though the decision to start with the person is a decision of the people."[110] A way of framing this conundrum is to see the jurisprudential response to the tensions resulting from these two types of rights-based principles as entailing an acceptance of conflict as an enduring aspect of the constitutional predicament. Implicit in this understanding of a nation's constitutional identity is a dynamic of dialogical development entailing interpretative and political activity reflective of the inevitable disharmonies inherent in the experience of constitutional governance.

Even if by a significant order of magnitude Germany's role and importance within the evolving project of European integration differs from Ireland's, its greater prominence in this connection should not be allowed to obscure a common conceptual lens. Through this conceptual lens, a better appreciation might be obtained of how this project bears on the relationship between identity and constitutional revolution. This becomes clearer in the next section, where we look through this lens at the *Lisbon* decision, with particular emphasis on the constitutive significance of revolutionary principles.

The Revolutionary Achievements of the Constitutional Future: The Problem of Dignity

Again, the abortion issue in Ireland possesses a meaning that transcends its religious and cultural significance; fully to apprehend its true importance is to place it within the context of the lengthy revolutionary struggle to achieve sovereign republican identity status. In Germany, the constitutive domain is more multilayered and complex, but at its core are the fundamentals of identity, what in the nation's jurisprudence has come to be known as "an objective order of values" (*eine objective Wertordnung*).[111] The substance of this objective order—notably, the human dignity principle prioritized in Article 1 of the Basic Law—is hardly unique to Germany; it figures prominently in other EU member states' constitutions, and its main precepts would appear to have been embraced within the governing treaties of the EU itself. The fact, however, that it is a common and prominent presence in many of the neighborhood's other constitutional identities, both national and supranational, does not diminish its distinctive symbolic weight in a political order whose revolutionary break with the past was the basis for the nation's political transformation. Thus, to compare and assess the constitutive meanings of different documents' inscribed commitments requires more than simply observing the parchment use of identical language. Scholars and jurists should be skeptical, therefore, of extrapolating identity directly from the words in a constitutional text. The text is a beginning point, but in Hanna Pitkin's wise framing, "How we are able to constitute ourselves is profoundly tied to how we are already constituted by our own distinctive history."[112] There are principles and values that embody precepts of political morality rooted in a nation's past, whose meaning derives from experience within a specific political and cultural context, and whose reach may or may not extend beyond that local context. When they do, they make a claim of universality: the moral truths they are said to embody are precisely the ones whose recognition is required for a constitution to exist in more than name only. Such recognition, however, should not elicit a strategy of passive validation; instead, it calls for continuing efforts to discover the fullest and most comprehensive expression of these fundamentals' universal significance.

To understand what this means in the context of the *Lisbon* ruling's singular preoccupation with German constitutional identity, and so to bring together the threads of this chapter, we focus on the problem of human dignity. If its centrality in the objective order of German values makes it an object of obvious interest, its similar standing in the European scheme of codified values—Article 1 of the Charter of Fundamental Rights of the European Union replicates the Basic Law's language—imbues it with irresistible appeal.

Initially, however, we confront an objection that speaks directly to the process-substance distinction in our theorizing of the constitutional revolution. Bruce Ackerman views the Basic Law as the product of "elite construction," which in his account means that it is "not a revolutionary creation."[113] Ackerman refers to the fact that unlike other "paths to constitutionalism," the German framing experience was neither a revolutionary event in which outsiders successfully mobilized against the existing government (as happened, for example, in India and South Africa), nor a story of insider pragmatism in which strategic concessions were achieved through the adaptation of preexisting lawmaking institutions (as happened in Great Britain).[114] Rather, it is a prime example of a constitutional order emerging from the embers of an old regime through the efforts of previously excluded political and social elites, who, despite their claims to have acted in the name of the people, generate a new constitutional order in the absence of any genuine popular participation. Once established, these regimes confront an "authenticity problem," since they lack "the broad popular legitimacy earned by revolutionary constitutionalism."[115]

Ackerman then asks, "Within this context, the Basic Law's famous 'eternity clauses' have a very curious ring. What does it mean for an emphatically provisional document to proclaim the 'eternal value' of human dignity? What does it mean for it to proclaim 'democracy' as an eternal value when its proponents refuse to submit the Basic Law to a vote?"[116] One answer that attaches more significance to the substance of these proclamations than to the method through which they were adopted is supplied by a former member of the FCC, a Court that in Ackerman's account "did not root the Basic Law in the revolutionary achievements of the constitutional past, since there weren't any."[117] Thus Ernst Benda writes, "If one takes the principle laid down in article 1 seriously (there is no doubt this is the purpose of the provision), and if it is also the clear jurisdiction of the Constitutional Court, then it is not an idea for a period of transition, but a fundamental guideline for all times. It could be abolished only by a revolution."[118]

Benda adds that once unification was accomplished, many years later, the former East Germany was admitted under the Basic Law rather than the auspices of a new constitution. The implication is that had the latter occurred without inclusion of the human dignity provision, it would have been a moment of revolutionary significance. Still, Ackerman's idea that Germany's constitutional past is bereft of revolutionary meaning comports with a scholarly effort that has recently gotten some traction, namely, questioning the importance of the Nazi past in the framing of the Basic Law, including the Federal Constitutional Court's role in ensuring that history does not repeat itself. Thus, the concept of dignity, "instead of being a reaction to Nazi ideology," is better viewed in connection with its signification in ancient Roman law of honor and social status.[119] What is more, "in those few cases where non-amendable principles are at stake, such as the Court's recent protection of German sovereignty vis-à-vis the European Union, it hardly fits with the kind of idea the Nazi thesis seeks to convey."[120]

Others differ from this account, but a simple recitation of the many assertions of the conventional view of the dignity provision of the Basic Law as representing a conscious repudiation of, and separation from, the monstrous practices of the Third Reich, in which its "underlying nature can be summarized in the words 'Never again,'" only gets us so far.[121] Precisely because, as Dieter Grimm pointed out, originalist theories of constitutional interpretation have only minimal purchase in German jurisprudence, one needs to ask how a given provision in the Basic Law fulfills a specific purpose within the broader constitutional order, whatever may have been the intentions of its authors.[122] Depicting human dignity in the constitutional text as symbolic of "a new constitutional beginning," with the FCC playing a central role in upholding the inscription's revolutionary implications for German constitutionalism, is not incompatible with the unconventional understanding—whatever our misgivings about its major premise.[123]

How does all of this fit with our theory of constitutional revolution? In her provocative pushback against the "Nazi thesis," Hailbronner argued, "The Court was . . . by no means *specifically* entrusted with the task of preventing a relapse into fascism."[124] The same might be said of the Indian Supreme Court, which in its formative postindependence record can hardly be described as having advanced the transformational agenda of the nation's newly minted Constitution. In Ackerman's typology of ideal types, the Indians, unlike the German elite constructionists, pursued a revolutionary path to constitutionalism, but in both places the apex courts did not for the most part distinguish themselves as enforcers of national constitutional identity. These tribunals eventually took on this role—the Indian Supreme Court by intervening more aggressively to pursue egalitarian goals, the German Court by emphasizing the objective order of values—to the extent that these high-visibility judicial priorities acquired wide recognition as basic features of each nation's constitutional order.[125] Each represented a paradigmatic shift in the way constitutionalism was experienced (or in the case of Germany, not experienced) in their polities. The symbolic import of each connoted aspiration as much as accomplishment: or to reverse Ackerman's construction, their constitutional identities were tethered to revolutionary achievements in the constitutional future.

Whether the German Court was specifically tasked with the job of "relapse into fascism" prevention is, in a sense, beside the point.[126] The entrenchment of human dignity, much like the commitment to secularism in India, has to it an aspirational aspect embedded in clear-eyed realism. A dignitarian culture does not suddenly descend on a country emerging from the depths of nightmarish inhumanity, just as egalitarianism does not abruptly take hold in a society shaped by centuries of religiously inspired inequities of grotesque proportion. As the Indian Court stated, "The main object behind the theory of . . . constitutional identity is continuity and within that continuity of identity, changes are admissible depending upon the situation and circumstances of the day."[127] Another way of putting this is that a constitutional identity is not made; rather, it is grown into. The constitutionally inscribed marks of identity that signal a revolutionary break with the past require, as we have said, an extended period of time for an actual displacement in constitutional orientation to occur. Whether "situation and circumstances" lead to such a revolutionary consolidation depends on many factors that cannot be known in advance, including the nature and quality of judicial engagement in the protracted growth process. That such engagement might commence well past the moment of formal constitutional transition says very little about the ultimate impact that a court could have in the realization of revolutionary aspirations.

It is in this respect that the *Lisbon* decision invites close scrutiny. As seen earlier, the ample criticism of the Court's opinion centered on the ruling's sovereigntist bent, which was subsumed in its preoccupation with constitutional identity. This emphasis has not gone unnoticed in the challenge to the "never again" argument concerning the Basic Law's historic significance; hence: "In those few cases where non-amendable principles are at stake, such as the Court's recent protection of German sovereignty vis-à-vis the European Union, it hardly fits with the kind of idea the Nazi thesis seeks to convey."[128] The claim here is that vigorously protecting national sovereignty from supranational violation is reminiscent of pre–Basic Law notions of state sanctity that effectively immunized the ruling power from legal restraints. But what if, again borrowing from Indian jurisprudence, we associate identity with "the principle of constitutional sovereignty" rather than with its more familiar and traditional state-centered nexus?[129] The principle of constitutional sovereignty refers to the existence of constitutional commitments that are unamendable; thus, abrogation of secularism in India is unacceptable precisely because it represents an illegitimate exercise of sovereign political power.

Critical, however, to the distinction between constitutional and national sovereignty is acceptance of the mutability of identity within entrenched principled parameters. Not only are "changes admissible," but the Indian Supreme Court's protection of secularism as an unamendable part of the basic structure of the Constitution also presumes the existence of a dynamic synergy between competing philosophical strands—reformist and communal—that drives the process of secular-identity refinement and maturation. As noted earlier, such a presumption is largely missing from the *Lisbon* opinion, leaving its defense of constitutional identity readily translatable into a conventional discussion of sovereignty. In the case of dignity, it is, accordingly, sufficient in the Court's calculations to invoke the text of Article 1 as if the inviolability of the principle codified therein established a clear and immutable essence whose safeguarding is the principal responsibility of the FCC.[130] The Court in *Lisbon*, a German court after all, is not to be faulted for its assertion of vigilance in relation to the potential threat—however unlikely—of a radical revision of constitutional identity. Functionally, when the Court performs a counterrevolutionary role in German constitutional politics, it tacitly affirms and advances the revolutionary meaning of the postwar constitutional settlement. Ultimately, however, the limitations in the Court's reasoning have less to do with the protective curtain it drew around the national constitutional identity than with a failure to think creatively about what is behind the curtain.

Consider, then, the question of dignity, whose philosophical and legal aspects scholars have explored extensively. One of this literature's most obvious lessons is that much like the commitment to secularism in India, dignity's perceived scope and significance are not the same in all legal systems. What is more, as Michael Rosen noted, "History shows the existence of different strands in the meaning of dignity, strands that come together and move apart at different times."[131] Such is prominently the case in Germany, where the dual histories of Kantian and Catholic thought have come to shape and define the concept, sometimes as competitive traditions with contrasting policy and constitutional implications (for example, on the abortion question), and sometimes in ways that converge on a similar place. And as Samuel Moyn argued, the German embrace of the human dignity principle owes much to the permeability of its constitutional borders, since "constitutional dignity for the individual [in Germany] was . . . founded as part of what became the unanticipated post–Second World War supremacy of Christian democracy."[132] More specifically, it was in Ireland that the incorporation of dignity as a fundamental anchor of constitutional design first took hold, eventually influencing, through the conduit of Christian-democratic networks, the constitutional theorizing that made the commitment to human dignity a cornerstone of the Basic Law.[133] In essence, this experience in the constitutional migration of ideas represents an early lesson in how the development of constitutive principles may benefit from the infiltration of ideas from without.

Another facet of this dynamic of infiltration resonates with German history, particularly as it relates to the question of identity. Matthias Mahlmann rightly points out that "under the cover of lofty 'dignity,' all kinds of subjective, relative, and heterogeneous ideas could infiltrate human rights regimes."[134] Thus there is a sense in which the constitutional revolution in Germany can be conceptualized as the replacement of a brutally antiegalitarian idea of dignity with one in which equality and human rights became the measure of its true meaning, which suggests that those charged with preserving the ascendant understanding should guard against complacency. Yet since the concept of human dignity in Germany "is more contested than the interpretation of any other fundamental right," even this depiction of repudiation and replacement is open to challenge.[135] Indeed, James Q. Whitman makes a spirited claim that the ugliness of the earlier rendering should not be viewed as discontinuous with what followed the Nazis' downfall: "'Dignity' as it is protected in contemporary German law is not in this account just the product of a reaction against Nazism; seen in proper sociological perspective, 'dignity' as it is protected today, is the product of an evolution that partly took place *during* the fascist era."[136] One need not buy into Whitman's linkage of the contemporary outlook on dignity with its less attractive—even repulsive—antecedent, which was rooted in the social honor owed to an ascriptively defined class of people, to appreciate that a formal acceptance of dignity is no guarantee that its substantive meaning will resonate in comparable ways across borders, or even within them at different times. The disparate array of responses in Europe to the 2015 refugee crisis is a revealing case in point.[137]

If, then, the FCC were to exercise its *Lisbon*-derived identity review in connection with a purported threat to the inviolability of human dignity, several suppositions not easily reconciled with the static view of constitutional identity manifest in the jurisprudence of that case are worth considering.[138]

First, the inviolability of a principle and its subsequent constitutional entrenchment do not signify that a defense of the principle requires acceptance of its unchanging meaning. As the Court once said: "[We] cannot separate our recognition of the duty to respect human dignity from its historical development. . . . Any decision defining human dignity in concrete terms must be based on our present understanding of it and not on any claim to a conception of timeless validity."[139] The present understanding of human dignity as a constitutive principle is, as Pitkin's observation reminds us, "profoundly tied to how we are already constituted by our own distinctive history."[140] Thus, through experience we may come to know what a commitment to human dignity *cannot* tolerate or accept, without fully comprehending in advance the ultimate contours and reach of such a commitment.

Next, however much the Court chooses to be guided by the intentions of the framers of the Basic Law, it should at least incorporate in its jurisprudence the view of one of that group's most prominent members—Carlo Schmid—who believed "human dignity [to be] a political commitment to the process of a democratic re-establishment of Germany."[141] More generally, such a commitment comports with the recognition of constitutional identity as a dynamic phenomenon that evolves as a function of a dialogue among different and sometimes disharmonic strands within a given polity. In connection with the project of supranational legal development and the Basic Law's declared openness to the advancement of European integration, the evolution of identity-laden provisions—in particular, those notable for their entrenchment in the document—ought not to be isolated from parallel efforts in the broader community. "The necessity to define more precisely the scope of human dignity in a manner oriented toward democracy" should thus lead to a salutary expansion of the "scope of conflict" within which such definitional work occurs.[142]

Finally, this expansion is not risk-free. What the political scientist E. E. Schattschneider wrote about democratic politics provides a cautionary note when reflecting on the interface between national courts and the European Union: "So great is the change in the nature of any conflict likely to be as a consequence of the widening involvement of people in it that the original participants are apt to lose control of the conflict altogether."[143] In addition, any significant change in a political system's scope of conflict "may take on a semi-revolutionary character."[144] Accordingly, the FCC's expressed concerns about how the Treaty of Lisbon's expansion of the EU's competences could affect German constitutional identity are reasonable insofar as such an expansion of scope could, especially if unmonitored, lead to a fundamental reorientation—that is, to a revolutionary displacement—in constitutional practice and understanding. Consequently, the line drawn by the Court is critical: "The Basic Law does not grant powers to bodies acting on behalf of Germany to abandon the right to self-determination of the German people in the form of Germany's sovereignty under international law by joining a federal state."[145] In marking this red line, however, the Court, by implication, retained control over the expansion of the scope of conflict in the European legal arena in order to avoid, if that is its preference, a constitutional revolution of the sort that fundamentally transformed the American constitutional polity through the nationalization of its federal structures of power. Indeed, because its constitutive choices are not dictated by a higher legal authority within a single sovereign entity, it can afford to take risks by encouraging an expansion in the scope of legal contestation, even with regard to things that matter dearly, such as human dignity. Its challenge is to welcome the possibility of an extra-sovereign dialogical refinement of constitutional identity, knowing that it need only accept such modification to the extent that it comports with its definition of revolutionary change.

* * *

In the keynote address quoted at the outset of this chapter, Gerhard Casper cited his old teacher and former member of the Constitutional Court Konrad Hesse: "[A constitution] must, if possible, restrict itself to a few basic principles, whose implications . . . can be developed anew in each individual case, but with regard to these essential principles."[146] Casper described this activity as "the continual definition of the polity with reference to essential constitutional principles."[147] In this regard, he celebrated the Court for its "participa[tion] in regime transformation," most notably in connection with the nation's "new beginning" in 1949 and its national reunification after 1990.

Critical and profound as these two moments were as turning points in modern German history, they are distinguishable as constitutional transformations in the sense that the first introduced a wholly new constitutional order, and the second expanded the reach of that order without deeply upsetting its way of doing things. The extraordinary change that was reunification occurred without the adoption of a new constitution. The point is not that revolutionary constitutional transformation is present only in circumstances of formal constitutional change; rather, it is that producing the evidence for its existence clearly presents a challenging task in the absence of any exertion—even one with notable defects—of the nation's constituent power.

The focus of this chapter is on the third transformation, German participation in the European Union. This integration, which did not culminate in the formal adoption of a federal state, has surely been a very different kind of transformation from the one in 1949, yet in the Basic Law's provision for the optional "transfer [of] sovereign powers to international organizations," it diverges also from the challenge of 1990, which was about assimilating a part of the historic German nation into the whole without abandoning or significantly revising the constitutional essentials operative in the West before unification. There is, however, some similarity between the last two transformations, since the treaties governing membership in the European Union present vexing assimilation issues in which national courts are effectively tasked with the responsibility of guarding against external threats to local constitutional identity.

But what is a threat to constitutional identity? Casper's allusion to the role of constitutional essentials in the "continual definition of the polity" speaks to the problem addressed in this chapter. Following Hesse, who found in the polity's essential principles the potential for developmentally discovering fresh implications, Casper's "continual definition" must be able to accommodate the idea of redefinition. Relatedly, to participate in "regime transformation" could mean contributing to the achievement of revolutionary change or, in its less radical connotation, facilitating renovative or restorative renewal. Both possibilities entail modifications in constitutional identity, but it would be strange to view the latter kind of transformation in the menacing sense conveyed by the specter of threat. On the other hand, the first kind of transformative displacement clearly conjures up just this sort of danger, which in principle is something that can be anticipated favorably or not.

Our consideration of the German Constitutional Court's *Lisbon* jurisprudence—that part of it that features the guardianship of constitutional identity—amounts to a quite mixed assessment. To the extent that the Court's defense of identity recognized that a fundamental reorientation in constitutional essentials can have revolutionary consequences, and further that these may come about through an incrementally fashioned pathway, it rightly underscored a critical—and, we think, correct—interpretative strand in the conceptualization of a constitutional revolution. To the degree, however, that this preoccupation with identity is rendered in a manner that is impervious to the dynamic aspect of constitutional identity, that ignores its adaptive potential and hence its significance to the salutary process of nonrevolutionary regime redefinition, the German Court limited the reach of its extraordinary contribution to constitutional theory and practice. In the next chapter, we examine a setting where the constitutionally articulated aspirations of a polity have a decidedly revolutionary meaning, and where these dynamic features of identity may be critical to the transformation of the constitutional order.

5
India's Dynamic Constitution: Revolution "Step by Step"

> When society requires to be rebuilt, there is no use in attempting to rebuild it on the old plan.
>
> John Stuart Mill

INDIA'S FIRST PRIME MINISTER, JAWAHARLAL NEHRU, used the occasion of an early parliamentary debate to elaborate on the document that had only recently brought forth a newly independent nation: "The whole purpose behind the Constitution which was meant to be a dynamic Constitution leading to a certain goal step by step, is somewhat hampered and hindered by the static element being emphasized a little more than the dynamic element and we have to find out some way of solving it."[1] Nehru had been a prime mover in the Constituent Assembly, which framed the Constitution. What concerned him in this debate was that the dominant egalitarian vision embedded in that effort was being undercut by a misreading of the text abetted by an improper assertion of judicial power. In essence, he argued that Parliament was obliged to rescue the Constitution from those who would set it upon an errant course, a possibility that he had clearly imagined when he said in the Constituent Assembly: "No Supreme Court and no judiciary can stand in judgment over the sovereign will of Parliament representing the will of the entire community."[2]

The problem Nehru was intent on solving arose from a series of early judicial decisions that presented a clear threat to the government's ambitious land reform agenda. The proposed solution entailed the use of the amendment power to restrict the judiciary's power to interpret the Constitution in a way that upheld the property rights of the landed wealthy. Such a specific intention conflicted with "the whole purpose behind the Constitution," the thrust of which was to achieve a radically more just society through incremental advancement toward that goal over time. However distant an achievement of such magnitude might be, for Nehru and his many compatriots at the Constituent Assembly and later in his government, the obligation to reach that goal was a revolutionary-inspired aspiration that implicated a crucial element in the nation's constitutional identity.

It also implicates our effort to understand constitutional revolution. Thus, the "constitutional moment" that was independent India's creation gave rise to a bewildering array of countervailing commitments that to some degree obscured the singular significance of that moment. That the revolutionary component in the country's emerging constitutional identity was accompanied by other, more preservative pieces is unsurprising, but also helpful in gaining insight into the evolution of an important variant of constitutional displacement. Thus, the "static element" in Nehru's comment was a reference to the presence of certain fundamental rights that were, in Granville Austin's well-known formulation, in tension with "the [constitutional] demands of the social revolutionary strand."[3] Also, a clearly articulated guarantee of formal equality coexisted uneasily with provisions designed to produce a greater measure of substantive equality by enabling officially sanctioned preferential treatment for disadvantaged groups. These specific dissonances were incorporated in a constitutional text embodying a capacious disharmonic reality reflecting two powerful claims on Indian constitutional identity, both firmly rooted in centuries of conflict and contestation. Since independence, one of these claims—for a secular composite-culture nation—has been in ascendance, but the other claim, for a Hindu nation, has influenced the aspirational content of constitutional identity, and at times (as with the elevation of Prime Minister Narendra Modi in 2014) posed a distinct threat to the supremacy of the predominant view.

In this chapter, we turn our attention to India's constitutional revolution. Since one of our principal claims is that the constitutional significance of a radical departure from earlier practice ought not to be minimized or negated by the extended period that often accompanies the consolidation of revolutionary aspirations, the example of India is illuminating. As in the previous chapter, we focus on both the static and the dynamic dimensions of the revolution-identity relationship; with the example of Germany in mind, we highlight the fact that revolutionary constitutional changes may present contrasting imperatives for political actors responsible for steering the constitutional ship of state. If, for example, the prospect of paradigmatic displacement were to be regarded as something plainly to be avoided, then playing the identity card could work as a buffer against any radical transposition. On the other hand, to the extent that realizing the benefits of a constitutional revolution looked like an advancement keenly to be anticipated, then the dynamic properties within an extant identity may be found expedient for achieving the desired result.

Germany and India are two polities that have provided unusually fertile ground for constitutional theorizing about identity and revolution. What is more, through the exertions of these nations' powerful constitutional courts, this theorizing has been refined by critical cross-fertilization, mostly evident in relation to the question of unconstitutional constitutional amendments. In Germany, the Basic Law's explicitly preservative entrenchment provisions became the touchstone for the postwar Constitutional Court's recognition of its authority to invalidate an identity-nullifying amendment, a move that in time figured prominently in the development of Indian jurisprudence.[4] Under the theory that constitutional change cannot destroy what it modifies, the Indian Supreme Court deliberately followed the German example by in effect arrogating to itself a supervisory role over any codified transformation that threatened regime essentials. With conviction, it memorably declared, "The Constitution is a precious heritage; therefore you cannot destroy its identity."[5] Extending its review authority beyond the confines of ordinary law was tantamount—or so it appeared at the time—to rejecting the exercise of the amendment power as a means of accomplishing revolutionary change. Once ensconced, however, in Indian constitutional thought and practice, the commitment to identity as a barrier to radical change was eventually adapted to the reconstructive aspirations of the polity. With this modification, the concept of identity's dynamic potential could inspire constitutional actors to imagine it as a vital resource for facilitating as well as hindering dramatic changes in constitutional development. What we argue below is that they could envision a political and jurisprudential path that led to a place where the early revolutionary promise of constitutional design was vindicated through the significant attainment of its reconstructive goals.

Following this path reveals that Nehru's original amendment solution has arguably succeeded in advancing his revolutionary goals, but only through a historic jurisprudential intervention originally designed to turn the path back on itself by challenging its founding conception—the idea of a "dynamic Constitution." The result of the intervention was the "basic structure doctrine," which became the source of the judiciary's authority to strike down a constitutional amendment on substantive grounds. As initially posited in the landmark *Kesavananda* ruling, it rested on one key assumption: "The word 'amendment' postulates that the old constitution survives without loss of its identity despite the change and continues even though it has been subjected to alterations."[6] Indeed, such a postulate can lead one plausibly to conclude that the "[basic structure] doctrine represents an effort to distinguish between a constitutional amendment and revolutionary action."[7]

Yet if on its face the doctrine is imbued with a preservative meaning, at a deeper contextual level the doctrine is also congruent with Nehru's insistence at the Constituent Assembly that "the Constitution . . . was meant to be a dynamic constitution."[8] We use the Indian experience to demonstrate not only that "revolutionary action" is possible within the constraints of the constitutional order, but also that in certain circumstances—namely, where a formal constitutional change has held out the promise of fundamental societal transformation—it can be viewed as indispensable. Consistent with the emphasis on substance over process in our conceptualization of constitutional revolution, the determination of a constitutional amendment's standing as a legitimate or illegitimate exercise of the formal amendment-adopting mechanism depends less on whether it is or is not a genuine expression of the constituent power than on whether it advances or impedes the fulfillment of "the purpose behind the Constitution."

To the extent that the concept of basic structure is assigned a meaning that encapsulates the aspirational content of the social revolution that Nehru and others saw as the "whole purpose" of the Constitution, its deployment by the Court has a dynamic component focused on the constitutional revolution's steady and continuing actualization. Constitutional identity in Germany functions in large part as a manifestation of how the postrevolutionary German nation conceives of itself in relation to a discredited past; in India, it serves as a foundation for the construction of a social order embodying the transformative hopes of its revolutionary promise. That the attainment of a democratic revolution was a major component in the vision animating many of the framers of the Constitution is undeniable and abundantly manifest in some—but by no means all—key provisions in the document. Even as an unfulfilled aspiration, it must be considered highly germane to any assessment of Indian constitutional identity; its fulfillment would remove any tentativeness from an assessment of its relevance.[9]

This chapter touches on several key themes in our understanding of constitutional revolution. First, difficult as it is to disentangle the procedural and substantive strands of fundamental constitutional change, the Indian case suggests that an emphasis on the aspirational commitments embedded in the document will ultimately prove more instructive than accentuating the specific character of the constituent power that framed the document. Whether India's founding constitutional moment is properly interpreted as the expression of the popular sovereign will is ultimately of less import than the "long democratic revolution" that developed out of that moment.[10] Next, the "step by step" progression of the protracted revolutionary unfolding is not simply a manifestation of the cautious incrementalism that can be expected to accompany the societal implementation of massive reconstructive work; rather, it is the inevitable consequence of the disharmony that is inherent in the constitutional condition. Indeed, Nehru's early amendment strategy was an implicit acknowledgment that his goal-oriented "step by step" constitutional understanding entailed the taking of steps backward and forward as conflicting interests and constituencies struggled for ascendancy in light of divergent readings of the Constitution. As András Sajó stated, "The [constitutional] text itself has only limited potential for forging identity. A legally binding document is but a first step on the long and winding road from a political design for collective identity to a socially embedded institution that actually fosters such identity."[11] Finally, the famous Lincolnian option of either amending a constitution for the purpose of improving it, or engaging in a revolution for the purpose of overthrowing it, leaves out a possibility that speaks directly to the phenomenon of constitutional revolution. As shown in our account of the basic structure doctrine's evolution from a defensive canon of extraordinary politics to an affirmative dictate of ordinary politics, a constitutional amendment can become a redemptive instrument for the fulfillment of transformative change. Familiarity with the German and Indian experiences with the amendment issue may not prepare one for an identity-enforcing assertion of judicial power in support of paradigmatic constitutional change. An amendment might be upheld on a finding of inoffensiveness to constitutional identity, or it might be invalidated for its presumed damage to constitutional identity, but we are not accustomed to seeing an amendment sustained for being a salutary advancement of the revolutionary mission that lies at the core of constitutional identity. The consideration of just such an amendment later in this chapter focuses our attention on the dynamic imperatives of constitutional revolution.

The Semirevolutionary People

The Constitution of India is hardly remarkable for its opening words: "We the people of India." A majestic innovation when introduced by secessionists from the British Empire in 1787, invocation of the people has become a staple of constitution making in the modern era.[12] In his draft of the Objectives Resolution, the famous document that outlined the aims of the Indian Constituent Assembly, Nehru explicitly drew a connection between that earlier exit from British colonial rule and the one over which he was presiding: "Wherein all power and authority of the Sovereign Independent India, its constituent parts and organs of government, are derived from the people."[13] As a practical matter there really was no other way to constitute a newly independent nation, for as Nehru also said, "An Assembly meeting on the sufferance of the British Government *or others* would be a negation of the very principle and meaning of a Constituent Assembly."[14]

While it is easy to see how the political necessities of legitimacy creation compel a reliance on a "We the People" story line, to what extent do the analytical requirements of conceptualizing constitutional revolution entail a similar dependency? Or put another way, would a refutation of the popular-sovereignty-framing scenario effectively pull the rug out from under a cogent explanation of what occurs when constitutional development takes a radical turn? Thus, according to one account, "The founding [in India] serves as an example of how fundamental political changes can occur in the future through the emergence of new forms of popular exercise of sovereign power."[15] In this vein, Sarbani Sen adopted an Ackermanian model to explain the occurrence of a revolutionary break with a prior regime: "The revolutionary phenomenon is understood in primarily political terms. In this characterization, a revolution need not be measured in terms of social outcomes, but as an affirmation of the independent value of politics and of the citizens' involvement in debating the validity of new ideas."[16] Specifically in relation to India: "My framework assumes the crucial question is the extent to which a revolution inspires the people to invest their energies and identities in the collective process of political redefinition. If this transformation in political consciousness occurs, it marks out a distinctive revolutionary situation, regardless of the polity's success in social transformation."[17]

An alternative framework might be constructed around a more substantive account of the revolutionary meaning of what transpired at the Constituent Assembly. Uday Mehta, for example, argued: "The dominant temper of mind in the assembly was revolutionary, in which the challenge was to build a new society on the ruins of the old. It was this thought that guided the Assembly from its start to its conclusion, and for which the State and political power was deemed to be the necessary instrument."[18] This version echoes Granville Austin's descriptive summary of that body's achievement, according to which "the theme of social revolution runs through the proceedings of the Assembly."[19] Interestingly, Austin's emphasis draws on the same document—the Objectives Resolution—from which the theme of popular sovereignty derives, to contend that it was "the social revolution that was put at the top of the agenda by the Constituent Assembly."[20]

To claim that a revolutionary agenda featuring major societal reconstruction was the highest priority of the attendees at the assembly is compatible with the idea that the document resulting from those deliberations was the pronouncement of "We the People." There is also the possibility, however, that one or both of these "objectives" were unmet, or at least that the claims made on their behalf have been greatly exaggerated by subsequent commentators. Such is the conclusion reached by Rajeev Dhavan, a prominent constitutional scholar and Senior Advocate of the Supreme Court of India, who, in a critique of Sen's application of Ackerman's thesis to his country, insisted: "The Constitution was not a revolutionary Constitution of the people. It was not a 'We the people' Constitution. It was a 'We the rulers' Constitution."[21] In this respect, he found Sen's reliance on the American experience inadvertently instructive, given the inclusionary deficiencies of that nation's homage to the sovereignty of the people. In this respect, too, he followed the prominent account of the historian Edmund S. Morgan, who provocatively argued, "The popular governments of Britain and the United States rest on fictions as much as the governments of Russia and China."[22] For Dhavan, this categorical rejection of the popular-origins thesis amounted to more than a statement about the unrepresentative character of the assembly, in which members were indirectly elected by provincial legislators whose selection had been decidedly unrepresentative. His refutation extended to the product emerging from the assembly, which, while incorporating a textual commitment to radical change, should be seen as having "adopted a bourgeois concept of human rights [and] equality."[23]

Dhavan in the end is not as gloomy or pessimistic as these comments might suggest. Much as Nehru did, he views the Constitution as a "site of struggle."[24] He maintains that out of this struggle—what we refer to as disharmony—meaningful social and economic transformation is possible, albeit as a testament to elite politics rather than to popular sovereignty. That disharmony, as explained earlier, exists not only in the form of contradictions and imbalances within the Constitution, but also in the sharp discontinuities that frame the document's relationship to the surrounding society. Nowhere was this point more sharply articulated than in the oft-quoted remark of B. R. Ambedkar during the period leading up to the Constitution's implementation: "On the 26th of January 1950, we are going to enter into a life of contradictions. In politics we will have equality and in social and economic life we will have inequality. In politics we will be recognizing the principle of one man one vote and one vote one value. In our social and economic life, we shall, by reason of our social and economic structure, continue to deny the principle of one man one value. How long shall we continue to live this life of contradictions?"[25]

How should we think about these positions in light of our conceptual question concerning constitutional revolution, specifically whether the phenomenon is best understood in political terms or social outcomes? There is explanatory room for both, but consider how dependent the "We the People" story is on the fulfillment of substantive goals. In this connection, Nehru's thinking can help us. As leader of the Indian National Congress (INC), he predicted in a major address delivered a decade before the convening of the constitution-drafting body, "[The Constituent] Assembly will not come into existence till at least a semi-revolutionary situation has been created in this country and the actual relationship of power, apart from paper constitutions, are such that the people of India can make their will felt. When that will happen I cannot say, but the world is too much in the grip of dynamic forces today to admit of static conditions in India or elsewhere for long. We may thus have to face this issue sooner than we might expect."[26] And as the call-to-action section of the address made clear, sooner or later would depend on how quickly "the defeatist mentality of some people" could be eradicated.

A decade later, that moment arrived. Nehru observed, "It is true that the Constituent Assembly is not the result of a revolution although there were a good many revolutionary influences at work for years. . . . The Constituent Assembly in which we are going is not a revolutionary body."[27] To be sure, the context for these remarks indicates that their purpose was to stress that the proceedings about to be conducted represented a peaceful alternative to violent revolution. Their meaning is understandable within the conceptual framework of revolution's standard instance, not within the more specific instance of the term's constitutional variant. Indeed, juxtaposed against the statements from Nehru's 1936 address to the INC, the difference is clear. In referring earlier to "a semi-revolutionary situation," Nehru was projecting the intentions of the movement he led to use the occasion of the Constituent Assembly to frame a constitution that would become pivotal in moving the country in a radically different direction. Accomplishing this goal would not require violent upheaval; rather, it would demand a suitably constituted collective mind-set as a predicate for pursuing the goal of societal reconstruction.[28]

The Constituent Assembly, according to Nehru, was to be a place where "the people of India can make their will felt." But who exactly were the people? Did the designated precondition of "a semi-revolutionary situation" effectively mean that the new beginning for independent India could be launched if its revolutionary promise was only partially shared by the totality of the population to whom the novel experiment would apply? If so, it might be instructive to speak of a semirevolutionary people. This makes sense for two reasons. First, imagining the people in this way feeds into the Nehruvian conception of a dynamic but incrementalist constitution. It implies that the impulse to infuse the document with a transformative purpose will fill only a partial space in the constitution, which is to say, however dominant this commitment might be within the entire scope of constitutional aspiration, achievement of its ends will be, as Dhavan suggests, a constant struggle. The frequent references in Nehru's public statements to the opposition between dynamic and static forces and conditions reflect the inevitable predicament of a constitutional revolution: its revolutionary thrust is accompanied by the presence of resistant interests, some of which remain uncommitted to the ascendant agenda, which in the Indian case promised transformational change. In this respect, too, Ambedkar's "life of contradictions" is an apt characterization of the constitutional challenge confronting a semirevolutionary people. Thus, the fundamentals of the status quo are embedded in the fabric of society even as a formal commitment to equality emerges from the charter adopted for its governance. As Ambedkar elsewhere insisted, "Constitutional morality is not a natural sentiment. It has to be cultivated. We must realize that our people have yet to learn it. Democracy in India is only a top-dressing on an Indian soil, which is essentially undemocratic."[29]

The second way in which the notion of a semirevolutionary people of India speaks to our immediate concerns goes to the frequently unexamined assumption of the constituent power's popular underpinning. As Chaihark Hahm and Sung Ho Kim point out in their illuminating study of the Japanese and South Korean Constitutions, "How the constituent people has come into existence, and in what shape, is often taken for granted as a historical accident that defies normative evaluations"; indeed, "most conventional views tend to assume the existence of an immutable constituent people with predetermined identity."[30] And so "it is incumbent on any theory of constitutional founding to cast a suspicious eye onto the assumption that the sovereign people with a clearly legible boundary exists prior to the constituent moment."[31] True as this is for two countries known for the homogeneity of their inhabitants, arguably it is all the more so when reflecting on the constitution of possibly the most religiously, ethnically, and linguistically diverse population in the world.

Skepticism toward the existence of a sovereign people as the driver of the constituent power is not quite the same as distrust of the inclusiveness of the "We the People" affirmation. In addition to whatever empirically grounded reasons there may be for harboring misgivings over the latter, there is a conceptual obstacle that can make a full embrace of the former problematic. In Hahm and Kim's account, it is the activity of constitution making that constitutes the people. Until the choices and actions made in the process that produces a constitution become part of the historical record, the identity of the people cannot be known. Even then it is premature to establish its content, since "the identity of the constituent people cannot properly be understood without a dynamic, or temporally extended, perspective."[32] At best, then, the drafting of a constitutional document is a historical moment in which structures are created to enable a newly constituted people to shape their identity over an extended period, a time that could very well include subsequent moments of recalibration or redefinition.

It is, however, not necessary to accept all the reasoning and assumptions in this account to see how it might still be instructive for the purpose at hand. Thus, to extrapolate from Hahm and Kim and say, for example, that the large following for whom Nehru and others spoke during the lead-up to the Constituent Assembly required the actual experience of the framing process to certify or legitimate their identity as a people could easily be misconstrued. A more precise formulation would be that to the extent that they held to a specific vision of India's constitutional future, their identity as a semi-subset of the population at large made them a significant, perhaps dominant player in the ongoing battle to determine the nation's constitutional identity. The revolutionary importance of the founding resided mainly in the substance of that dynamic vision, and not so much in the fact that one could claim authority for it as the epitome of the Indian people's sovereign will.[33] As Nehru and Ambedkar surely knew, "As a process of self-constitution, the initial founding action may . . . take years to be successfully carried out."[34] In the remainder of this chapter, we look at some of the events in those subsequent years that provide retrospective insight into the specific revolutionary character of the framers' founding achievement.

The Judiciary and the Constitutional Revolution

Just as it is tempting to locate constitutional identity in the text of a constitution, it is similarly alluring to imagine finding a definitive articulation of its meaning in the decisions and opinions of the judiciary. Yet the text can provide at best only limited service in delivering what we want, and it is much the same when we look to the judiciary. The reason for this is only partly accounted for by the wrongness of assuming that, as was famously proclaimed by a U.S. chief justice, the "constitution is what the Supreme Court says it is."[35] At least as significant as the acknowledgment of a court's fallibility is the unyielding fact that its interpretative powers are constrained by the decisions of other institutional actors involved in the writing of a nation's constitutional narrative. Indeed, the absence of monopolistic authority over the shaping of constitutional identity and the pursuit of a constitutional revolution are amply illustrated in Indian politics and jurisprudence.

That said, the Indian Supreme Court has been depicted as an institution envisioned by its creators to function as "an arm of the social revolution"[36] whose mission, according to a prominent former justice of that tribunal, was to serve as a "radical fiduciary and redemptive institution of the people."[37] Yet, although a transformative remedial jurisprudence may seem to some implicit in the militant folds of the Constitution, the Court did not embrace the mission effortlessly or consistently. As Nick Robinson pointed out, "The original, narrow judicial role of the Court . . . sits in incongruity with the Constitution's transformative vision for Indian society."[38] Indeed, in its early years the judiciary, as Nehru's comment about the Court's initial pro-landowner actions suggests, showed contempt for "the sovereign will of Parliament" and impeded the implementation of much of the framers' constitutionally grounded egalitarian vision.[39]

Much has transpired since those early years, and the Court has become widely and properly singled out for its activist promotion of broad-based societal change. The story of its institutional evolution can be told in several ways; ours depicts it as exemplifying important characteristics of constitutional revolution, which is to say, as one of "India's public institutions function[ing] in the context of a 'long democratic revolution.'"[40] During the course of this extended "controlled revolution," the Court became the perfect embodiment of the disharmonies within the Constitution, and it found itself over time on both sides of the tension inherent in the dual commitment to socioeconomic transformation and liberal democratic rights.[41] Nowhere is this better illustrated than in its most notable jurisprudential innovation—the invalidation of a constitutional amendment on substantive grounds—in which the static elements in play when the controversial practice was introduced were eventually displaced by dynamic elements that facilitated the progress of the revolutionary constitutional promise.

The saga begins with Prime Minister Nehru arguing for constitutional changes that would counter the judiciary's actions in upholding property rights over the government's ambitious land reform efforts. "We have found," Nehru insisted, "this magnificent Constitution . . . was later kidnapped and purloined by the lawyers."[42] The Indian Parliament, many of whose members had served in the Constituent Assembly and could therefore be considered victims of these purported crimes, needed to adopt an amendment that would in effect reinstate the assembly's transformational program. As Nehru put it: "The House has to keep in mind the traditional and revolutionary aspects of the problem, because, when you think of the land question in India today, you are thinking of something which is dynamic, moving, changing and revolutionary."[43]

For Nehru, the textual source of constitutional dynamism was the Directive Principles of State Policy, just as the preceding section, Fundamental Rights, was the basis for the countervailing static conception: "Both . . . are right. But sometimes it might so happen that that dynamic movement and that static standstill do not quite fit into each other."[44] Inherent in the Indian constitutional condition was a plainly articulated gap between foundational ideals and existing realities; the question for Nehru's government was whether the radical disharmony between law and society established a constitutional obligation for the state to resolve the severest of these contradictions. Arguably, this obligation was inscribed in the Constitution in several ways, including the invitations extended to the state to regulate religious practices in the interest of social welfare and equality.

But the most visible constitutional expression of the aspirations that stamped the document with a distinctive identity was Part IV's Directive Principles. They were, as B. N. Rau, an influential member of the assembly, put it, "instructions from the legal sovereign, namely, the people of India, speaking through their representatives in the Constituent Assembly to the authorities."[45] Although the provisions contained in this section were not accorded the power of judicial enforcement, as was stated in Article 37, "the principles therein laid down are nevertheless fundamental in the governance of the country and it shall be the duty of the State to apply these principles in making laws."[46] What is more, according to the next article, "The State shall strive to promote the welfare of the people by securing and protecting as effectively as it may a social order in which justice, social, economic and political, shall inform all the institutions of the national life." As Tarunabh Khaitan points out, "Article 38 may even be considered the master directive, its abstract pursuit of welfare and justice never contested. Every transformative visionary believed that their preferred route would lead to this ultimate utopia. It might even be seen as having some controlling impact on how all other directives were justified in the assembly, i.e., as particular manifestations of this overall goal."[47] Thus, it could be said with only slight exaggeration: "[The] Directive Principles of State Policy constitute the soul, the very spirit of the ethos of the Constitution. These principles are the epitomes of social policy whereupon the State has been enjoined to embark on the goals of distributive justice."[48]

Courts, however, are more comfortable with adjudicating enforceable rights, even if that means not exhibiting due deference to the underlying spirit of a constitution. The adoption of the First Amendment in response to the judiciary's defense of the right to property established a precedent unique in the annals of constitutional jurisprudence, as did the more renowned novelty of the unconstitutional constitutional amendment initiated some years later. Much of what this first formal revision did was to immunize laws targeting inequitable land holdings from constitutional challenges, thereby prioritizing the egalitarian vision of the Directive Principles over the purportedly less valued fundamental right to property.[49] Laws so protected were to be placed in the Ninth Schedule, a repository for all things not to be invalidated by judicial review: "The clash as to the relative normative hierarchy of Fundamental Rights and Directive Principles of State Policy led to the birth of saving clauses and also set the tone for several decades of battle for supremacy between the Supreme Court and Parliament."[50] Although used in later years in ways that were increasingly controversial and doubtless unforeseen by the First Amendment's proponents, its unorthodox way of addressing the widely held view of the judiciary's distortion of the Constitution's revolutionary vision "established the precedent of amending the Constitution to overcome judicial judgments impeding fulfillment of the government's perceived responsibilities to . . . particular policies and programs."[51]

Ironically, it was the landowners' legal challenge to this amendment that opened the jurisprudential pathway to an eventual acceptance by the judiciary of a prominent role for itself in attaining the substantive goals of the constitutional revolution. In responding to this challenge, the Supreme Court's freshly demonstrated authority to nullify acts of ordinary legislation did not lead it to accept the more radical notion that the proclaimed constituent power underlying Parliament's amending power permitted a comparable act of nullification with respect to that power.[52] While the Court's deference to the constituent power of Parliament had the appearance of a conservative exercise of self-restraint, it in effect served to legitimate a radical legislative undertaking of constitutional clarification. That this parliamentary initiative had itself been a response to earlier, assertive judicial decisions on behalf of a conservative cause makes for a dizzyingly fascinating sequence of events. The upshot of all this thrust and counterthrust was to sustain the vulnerability of landed interests in the face of determined governmental efforts to achieve a more equitable property regime.

Yet this exposure to the egalitarianism-inspired assaults on vested interests was short-lived. In its landmark *Golak Nath* decision of 1967, the Court issued a "conservative ruling" by means of a radical rethinking of its understanding of the constituent power.[53] No longer was a constitutional amendment to be distinguished in its legal quintessence from ordinary legislation and thus to be accorded the submissiveness appropriate for creations of the constituent power: "One need not cavil at the description of an amending power as sovereign power, for it is sovereign only within the scope of the power conferred by a particular constitution."[54] Had Nehru been alive to witness this historic constitutional turn, one could well imagine his disappointment at a "static" ruling that protected fundamental rights—in this instance, the property guarantee—from a corrective, vision-inspired exercise of parliamentary sovereignty that also embodied the legitimating authority of the constituent power.

Seen within an extended outward perspective, however, the decision in *Golak Nath* is of a piece with the "step by step" logic of a dynamic constitution and its Indian corollary, the "long revolution." Predictably, it led to an emphatic parliamentary reaction and the adoption of more amendments, including the Twenty-Fourth (the Constitution Act of 1971), which provided that there are no restrictions on Parliament's power to amend the Constitution. It specifically referred to this amending function as an "exercise of [Parliament's] constituent power," thereby explicitly reinstating the Court's earlier distinction between ordinary legislation and enactments whose purpose was to revise the Constitution. Most controversially, it brought the document's Fundamental Rights section within the scope of the amending power, thereby leaving the liberties of the Indian people exposed to the vagaries of the political process. And as was underscored by the subsequent curtailing of the right to property by the Twenty-Fifth Amendment, this prospect was more than a theoretical possibility.

The Supreme Court's response came in *Kesavananda Bharati v. State of Kerala,* a watershed moment in Indian constitutional development and by most accounts that nation's iconic constitutional judgment.[55] In its assertion of review power over the process and substance of constitutional amendments—the Twenty-Fourth and Twenty-Fifth Amendments were at issue—the Court, as Upendra Baxi said, expanded the reach of judicial activism to an extent never before accomplished in India or anywhere else.[56] Of course, an achievement of such noteworthiness—particularly one enhancing the political power of the judiciary—engendered mixed reviews. For example, a not atypical negative assessment worried about the effect of the judgment on the very fabric of constitutional government: "Prior to *Kesavananda Bharati,* the Constitution, with all its checks and balances, was considered supreme. The Supreme Court has emerged as the strongest wing of the state with unlimited and illimitable power."[57]

Again, for followers of Nehru, who had insisted that no court could stand in judgment over the sovereign will of Parliament, the result in *Kesavananda* would on its face appear to be a deeply troubling and reactionary development. While overruling *Golak Nath*'s precedent holding specific textual provisions immune from the power to amend, a divided Court settled on a more principle-based limitation on this power. At the core of *Kesavananda* is the "basic structure" doctrine, according to which specific features of the Constitution are deemed sufficiently fundamental to the integrity of the constitutional project to warrant immunity from drastic alteration. Under the theory that constitutional change must not destroy what it modifies, the Court affirmed its institutional authority to invalidate any constitutional amendment whose adoption would, in its judgment, result in radical transformation of regime essentials. The political and jurisprudential implications of this unenumerated power were extraordinary, easily making the countermajoritarian difficulties of conventional judicial review pale in comparison. Armed with its new doctrine, the contents of which would be determined over time, the Court in effect designated itself enforcer of constitutional entrenchment at its deepest level.

That this enforcement authority might not have seemed at the time to encompass revolutionary implications is understandable. The framers of India's Constitution, unlike Germany's, did not include eternity clauses in their handiwork, yet they clearly saw themselves as exercising the constituent power of the Indian nation. As formulated by Dietrich Conrad, the German theorist and scholar of India whose work was instrumental in shaping the judgments in *Golak Nath* and *Kesavananda,* the relevant question became, "Has the original constituent power been spent in the effort, or have the people retained it, to exercise it, if they wish to replace the existing Constitution by a new one?"[58] Conrad's answer is apparent in the Indian Court's amendment jurisprudence: "An ordinary legislative assembly can never be said to exercise the original constituent power."[59] This logic sits comfortably with what Nehru would characterize as static, as opposed to dynamic, interpretation of constitutional development. Thus, Dawn Oliver and Carlo Fusaro concluded, "[The Indian Supreme Court] accurately differentiate[d] *pouvoir constituant* from *pouvoir constitue.*' . . . By doing so [the Court] rather than being [an] instrument of change, adopt[ed] a conservative approach to interpretation and act[ed] as the ultimate guarantor of the constitutional arrangements then in force."[60]

We, however, see things differently. The underlying assumption in these cases and others in this vein that followed is that Parliament's Article 368 amending power is subordinate to the creative authority that first established the Constitution's basic structure. Another way of putting this is that the implicit substantive limits to the amending power are inscribed in constitutional provisions in whose contents are to be found an articulation of a nascent constitutional identity. As Bhikhu Parekh has observed, "There was an extensive debate . . . in the Constituent Assembly, resulting in the Indian Constitution, which provides the clearest statement of the country's self-given identity."[61] Still, as Dhavan reminds us, the assembly was a site of struggle in which the contours and substance of this identity were at least contestable, even if the "semi-revolutionary" articulation of its socially reconstructive content had assumed ascendancy and subsequently taken over many of the reins of power. Adopting the basic structure doctrine laid the jurisprudential foundation for the Court—and ultimately not only the Court—to elaborate, shape, and extend this version of identity to the point where its proponents could empirically and legitimately lay claim to stewardship of the constitutional revolution. As "an approach that asks what values and principles must exist for constitutionalism itself to exist," the judiciary, no longer tethered for its enlarged role to specific provisions in the text, would have "greater freedom to use [the doctrine] in a political manner."[62] So, for example, progressive amplification of the substance of fundamental constitutional principles would provide the judiciary with the confidence and eventual authority to mandate enforcement of the transformative rights contained in the theretofore nonjusticiable Directive Principles.[63]

The Court's ability to facilitate the entrenchment and advancement of the constitutional revolution required an adaptation of the basic structure doctrine to the exigencies of ordinary politics. Precisely because *Kesavananda* was not about everyday governance, the impact of basic structure jurisprudence was likely to be experienced more symbolically than tangibly.[64] The great challenge for Indian constitutionalism has been to deliver on the promise of its transformative aspirations. That arguably requires a Court performing more ambitiously than in its familiar naysayer role in the orthodox judicial-review model, but in a role attuned to the limitations of judicial power and the hollowness that is often the fate of the more grandiose hopes for judicial interventions in policy making.[65] It also requires a Court that with genuine conviction can reaffirm the meaning and import of what Nick Robinson rightly referred to as the only constitutional moment in India's history—the founding—when "the people of India came together to cast the future of the country in a markedly different direction."[66] Regardless of whether that moment was an authentic exertion of the sovereign power of the people, the identification of the assembly's constituent power with a specific substantive vision for constitutional development was a critical moment in the progress of the constitutional revolution. And so the declaration in *Minerva Mills, Ltd. v. Union of India,* the case that solidified the standing of *Kesavananda* as the linchpin of Indian constitutional jurisprudence, must be given its due: "The Constitution is a precious heritage; therefore you cannot destroy its identity."[67] More specifically, "Parts III [Fundamental Rights] and IV [Directive Principles] together constitute the core commitment to social revolution and they, together, are the conscience of the constitution."[68]

Revolutionary Adaptation

The framing of India's Constitution falls somewhere between the Lincolnian options set forth in his First Inaugural, since it was neither an exercise in amending a flawed document nor one of revolutionary dismemberment. It consolidated the securing of independence and the withdrawal of Britain, both of which were facilitated by countless acts of illegality. But the emergence of a new constitutional order was in the end not predicated on a violent severance of ties with a prior regime whose leaders contested the legitimacy of its successor. The creative experience may nevertheless be considered a constitutional revolution in that the predominant intentions behind the Constitution were confrontational, which is to say, its incipient identity was in large measure defined by a commitment to reshape key structures of the existing social order. In this sense, it assumed a stance of militancy analogous to that of the post–Civil War amendments in the United States, which, unlike the mainly acquiescent features of the polity's broader document, were directed at the eradication of entrenched social inequities.[69]

For the same reason that a person's identity is not fixed in the distinctive makeup of the infant who emerges from the womb, the identity of a constitution is only imperfectly knowable through the provisions promulgated during its framing and adoption. As the Indian constitutional experience demonstrates, the early years of a newly independent nation do not always highlight what its founding document anticipates with respect to the consolidated identity of a mature constitutional order. While, therefore, the first battles between the judiciary and the legislature concerned issues of economic inequality that the prime movers of the social revolution saw as critically important, these clashes were in a sense peripheral to the root cause of society's systemic injustices. As many of the framers understood, the goal of social reconfiguration could not be effectively addressed without official recognition of the constitutive significance of the spiritual realm for the condition of the body politic. So deep was religion's penetration into the fabric of Indian life, and so historically entwined was it in the shape of a social structure that was by any reasonable standard grossly unjust, that the framers' hopes for a democratic polity and a just society meant that state intervention into religious life could not be constitutionally foreclosed.[70] As a former Indian chief justice observed, "The multi-dimensional jurisprudence woven around the Preamble has a revolutionary thrust as it seeks to transform the socio-economic structure of our society."[71]

In *Kesavananda*, the Supreme Court invoked basic structure as a defensive move to preserve what it designated the Constitution's identity. On paper, at least, this breakthrough was enough to vault the Court to the forefront internationally of the most activist judiciaries. As Upendra Baxi noted, the Court performed "a remarkable feat of judicial activism, unparalleled in the history of world constitutional adjudication."[72] But for its jurisprudence to be transformative in the dynamic sense required by the Constitution's revolutionary acceptance of a novel identity, the Court, in collaboration with other political actors, would have to adapt the basic structure doctrine to the politics of day-to-day governance, establishing it not only as a standard against which the Court could judge the constitutionality of others' actions, but also as a potential touchstone for directing the course of actions yet to be taken.

The shaping of the doctrine to achieve this result is perhaps best told as a story of disharmonic constitutional politics in which the revolutionary component in the country's emerging constitutional identity struggled to prevail against other, more preservative elements that, much like their radical adversary, were rooted in a centuries-old history of inter- and intrareligious conflict and contestation.[73] Presenting any version of this history would take us well beyond the specific aims of this chapter, but in the depiction of two extraordinarily revealing constitutional milestones, the first, a response to the worst bloodbath of sectarian violence in India since Partition, and the second, a controversial amendment that sought to advance the interests of historically oppressed groups in the society, we will see how the interplay between jurisprudential development and political engagement can function to advance the realization of founding revolutionary aspirations. Whether this advancement culminates in consolidation, such that constitutional redemption and constitutional revolution converge to provide us with a sufficient basis for the latter's conceptual certification is, alas, a separate question.

A Radical Fiduciary?

In what can without exaggeration be described as India's most important judicial decision since *Kesavananda*, a justice of the Supreme Court wrote, "The Indian Constitution is both a legal and social document. It provides a machinery for the governance of the country. It also contains the ideals expected by the nation. The political machinery created by the Constitution is a means to the achieving of this ideal."[74] The case, *S. R. Bommai v. Union of India*, is famous for its serial clarifications of the essentials of secularism and its detailed discussion of the nature of emergency power, but its eminence in the canon of Indian constitutional law may ultimately rest with the transformative potential of the ruling's deployment of the basic structure doctrine. It is a linchpin in Nehru's step-by-step progression through which revolutionary ideals are provided the dynamic thrust indispensable to their practical realization. If one mark of a decision's ultimate significance is that it both fits within the aspirational DNA of a constitution and that it elevates the Court as a potentially vital institutional actor in the realization of the document's constitutive goals, then *Bommai* surely warrants such recognition.

The principal result in this landmark case was the approval given to the dismissal of three elected state governments deeply implicated in the orgy of Hindu-Muslim violence that followed the destruction of a mosque in the northern city of Ayodhya. Yet the broader meaning of the decision may be found in the connection drawn between the basic structure doctrine—specifically as it relates to secularism—and the responsibility of the state to advance the constitutional essentials of the polity. The immediate outcome of the ruling was to affirm the central government's finding of a "failure of constitutional machinery" in the States. More arresting were the decision's long-term prospects: that the Indian political system had a positive responsibility to abide by the spirit of the Constitution, that the Directive Principles of State Policy would henceforth be imbued with more than hortatory significance, and that the counterrevolutionary jurisprudence of an unconstitutional amendment might somehow be refashioned into a vehicle for revolutionary fulfillment.

The specific exercise of power that triggered the litigation in *Bommai* was the implementation of President's Rule. Under Article 356 of the Indian Constitution, "If the President . . . is satisfied that a situation has arisen in which the government of the State cannot be carried out in accordance with the provisions of this Constitution," he may "assume to himself all or any of the powers" of the government in question. The constitutional provision has been called "the cornerstone of [the] Indian Constitution," since it "constitutes the crux of the entire Centre-State relationship."[75]

For our purposes, its main significance lies in its implications for the marking and affirming of constitutional identity. Article 356 was expressly modeled after the Guarantee Clause in the U.S. Constitution. The language is not the same, but it incorporates an idea similar to Article IV's mandated assurance by the federal government of a republican form of government in the states, as is clear from what B. R. Ambedkar, the James Madison of India, said at the Indian Constituent Assembly: "When we say that the Constitution must be maintained in accordance with the provisions in the Constitution we mean what the American Constitution means, namely that the [republican] form of the constitution prescribed in this Constitution must be maintained."[76] The Supreme Court's ruling in the wake of the Ayodhya debacle and subsequent dismissals was framed within an explicitly articulated commitment to the protection of certain substantive principles against assaults that threatened to undermine their privileged status in the constitutional order. What is more, the decision in *Bommai* affirming principle-based state removals was directly related to the politics of constitutional entrenchment. By linking the "basic structure" argument of *Kesavananda* with Article 356's requirement that the states adhere to republican principles, the Court effectively upheld the designation of threshold constitutional essentials as the predicate for their uniform application within a federal system: "We do not know how the Constitution can be amended so as to remove secularism from the basic structure of the Constitution. Nor do we know how the present Constitution can be replaced by another; it is enough for us to know that the Constitution does not provide for such a course—that it does not provide for its own demise."[77]

The contrast between the American and Indian approaches in these matters is instructive. The American model for the Indian provision also provided the occasion for originating the doctrine that the Court should be careful to avoid "political questions."[78] Indeed, the difference in the two nations' approaches is evident in *Kesavananda*. Thus the Indian Court's linking in *Bommai* of "basic structure" limitations on the amending process with Article 356 responses to failures of constitutional machinery in the states had the effect of casting political and judicial institutions as proactive players in the explication and enforcement of the Indian republic's constitutional identity. By contrast, the U.S. Supreme Court, which studiously avoids all temptations to declare an amendment unconstitutional, has over the years embraced a distinctly positivist approach that is much more congenial to process than to substance. Accordingly, the same deference that must be extended to the constitutional amendments emerging from the procedures of Article V is to be provided to the governments that are elected by popular voting in the states. These alternative judicial perspectives reflect fundamental conceptual differences over whether to confer on the Court the role of guardian of the nation's public philosophy. To maintain what they perceive as the requisite neutrality associated with the liberal state, American judges have been as eager to avoid defining republicanism as their Indian counterparts have been to engage with that subject under the banner of basic structure.[79]

How did such engagement manifest itself in *Bommai*? Here again a look at *Kesavananda* is illuminating. There the attorney general of India argued: "[The State] is under an obligation to take steps for promoting the welfare of the people by bringing about a social order in which social, economic and political justice shall inform all the institutions of the national life."[80] In its decision in that case, the Court did not directly affirm such an obligation, but in establishing the basic structure doctrine, it created the constitutional underpinnings for doing so in the future. *Bommai* rests on the jurisprudence of *Kesavananda*; additionally, it allows for an extraordinary expansion of the authority of "the institutions of the national life"—perhaps unanticipated in 1973, yet consistent with the argument advanced by the attorney general then.

S. P. Sathe captures the distinction very well: "When a constitutional amendment is challenged [as in *Kesavananda*], the question for the Court's determination is whether it destroys the basic structure. When the Presidential action under Article 356 is examined, the Court considers whether such action was necessary for saving the basic structure."[81] The distinction is exemplified in what the Court concluded after reviewing the disturbing account from Ayodhya: "The destruction of [the] mosque was a concrete proof of the creed which the party in question [the Bharatiya Janata Party, BJP] wanted to pursue. In such circumstances, the Ministries formed by the said party could not be trusted to follow the objective of secularism which was part of the basic structure of the Constitution and also the soul of the Constitution."[82] As the narrative in *Bommai* turned to secularism, federalism's bias in favor of the central government emerged as the critical variable in maintaining and furthering the aspirational commitments of the Constitution. As Sathe put it: "The law was laid down that if a State government acted in disregard of the basic structure of the Constitution, it could be dismissed by the President under Article 356."[83]

But what does it mean to act in disregard of the basic structure? Does it require that the state be implicated in some positive way in actions that threaten an essential feature of the Constitution? The official reports to the president from the governors of the three suspect states included evidence pointing to specific activities undertaken by officials of those governments that in blatant and obvious ways challenged the Constitution's formal commitment to secularism. The Court's response to these provocations was noteworthy, in that "for the first time the Supreme Court used secularism as a reference for judging the validity of State action."[84] Yet significant as this breakthrough was, its long-term impact would remain indeterminate without a clarification of the meaning of state action. Were the meaning to incorporate governmental inaction, that is, the failure of a state to commit itself to achieving the aspirational content of secularism as a basic feature, the impact of the decision could potentially be quite extraordinary.

It is therefore important to take note of the Court's chosen emphasis in discussing religion and law: "*Secularism is . . . more than a passive attitude of religious tolerance. It is a positive concept of equal treatment of all religions.*"[85] Several justices (Ramaswamy, Reddy, Sawant) were clear in tying this non-passive sensibility to the deepest of constitutional commitments—societal transformation. According to Justice Ramaswamy, "The Constitution has chosen secularism as its vehicle to establish an egalitarian social order. . . . Secularism, therefore, is part of the fundamental law and basic structure of the Indian political system to secure to all its people socio-economic needs essential for man's excellence and of his moral well-being, fulfillment of material prosperity and political justice."[86] The point's relevance to state action is more transparent in Justice B. P. Jeevan Reddy's opinion. The justice reminds us that Article 356 demands state compliance with the provisions of the Constitution, and that this, following *Kesavananda,* "take[s] in all the provisions including the preamble to the Constitution."[87] That language speaks of the resolve of the Indian people to secure the "social, economic and political justice" appropriate to the Constitution's establishment of a "secular Democratic republic." Then, quoting from an address given by one of his predecessors on the Court, Reddy wrote of the Constitution: "Its material provisions are inspired by the concept of secularism. When it promised all the citizens of India that the aim of the Constitution is to establish socio-economic justice, it placed before the country as a whole the ideal of a welfare state."[88]

This conceptual linkage of secularism and egalitarianism creates constitutional obligations with important interpretative consequences. Justice Reddy added that the relevant provisions of the Constitution included, besides the Preamble, the Fundamental Rights chapters and Directive Principles of State Policy.[89] Recall that in the Constitution, the Directive

Principles were designated "unenforceable by any court," yet "fundamental in the governance of the country." The vagueness of that language was heightened by the concluding words of Article 37, which stipulated "it shall be the duty of the State to apply these principles in making laws." Presumably, that meant the sanctions behind the provisions in this section were political, an inference supported by Ambedkar's observation at the Constituent Assembly: "If any Government ignores them, they will certainly have to answer for them before the *electorate* at the election time."[90]

But what about legal accountability? Is an additional inference now reasonable, namely, that a government will also have to answer for ignoring the Directive Principles in a court of law? *Bommai* became the occasion for the Court to use the ameliorative objectives of secularism to adapt the doctrine of basic structure to the desiderata of ordinary politics. According to Justice Reddy, "Any State government which pursues unsecular policies or an unsecular course of action contrary to the constitutional mandate renders itself amenable to action under Article 356."[91] That such an instance has yet to occur does not detract from the potential long-term meaning of *Bommai:* positive secularism is a component of the egalitarian mandate incorporated in the Directive Principles; as a staple of basic structure, it stands as an important incentive for a more intrusive judicial presence in the affairs of state, enabling it to serve, as Justice Iyer put it, as a radical fiduciary of the people.[92]

What is also true, however, is that the performance of such a role requires a judiciary whose independence will enable it to withstand the pressures of political forces that do not embrace the transformative commitments of *Bommai*'s concept of secularism. If the egalitarian mandate is to be maintained as indispensable to the Constitution's basic structure, then that structure might be deemed necessary to guarantee the Supreme Court's autonomous standing within the constitutional order. This was made very clear in 2014 with the electoral ascendance of a BJP government that viewed the Court as the most important potential obstacle to its Hindu-focused agenda. And so it is significant that in 2015 the Court invalidated a government-sponsored constitutional amendment—the Ninety-Ninth—that would have established a new method for selecting members of the Court, one that would have markedly increased the power of the government over the appointment process.[93] In doing so, the Court invoked the basic structure doctrine, finding it implicated in the effort to undermine the independence of the judiciary.[94] The fact that the government in power, headed by Prime Minister Narendra Modi, was one whose principal base of support subscribed to an agenda antithetical to the thrust of the *Bommai* ruling underscored an entrenched political reality: the judiciary's role in fulfilling the goals of the constitutional revolution can never be taken for granted.

Theseus Redux

To further illustrate that role, in 2011 the Indian Supreme Court decided a case highlighting a "constitutional logic" that holds state intervention in support of constitutionally prescribed revolutionary goals to be "a categorical imperative."[95] The decision in *Indian Medical Association v. Union of India* concerned a critical public policy issue—higher-education admissions—that followed the reasoning of *Bommai*; yet its principal value for us resides as much in its rich theoretical content as in whatever may ultimately be its significance for reservations policy. Much like *Kesavananda,* it wrestled with basic-structure principles as they might apply to the validity of a constitutional amendment, with this key difference: in *Indian Medical Association,* the Court invoked the doctrine for the express purpose of upholding the contested textual modification. Its reason for doing so—to protect Indian constitutional identity—is reminiscent of its analysis in *Kesavananda,* but in this instance its defensive exertion had an explicitly revolutionary purpose.

More specifically, that purpose lies at the core of the transformational constitutional commitment to ameliorate gross injustices resulting from centuries of entrenched cultural and religious practices. That an important next logical Nehruvian step in the crystallizing of India's constitutional revolution would have an affirmative action component was perhaps foreseeable following the egalitarianism-inspired basic-structure standard established in *Bommai* for judging governmental compliance with the positive concept of secularism. Thus, among the Directive Principles of State Policy is Article 46, which states: "The State shall promote with special care the educational and economic interests of the weaker sections of the people, and, in particular, of the Scheduled Castes and the Scheduled Tribes, and shall protect them from social injustice and all forms of exploitation." With the jurisprudential legitimation of basic structure and the adaptation of its identity-affirming properties to the responsibilities of ordinary politics, this presumptively unenforceable injunction acquired a greater sense of urgency with respect to the consolidation of revolutionary aspirations.

To be sure, the Fundamental Rights section that emerged from the Constituent Assembly included a provision (Article 15-1) that seemed to push against the Article 46 directive, since it prohibited the state from "discriminat[ing] against any citizen on grounds only of religion, race, caste, sex, place of birth or any of them." But as part of the First Amendment, adopted in 1951, an additional section (4) was added, stipulating that nothing in the article "shall prevent the State from making any special provision for the advancement of any socially and educationally backward classes of citizens or for the Scheduled Castes and Scheduled Tribes."[96] Marc Galanter, the leading scholar of India's system of preferential treatment of historically deprived population sectors, captures well the tensions reflected in the document's "embrace of antagonistic principles": "In the Constitution the compensatory theme appears juxtaposed with the theme of formal equality. The provisions for compensatory preference appear as exceptions within a framework of enforceable fundamental rights which attempt to curtail the significance of ascriptive groups and guarantee equal treatment to the individual."[97]

Accompanying the coexistence of antagonistic equality principles is a further disharmonic juxtaposition quite common to the liberal constitutional experience, namely, the issue whether the reach of constitutional principles extends beyond the public domain to order relationships and conduct in the strictly private sphere. Thus clause (1) of Article 15 can easily be read in the way the Fourteenth Amendment has been interpreted by the U.S. Supreme Court, that is, as pertaining only to state action, leaving the domain of private activity beyond the scope of public concern and influence.[98] Such a reading is consistent with the general position of the Indian Supreme Court concerning the provisions in Part III of the Constitution, which is that they apply to the government and not to individuals.[99] On the other hand, clause (2) of Article 15 bans discrimination of any kind in places such as shops, hotels, and restaurants, a provision similar to the prohibition in the United States incorporated in the Civil Rights Act of 1964. The law was upheld nearly one hundred years after a similar effort had been declared unconstitutional in the profoundly important *Civil Rights Cases,* leading an Indian commentator to note with evident satisfaction, "It redounds to the wisdom of the Indian Constitution-makers to have provided in the Constitution itself, without leaving to chance, for the social equality, which is vital for the exercise of freedoms guaranteed in the Constitution."[100]

Still, the belief that the document that emerged from the deliberations of the Constituent Assembly delivered an unequivocal ratification of the egalitarian aspirations of the more visionary members of that gathering is not very credible. Dhavan's depiction of the Constitution as a "situs of struggle" is more convincing, and no more so than in connection with the issue of reservations. Thus, the addition of the First Amendment's clarification of Article 15's compatibility with the official reservation of seats in state educational institutions for members of specified deprived groups represented a step forward in the dialogical advancement of a dominant, though not indisputable, view about achieving distributive justice in the polity. Yet even as it provided additional constitutional legitimacy for governmental policies to advance the status of historically oppressed groups, and with it the increasing acceptance by the judiciary of such efforts, critical matters having to do with the criteria for determining the specific beneficiaries were left unresolved. And so, for example, sorting out thorny issues of caste and class required years of complex litigation to clarify the real egalitarian meaning of the evolving constitutional commitment. Deciding how and to what extent the reference to "social" in Article 15 (4) included economic considerations turned out to be one of the more vexing questions in the ongoing debate over reservations.

Similarly vexing was the question at stake in the *Indian Medical Association* case: Did the scope of the Constitution's affirmative action provisions extend to private as well as public institutions? The question had assumed increased salience in light of a pronounced political drift in the 1990s toward economic liberalization and privatization, a development whose impact was experienced with particular force in higher education. Thus, regardless of how one assessed the broader aggregate costs and benefits of liberalization policies, a marked decline in the state's investment in education held out the distinct possibility of a dilution of the constitutional commitment to the weaker sections of the population if that promise extended only to institutions funded from the public treasury. Moreover, the likelihood of such dilution occurring was hardly diminished by a Supreme Court ruling in 2005 that barred the state from imposing its reservations policies on unaided private colleges.[101] And consistent with the history of constitutional revision in this contentious policy sphere, the decision was the trigger for a forceful parliamentary response, in this instance taking the form of the Ninety-Third Amendment.

The amendment added a fifth section to Article 15, stating: "Nothing in this article or in sub-clause (g) of clause (1) of article 19 shall prevent the State from making any special provision, by law, for the advancement of any socially and educationally backward classes of citizens or for the Scheduled Castes or the Scheduled Tribes in so far as such special provisions relate to their admission to educational institutions including private educational institutions, whether aided or unaided by the State, other than the minority educational institutions referred to in clause (1) of article 30." The legalistic sound of this language can easily deflect attention from its relevance to the more elusive question of constitutional identity. To be sure, there is much in it, including its two allusions to other equally legalistic provisions in the document, which have provided attorneys and judges with ample opportunity to ply their lawyerly skills. But what Marc Galanter pointed out long before the adoption of the Ninety-Third Amendment bears directly on the significance of Article 15 (5): "The compensatory discrimination policy is not to be judged only for its instrumental qualities. It is also expressive: through it Indians tell themselves what kind of people they are and what kind of nation."[102]

It is therefore not surprising that a case concerning this issue would produce what may be the most deeply reflective judicial rumination about constitutional identity in Indian constitutional jurisprudence. The Supreme Court had confirmed the Ninety-Third Amendment's compatibility with basic-structure criteria before 2011, but it was not until the decision in the *IMA* case that the strongest expressive implications of this formal constitutional change were articulated. Thus, the Court's decision in 2008 in *Ashoka Kumar Thakur v. Union of India,* in which the government's reservations policy was challenged for its alleged infringement of equality guarantees, found no "basic structure" violation of the Constitution in the Ninety-Third Amendment's new provisions for admission to educational institutions. Its ruling, however, applied only to state-maintained institutions and state-aided educational institutions, and the question whether the amendment was constitutionally valid with respect to "private unaided" educational institutions was left for a later date when the specifics of that configuration of the problem could be appropriately presented to the Court. Since the greatest potential societal effect of group-based admissions policies implicates the private domain, it was appropriate that a case confronting that issue directly became the occasion for instructive reflection on India's constitutional revolution.

The case concerned the admissions regimen of the Army College of Medical Sciences (ACMS), a private, unaided, nonminority professional school. Justice B. Sudershan Reddy's first sentence announcing the Court's decision made clear that establishing entry into the limited space of the higher-education sphere was hardly a new issue for his country: "The vexed question of access to education has hounded India from times immemorial."[103] Here the problem arose out of the college's policy of admitting only students who were wards or children of current or former army personnel and widows of army personnel, who, the school's defenders claimed, had experienced educational disadvantages relative to the civilian population. To counter this claim, it was argued that implementation of this highly restricted admissions policy violated a 2007 Delhi law mandating admissions according to criteria more broadly conceived in light of the Constitution's encouragement of the state to secure the advancement of socially and educationally backward citizens for their entrance into both public and private academic institutions.[104] The Court was asked to declare the Delhi Act of 2007 unconstitutional, which meant also addressing the validity of the Ninety-Third Amendment, under whose authority the legislation had been enacted.[105] Of paramount importance for us, the Court was invited to rule on whether the amendment was unconstitutional as an abrogation of the basic structure of the Constitution.

The judicial response was unequivocal: "We find that if we were to [nullify clause (5) of Article 15] we would have set ourselves on the path to ineradicably alter the identity of the Constitution, damage its very purposes and the national project, and wipe out decades worth of jurisprudence with regard to the Directive Principles of State Policy."[106] The Ninety-Third Amendment's insertion of that clause into the Constitution advanced "the broad egalitarian objectives of the Constitution" and in so doing satisfied "the theory of basic structure [which] is based on the concept of constitutional identity."[107] In answer to the question left unresolved in *Ashoka Kumar Thakur* (a 2008 precedent in which the government's reservations policy was challenged for its alleged infringement of equality guarantees): "The same concerns of national purpose . . . that inform the constitutional identity [do not] miraculously disappear in the context of the private sector."[108]

Upholding the amendment was a critical step in the progression of the constitutional revolution. Justice Reddy asked rhetorically: "If there is an activity that conflicts with an amendment that intends to strengthen the process of achievement of one of the main navigational tools and thereby the goals of the nation-state itself, should such an amendment be declared to be unconstitutional and against the basic structure?"[109] The question then invokes a familiar foreign import: "The doctrine of basic structure has emanated from Germany."[110] Yet in India the doctrine has played out quite differently, in ways that underscore a distinctive, more dynamic approach to the jurisprudence of constitutional identity. Recall that in Germany there are specific deeply entrenched provisions—most prominently, regarding dignity—that are immune from alteration through the amendment process. While determining their meaning as identity-carrying essentials of the Constitution could benefit from some resourceful dialogical interpretative exercises, the very status of these "eternity" provisions creates a judicial imperative for anchoring them in a safe harbor where the risks of separation from the larger constitutional structure are greatly minimized. In contrast, the basic structure doctrine in India is less moored to specific constitutional provisions: "It is not the identity of any one element . . . but rather whether the over-arching principles that connect one fundamental right to the other that are so abrogated as to change the very identity of the Constitution which is the true test to evaluate whether a constitutional amendment has violated the basic structure."[111] Drawing explicitly from the rationale in *Bommai*, the opinion notes that "the recognition of a basic structure in the context of amendment provides an insight that there are, beyond the words of particular provisions, systematic principles underlying and connecting the provisions of the Constitution."[112] This reference to overarching principles is meant to evoke the "social revolution," which was formulated by the framers as the inspiration for subsequent constitutional development.[113] And relying again on *Bommai,* the decision notes that there are "positive rights, which obligate the State to achieve egalitarian and social justice objectives."[114] Amending the Constitution advances that goal.

The navigational metaphor that courses through the Court's opinion shows how. Its deployment by Justice Reddy seeks to elucidate the substance of basic structure by linking Indian constitutional identity with its revolutionary wellspring. But before embarking on his allegorical journey, the justice recalls the claim in *Kesavananda* that "the theory of basic structure is based on the concept of constitutional identity."[115] As the "primordial issue" of Indian constitutionalism, it can benefit from an ancient literary account whose unconventional placement in a legal opinion may be just what is required to render accessible and indelible a foundational insight that would easily *be obscured* by a more orthodox judicial presentation.[116]

Enter Theseus's paradox, Plutarch's classical narrative about the problem of identity. It features an Athenian ship that was successfully involved in a vitally important mission, leading the Athenians to want to preserve it in their harbor for generations. The relevant passage in Plutarch reads as follows: "The ship wherein Theseus and the youth of Athens returned had thirty oars, and was preserved by the Athenians down even to the time of Demetrius Phalereus, for they took away the old planks as they decayed, putting in new and stronger timber in their place, insomuch that this ship became a standing example among the philosophers, for the logical question of things that grow; one side holding that the ship remained the same, and the other contending that it was not the same."[117] Did the identity of the ship change after newer parts had replaced all its older ones, or did it remain the same, given the functionally identical attributes of the replacement parts?

The Court avoided the metaphysical speculation necessary to engage directly with this question and instead launched an alternative voyage of discovery, likening the Constitution to a ship that, unlike Theseus's, "was never intended to remain in the harbor and was intended to set sail."[118] The identity of that ship-constitution was established at its port of origin, but its preservation was attainable only through resolute navigation, which is to say, in less metaphorical terms, "follow[ing] certain principles" to achieve the goals of the social revolution: "In this regard, it was recognized early on as we, as a nation-state, set sail that . . . revolutionary change, using the force and might of the State, might bring about the realization of [the] state of equality much faster."[119] As for the constitutional component of revolutionary change, an extended journey is an apt analogy for its long revolution: "We were enjoined to roam the high seas until we achieved a state of acceptable achievement, neither knowing the length of time nor the length of that journey. . . . We also knew that along that journey, many of the boards, and indeed even certain parts of the main structure may appear to be or actually become a detriment to our progress. Hence, we were also given liberty to change some of those parts in terms of replacing those parts with exact same ones, or mostly similar ones, or even radically differently designed ones."[120]

In the Court's imagining, Theseus's paradox became—or so it seems—the Indian constitutional paradox, in which the defense of identity could occur only if consequential change happened: in the case at hand, through an amendment that fittingly had to be upheld against the objection that it violated the Constitution's basic structure. "If inappropriate changes were made, the ship would sink; and if the appropriate changes were to not be made the ship would sink. Neither wrong action [an unconstitutional amendment?], nor abstinence from action [adopting an essential amendment?] was permissible."[121] But of course there is nothing paradoxical here if one follows the navigational logic of constitutional revolution. The Court's opinion singles out B. R. Ambedkar, who, as the James Madison figure at the Constituent Assembly, can rightfully be described as the foremost master builder of the constitutional ship of state. The ship's identity was officially marked "in the form of formal equality," but Ambedkar understood that unless real progress was achieved in addressing the rampant substantive inequalities that prevailed in Indian society, "the ship itself would be torn apart."[122] This understanding comports with our conceptualization of identity and revolution. A constitution is a large piece of a nation's constitutional identity, but it is not coterminous with it. In most cases, it lays down key markers of that identity, which are then to be adapted to changing political and social realities in ways that modify, clarify, or reinforce it through the dialogical engagement of public and private sources of influence and power. Until a convergence is apparent between constitutional rules and principles on the one hand and actual constitutional practices on the other, one would be well advised to withhold definitive conclusions about a nation's constitutional identity.

Circumspection in this regard is particularly warranted in India, where the question of identity is tightly linked with transformative aspirations. The very notion of a confrontational constitution hints at the magnitude and daunting nature of the challenge of reconstruction; what an Indian jurist once called a "militant environment" is unlikely passively to submit to the transformative designs of a hostile constitution.[123] For that reason, the success of such a constitution in delivering on its promise of radical change is by no means assured. Indeed, the one explicit mention of revolution in the Indian Constitution is quite revealing in this respect. It appears in the Statement of Objects and Reasons that serves as a preamble to the Forty-Second Amendment, adopted in 1976: "The question of amending the Constitution for removing the difficulties which have arisen in achieving the objective of socio-economic revolution . . . has been engaging the active attention of Government and the public for some years now."

In the context of "the long revolution," the Ninety-Third Amendment may thus be viewed as a stride toward fulfillment of the constitutional revolution's promise,[124] "or in terms of the analogy to [the] Ship of Theseus, Clause (5) of Article 15 may be likened to a necessary replacement and in fact an enhancement in the equality code, so that it makes our national ship, the Constitution, more robust and stable."[125] The Court's avowal that through the amendment "the goals and objectives that inform the constitutional identity" were applied to "the private sector" (that is, to nonstate educational institutions) underscores its dynamic approach to the identity-revolution question.[126] Providing constitutional legitimacy to the guarantee of greater access to higher education to the weaker sections of the population pursues the transformative mandate of the Directive Principles of State Policy, as outlined in Article 46, to promote the educational advancement of lower-status citizens. Upholding the amendment on basic-structure grounds was a calculated effort to give fuller meaning to what was at best only an inscribed embrace of revolutionary constitutional identity. Indeed, as mentioned earlier, well before the convening of the Constituent Assembly, Nehru had projected its commencement as occurring at a time when "a semi-revolutionary situation has been created in this country." Viewed from the perspective of one looking back at the work of that assembly, the term "semi-revolutionary" may be seen also to embody the incomplete or unfinished work of the constitutional revolution codified at that convention. So while it is true that on its face the basic-structure doctrine effectively distinguishes between a constitutional amendment and revolutionary action, at a deeper level it certifies that there is a fundamental connection between the two. As the Court concluded in the *IMA* case, "State intervention is a categorical imperative, both morally and within our constitutional logic."[127]

A constitution can be both a revolutionary moment and the commencement of measured and continuing change. Particularly in the case of constitutional revolutions not connected with certifiable revolutionary upheavals, their aspirational character necessarily entails a high degree of uncertainty in establishing their ultimate transformative impact. Conceptually, the designation "constitutional revolution" has been used as a way of marking the onset of a new departure in a nation's constitutional narrative, reflected both in the novelty of what will be as well as the repudiation of what has been. Adopted within six months of each other, the German and Indian Constitutions were in this sense notable revolutionary achievements—the first for having replaced tyrannical rule with constitutional governance, and the second for having severed the bonds of colonial rule with an accompanying commitment to undo the structures of social oppression that had been nurtured under that rule. The highest courts in both countries were also notable for their pioneering work in establishing the authority of the judiciary to invalidate duly passed constitutional amendments on substantive grounds—Germany for first acknowledging the legitimacy of doing so, and India for being the first to accomplish the task. A result of these efforts is that the concept of constitutional identity has been elevated to a position of jurisprudential significance.

As we have seen in this chapter and the previous one, novelty and repudiation are associated with identity-based adjudication in the sense that a constitutional revolution—legal change that brings about a displacement in the way constitutionalism is experienced in a given polity—yields contrasting sets of juridical priorities. Preservation and change are inherent in both, but where the dominant concern is to affirm the repudiation of a horrific past, the determination to fasten the new attributes of constitutional identity to a fixed and secure place may subordinate the commitment to refine that identity in accordance with the underlying principles of the revolution. In contrast, where the embrace of a new constitutional identity clarifies the urgent need to make of that novelty a genuine societal transformation, the launching of an extended collective mission to translate the formal attributes of identity into lived experience will likely follow. Yet in pursuing the dynamic implications of postrevolutionary constitutional identity, the mission will, if successful, preserve the underlying precepts of the constitutional revolution.

Hence the obvious appeal of the Theseus paradox story to the Court in the army medical college case. Justice Reddy's sustained attention to constitutional identity led him to the legendary king of Athens and his famously decaying ship, as it has many others captivated by questions of identity. Along the way, he might also have found himself moved by the portrayal of Theseus's broader appeal. Thus, in his depiction of the Greek hero's final resting place, Plutarch notes, "His tomb is a sanctuary and refuge for slaves, and all those of mean condition that fly from the persecution of men in power, in memory that Theseus while he lived was an assister and protector of the distressed, and never refused the petitions of the afflicted that fled to him."[128] Celebrated in Greek mythology as both a founder of democracy and a champion of the poor and oppressed, his most illustrious triumph—the slaying of the Minotaur—has among its several popular story lines the victory over a socially repressive religious order.

Nehru once observed: "India is far nearer in spirit and outlook to the old Greece than the nations of Europe are today, although they call themselves children of the Hellenic spirit. . . . Both developed a mythology which was indivisibly mixed up with history, and it was not possible to separate fact from fiction."[129] For an Indian judge, however, it is hardly necessary to reach back to ancient Greece to find inspiration for noble undertakings. Nehru, like many others at the Constituent Assembly, found it in the ancient (and not mythological) figure of the great reformer Emperor Ashoka, "one of the most magnificent names in Indian history."[130] In that gathering, he made the case for the Ashokan wheel to be the centerpiece of the flag of his newly independent nation. It was, Nehru maintained, the symbol of India's ancient culture; because of its historic connection with the cause of social justice, he urged that it become emblematic of the Constitution's goals and identity. As his colleague S. Radakrishnan, the distinguished philosopher and future president of India, said, "This wheel, which is a rotating thing, indicates to us that there is death in stagnation. . . . With regard to our social conditions it is essential to move forward."[131]

In this chapter, we have seen this forward movement proceed haltingly, or in Nehru's words, through a "step by step" pursuit of a constitutional vision whose ultimate goal was the revolutionary transformation of Indian society. Nehru understood that the Constitution, as words on paper, was hardly a guarantee of progress, revolutionary or otherwise. We might think in this regard of James Madison's famous question in *Federalist* 48: "Will it be sufficient to mark, with precision, the boundaries of these departments, in the constitution of the government, and to trust to these parchment barriers against the encroaching spirit of power?"[132] If Madison's challenge to the efficacy of written guarantees in protecting a people's rights calls attention to the restricted potential of a constitutional text, then it surely must stimulate a similar concern for parchment promises of societal transformation. It follows that whatever the nature of the paradigmatic displacement that is inscribed in the provisions of a constitution, the actual authentication of any accompanying claim to have achieved a constitutional revolution of socially transformative significance must await developments over time.[133]

How long? In India, or more generally where the reconstructive aspirations of constitutional framers are codified in rules and principles that confront recalcitrance in deeply entrenched social institutions not lacking in textual resources, the confirmation that a constitutional revolution has occurred requires considerable time. This is what Nehru understood. And as Michael Walzer has astutely noted, "National liberation, like every other form of liberation, is a very long process, not a single battle but a series of battles that extends over many decades."[134] With India as a principal example, he focuses on secular political movements that achieved statehood only to be challenged by religious movements in the decades that followed. While constitutional disharmony is not central to his inquiry, what we have seen in this chapter is that the intense political and cultural divisions that he vividly portrays within a broader society are all reflected in the constitutional struggles that commence from the moment of liberation. In this connection, Marc Galanter's distinction between "horizontal and vertical perspectives" on equality and compensatory discrimination captures the time dimension very nicely: "In the horizontal view, the relevant time is the present. In [the vertical view] the present is seen as transition from a past of inequality to the desired future of substantive equality; the purpose of compensatory discrimination is to promote equalization by offsetting historically accumulated inequalities. . . . It is seen as requisite to the fulfillment of the nation's long-range goal of substantial redistribution and equalization."[135]

Indeed, fulfilling that long-range goal was what Nehru and his compatriots saw as "the whole purpose" of India's "dynamic constitution." Our emphasis on the substance of the "long democratic revolution" has taken precedence over the question whether India's founding moment and subsequent moments of formal constitutional change are properly to be regarded as true expressions of the sovereign popular will. Ran Hirschl argued that "the vast majority of constitutional revolutions in the last few decades were culminations of elite bargains, or otherwise do not fit [the] bottom-up narrative."[136] He is skeptical of "the romantic notion of constitutionalization as reflecting massive political mobilization and genuine popular will."[137] Surely such skepticism is warranted in the case of India, even if a credible account built around the romantic view can also plausibly be constructed. Indeed, in chapter 7 we address the problem of what might be called participatory deficit in an examination of the vexed topic of the constituent power. Yet interesting as may be the outcome of the top-down–bottom-up debate, what ultimately matters more with respect to constitutional change that can legitimately lay claim to being revolutionary is the substance of what has demonstrably changed. As Nehru said, "So far as the basic nature of the Constitution is concerned, it must deal with the fundamental aspects of the political, the social, the economic and other spheres. . . . You will find that if you go into too great detail and mix up the really basic and fundamental things with the important but nevertheless secondary things, you bring the basic things to the level of the secondary things too."[138]

In India the "long democratic revolution" has proceeded, however haltingly, with the active involvement of the judiciary. The next chapter tells a constitutional revolution story in which a nation's highest court is not just an expediter of the transformational agenda of a formal document's inscribed aspirations, but also the principal actor in the remaking of a new constitutional order. But the centrality of the Israeli Supreme Court in the events that culminated in that nation's constitutional revolution was pregnant with implications for the long-term prospects of transformations that unfold in this most "unromantic" of ways.

6

Constitutional Revolution Through Adjudication: The Case of Israel

When confronted by a lion, do we need to gather evidence and construct doctrines to prove that it is a lion? If that is the case with a lion, should it not be the case with regard to the very existence of authority to frame a constitution? It should be self-evident.

Justice Mishael Cheshin, *Mizrahi Bank* case

CONSTITUTIONS CHANGE WITH TIME, and such change happens in multiple ways. Beyond the realm of constitutional law, it can occur in the social sphere, for instance, "by gradually shifting the rank and importance of constitutional factors . . . and norms."[1] As seen in chapter 3, within constitutional law the text of a constitution can be formally modified according to an amendment procedure stipulated within it, often in a transformative manner. While formal constitutional amendments are an essential means of constitutional change, constitutional transformations, even important ones, may occur without an alteration of the constitutional text, for instance, through judicial interpretation or practice.[2] When the enforceable meaning of the constitution changes outside the amendment process, we have "an informal constitutional change" or "an informal amendment."[3] Indeed, a judicial decision that purports merely to interpret or resolve the ambiguities of a constitutional text can have a greater effect on a constitutional system than a formal constitutional amendment.[4]

In the U.S. context, judicial decisions are commonly viewed as instruments of constitutional change. Some scholars have even suggested that certain judicial interpretations of the Constitution are best understood as constitutional amendments.[5] In the famous *Lochner v. New York* case, for example, the U.S. Supreme Court invalidated a state statute restricting bakers to a ten-hour maximum workday, which was later regarded as a policy adjustment that resulted in the "amendment" of the document through interpretation.[6] It is for good reason that President Woodrow Wilson once described the U.S. Supreme Court as a "constitutional convention in continuous session."[7]

Besides creating constitutional change, a judicial decision can completely transform the core values of the constitutional order. Consider a recent informal constitutional change in Honduras. One of the basic principles in the Honduran Constitution of 1982 is the presidential term limit.[8] In 2014, a group of fifteen representatives in Congress belonging to the National Party challenged the constitutional rules regarding presidential reelection. Later, in early 2015, the former president of the National Party, Rafael Callejas, challenged the rule against presidential reelection by claiming it should be inapplicable. According to the challengers, the prohibition on reelection infringed on fundamental rights such as the right to be elected, the right to vote, and freedom of expression. A unanimous judgment of the Constitutional Chamber of the Honduran Supreme Court held unconstitutional the constitutional provisions banning reelection, the unamendable nature of those provisions, and the invalidation of citizenship for promoting reelection.[9] In essence, the judicial decision completely eradicated the presidential term limit that had been at the core of the 1982 Constitution, and allowed for the possibility that presidents could stay in office ad infinitum. This judicial decision was seen by commentators as "a fundamental change to the core of the Constitution."[10]

So constitutional change, even fundamental transformation, can materialize through judicial decisions. In the preceding chapter, we saw how the Indian Supreme Court embraced a role that allowed it to pursue a jurisprudential path toward the greater advancement of the revolutionary goals of the Constitution. In its deployment of the aspirational content of the document, the Court appropriated the dynamic component of Indian constitutional identity to secure a fuller attainment of the transformative hopes of the Constitution's revolutionary promise. But can a constitution in effect be created by a judicial ruling? Since, as in the Indian case, constitution making typically results from a special constitution-making body, at a special, celebrated moment, one might be inclined to think not. In his famous "Tryst With Destiny" speech delivered to the Indian Constituent Assembly on the eve of independence, Nehru said, "A moment comes, which comes out rarely in history, when we step out from the old to the new, when an age ends, and when the soul of a nation, long suppressed, finds utterance."[11] Justice Mishael Cheshin seemed to have such a moment in mind when he wrote in his minority opinion in the landmark Israeli *Mizrahi Bank* case, "The day of giving a constitution is a day of pomp and circumstance. Everyone knows that the authorized body is about to enact a constitution, for behold a constitution is about to be given, and behold a constitution is now given."[12] Justice Cheshin compared constitution giving to the revelation on Mount Sinai, where the Jewish people purified themselves for three days in anticipation of receiving their first constitution. Said Cheshin, "This is the Sinaitic theophany, the awesome grandeur of receiving the Law; the ceremony of bestowing a constitution upon Israel." He elaborated:

> There is no doubt as to who grants the constitution; there is no doubt as to the authority of the giver of the constitution; there is no doubt as to the language of the constitution, and there is no doubt that a constitution has been given. The authority is not disputed, its language is not disputed, and the giving of the Torah is not disputed. . . . This is the Torah of thunder and lightning, of thick cloud and the mighty sound of the trumpet, and this is the Torah of the still small voice. Indeed, this is the hallmark of a constitution, and to the best of my knowledge it has been the hallmark of constitutions throughout human history.[13]

Justice Cheshin wrote this intrepid minority opinion in strong support of an extraordinary constitution-making moment and in robust opposition to the majority's view that the Israeli parliament, the Knesset, possessed constituent authority. The Supreme Court of Israel retrospectively acknowledged the superior constitutional status of the Basic Laws on human rights, enacted three years earlier. This dramatic judicial decision marked a dividing line between the previous constitutional order, one featuring the principle of parliamentary sovereignty, and a new constitutional order distinguished by constitutional supremacy.[14] This judicial recognition of constituent authority, we claim, was the decisive act in the idiosyncratic "constitutional revolution" story in Israel.

It is a story whose beginning and end are shrouded in mists of uncertainty and ambiguity. In this chapter, we outline the peculiar course of constitutional development in Israel, finding that the particular characteristics that make it a unique chronicle of legal and political accretion conform to some of our general expectations regarding the concept of constitutional revolution. Most obvious is the absence of the constitutional moment, or at least the failure to exploit the occasion of a political rupture in political continuity by constitutionalizing it for the long-term benefit of society. "The challenge for statecraft," wrote Bruce Ackerman, "is to use these fleeting moments to build new and stronger foundations for liberal polities before the opportunity for self-conscious transformation is lost in the centrifugal whirl of liberal society."[15] To be sure, constitutional revolutions often begin this way, but even when they do, the consolidation of revolutionary aspirations often proceeds over an extended period of time, as has happened in India. Ackerman pointed to the Indian constitutional document as "a paradigmatic achievement of the first great age of liberal revolution."[16] Since, however, "the long-term costs of a short-term failure to act at the moment of revolutionary triumph are easy to underestimate," the Israeli example must, in this account, be appraised as a failure of the first order.[17]

A calculation of the possibly prohibitive costs of adopting a constitution at the independence moment resulted in an indefinite postponement of such a codification. Ackerman is not the only one who has questioned this early reckoning. But even those who defended the benefits of postponement came to see the desirability of getting on with the business of constitutional creation. But how? Would it require a clear and unambiguous exertion of constituent authority to achieve the establishment of a new constitutional order, or would a questionable constitutive undertaking of legislative activity, retrospectively sanctified by the Supreme Court, be a sufficient basis for proclaiming a constitutional revolution? This question was debated by the two leading figures on the Court in a landmark case in Israeli jurisprudence. In presenting the opposing views of Justices Barak and Cheshin, we show how the theoretical conundrum concerning process and substance played out in the vortex of legal and political contestation. Thus, without conceding the procedural high ground to his colleague on the Court, Justice Barak found in the substantive regime transformations attained through dialogical interaction between the legislative and judicial branches in the 1990s ample reason for certifying the legitimacy of the constitutional revolution. For Justice Cheshin, on the other hand, the predicate for such certification was lacking, given the clear absence of the appropriate activity mandated for regime-altering constitutional transformation.

The Barak-Cheshin debate can be framed as an argument over judicial power, and more specifically as a disagreement about the pros and cons of an activist court. But inevitably in Israel, questions about institutional power coincide with the disharmonic constitutional politics that has been present since the inception of the state: whether the polity's essential character is to be understood mainly as the embodiment of democratic—predominantly Western—attributes, or as the fulfillment of the national ambitions of a particular people. As Ran Hirschl noted, the Supreme Court serves as the main, perhaps the exclusive, recipient "of core collective identity questions."[18] As the Israeli case epitomizes, disharmony is the critical variable behind the dynamics of the constitutional revolution. So it is not entirely surprising that Israel serves as our exemplar of a constitutional revolution that was driven by the judiciary.

Preconstitutional Revolution

The establishment of the State of Israel in 1948 seemed like an appropriate time to write a constitution for the nation. As was said of Canadian constitutionalism, "No liberal democratic state has accomplished comprehensive constitutional change outside the context of some cataclysmic situation such as revolution, world war, the withdrawal of empire, civil war, or the threat of imminent breakup."[19] Indeed, with the termination of the British Mandate and the establishment of the state, it was widely assumed that a formal constitution would be adopted. Such a document was among the criteria discussed by the United Nations and promoted in a UN General Assembly decision of November 29, 1947, which stated: "The Constituent

Assembly of each State shall draft a democratic constitution for its State and choose a provisional government to succeed the Provisional Council of Government appointed by the Commission." The resolution further elaborated on the essential components of the future constitution.[20] In accordance with Resolution 181, Israel's Declaration of the Establishment of the State of Israel, proclaimed on May 14, 1948, anticipated a formal constitution-making process and declared that an elected constituent assembly would adopt a constitution no later than October 1, 1948: "We declare that, with effect from the moment of the termination of the Mandate being tonight, the eve of Sabbath, the 6th Iyar, 5708 (15th May, 1948), until the establishment of the elected, regular authorities of the State in accordance with the Constitution which shall be adopted by the Elected Constituent Assembly not later than the 1st October 1948, the People's Council shall act as a Provisional Council of State, and its executive organ, the People's Administration, shall be the Provisional Government of the Jewish State, to be called 'Israel.'"[21] The declaration thus anticipated the following three stages: first, the "Provisional Council of State" was to act as a temporary legislative branch; second, elections were to be held for a "Constituent Assembly" that would draft the constitution, after which the body was to disperse; third, elections would be held for a legislative branch, following which the Provisional Council of State would disperse as well.

Several months after this announced deadline, on January 25, 1949, a constituent assembly was elected.[22] Despite the declaration's plan that the assembly's sole role would be to draft a constitution, the Provisional Council of State decided several days before the elections that with the convening of the Constituent Assembly, it would cease to exist. Its legislative powers would be transferred to the elected Constituent Assembly, which would, as planned, exercise the constitution-drafting role as well.[23] Soon after its formation, on February 16, 1949, the assembly enacted the Transition Law, which provided that the legislative body would be called the Knesset and the Constituent Assembly would be called the First Knesset.[24] Although it held this dual capacity—legislative and constitutive—the First Knesset did not execute its constitution-making task, and the plan to draft a comprehensively written constitution for the State of Israel was never realized.

A central feature—perhaps *the* central feature—of Israel's abortive constitution-making process was the disagreements and controversies surrounding the formal question whether a constitution was needed at that time, and the substantive questions concerning the core values, characteristics, and arrangements to be included and secured in the constitution. Disagreements, of course, are part of Jewish history, often concerning conflicting visions and ideologies respecting humanistic universal values and particularistic Jewish values.[25] From May 1949 until June 1950, the First Knesset was besieged by heated debates surrounding the adoption of a constitution as explicitly stated in the Declaration of Establishment.[26]

The objections to a formal constitutional arrangement were of several kinds. The constant threats to the nation's security, to its very survival in the early years, led Israel to consider itself to be in a state of emergency, a condition that complicated the drafting and adoption of a formal constitution. Additionally, the religious community viewed the Torah, or Jewish law, as supreme, and thus viewed a formal constitution as not only unnecessary but also as potentially hostile to important religious rules, institutions, and customs. The religious groups that did not categorically reject the idea of a constitution thought that it ought to be based on the principles of the Torah and provide for the supremacy of Jewish law in matters concerning marriage and divorce, the provision of kosher food in state-funded institutions, and the securing of the Sabbath and religious holidays as national holidays. In contrast, the left-wing political parties, notably Mapai, favored a secular state.[27] Critical opposition came from Prime Minister David Ben-Gurion, who claimed that the Knesset was not required to immediately adopt a constitution and could postpone its implementation until a later date. Ben-Gurion's opposition derived from his determination to prevent a struggle between the society's rival segments and political parties, antagonism that, he believed, would threaten the goal of state building.[28] Since most of the world's Jews were still in exile, it was felt that constitutional entrenchment of the state's vision, basic characteristics, and values should not precede the "Ingathering of the Exiles." Instead, the constitution-drafting process should occur after their arrival in Israel.[29] There was also a realpolitik rationale for Ben-Gurion's opposition to a constitution, namely, his reluctance to curtail his powers through the imposition of constitutional limitations.[30]

One can reasonably assume that had there been support from Ben-Gurion, a written constitution could have been achieved.[31]

Entwined in the question whether the time was ripe to constitute a constitution were "substantive disagreements" between the political groups concerning policies, conceptions of the "good," and the rights to be protected by the constitution. Should the state's fundamental character be secular, as the left-wing parties contended, or sectarian, as advocated by the religious factions? Should the constitution entrench social and economic rights, as desired by the socialist factions, or allow private ownership of property and free enterprise, as the General Zionists favored? Should the constitution support a particular nationalist ideology and envision territorial expansion, as propagated by the Revisionist and Herut parties, or endorse the protection of the Arab minority, as the Communist Party desired?[32] These and other disagreements concerning governmental structure proved resistant to resolution. This stalemate led to the adoption of a compromise formula known as the Harari Resolution (named for Yizhar Harari, its proposer), according to which the constitution-drafting process would evolve in stages in the guise of Basic Laws that would, at the end of the process, culminate in a full, formal constitution.[33] In essence, the Knesset, holding both legislative and constitution-making powers, decided to make the constitution-making process an incremental enterprise by which the constitution would be enacted in stages through a series of Basic Laws.[34] By adopting the Harari Resolution, an internal document lacking any constitutional status, the Knesset decided not to decide. To be sure, while it is common for constitution drafters to leave certain constitutional issues undecided, either by gag rules, vague language, or delegation to future legislators, it is exceptional to leave the entire constitution-making process undecided.[35]

Parliamentary Supremacy

During its entire term, the First Knesset did not enact any Basic Laws. The law that provided for the transition of power to the Second Knesset did, however, explicitly transfer all powers of the Knesset, that is, both constituent and legislative powers, to the Second and all subsequent Knessets.[36] The fact that the First Knesset, the Constituent Assembly, did not adopt a constitution raised the question whether subsequent Knessets were in possession of the constituent power. Some scholars questioned the Knesset's ability to transfer its constituent power to succeeding Knessets, concluding that the unused constituent powers of the First Knesset vanished with its dissolution.[37]

The Second Knesset, too, failed to ratify any Basic Laws. Finally, eight years after the adoption of the Harari Resolution, the Third Knesset enacted the first Basic Law (Basic Law: The Knesset). Besides being the first to carry the title Basic Law, this legislation included certain formally entrenched provisions. For example, section 4 of the enactment governed the form of elections to the Knesset and could be changed only by approval of a majority of its members. From then until 1992, the Knesset enacted an additional eight Basic Laws that regulated governmental structure.[38] None of this legislative activity, however, concerned a constitutionally inscribed bill of rights or, crucially, a comprehensive, formal constitution. Perhaps the "political leaders," as Benjamin Akzin noted, "got used to the convenience of having no Constitution to check them."[39]

Whereas the Harari Resolution enabled the postponing of the constitution-making process and provided some constitutional flexibility, it left behind many unresolved issues.[40] It stipulated neither a procedure for the acceptance and ratification of the full constitution nor a timetable for the enactment of each Basic Law and the fusion of all of them into a single document. Could the constitution-making process last decades? Additionally, it was unclear whether the process described in the resolution was limited to the term of the First Knesset—the Constituent Assembly—or whether it allowed or even imposed a duty upon succeeding Knessets to enact a constitution. Moreover, the normative status of each Basic Law and its enforceability in the courts remained unclear.[41] This ambiguity allowed some to claim that the Harari Resolution entailed a gradual process that would ultimately allow for the adoption of a constitutional system like that of the United States. Others, however, argued that the resolution implied the adoption of the British parliamentary supremacy model, according to which the prevailing doctrine would be "Knesset sovereignty," with the Basic Laws carrying a status similar to that of ordinary legislation.[42] Indeed, according to the early jurisprudence of the Supreme Court, until the Basic

Laws were integrated into a unified constitution, their normative status had to be considered equivalent to that of ordinary statutes—ergo, the Basic Laws could be changed by ordinary legislation.[43] The prevailing approach was thus similar to that of the Westminster model of parliamentary supremacy, according to which the Knesset held unlimited legislative power, as the Supreme Court repeatedly emphasized: "The Knesset is sovereign and has the power to enact any law and give it content—as it pleases. It is entirely inconceivable that a duly enacted Knesset law, or any provision thereof, should for any reason by deprived of validity."[44]

During this period, the main legal debate concerned the question whether the formal entrenched provision found in Basic Law: The Knesset was binding on the Knesset. In 1969, the prominent legal scholar Amnon Rubinstein argued that "Basic Law: The Knesset is the loyal expression of the Knesset's constituent power" while contrasting it with the more questionable normative status of the unentrenched Basic Laws.[45] A year later, another influential scholarly voice, Claude Klein, wrote that the entrenched and unentrenched Basic Laws should all be regarded equally; all were the result of the Knesset exercising its constituent power.[46]

In the background of this debate, the Israeli Supreme Court in 1969 decided the *Bergman* case, in which the Court acknowledged the validity of formal entrenchment provisions included in the Basic Laws. It held that the Financing Law of 1969 was in conflict with the formally entrenched section 4 of Basic Law: The Knesset. The Court ruled that the entrenched character of the latter provided the judges with the authority to overturn ordinary legislation that had not been passed by the required special majority. In other words, the Supreme Court ruled that the Knesset possessed the ability to limit itself through an entrenched clause in a Basic Law, thereby authorizing the Court to invalidate an ordinary statute that contradicted such an entrenched provision.[47] The case marked a significant development in the evolution of judicial review in Israel, since it was the first time the Supreme Court invalidated a law of the Knesset. For some commentators, *Bergman* signified "a new era" in Israeli constitutional law, although it remained debatable whether it represented a deep rupture in the Court's jurisprudence.[48] Indeed, the opinion of Justice Moshe Landau notably understated the judgment's significance, stating that the Court intentionally avoided ruling on "weighty preliminary questions of a constitutional nature, relating to the status of the Basic Laws, and to the justiciability before this court of the issue of the Knesset's actual compliance with a self-imposed limitation."[49]

In an academic article, the petitioner, Dr. Bergman, emphasized that the "procedural question—whether its [the Knesset's] vote did result in the requisite majority—had nothing to do with parliamentary sovereignty."[50] Accordingly, the *Bergman* judgment left the many unresolved issues regarding the normative status of the Basic Laws unanswered. Still, the decision's expansive potential for judicial review was such that some observers regarded it as Israel's *Marbury v. Madison*.[51] At least one commentator found the work of the Supreme Court to have been more sweeping than that of its early-nineteenth-century American counterpart: "Where Chief Justice Marshall declared an Act of Congress void because it was in conflict with the Constitution, Mr. Justice Landau . . . declared an Act of Knesset void despite the fact that Israel has not yet adopted a written constitution."[52] Such an assessment was consistent with another's observation that *Bergman* "revolutioniz[ed] the Israeli legal system by introducing de facto judicial supervision of the constitutionality of primary legislation."[53] Indeed, following the *Bergman* case, the Supreme Court gave priority to formally entrenched provisions of a Basic Law over regular legislation.[54] In that respect, and by adopting and maintaining certain judicial review power, this was certainly a "Marbury Moment."[55] But in a constitutional system lacking a formal bill of rights, this judicial supervision was limited to a very few specific provisions in the institutional Basic Laws that had no formal entrenchment.

Ultimately, the *Bergman* case did not change the prevailing approach of parliamentary sovereignty, or legislative supremacy. It was generally accepted that the Knesset had no limitations on its legislative powers, except regarding a few formally entrenched provisions in Basic Laws, and was regarded as equivalent to the British Parliament.[56] Yet the lack of a bill of rights did not prevent the Supreme Court from protecting individual rights through interpretative exercises.[57] The Court derived fundamental rights from the democratic nature of the state and from the Declaration of Establishment; like every modern democracy, the state recognized the human rights that have come to characterize such regimes.[58] It developed an interpretative orientation in which every statute (primary or secondary legislation) would be interpreted according to the presumption that its purpose was to advance human rights. To rebut this presumption and permit the infringement of human rights, a statute would have to contain explicit and clear language to that effect.[59]

Thus, "over the years Israeli justices managed to maneuver quite effectively within the limitations of parliamentary supremacy, employing various interpretive strategies to enact and enforce a de facto judicial bill of rights."[60] In essence, the result was tantamount to a "'constitution without a Constitution" or an "unwritten constitution."[61] Still, this judicial protection of human rights remained limited, since the Knesset retained legislative supremacy. When a clear statute of the Knesset infringed a fundamental right, even one recognized in the Declaration of Establishment, the conflicting statute of the Knesset prevailed.[62] Accordingly, the debate going forward centered on the need to constitute a formal bill of rights enforceable through the exercise of judicial review.[63]

The Constitutional Revolution

The 1970s and 1980s saw recurring attempts to enact a comprehensive constitution, all of which failed.[64] In 1989, the minister of justice, Dan Meridor, presented the government with a draft Basic Law: Human Rights. When the deliberations on this proposal began, it appeared that the religious parties would object to it. This led Amnon Rubinstein, then a Knesset member, to submit the proposal as a private bill in case the governmental proposal failed to proceed. Also included was an explicit provision pertaining to judicial review. Rubinstein's submission (Basic Law: Human Rights) passed a preliminary reading in the Knesset, but did not survive the dissolution of the government.[65] After the establishment of the new government, Rubinstein resumed his efforts, now painfully aware that the principle of equality was the main bone of contention. This prompted him to adopt an approach that has come to be known as "atomization," in which the proposed Basic Law on human rights would be divided into several components. Rubinstein took a gradual approach; instead of attempting to push for a full bill of rights, which the religious parties would have opposed, he advanced less contentious basic rights for enactment into a basic law. As a result, four Basic Laws on human rights were proposed. These were Basic Law: Human Dignity and Liberty, Basic Law: Freedom of Occupation, Basic Law: Freedom of Speech, and Basic Law: Freedom of Association. Two of these bills were successfully ratified in March 1992—Basic Law: Human Dignity and Liberty, which protects the rights to life, dignity, privacy, liberty, and property, as well as the right to enter and exit Israel; and Basic Law: Freedom of Occupation, which protects the freedom of professional occupation.

Absent from the list of protected rights were several important human rights, such as equality and freedom of religion and conscience. Again, these omissions were intentional, since their inclusion would have been considered unacceptable by the religious parties. The two new Basic Laws thus reflected a political compromise concerning the specific rights that would receive heightened protection under Israeli law.[66] To placate the fears of the religious parties, the introductory sections of the two Basic Laws stated that the laws' purpose was to protect rights "in order to stipulate the values of the State of Israel as a Jewish and democratic state, in a Basic Law." The addition of the word "Jewish" as a counterbalance to the democratic character of the state contributed, according to Rubinstein, to the religious parties' willingness to support the two Basic Laws.[67] Also, because of the difficulties in reaching a national consensus—in particular, the intense opposition of the religious parties to any change in the status quo regarding the relationship between religion and the state (for example, the authority to determine issues concerning marriage and divorce is in the exclusive jurisdiction of the rabbinical courts)—the Basic Laws not only excluded certain rights from protection, but also included "saving provisions" that preserved the force and validity of statutes enacted before 1992.[68]

Perhaps most importantly, the two new Basic Laws constitute a partially entrenched bill of rights. Each includes a limitation clause that specifies four cumulative conditions that, if met, could legitimate the infringement of protected rights: "There shall be no violation of rights under this Basic Law except by a law befitting the values of the State of Israel, enacted for a proper purpose, and to an extent no greater than is required or by regulation enacted by virtue of express authorization in such law."[69] This was the first time in the history of Israeli constitutional law that a Basic Law included a substantive entrenchment mechanism. According to another clause, "all governmental authorities must respect these human rights."[70] It appeared as if these clauses were primarily directed at the legislature, since they are intended to prevent it from enacting certain statutes.[71] Consistent with the *Bergman* case's rationale, the two Basic Laws were formally entrenched initially, requiring approval by a majority of Knesset members for their amendment. But the entrenchment provision in Basic Law: Human Dignity and Liberty was voted down in the second and third readings of the bill, leaving only Basic Law: Freedom of Occupation formally entrenched; Basic Law: Human Dignity was left open to change by a simple majority in the Knesset.[72]

After the ratification of the two Basic Laws on human rights in March 1992, some scholars claimed that a "revolution" had occurred within Israel's constitutional order. Notably, it was Claude Klein, the pioneer behind the theory of the Knesset's constituent power, who first used the term "constitutional revolution," in 'The Quiet Constitutional Revolution," an op-ed published shortly after the passage of the Basic Laws.[73] Regarding the Basic Laws as an exercise of the Knesset's constituent power, Klein contended they were constitutional norms superior to ordinary legislation.[74] A few days later, the "executor" of the constituent power, Amnon Rubinstein, published an op-ed in which he announced that "a big constitution [has] arrive[d]."[75] Or as summed up by another commentator, "the two new Basic Laws have introduced a mini-revolution into Israeli constitutional law by providing a sound basis for judicial review of legislation on grounds that it is inconsistent with human rights."[76]

Most significantly for Israel's constitutional development, Justice Aharon Barak, the president of the Supreme Court, pointed to the revolutionary character of the two Basic Laws on human rights.

> Not everyone knows this, but recently a revolution has occurred in Israel. I am speaking of a constitutional revolution, in which the Knesset, as the constitutive branch, enacted Basic Law: Human Dignity and Liberty, and Basic Law: Freedom of Occupation. . . . By virtue of this basic legislation, human rights in Israel have become legal norms of preferred constitutional status much like the situation in the United States, Canada and many other

countries. . . . The revolution is not one of content so much as of force. With the enactment of the Basic Laws, these fundamental rights have become "inscribed in the book." From now on, they bind not only the citizens and residents, and not only the administrative authorities, such as the government and local authorities. From now on, they bind the Knesset itself. Above the Knesset as the legislative branch stands the Knesset as constitutive branch, and above the ordinary law of the Knesset stand the two Basic Laws.[77]

On this account, a historic event occurred in 1992. Israel's constitutional order was transformed from a model of parliamentary sovereignty to one of constitutional supremacy. In other words, Israel adopted a constitution, albeit one that did not correspond with a unique historical moment in the life of the nation: a "constitutional moment" in which, as Ackerman argued, the public becomes aware of and collectively deliberates over its constitution.[78] Yet from the outset, the legal status and significance of these Basic Laws was unclear and controversial, an uncertainty that rested upon several grounds.

First, the two Basic Laws on human rights passed by only slim majorities and with a small number of Knesset members present for the votes.[79] The votes occurred shortly before primary elections, which may explain the low legislative turnout. Whatever the reason, the absence of Knesset members raises a question of legitimacy—can or should a constitution be adopted by such a process?[80] Second, the issues raised by the Basic Laws gained minimal media coverage before and after their enactment. For example, Rubinstein, the "father" of these Laws, pointed out that "most of the media never told their readers that the Knesset had passed a law as revolutionary as Basic Law: Human Dignity and Liberty."[81] Third, it was questionable whether the Knesset members were attentive to the "revolution" they were producing. There was, in short, very little evidence of any public or political awareness of the Basic Laws' transformative importance, thus raising serious doubts about whether human rights enactments, ratified by an ordinary legislative procedure and by rather slim majorities of the Knesset, without public engagement or support, could achieve constitutional status.[82]

From a different perspective, the 1980s and early 1990s signaled the advent of a constitutional moment reflective of a substantial movement for revolutionary reforms challenging traditional constitutional principles. By the mid-1980s, the misdeeds of the Israeli multiparty structure had generated high levels of public distrust in the political system. Small parties were seen as the beneficiaries of the distortion that resulted from their leverage over governing coalitions.[83] During the later years of the decade and against this backdrop, a broad consensus emerged on the need to achieve a far-reaching reform of the political system. This led to the creation of a broad-based civil movement, "A Constitution for Israel," aspiring to implement a comprehensive formal constitutional document.[84] According to Daphne Barak-Erez, later a justice of the Supreme Court, the enactment of the Basic Laws cannot be abstracted from this reform-filled background. In language tinged with an Ackermanian accent, Barak-Erez noted: "[This is] a new constitutional moment, which is an appropriate time for fundamental constitutional changes, such as a new approach to judicial review. The new Basic Laws express the general expectations of the public amidst this constitutional moment."[85]

Significantly, the Constitution for Israel movement focused mainly on the relationship between the government and the legislature, advocating for direct election of the prime minister. The proposal that emerged from its efforts was entirely different from the two Basic Laws on human rights. Also, the movement supported the enactment of the proposed constitution by a two-thirds majority vote of the Knesset and its ratification by popular referendum, neither of which occurred.[86] Ultimately, as Gideon Sapir observed, "Clear evidence of a constitutional moment in Israel before the adoption of the Basic Laws and of marked public support for their enactment . . . is hard to find. The claim arguing that a crisis of trust prevailed between the public and the political system during the relevant period appears to be substantiated. No evidence, however, supports the claim stating that the significance of the constitutional revolution was presented to, discussed, and broadly supported by the public prior to the Knesset vote on the adoption of the new Basic Laws."[87]

We agree that there was no discernible constitutional moment. While, as Ran Hirschl pointed out, "the 1992 constitutionalization was a major catalyst in bringing about the unprecedented judicialization of politics in Israel," his controversial thesis concerning the constitutional revolution—that "[it] was driven primarily by a self-interested agenda"—underscored the absence of popular engagement that one would expect to find if the development had been a genuinely momentous constitutional departure.[88] One need not agree with Hirschl's rendering of the constitutional revolution as an effort by elites to insulate their policy preferences from the vicissitudes of democratic politics to find his depiction of the legislative process to be compatible with alternative accounts similarly dismissive of any necessary nexus between revolutionary constitutional transformation and self-conscious popular mobilization. In retrospect, the stirrings of a constitutional revolution can be seen in the modest but significant claims made in the *Bergman* case and in the more definitively delineated ambitions of the 1992 Basic Laws. It required an additional step, another Supreme Court case with *Marbury* overtones, to fully reveal the magnitude of the constitutional transformation that had occurred in Israel. Indeed, without this judicially driven effort there would have been no constitutional revolution.

The United Mizrahi Bank *Case*

In the years following enactment of the two 1992 Basic Laws, their legal status remained undecided. Without any provisions regarding their normative constitutional status, the prevailing understanding was, consistent with the earlier jurisprudence of the Supreme Court, that they have no superiority over ordinary legislation and should be treated as ordinary legislation until their unification into a full constitution.[89] This changed in 1995.

November 1995 stands out as one of the more consequential months in Israeli history. Prime Minister Itzhak Rabin was assassinated on November 4, in Tel Aviv, and five days later the Israeli Supreme Court decided the *United Mizrahi Bank* case.[90] Through its many pages, the constitutional revolution came into full view as nine judges confronted the fundamental questions regarding the legal status of the Basic Laws.[91] The Court's landmark judgment was delivered by Justice Aharon Barak. The Basic Laws, he argued, were enacted by the Knesset as the constitutional authority of Israel. Accordingly, the Basic Laws enjoyed a superior normative status in relation to ordinary legislation. The Knesset has limited legislative powers and is therefore unauthorized to enact statutes other than those that conform to the provisions of the Basic Laws. Finally, the Court possesses the authority to conduct judicial review of legislation and to invalidate laws that contradict the substantive provisions in the Basic Laws. While each of the justices wrote a separate opinion, in the following section we focus on the fundamental question of the Knesset's constituent authority as it was considered and debated in the opinions of Justices Shamgar and Barak, and in the dissenting opinion of Justice Cheshin. In particular, in highlighting the disagreement between Barak and Cheshin, we gain further insight into some of the challenging complexities encountered in the attempt to elucidate and clarify the concept of constitutional revolution.

THE "TWO CROWNS" THEORY

The nature of constituent power—the power to make a constitution—is one of the most complex ideas in constitutional theory. (It is the subject of the next chapter.) It is no wonder, then, that a principal question addressed in the *United Mizrahi Bank* case concerned the constituent power of the Knesset, that is, the authority of that body to enact constitutional norms that hold a higher normative status than that of ordinary legislation. The recognition of such a power would allow the Knesset to self-impose substantive limits on future legislation. It is hardly an exaggeration to say that the issues raised by the question were perhaps the most important ones ever deliberated on by the Court. As Justice Cheshin wrote, "The question of the Knesset's authority to limit itself (by constitution or law) is the most important question arising before the Court in the present case, and its importance far exceeds that of the other matters confronting us. In comparing them, I would say that this is one of the giants while those are Lilliputians. Furthermore, I dare say that since Israel has had a Supreme Court—from its inception to this very day—no greater or more important question has come before it than the question of the Knesset's constituent authority to frame a constitution for Israel."[92]

The Court was confronted with this challenge: Does the Knesset possess the authority to enact a constitution for the State of Israel? In accordance with its importance, the justices devoted over 350 pages to this crucial question. All the justices, with the exception of one member who did not address the issue, agreed that the Knesset had the power to bind itself in the future. Apart from Justice Cheshin, all the justices agreed that the Knesset possesses constituent power and thus has the authority to constitute constitutional norms having a higher normative value than ordinary laws. Most of the justices accepted Justice Barak's analysis—"the two crowns (or hats) theory"—according to which the Knesset holds both legislative authority and constituent authority, making it the authorized organ to constitute a constitution.[93]

Before discussing Barak's thesis, we must briefly consider Justice Meir Shamgar's alternative approach. Justice Shamgar rejected the "two crowns theory," arguing instead that the Knesset embodies absolute sovereignty and thus is entitled to create norms carrying different normative status. Instead of Barak's "dualist approach," Shamgar preferred a "monist" view that holds the Knesset to be sovereign and omnipotent.[94] Since the Knesset has the authority to enact ordinary laws, so too in this account does it have the authority to enact constitutional norms that would limit its own ordinary legislation.[95] Accepting the proposition that the omnipotent Knesset has absolute sovereignty leads one to the familiar paradox of how an omnipotent organ can bind itself.[96] If it can bind itself, then it is not omnipotent; if it cannot bind itself, then in like manner, it is not omnipotent. At a certain point in Shamgar's opinion, the concept of parliamentary omnipotence was further challenged by his own avowal that the Knesset's ability to bind itself might have its limits. He then raised a question for which no answer was provided: To what extent can the Knesset, either in its legislative or constituent capacity, infringe a basic right?[97] In the end, Justice Shamgar's theory did not illuminate the source of the Knesset's constituent authority.[98]

For Justice Barak, the Knesset wears two hats or crowns—the crown of legislative authority and the crown of constituent authority.[99] His starting point was that sovereignty belongs to the people. Accordingly, the question of the existence of constituent authority cannot be answered by the actions of the Knesset, but rather: "In order to frame a constitution, which will be placed above the law in the normative hierarchy, there must be an Archimedean foothold located outside the constitution or the law, which provides the Knesset with the authority to adopt a constitution. The constitution cannot create the authority by which it will be created."[100] To answer the key question whether the sovereign people provided the Knesset with a constituent authority, Justice Barak drew on the work of three of the twentieth century's most important legal philosophers: Hans Kelsen, H. L. A. Hart, and Ronald Dworkin. In all three theories, Barak found a positive answer to the fundamental question surrounding the derivation of constituent power.

Justice Barak first invoked Kelsen's *Grundnorm,* tracing constitutional continuity from the Provisional Council of State's Declaration of Establishment to the Constituent Assembly (the First Knesset), which then transferred its constituent power to future Knessets.[101] This historical survey directed him to conclude that "the constituent authority of the Constituent Assembly has rested continuously in the hands of the Knesset."[102] Hart's "rule of recognition" provided Barak further support for the Knesset's constituent power.[103] This is a rule concerning the legal validity of other rules, a secondary rule that determines how primary legal rules are created, and hence their normative status. According to Barak, "The rule of recognition of the State of Israel is that the Knesset is endowed with both constituent and legislative authority. This determination does not reflect a subjective judicial position. It reflects an objective position as to the 'system of national life' of the State of Israel. . . . The basic understanding of today's Israeli community—expressing our entire national experience—is our national consciousness that the Knesset is the body authorized to enact a constitution for Israel."[104] Then Justice Barak turned to Dworkin's work, in which "a given body . . . is empowered to enact the constitution for a country if that conclusion is the best interpretation of the body of social and legal history of that country."[105] Applying this model to Israel, "the most fitting interpretation of our history is that the Knesset is endowed with constituent authority."[106]

For Barak, then, the Knesset's embodiment of constituent authority legitimates the enactment of Basic Laws that represent different chapters in a cumulative constitution. Each chapter is positioned at the peak of the pyramid of norms. Ordinary legislation produced by the Knesset's legislative authority holds an inferior status to Basic Laws, products of the Knesset's constituent authority.[107] Consequently, a Basic Law, or any of its provisions, can be amended only by a norm carrying a similar normative status—another Basic Law or an ordinary law if the Basic Law expressly allows for it.[108] Similarly, ordinary legislation cannot affect the arrangements set forth in a Basic Law unless the Basic Law permits it.[109] The Basic Laws on human rights, for example, include limitation clauses, meaning that no legislation may infringe the rights protected in them unless certain substantive requirements are met. This is a substantive entrenchment. Therefore, an ordinary law that infringes the Basic Laws without meeting the substantive requirement of the limitation clauses is unconstitutional.[110]

Apart from recognition of the Knesset's constituent authority and the Basic Laws' constitutional status, central to the ruling in *Mizrahi Bank* was the acknowledgment of the Court's power to conduct judicial review. By concluding that the Basic Laws carry a superior constitutional normative status and that ordinary legislation cannot infringe their provisions, Barak insisted on the necessity of this power, citing *Marbury v. Madison* and its affirmation of the power to invalidate acts of a coordinate branch of government without express constitutional authorization.[111]

The justice then derived three rationales from the American experience. First is the "rule of law," or "rule of the constitution." When a legal system includes a constitution, the rule of law requires that the supremacy of the constitution be protected. Ordinary legislation that clashes with the constitution—in Israel, with a Basic Law—must be invalidated: "Strip the constitution of judicial review and you have removed its very life."[112] Second is the separation of powers, which legitimates the Court's obligation to interpret the constitution. This responsibility entails adjudicating disputes in accordance with the constitution, which may lead, in turn, to the invalidation of legislation.[113] Third is democracy itself. In relying on *Federalist* 78, Justice Barak, following Alexander Hamilton, claimed that when the Court reviews the constitutionality of legislation, it protects the superiority of the people, as declared in the constitution, over the legislative powers. Democracy rightly understood includes basic values and rights expressed in the constitution. When the Court conducts judicial review and invalidates laws that contradict the constitution, it expresses fundamental values of society that have developed over time.[114] As detailed in *Federalist* 78: "Nor does [judicial review] by any means suppose a superiority of the judicial to the legislative power. It only supposes that the power of the people is superior to both . . . which are not fundamental."[115]

The citation to *Marbury v. Madison* has telling significance when viewed within the broader revolutionary aims of Barak's transformative constitutional agenda. Thus, it is likely, for example, that he was familiar with the role that judicial review played in the progress toward the revolutionary break by the American colonies with their colonial rulers. In James Otis's famous argument in the *Writs of Assistance Case,* he penned these defiant words: "As to Acts of Parliament, an Act against the Constitution is void: an Act against natural equity is void: and if an Act of Parliament should be made, in the very words of this Petition, it would be void. The Executive Courts must pass such Acts into disuse."[116] Upon reading these words, the young John Adams declaimed, "The Child Revolution was born."[117] To the extent, then, that Justice Barak's *Mizrahi Bank* case opinion represented the culmination of the constitutional revolution precipitated by the enactment of the Basic Laws, his effort contained echoes of a similar exercise surrounding the adoption of what is now the world's oldest constitution. But that exercise did not go unchallenged, for the legitimacy of judicial review in U.S. constitutional development was contested from the outset by voices dissenting from the underlying assumptions about judicial review in the writings of John Marshall and Alexander Hamilton. These dissents had their parallel in Israel's constitutional revolution, beginning with the powerful dissent of Justice Mishael Cheshin.

"THE CONSTITUENT AUTHORITY—WAS IT YOU OR WAS I DREAMING?"

Cheshin's strong dissent insisted that the Knesset does not possess constituent power.[118] The First Knesset's constituent power could not possibly be passed on to future Knessets. For Justice Cheshin, the Knesset does not hold constituent power and Israel has no formal constitution. A constitution, after all, is launched at a celebrated event accompanied by "thunder and lightning, of thick cloud and the mighty sound of the trumpet," and not in a "still small voice."[119] It must be an occasion widely acknowledged by the people and the constitution-making body.

> Perhaps our perspective is limited, but to date we have yet to hear of a dispute over whether a particular body has the (historical and legal) authority to grant a constitution to the nation. And we certainly have not heard of this question arising as a legal issue given to judicial resolution. We have enough—more than enough—questions pertaining to the interpretation of the law and the interpretation of the constitution. We would at least have expected there to be dispute over the actual authority to enact a constitution. The very existence of disputes on this question indicates the tenuousness of the conclusion that the current Knesset possesses constituent authority.[120]

Justice Cheshin's argument begins with the Constituent Assembly, which he regards as singular, exceptional, and unique. While he does not dispute the constituent authority held by the Constituent Assembly (First Knesset), he views that body as the specifically designated master of the constituent power.[121] When it dispersed before framing a constitution, the Knesset's constituent power expired and the power it transferred was its ordinary legislative power, not its constituent power:

> The task of the Constituent Assembly to write a constitution was a specific, one-time mission. The authority of the Constituent Assembly to write a constitution could not be viewed as a property right, transferable at its owner's will. It was a kind of trust that the People's Council entrusted to the hands of the Constituent Authority, and a trust—as is known—is not transferable from person to person at the trustee's behest. . . . The Constituent Assembly was not empowered to transfer its constituent authority to another. . . . Neither the People's Council nor the people authorized the Constituent Assembly to transfer its authority to another body.[122]

What is more, how can an organ that possesses inferior authority transfer the sacred powers of a superior authoritative body? "Just as a person cannot save himself from drowning by pulling himself up by his own hair," Cheshin wrote, "the Knesset cannot empower another body to establish a constitution to which the Knesset would be subordinate."[123] Thus, in contrast with Justice Barak's majority opinion, Justice Cheshin rejected the notion of constitutional continuity.

To the claim that the Knesset understood that it maintained its constituent authority, Cheshin cited numerous comments made by Knesset members expressly stating that they lacked constituent authority. In response to Justice Barak's assertion that the vast majority of the Israeli legal community believed in the Knesset's constituent authority, a conclusion also evident from the Court's earlier judgments, Cheshin disputed that a scholarly consensus supported the two-crown doctrine, or that earlier case law compelled recognition of the Knesset's constituent authority. He pointed to previous cases acknowledging the Knesset's authority formally to entrench laws against changing a Basic Law, as well as its authority to invalidate laws that violate entrenched provisions. Yet he found no references in case law affirming the constituent authority of the Knesset as the basis for the Knesset's decisions. As for the "national consensus" of Israeli society, the justice maintained that the Court simply did not know the current views of society, even as he then opined that no such consensus existed regarding the Knesset's constituent authority.[124]

To be clear, Justice Cheshin opposed the Court's creation of a constitution, not the desirability of having a constitution:

> Let the act be done and let a constitution be adopted. But it should be performed in the way of all the nations. Let a constitution be drafted and submitted for a referendum. Let the constitution be adopted in a process of six readings spread out over the two Knessets. Let any act be done, provided that it involves a substantial deviation from regular legislative proceedings, and provided that the people are involved in the enactment of the constitution. All of these are legitimate acts, and we will acquiesce to them and cherish them. But with all my might I will oppose our recognition of the Knesset's authority to enact a constitution by force of a judicial ruling, via a legal analysis of a document dating back forty-seven years, in reliance on disputed conceptions which have no firm roots in Israeli society.[125]

In effect, Justice Cheshin was demanding a constitutional moment: "We must remember that a constitution is and should be written at a propitious hour, when the heavens open to hear our petitions, at a momentous turning point in the life of the nation."[126]

Notwithstanding Cheshin's disagreements about fundamental issues, at the core of which was his rejection of the existence of constituent authority in the Knesset, in cases following the *Mizrahi Bank,* he no longer questioned the Court's controversial ruling.[127] For example, in a case in which Justice Barak wrote an opinion invalidating provisions of a law based upon its violation of Basic Law: Freedom of Occupation, Cheshin wrote, "I agree with my friend President Barak's judgment, and I have nothing to add."[128] His statement was interpreted as endorsing the decision in *Mizrahi Bank,* and indeed while still a member of the Court, Cheshin never repeated his belief that the Basic Laws lacked the elevated constitutional status he had earlier contested.[129]

After his retirement, however, the justice maintained that he had not in fact changed his mind about the views he expressed in *Mizrahi Bank*. Respecting the question of constituent authority, he affirmed that he still had not heard anything to dissuade him of his previously articulated position. In characteristically vivid terms, he argued that the granting of constituent authority to the Knesset in *Mizrahi Bank* was comparable to "witchcraft," "alchemy at its best," or "the creation of something from nothingness": "One night we went to sleep without a constitution, and the next morning the sun has wakened us and notified us that we had been awarded a constitution. I believe there is not, and never has been, a nation—in all of human history—in which a court granted a constituent authority to one of the state's authorities. This is not the manner to constitute a constituent authority. This is not the manner to adopt a constitution."[130] Cheshin repeated his view that the Constituent Assembly, under the name it gave itself—the First Knesset—was therefore not authorized by the people to pass its constituent authority to another organ. Consequently, the time to establish a constitution had passed. As for the renowned theories of H. L. A. Hart, Hans Kelsen, and Ronald Dworkin: "I allow myself to assume that Hart and Kelsen, RIP, were turning in their graves with amazement, and Dworkin was shrugging his shoulders uneasily, when hearing the theory concerning the Knesset's constituent authority."[131] Nonetheless, despite his serious misgivings concerning the Court's groundbreaking reasoning, the fact that the constitutional revolution had been accepted—however grudgingly while Cheshin was still adjudicating—by its strongest opponent on the bench suggests how profound was the shift in the underlying assumptions of Israeli constitutionalism.

But the legitimacy of the shift would remain a much-contested issue. We can see in the judicial encounter between the two justices more than a disagreement over the number of hats the Knesset is entitled to wear, or the authority of the Supreme Court to decide that it is either one or two. Their dispute in the *Mizrahi Bank* case was also about the deeper, theoretically vexed issues surrounding the legitimacy of the constitutional revolution. In denying that the Knesset in 1992 could rightfully possess and exercise constituent authority, Justice Cheshin took the position that any such authority had to be grounded in a clear and specific decision to transfer the constitution-making power from one Knesset to another. In the absence of such a decision, which for Cheshin was surely the case in Israel, the only way in which the constitutional order could legitimately undergo radical transformation was if the regime modification emerged from a process "involv[ing] a deviation from regular legislative proceedings."[132] Such a process could take different forms—maybe through the use of a referendum—as long as it made the people the source of constitutive reordering. Hence, the idea that the judiciary, an institution without any generally recognized popular connection, should take up the task of constitutional enactment was simply unacceptable. Regardless, then, of the substance of the changes that might accompany a procedurally incorrect restructuring of constitutional arrangements, the constitutional revolution would be burdened with the taint of its illicit origins.

For Justice Barak, things were more complicated. He did not concede the elevated ground of popular sovereignty to Justice Cheshin, invoking Kelsen and others to argue for the continuity of constituent authority, all traceable to the "Archimedean foothold located outside the constitution or the law," namely, the people. Thus, it cannot be said that Barak was indifferent to a process-based criterion for affirming the reality of the constitutional revolution. But that affirmation was made by the Supreme Court through an interpretative exercise resulting in a fundamentally transformed constitutional order. At the core of the new order was the elevation to constitutional status of human rights in Israel. That they were now functioning parts of the nation's constitution took precedence over their derivation, which, as was evident from Barak's disagreement with both Cheshin and Shamgar, was a highly contestable matter. As Cheshin pointed out, the very controversy rendered tenuous any conclusion about the Knesset's constituent authority. Nonetheless, at least for Justice Barak, there was nothing tenuous about the newly achieved normative status of dignity-based rights or about the authority of the judiciary to ensure their protection. It was the substance of these changes that legitimated the constitutional revolution.

The Revolution Continued

The enactment of the Basic Laws on human rights in 1992 and the *Mizrahi Bank* decision, which provided these Basic Laws with a constitutional status and a judicial enforcement mechanism, together marked a revolutionary development in the advancement of the Israeli constitutional order. Nevertheless, with the inclusion of limitations on the Knesset's legislative powers in the two Basic Laws on human rights, judicial acknowledgment of the substantive entrenchment had only a limited effect. The rest of the institutional Basic Laws did not include any substantive entrenchment, and only a few provisions included formal entrenchment. Since the *Mizrahi Bank* decision focused on those Basic Laws that included substantive entrenchment in the form of limitation clauses, the answer to the question whether—and by which manner—ordinary legislation could infringe a provision in an institutional basic law that did not include a limitation clause remained ambiguous.

A jurisprudential step to resolve this uncertainty occurred some years later. In the *Herut* case of 2003 concerning Basic Law: The Judiciary, Justice Barak held that the Basic Law is a "constitutional, superior law." He asserted, "An ordinary legal provision does not have the power to change a provision of a Basic Law. . . . Similarly, a regular law does not have the power to infringe upon the provisions of a Basic Law, unless such is allowed by the limitations clauses which are part of the Basic Laws themselves."[133] Accordingly, as legal scholars noted, the Court had changed its previous approach: an ordinary statute could no longer violate a Basic Law even if the latter did not include a limitation clause. Amnon Reichman suggested that the effects of this judgment amounted to a revolutionary transformation; another commentator, Ariel Bendor, considered the significance of what transpired to be nothing short of a "constitutional revolution."[134] Others considered it unlikely that this sort of revolution could occur as a result of a single vague phrase that purportedly contradicted earlier jurisprudence.[135]

On balance, it is hard to deny that what occurred amounted to a fundamental change in jurisprudential understanding. The judgment elevated the ranking of the older, institutional Basic Laws to a supralegal constitutional status, thus expanding the *Mizrahi Bank* ruling to all Basic Laws. Indeed, in other judgments it was stated that all Basic Laws—not only those concerning human rights—carry a superior constitutional status.[136] Their status thus became equivalent to that of the Basic Laws on human rights, and therefore an ordinary statute could no longer change or violate any Basic Law. Henceforth, this would be the governing understanding concerning the relationship between statutes of different hierarchy.

One persistent problem, however, was that the institutional Basic Laws did not include limitation clauses. This difficulty was raised in a case concerning the equality of elections principle provided in Basic Law: The Knesset. Justice Yitzhak Zamir suggested that infringement of the constitutional right to equality in elections was one that did not conform to the conditions of the limitation clause as provided in the Basic Laws on human rights. This suggestion, Justice Barak replied, could lead to the development of a "judicial limitation clause" in situations where the Basic Law does not include such an explicit provision.[137] Against the backdrop of this case, this phase of the constitutional revolution reached its apex in the *Mofaz* case, which concerned regular legislation infringing the right to be elected and the right to equality in elections, both constitutional rights enumerated in Basic Law: The Knesset.[138] In his ruling, Justice Eliyahu Mazza held that the infringement was constitutional because it complied with the tests of the limitation clause. The Court thus created an implied limitation clause in the older Basic Law.[139]

According to (now) Professor Barak, the "importation" of the limitation clause into the institutional Basic Laws was the natural outcome of the acceptance of the Knesset's status as a constituent authority. Thus, for Barak, the *Herut* judgment should not be regarded as another "constitutional revolution," as some claimed, but rather as a development of the original constitutional revolution's inner logic. Whether viewed as a stand-alone constitutional revolution or the extension of an earlier break, it represented a major component of the paradigm shift in constitutional understanding.

This revolutionary departure was accompanied by another important constitutional transformation concerning the constitutional status of unenumerated rights. Recall that for historical-political reasons, the Basic Laws concerning human rights did not include a comprehensive list of political and social human rights. Thus, the two Basic Laws explicitly excluded equality, freedom of expression, freedom of religion, and other rights.[140] This was the main compromise that enabled the enactment of the Basic Laws on human rights. Notwithstanding this explicit omission, the Court began expanding the scope of the rights protected by the Basic Laws, focusing on the right to dignity as a framework right that encompassed other basic rights.[141] The Supreme Court took the position that at the core of dignity is the autonomy of the person. Dignity means recognizing a person as a free being who develops his or her body and mind as he or she sees fit.[142] This was the backdrop for judicial affirmations of the constitutional right of human dignity as inclusive of the right to equality, freedom of expression,[143] and protection from the degradation of discrimination.[144] So, for example, a hungry person is a person whose human dignity has been impaired, as is a person without shelter or access to basic medical treatment. And so the right to human dignity included properties of social rights.[145]

In a series of judicial decisions that followed the *Mizrahi Bank* case, the Supreme Court decided that regardless of the fact that certain fundamental rights, such as equality, were not explicitly included in the two Basic Laws on human rights, certain fundamental aspects of these rights should be inferred from the explicitly protected right of human dignity. On the basis of this capacious interpretation of human dignity, the Court ruled that elements of the rights to equality and freedom of expression carry a constitutional status.[146] Congruently, any new legislative enactment by the Knesset that violated equality, for example, would have to meet the terms set forth in the Basic Law: Human Dignity and Liberty. As aptly noted by Suzie Navot, this dramatic development "is surely a revolution in itself."[147]

Constitutional Revolution by Whom?

How should one describe the constitutional changes in Israel? Some argued that "the proper way to characterize these developments is as a 'Constitutional Evolution' rather than a 'Constitutional Revolution.' "[148] Others, such as Justice Yitzhak Zamir, contended that the constitutional revolution did not occur when the Basic Laws regarding human rights were passed, but many years before, in the *Bergman* case.

> Justice Landau's opinion in that decision began a revolution, because it came to the legal community as a complete surprise and introduced a fundamental change: it reversed what had until then constituted the axiomatic view of the status of the Knesset, the status of the Court, and the relationship between them. . . . The constitutional revolution of the Bergman decision

> was, like all successful revolutions, only the first stage in a long, complex process. It paved the way for the second stage of the revolution, which commenced approximately three years ago, with Basic Law: Human Dignity and Liberty and Basic Law: Freedom of Occupation. Although the practical importance of this stage inestimably surpasses the importance of the first stage, it does not represent a theoretical breakthrough. . . . The laws expand the principle that was established in the Bergman decision, and that has since become generally accepted, that the Knesset can limit itself through a Basic Law.[149]

For both supporters and opponents of the constitutional revolution, it is clear that the governing legal regime that followed the *Bergman* case was dramatically altered following the *Mizrahi Bank* case.[150] The decision "revolutionized Israel's constitutional law."[151] A constitutional revolution occurred in Israel in the mid-1990s. But did the revolution occur in 1992 with the enactment of the Basic Laws on human rights, or in 1995 with the *Mizrahi Bank* case?

By one account, the constitutional revolution was traceable to the Knesset's enactment of the two Basic Laws on human rights, a move that explicitly limited the legislative powers of the Knesset through the limitation clause. The Court was simply a vehicle for fulfilling the legislature's will. According to this approach, in the *Mizrahi Bank* case the Supreme Court was merely *"la bouche qui prononce les paroles de la loi"* ("the mouth that pronounces the words of the law"), to use Montesquieu's formulation, simply applying the norms provided by the lawgiver.[152] Barak himself claimed that the constitutional revolution was brought about by the Knesset.[153] Similarly, Uriel Lin, the chair of the Constitution, Law and Justice Committee in the Knesset at the time of the enactment of the two Basic Laws on human rights, argued: "The constitutional revolution in Israel began when the Knesset completed in March 1992 the enactment of Basic-Law: Freedom of Occupation and following which Basic-Law: Human Dignity and Liberty."[154]

We contend, however, that this tells only part of the story. The revolution might have been triggered by *Bergman* and the enactment of these two Basic Laws, but it came to fruition only in the following years, through the purposeful efforts of the judiciary. Indeed, Barak said:

> [The Knesset's] constitutive action at the time was an essential condition to the constitutional revolution. Yet it was not sufficient. The constitutional revolution would have not taken place in 1992 had the court not recognized the power of the Knesset to constitute a constitution, and had it not held that the Knesset has exercised this power. . . . The constitutional revolution was enabled in 1992 thanks to the cooperation between the constituent branch and the judicial branch. Each of these two branches could not have brought about the revolution in its own action. Only the power unification between the Knesset and the court led to the constitutional revolution.[155]

For Barak, the enactment of the two Basic Laws was significant, even if it was not regarded that way by the Knesset members at the time. It enabled the Supreme Court to legitimize judicial review and establish the "normative superiority" of rights. It was a revolutionary achievement, even if it stemmed from the workings of the lawmaking system.

As we see it, the revolution coincided with the ruling in the *Mizrahi Bank* case. In each of the issues decided in that case—the Knesset's constituent authority, the legal status of the Basic Laws and their relationship with ordinary laws, and the judicial review power—the Court had considerable discretion and could have reached different outcomes. Such outcomes would have been eminently defensible and would not have led to a paradigm shift in constitutional practice and understanding. One need only imagine an alternative reality in which Justice Cheshin's opinion was the majority opinion. The Knesset would not possess constituent authority, leaving the Basic Laws without constitutional status. Hence, no constitutional revolution.

Important as the Knesset's role as constituent legislator undoubtedly was, it was the Court's activism that made possible the revolutionary changes in constitutional norms and practices. As one of us has previously argued, the revolutionary content of the Basic Laws on human rights inhered less in the substantive changes introduced by their enactment than it did in the possibilities latent within them for creative judicial intervention in the unresolved problem of regime definition.[156] Frank Michelman noted that "the onset of a formal constitution for Israel by a judicially cognized act of sovereignty authoriz[ing] higher lawmaking" was the "constitutional revolution."[157] In all three phases described in this chapter—the *Mizrahi Bank* case, the elevation of the constitutional status of the older, institutional Basic Laws, and the elevation of unenumerated rights (some of which were intentionally excluded from the Basic Laws on human rights) to a constitutional status—the Court's exercise of judicial discretion had profoundly consequential results for the development of Israeli constitutionalism.[158] The judicial recognition of the Knesset's constituent authority, of the constitutional status of the Basic Laws on human rights, of the power of judicial review, in addition to the series of judicial decisions concerning the constitutional status of the older Basic Laws and of unenumerated rights, have all produced a radical change in the overall structure of Israeli constitutional law, eventually transforming Israel from a "parliamentary sovereignty" system to a "constitutional democracy." As the late Justice Moshe Landau put it, the Israeli constitution is "the only one in the world created by the mouth . . . of the court."[159]

A Counterrevolution?

Justice Cheshin expressed his discomfort with the term "constitutional revolution" in the *Mizrahi Bank* case: "I find the label 'revolution' to be problematic. Is it not enough to say that there has been a 'change' in the legal system? And I say this because labels—in themselves—may sometimes blind us and make for self-fulfilling aspirations. . . . However, to what extent a 'revolution' has transpired, only time will tell."[160] It now appears that the revolution has had a substantial impact on the Israeli legal order. The human rights established in the two Basic Laws concerning human rights (including unenumerated rights) were accorded a constitutional, supralegislative status, and the legislative power of the Knesset was decisively limited.[161] From the *Mizrahi Bank* case to the present, the Court has invalidated eighteen statutory provisions for their unconstitutionality.[162] Viewed in its entirety, this development has amounted to more than a "human rights revolution," since it has had sweeping implications. Every branch of law and every legal norm has had to conform to this new constitutional regime. Israeli law was fundamentally constitutionalized.[163] In retrospect, whatever the members of the Knesset had understood or believed they had achieved with the enactment of the Basic Laws on human rights, a downstream result of their efforts was that the political branches have internalized the idea that their legislative and executive powers are now limited by constitutional norms. After the constitutional revolution, effective mechanisms of constitutional scrutiny were put in place within the government and within the Knesset itself, and the constitutionality of all legislative initiatives must be carefully examined by legal advisers to the Knesset and the government.[164] "Although of course still to this day contested in Israeli legal and political circles," Michelman correctly observed, Barak's account, by which the Knesset established a formal constitution for Israel by exercising constituent authority, "seems to have settled widely into daily Israeli political practice and legal argument."[165] The intensive involvement of legal gatekeepers in political decision-making processes and the countermajoritarian judicial defense of rights and freedoms were effectively established through tacit political consent. To be sure, the *Mizrahi Bank* case naturally attracted criticism from the political branches, triggering often-heated exchanges between the legislature and the judiciary.[166] Yet despite some sharp disparagement by opponents of the constitutional revolution, the Basic Laws on human rights have not been repealed;[167] indeed, their exalted status has led many to perceive the Israeli constitutional revolution as a liberal-democratic success story.[168]

Nevertheless, along with the many tributes engendered by the constitutional revolution, exertions by the Court have been attacked in both domestic and international arenas.[169] Critical observers at home and abroad often described the Israeli judiciary as perhaps "the most activist in the world."[170] Hardly, then, is it surprising that the constitutional revolution and the expanding scope of judicial review have been increasingly contested, first by narrow legal circles within Israeli society, and subsequently by political groups and in the public at large.[171]

As Yoav Dotan noted: "The wave of opposition to the court's activist policies intensified throughout the 2000s and reached its peak (at least for now) toward the end of that decade. Open attacks on the court's activism became commonplace within the Israeli media by politicians, bureaucrats, top columnists, and even law professors. This wave of criticism has been accompanied by a sharp decrease in public trust in the Court."[172] It was to be expected that the judiciary's dominant role in the broader constitutional project would raise substantial questions regarding its democratic legitimacy. As Wojciech Sadurski pointed out in relation to the Israeli case, it is a matter of profound significance whether constitutional judicial review is created through a contractual constitution (or with a significant constitution-making stage preceding it), or through a situation in which the most powerful tribunal essentially gives itself constitutional authority over the Parliament or the public. In the latter case, the very existence of judicial review becomes a focal point for contentious debate, and the supervisory function of the Court will always be exercised "in the shadow of this original sin."[173]

Many opponents of the constitutional revolution characterize it as an elite project featuring the creation of a constitution without popular input. Whether attributable to a self-serving "former hegemonic" elite or the new judicial elite, the idea that a constitutional revolution was engineered in the absence of wider public involvement hovers over constitutional development.[174] And this lack of contribution by the public can have ominous implications: "How much of a distance yet remains between the judicial elite and the body politic is a matter of immense importance to the fate of the 'constitutional revolution.' "[175]

Here we are reminded of the Hungarian case, an elite-led constitutional transition that produced a Constitutional Court whose activism contributed to the seismic backlash that culminated in 2010 in what many have described as a "constitutional coup." The constitutional revolution suffered from a legitimation deficit, built as it was on a suspect democratic foundation and poor levels of popular participation. It thus proved to be inadequately prepared for the unsettling social and political forces aiming to counter the revolution. In Hungary as in Israel, there was a struggle between the universalist liberal-secular values advanced by the constitutional revolution, and particularistic national-religious values promoted by those who were determined to counter it. This struggle of values was exacerbated when the organ aiming to advance the revolution was the judiciary. The Hungarian Constitutional Court's "invisible constitution" jurisprudence, much like the Israeli Supreme Court's expansive reading of human dignity, projected the idea that the judiciary and not the people or their elective representatives would determine the meaning of the constitutional revolution. Such activist intrusion into political conflicts naturally triggered a constitutional backlash.[176] In Hungary, the backlash resulted in the curtailing of the Court's power of judicial review and ultimately in the rise of an illiberal regime.

As in Hungary, the backlash in Israel manifested itself mainly in recurring demands for structural reforms to restrain the judiciary.[177] That the commencement of this backlash corresponded with the retirement of Justice Barak from the Court is doubtless not a coincidence.[178] Additionally, the emergence of new elites, coupled with the strengthening of a political right wing committed to promoting a more nationalistic vision of the state, has led to significant political and public assaults on the symbolic values as well as the functional outcomes of the constitutional revolution. At the time of this writing, Israel is experiencing a counterrevolution to the constitutional revolution, with the Supreme Court absorbing the most sustained political attack in its history.[179]

The constitutional revolution, it has been argued, "consolidated the religious and nationalist political and social groups that oppose the Court's liberal project." This coalition has been busy: "These groups have not only leveled persistent, sharp criticism of particular decisions of the Supreme Court, and continuously worked for undermining the legitimacy and credibility of the Supreme Court; they also came out with many initiatives meant to threaten the Supreme Court and by that to constrain its decision-making freedom."[180] Such counterrevolutionary tactics are perhaps most visible in the ever-increasing attempts to limit the Court's competence to conduct judicial review. These attempts involve multiple legislative proposals seeking a major curtailment of judicial power: by inserting an override clause into Basic Law: Human Dignity and Liberty; by limiting the Court's ability to review interparliamentary proceedings or the government's decisions; by limiting the ability to petition the Supreme Court in matters of constitutional rights violations; by changing the manner of voting in the judicial selection committee; by abandoning the seniority principle through which the most veteran Supreme Court justice takes over as president of the Court when its president retires. These attempts are abetted by a coalition of politicians arrayed against the Court, including the minister of justice, Ayelet Shaked, who has warned against judicial activism and has sought the nomination of conservatively inclined judges. Drawing upon increasingly accepted populist sentiments, she has portrayed the Supreme Court as an elite group that treats the people as the enemy: "In the eyes of the court the 'demos' has become a demon." The Court's invalidation of the Knesset's legislation reveals "a disconnect between some of the old elite from the realities of life."[181]

Consistent with this view, Shaked has declared that "Zionism should not continue, and it will not continue to bow down to the system of individual rights."[182] This declaration is reflective of a discourse that places national values above and superior to individual rights.[183] In line with this ascriptively inflected mind-set, the dominant political coalition has enacted the "Basic Law: Israel as the Nation-State of the Jewish People" (Basic Law: The Nation-State). While this controversial law declares the obvious—that Israel is the homeland of the Jewish people—it is notable for affirming that "the exercise of the right to national self-determination in the State of Israel is unique to the Jewish People."[184] Additionally, it lacks any mention of the democratic character of the state (in contrast with the Basic Laws on human rights, which stipulate that Israel is a "Jewish and Democratic" State); nor does it invoke the Declaration of Establishment's assertion that the State of Israel "will ensure complete equality of social and political rights to all its inhabitants irrespective of religion."[185] Enacted on the very last day of the Knesset's summer session in July 2018 by a slim 62–55 majority, the Basic Law targets the state's national and constitutional identity, seeking to shift the balance between the state's "Jewish and Democratic" commitments in favor of the former.[186] As Menachem Mautner noted, the adoption of Basic Law: The Nation-State occurred at the height of "the animosity of Israeli Religious-Zionists and Israeli nationalists to the constitutional project of the Court," and was a "measure aimed at offsetting the constitutional project on which the Court embarked in the years following the enactment of the two Basic Laws of 1992 and the Bank HaMizrahi decision of 1995."[187]

As of this writing, petitions attacking the constitutionality of the Basic Law have been submitted to the Supreme Court. As stated in one of them, "[The] act of grounding the constitutional identity of the state in exclusionary principles negates the legitimacy of the entire constitutional and political regime."[188] Borrowing from the conceptual tool kit of Bruce Ackerman, the petition portrays the Basic Law as a "constitutional moment" in Israeli history, a "new beginning" that represents the end of any pretense of democratic governance.[189] Unlike Germany, Israel lacks an explicit eternity clause, and unlike its Indian counterpart, the Supreme Court has never adopted the constitutional-amendment-nullifying methodology of the basic structure doctrine.[190] Indeed, the very authority of the Supreme Court to review the Basic Law is unclear. Although highly unlikely, should the Court intervene in agreement with the petitions, there could very well be a political response similar to what occurred in Hungary—enactment of an explicit constitutional provision prohibiting judicial review of constitutional norms. As former minister Shaked warned, if the Supreme Court invalidates Basic Law: The Nation-State, it would be "an earthquake that would start a war between the branches."[191]

In part, at least, the constitutional revolution represents an ambitious effort to reconcile the contradictions of the founding legacy of the Israeli polity, thereby rendering the universalistic and particularistic strands of that tradition more harmonious and whole. If so, then the political reaction to this judicially propelled campaign arouses concerns that the Court's expansion of its powers before the congealing of a popular consensus on fundamental issues of nationhood could undermine its clout as an institution within the broader political system.

While the Court has continued actively to intervene in many sensitive arenas of Israeli society—political, military, and religious—invalidating legislation deemed transgressive of constitutionally protected rights, it has developed a variety of judicial tools that allow it to proceed cautiously and with restraint as part of its ongoing and often contentious dialogue with the Knesset.[192] Still, Mautner argues, in retrospect, Justice Barak's use of "the most prominent instrument of liberal law: a written constitution," in order "to fixate the affiliation of Israeli law to liberal political theory and tradition," eventually "weakened the Israeli Supreme Court, the primary agent for the introduction of liberal values into Israel's political culture."[193] Because society has grown increasingly nationalistic and religious, the argument goes, the Court's constitutional revolution was "a grave mistake" in the "ongoing struggle to entrench liberal values in the face of a political culture."[194] On this, the verdict of history is not yet in. What can, though, be said with greater confidence is that the durability of Israel's revolutionary reorientation in constitutional priorities and practices will depend on the extent to which its advancement is pursued with circumspection and prudence.

Disagreements over foundational issues derailed the original plan to enact a comprehensive formal constitution in Israel. For over forty years, the polity operated under the principle of parliamentary sovereignty, leaving the significance of the two Basic Laws for the legal order extremely opaque at the time of their enactment. Yet after only three years, their constitutive centrality was judicially acknowledged in the *Mizrahi Bank* case. The justices declared the Basic Laws to be of constitutional status, superior to ordinary legislation, with the Court henceforth having the authority to conduct judicial review and to invalidate legislation conflicting with the Basic Laws. All that occurred without a formal, rigid constitution.[195]

The judicial decision shocked the legal community. Can a constitution-making process go on for decades? Can a court essentially proclaim the arrival of a constitution? As Suzie Navot wondered, "Is it even possible to create a constitutional text if the body that creates it is devoid of pouvoir constituant?"[196] While the enactment of the Basic Laws was a crucial step in Israel's constitutional revolution, a *conditio sine qua non* (indispensable condition) of the revolution, it was the judgment in the *Mizrahi Bank* case that ultimately constituted the transformation. What was only imaginable in 1992 came to fruition in 1995.

In the *Mizrahi Bank* case, Justice Barak, who championed the terminology of constitutional revolution, referred to the unique character of Israel's constitution making: "As in many countries . . . our constitution is the product of natural social development. It results from a continuing 'evolution,' not a one-time 'revolution.' . . . Moreover, preparation of the Israeli constitution took place over an extended period without parallel in the constitutional history of other countries. . . . It is unusual for the constitutional enterprise to continue for more than forty years. For a variety of political and social reasons this has occurred in Israel. . . . Indeed, we are different from other nations, even in the enactment of our constitution."[197]

The differences adverted to by Justice Barak speak to the particular characteristics of Israel's political and social history that led it to follow a path of constitutional development that is distinctive in form. But this path can also be seen as conforming to one of the two permutations outlined in chapter 2 for conceptualizing constitutional revolution. In pointing out that the Israeli constitution did not result from "a one-time revolution," Barak rightly distinguished what happened in his country from what occurred in places where constitutional revolutions took the form of a governing set of rules and principles establishing a constitutional order based on a political revolution that overthrew a previous regime. Instead, as Barak tacitly acknowledged, the Israeli experience was one in which, as we have seen in other contexts, major transformation in the constitutional order emerged from within the parameters of an extant legal-political setting. The "extended period of time" to which Barak referred in this connection was not a unique feature of this permutation; what stood out was the role of the judiciary as the lead revolutionary actor in the constitutional narrative.

Justice Barak was at the forefront of this endeavor, but his involvement, and indeed that of the other players in this effort, should be viewed against the backdrop of the dynamic driving the change in constitutional identity that is the essence of constitutional revolution. Specifically, the disharmonies of constitutional politics create the conditions out of which fundamental change sometimes occurs. In the case of Israel, this dissonance was embedded in the aspirations of competing political institutions, each of which embodied more fully than the other a foundational element of the nation's conflicted constitutional tradition. One way to comprehend the result in the *Mizrahi Bank* case is to see it as the ascendance of one of these institutions (the judiciary) relative to another (the legislature) with the enhanced possibility that this shifting power balance would culminate in a corresponding recalibrating of foundational priorities.

Exactly how? Justice Barak, in reflecting on the constitutional revolution, commented: "The judiciary must be aware of the fundamental values of the people. It must balance them in accordance with the values of the 'enlightened general public.'"[198] He went on: "[Constitutional] interpretation must base itself on the historical continuance of the nation's creation, with the intention of achieving unity and constitutional harmony." If the objective of judicial power was to achieve a value consensus consistent with the tenets of enlightened public opinion, then the counterrevolutionary exertions by political actors responsive to a decidedly different sector of Israeli public opinion—one less secular and more critical of an enlightened worldview—reveal just how challenging, perhaps even impossible, implementing Barak's intention may turn out to be.

The judiciary's approach, Mautner notes, "could not have been perceived by the Jewish religious groups other than as a unilateral, forcible and coercive move made by its rival—in the 'war of cultures' (kulturkampf), the secular group—with the aim of offsetting its losses in the political and cultural arenas by way of determining that even without an initiated, conscious and inclusive process of constitution-making, a liberal constitution had been created in Israel, nonetheless."[199]

Implementing the intention, however, is even more revealing with respect to our "disharmonic understanding" of the *Mizrahi Bank* case as the critical event in Israel's constitutional revolution. Thus, Basic Law: Human Dignity required upholding "the values of the State of Israel as a Jewish and democratic State." Recall that the tension between these values loomed large in explaining the First Knesset's failure to adopt a formal constitution. There were many who agreed with the sentiment expressed by one commentator who warned after the Court's ruling, "It is a mistake to embrace a constitution that in one swift move burdens the judiciary with the enormous responsibility of formulating the resolution of a schism that is an immanent feature of Jewish social existence."[200] Justice Barak was not one of them. As he wrote, "The content of the phrase 'Jewish state' will be determined by the level of abstraction which shall be given it. In my opinion, one should give this phrase meaning on a high level of abstraction, which will unite all members of society and find the common ground among them. The level of abstraction should be so high, until it becomes identical to the democratic nature of the state."[201] In essence, the purpose of Justice Barak and his Court in 1995 was to resolve the disharmonic dilemma of Israeli constitutional politics through a paradigmatic displacement in the way constitutionalism is experienced in Israel. Whatever one might think of what followed, these justices fashioned a constitutional revolution.

We conclude by returning to the words of Justice Mishael Cheshin that began this chapter, when in the *Mizrahi Bank* case he claimed that "the very existence of authority to frame a constitution" should be self-evident. But how likely is this to be the case? How real is such an authority? In the next chapter, we shift our inquiry to the nature of the constitution-making power in order to examine its complexities and to demonstrate how constitutional revolutions challenge some of the basic premises underlying the concept of the constitution-making power.

7
Constitutional Revolutions and Constituent Power

> Constitutionalism, and more especially Democracy, presupposes an active group of citizens who are ready to assume responsibility and become the "constituent power."
>
> Carl J. Friedrich

"REVOLUTIONS," HANNAH ARENDT WROTE, "are the only political events which confront us directly and inevitably with the problem of beginning."[1] For Arendt, as we noted in chapter 2, the term "revolution" is associated with a violent rupture in political continuity, and hence a "constitutional revolution" describes the postviolence liberation adoption of a constitution. Our concept of revolution in the constitutional sense does not require violence, since it shifts the focus from the process of change to the content or substance of the constitutive arrangements produced by that process, even if achieved legally, as in Israel, South Africa, and Hungary. There is an important link, though, between our concept of revolution and Arendt's; both confront us with the question of beginning—in Arendt, after a violent rupture, and in ours, after a new beginning often made under the rule of law. Consideration of the initiation or origins of constitutional ordering, regardless of the process whereby it is achieved, brings into play the concept of constituent power.

What is constituent power? Simply put, constituent power is the power to create and re-create the constitutional order. In democratic settings, this power is said to rest with "the people": "The constitution is . . . an expression of the constituent power of the people to make and re-make the institutional arrangements through which they are governed."[2] The idea of the people's constituent power has its origin in early modern legal thought, its first articulations having appeared in the English revolutionary debates of the mid-seventeenth century.[3] It was more fully articulated during the French and American Revolutions, so the concept of constituent power is commonly used in its French form: *pouvoir constituant*.[4] The notion of constituent power is usually traced back to the works of Jean-Jacques Rousseau and Emmanuel Joseph Sieyès.

While Rousseau is famous for the idea of the social contract, Joel I. Colón-Ríos has shown how Rousseau's political writings, though often missing from the literature on constituent power, actually center on a participatory conception of constituent power by, first, advancing a clear distinction—to which we return later in this chapter—between the sovereign people (holding constituent power) and the ordinary institutions of government (holding constituted powers), and by providing institutional alternatives to facilitate the exercise of constituent power.[5] Whereas Rousseau influenced the conceptualization of constituent power, the greatest theorist of constituent power and the one to whom the concept is often attributed is Abbé Emmanuel Joseph Sieyès, who developed a modern account of the people's constituent power.[6]

In a speech before the National Assembly in 1789, Sieyès famously declared that "a constitution presupposes a constituent power."[7] In his famous *Qu'est-ce que le Tiers état?* (*What Is the Third Estate?*), Sieyès wrote that "in each of its parts a constitution is not the work of a constituted power but a constituent power."[8] The latter is the extraordinary power to form a constitution, the immediate expression of the nation, and thus its representative. It is independent of any constitutional forms and restrictions. The former is the power created by the constitution, an ordinary, limited power that functions according to the forms and modes that the nation grants it in positive law.[9] These constituted powers are commonly the three governmental institutions of legislature, executive, and judiciary, which are separated and have a certain balanced relationship. Sieyès thus managed to apply Montesquieu's concept of the separation of powers to Rousseau's notion of sovereignty.[10]

Indeed, it was Montesquieu's theory of the separation of powers in *De l'Esprit des lois* that paved the way for constituent power; that the different governmental organs are created powers implied a superior and creative power.[11] Drawing on Rousseau's concept of the social contract and the idea of an indivisible and inalienable *volonté générale* ("general will"), Sieyès regarded constituent power as residing in the nation and, like the general will—which it expresses—as being inalienable and sovereign.[12] It was in this revolutionary context that the concept of constituent power, as a power that transcends constituted powers, was formulated to legitimize the revolution and the replacement of the old regime with a new one.[13]

Notwithstanding the immense importance of the concept to modern constitutionalism, for years it was overlooked in the English-language constitutional literature. Recently, however, there has been a revival of interest in constituent power, and insightful scholarly writings have attempted to explicate the meaning of one of the most abstract concepts of constitutional theory. The complexity of the concept was best illustrated by a Parisian law professor, Julien Oudot, in 1856. History can tell us much more about constituent power, Oudot wrote, than any a priori logical reasoning. Sometimes, he explained, constituent power is the act of a skillful and strong dictator, winning power because of his genius and clinging to it through the recognition or the habit of the governed; sometimes it is in part a riot, the beginning of a revolution that the general citizens accept; and in some places, constituent power is planned in advance through the organization of a special regular constituent power that settles the form in which the nation can make changes to the political mechanism (what we now call amendment power). The proper answer, according to Oudot, to the question "what is constituent power?" is "whatever you like it to be, reader!"[14]

In this chapter, we claim that constitutional revolutions provide additional case studies for thinking and rethinking about constituent power and perhaps better conceptualizing it. At the very least, as the different case studies demonstrate, constitutional revolutions challenge traditional distinctions between constituent and constituted powers, and between primary (original) and secondary (derived) constituent powers, but also shed light on some of the most obscure questions surrounding its exercise: Is constituent power necessarily external or internal to the constitutional order?

Can it be expressed directly by the people or also through representation? Who are "the people" that can exercise constituent power—a mythical, transcendent understanding of the people or the real, immanent people in a state? Constitutional revolutions may provide us with some answers to these vexing questions in addition to illustrating what might be considered a legitimate exercise of constituent power, in contrast to a merely successful one.

Constituent Power Under the Rule of Law

According to Sieyès, constituent power, unlike constituted powers, is free and independent of any formal bonds of positive law created by the constitution: "The nation exists prior to everything. It is the origin of everything. Its will is always legal. It is the law itself."[15] These two types of powers exist on different planes: constituted powers are inseparable from a preestablished constitutional order, while constituent power is external to a constitutional order and exists without it, and therefore is alien to the law.[16] Accordingly, for Sieyès, constituent power is unlimited, for "it would be ridiculous to suppose that the nation itself could be constricted by the procedures or the constitution to which it had subjected its mandatories," and therefore the nation is free of constitutional limits: "Not only is the nation not subject to a constitution," Sieyès insists, "it *cannot* be and *should* not be."[17] Sieyès thus positions the constituent power in a state of nature in which the sovereign people are exterior to their institutions.[18]

Expounding upon constituent power as an open, creative power, Antonio Negri explained that it could not be understood from the perspective of constitutionalism, since the latter is fundamentally a theory of limited government. In fact, constituent and constituted powers are not only strictly separate concepts, but also contrasting ones. Any legal approach to constituent power fails: "The radical quality of the constituent principle is absolute. It comes from a void and constitutes everything."[19] Negri proposes to understand constituent power as a purely creative and revolutionary power of the multitude that can disrupt constituted boundaries.[20]

Of course, some regard the external conception of a formless and limitless power of "the people" to break any constitutional or legal bounds at any time as a dangerous idea, open to abuse. Experience teaches us that dictators often seize governmental powers through revolutionary acts or coups, claiming to be the bearers of the constituent power.[21]

It is perhaps this danger that is the basis of the counterconception of constituent power that considers it to be internal to the constitutional order. In contrast to Sieyès, the French journalist and historian Louis-Marie Prudhomme wrote in 1790 that the distinction between the constituent power and legislative power is "childish" and a result of "the silly vanity of some of our politicians who invented this nonsense, in purpose to prevent legislatures from discovering their mistakes. It is a vile and despicable jealousy that makes them aspire to infallibility."[22] Providing a more analytical explanation, Raymond Carré de Malberg in 1922 took the view that constitution-making power and constitutional-amending power are two modes of *pouvoir constituant:* constituent power is first exercised in revolutionary circumstances, outside the forms and procedures established by the constitution; whereas during the lifetime of the state, a juridical concept of constituent power is exercised in peaceful circumstances according to rules established by the constitution. This juridical constituent power can achieve changes of any magnitude, or even entirely replace the constitution.[23]

Interestingly, it is this conception that has become prevalent in modern American constitutional theory. In the early years of the American Revolution, the people's constituent power was considered to be external to and above the constitutional order.[24] Indeed, the U.S. Constitution was adopted in violation of the Articles of the Confederation, which were virtually unamendable, since they required agreement in Congress and confirmation by the legislature of every state in the Union.[25] In the great debate between the Federalists and Anti-Federalists, James Madison and others invoked the people's constituent power to justify the ability to overcome the constituted powers of the federation and the states. James Wilson, for example, declared: "The people are superior to our constitutions. . . . The people may change the constitutions, whenever, and however they please. This [is a] right, of which no positive institution can ever deprive them."[26] And in *Federalist* 40, Madison invoked the higher constituent authority of "the people themselves" in response to Anti-Federalist claims that the Philadelphia Convention had exceeded its mandate.[27]

Upon the enactment of the Constitution, however, the prevailing approach held that constituent power had come to an end, since it was subsumed under Article 5, through which "the people" may amend the Constitution. As Stephen Griffin notes, the concept of constituent power "plays no direct role in American constitutionalism, other than through the amendment process."[28] In the American tradition, enactment of the Constitution was the turning point: "The constituent power went into abeyance, leaving the work of government to the authorities now constituted. The people, having exercised sovereignty, now came under government."[29] The approach described by Griffin is not accepted by all. A notable contrasting perspective is that of Akhil Amar, for whom the U.S. amendment procedure supplements but does not replace popular sovereignty. Thus, the people retain their power to revise the constitution themselves, outside the amendment process.[30] Similar voices to Amar's can be found among French constitutional theorists. Markedly, in contrast to Carré de Malberg, Olivier Beaud rejected the assimilation of the sovereign constituent power to the limited amendment power.[31] Elsewhere, one of us has taken a similar approach, in which there is a distinction between the people's constituent power and amendment power, so that even after the constitution's enactment, the people retain a nonexhaustive constituent power, and through its exercise they can establish and change their constitutional order and even overcome constitutional unamendability.[32] As Carl Friedrich noted, "No matter how elaborate the provisions for an amending power may be, they must never . . . be assumed to have superseded the constituent power."[33] Ontologically, constituent power maintains its energy "to bring about a fundamental break . . . in the nature of the governing regime."[34] Therefore, constituted organs, including the amendment process, cannot subsume the constituent power, which is neither exhausted nor bound by existing constitutional limitations. The authorizing constituent power remains in the constitutional background and can reemerge to assume its role, while the amending power, as a delegated authority, can be set aside, just as it can be created.

Now, even if one accepts the understanding of constituent power—the "slipping sovereignty at the back of the Constitution"[35]—as maintaining extralegal features, and being able to be expressed outside constitutional rules and procedures with power to modify even the basic principles or structure of the constitutional order, how can we explain such a change when it is brought about through the formal constitutional amendment procedure stipulated in the constitution? As shown in chapter 3, in jurisdictions such as Hungary, Japan, Taiwan, South Korea, and Chile, constitutional revolutions have occurred within the parameters of legality. In these instances of paradigmatic change through formal constitutional amendments, legal continuity was maintained, that is, although the prior constitutional order was not formally overthrown, a complete substantive displacement in the constitutional order was brought about. How are we to understand such constitutional revolutions?

According to one approach, such a process is an exercise not of constituent power but of the extant constituted power. Once constituent power is institutionalized, "it would not be 'constituent' but 'constituted.'"[36] This was the approach taken by Andreas Kalyvas:

> If the constituent power were to be determined by the previous legal order or if it were to derive its legality from a pre-existing constitution, it would not be a constituent power but rather a constituted power. This amounts to a logical impossibility that effaces the very meaning and existence of the term constituent power. In such a case, there is no constitution of an order but only a partial transformation, a re-constitution and re-articulation, that is, a revision of an already existing order.[37]

But the transformations we have described in places such as Chile and Hungary were neither "real" revisions of the constitution nor amendments to it. They replaced the existing constitutional order of an authoritarian or communist regime with a democratic one. They created a new constitutional order by using the old constitutional order's mechanisms. Such activities of extraordinary character are likely to be strongly challenged because of their questionable legitimacy, notwithstanding their facade of legality.

After all, the entire idea behind the theory of constitutional unamendability is that amendments establishing a "new constitution" or a new "constitutional identity" cannot be achieved through the regular amendment procedure but require a different constituent process—an invocation of the people's constituent power. In Germany and India, both constitutional orders have provided constitutional mechanisms for protecting constitutional identity from revolutionary rupture by constitutional means: in Germany through the famous eternity clause of the Basic Law, which expressly and absolutely entrenches the fundamental values of the constitutional order, protecting its core identity from amendments that might affect them; and in India (influenced by German theory and jurisprudence) through the judge-made basic structure doctrine, according to which Parliament cannot destroy the basic structure of the Constitution via constitutional amendments and thereby destroy its identity, "a precious heritage."[38] The Indian basic structure doctrine "represents an effort to distinguish between a constitutional amendment and revolutionary action."[39] Consequently, constitutional unamendability and its judicial enforcement proclaim that the power to change the fundamental values of the constitution, which comprise its genetic code or identity, does not reside in the constitutional amendment procedure, but rather is appropriately part of the constituent power of the sovereign people, from which all legitimate authority springs. Accordingly, it could be argued that a constitution radically revised by constituted powers would be illegitimate or even "unconstitutional."

But can it not be argued that in these instances it was not the illegitimate act of a constituted power but the legitimate act of a constituent power? The relevant constitutional amendments in Poland, Hungary, and Chile "invaded and destroyed the identity of the existing constitutional order," notwithstanding the fact that they were "adopted in a relatively simple parliamentary procedure"; but arguably, "it was quite obvious that, in the existing political context, such 'amendment-induced-destruction' of the old order constituted an expression of the 'will of the people.' So, in some situations, the primary constituent power did find its appearance in constitutional amendments."[40] Thus, an alternative approach would be that it was indeed constituent—rather than constituted—power that played the constitution-making role, but it simply chose to act according to the existing procedures for amendment rather than be obliged by them.[41]

Carl Friedrich gave the example of a constitutional change that occurred in Switzerland in 1874 when the Constitution of 1848 was "entirely overhauled and democratized" through the ordinary amendment procedure. In this instance, Friedrich maintained, the constituent power "manifested itself through the amending power; but that does not mean that it is identical with it; in fact even to say that it manifested itself through it is something of a misstatement. It would be more accurate to say that the group which might otherwise develop into the constituent power manifests itself through, acts through the amending power."[42]

As a conceptual matter, it appears to us correct to say that in these cases, constituent power was successfully exercised. True, constituent power has extrajuridical dimensions, and it cannot be fully regulated or stipulated legally. This means that by its nature, constituent power does not have to abide by constitutional rules and may be successfully exercised extralegally. This does not mean, however, that constituent power can be exercised exclusively in such an extralegal manner. In that respect, constitutional revolution necessitates a rethinking of Richard Kay's formulation that "a true constituent authority must act without the comfort of legal authorization."[43] Perhaps it would be more accurate to say that constituent power may act without the comfort of legal authorization, yet if it wishes, it may be manifested under the rule of law through constitutional mechanisms for constitutional change. As Mark Tushnet noted, "Behind every constitutional structure lies the possibility of revolutionary overthrow—peasants with pitchforks, so to speak. The constituent power can exercise itself through the forms of law, but those forms cannot ultimately constrain the constituent power."[44] Still, as we show later, the legitimacy of such an exercise may vary. Constitutional systems are more complex than the constituent-constituted dichotomy. They are polymorphic. Materials science shows that a solid material can exist in multiple forms, and so too do amendment procedures. Constitutions have different procedures, mechanisms, and actors involved in constitutional change, and a single constitution might incorporate different procedures for changing different provisions and principles. Constitutional amendment powers ought to be regarded on a spectrum of legitimacy. Amendment procedures carry an increased democratic legitimacy when they use formal mechanisms such as referendums and when they summon constituent assemblies to create an environment in which the people "awake," in a sense, to resume their role as constituent authors.

Post-Sovereign Constituent Power

As we noted in the previous section, constituent power has in some instances been exercised through constitutional mechanisms of amendment, bringing about revolutionary constitutional changes of the constitutional order. The ability of the constituent power to exercise itself through the forms of law is most visible in modern constitutional mechanisms aiming to institutionalize constituent power in constitutional forms. As mentioned in chapter 3, examples of such institutionalization are constitutions that attempt to regulate not only the amendment procedure, which is the most common mechanism, but also the exercise of constituent power by establishing rules for their own replacement. For instance, the Constitution of Venezuela of 1999 establishes a formal constitutional procedure for the creation of "a new juridical order" and "drawing up a new Constitution." Similar mechanisms providing for a "total reform," "complete revision," or "adopting a new constitution" exist in Argentina, Bulgaria, Nicaragua, and Switzerland.[45] Such legal procedures carry the benefit of creating an ordered, inclusive, multipart procedure of participation and deliberation, which may preserve the credibility of the constituent power by allowing the divided people's will to be pronounced.[46] Such special mechanisms not only allow the people to participate and feel that it is their will—and not some "will of a mysterious People"—that is being exercised, but also ensure "that participants in the exercise of power understand the significance of their actions, prodding them to understand that they are not merely tinkering with the details of the constitution but proposing to transform it."[47]

Again, these mechanisms should not be regarded as negating or confining constituent power in constitutional form. By its nature, constituent power is unbound by any constitutional rules; it cannot be contained or fully expressed by existing laws and institutions. As Carl Schmitt argued, "No constitutional law, not even a constitution, can confer a constitution-making power and prescribe the form of its initiation."[48] That said, attempts to constitutionalize constituent power should not "be dismissed as rhetorical decoration."[49] Instead of dismissing such provisions, it might be more valuable to regard them not as constituting constituent power, but rather as recognizing or declaring it. Thus, even if one accepts the idea that constituent power cannot be regulated, a constitution could still attempt to stipulate the means for constituting a new constitution; constituent power would not be bound by it, but might act accordingly if it so chose. Therefore, these mechanisms can be viewed as vehicles for the exercise of constituent power. Such *ex ante* mechanisms, which may not prevent constituent power from being exercised in an extralegal manner, may still strengthen the legal legitimacy of the exercise of constituent power.

By taking this approach, we do not claim that constituent power is purely legal. We still maintain that constituent power has extralegal dimensions, yet we reject the positivist approach, embraced by some scholars, that constituent power is "a pure fact" that has nothing to do with law.[50] Constituent power is strongly linked with law. At its core, constituent power has a legal aim—the creation of a legal constitutional order. Ultimately, this is a juridical exercise. Constituent power, Kalyvas rightly claimed, has a "juridical character": "Its true finality, is to fulfil the idea of law."[51]

If constituent power, which is never completely absorbed into constituted organs or permanently stabilized, may nonetheless be exercised through constitutional mechanisms such as amendment or total replacement, this necessitates a new thinking of the concept of a sovereign extralegal constituent power. Andrew Arato is perhaps the most persistent theorist in calling for a reconceptualization of constituent power. According to Arato, we are now living in an era of "post sovereign constitution-making" in which constituent power takes an institutional form. Following the recent experiences of constitution making in places such as eastern Europe and South Africa, Arato presented a "post sovereign, post-revolutionary, round-table-led and multistage paradigm of constitution-making," which allows for constituent power to survive and at the same time be regarded as a limited power, receiving its authority from its legitimacy and legality. Post-sovereign constitution making does not vest constituent power in a single individual or institution; rather, it is based on values such as pluralism, inclusion, publicity, compromise, and legality, and emphasizes the role of interim constitutions as parts of a multistage process.[52]

The Hungarian case is an example of such planned constitution making in process, which was not altogether fulfilled. The 1989 revision to the old, communist Constitution of 1949 brought about a new constitutional order, which was meant to be only temporary, although it did not provide any rules of procedures for the making of a new constitution (similar to Article 146 of the German Basic Law). Yet Hungary, unlike Poland, failed to produce a permanent constitution and complete the process of constitution making in the mid-1990s. A more successful experience, and the one that has perhaps become the paradigmatic case, is the constitution-making process in South Africa. There, an interim Constitution was negotiated in the Multiparty Negotiating Forum and adopted by the last apartheid-era South African Parliament in 1994, according to the procedural rules of constitutional change stipulated in the 1983 Constitution. Clear, predetermined rules for the constitution-making process were set in sections 68–73 of the interim Constitution, and the final Constitution was adopted by an elected Constitutional Assembly, a process that overcame the lack of democratic legitimacy of the sort that was experienced in Hungary. The entire process was explicitly bound by thirty-four predetermined principles listed in Schedule 4 of the interim Constitution. The Constitutional Court was entrusted with the task of certifying the new Constitution's compliance with these predetermined principles. In an unprecedented ruling in 1996, it declared the new Constitution to be unconstitutional, demanding its revision. Only after the assembly revised the Constitution did the Constitutional Court approve it.[53]

The process successfully produced a constitutional revolution within legal continuity, since the amendment rules of the old regime were used until replaced in a legal manner. Arato claimed that in the South African case, "we should be speaking about 'regime change' rather than reform or revolution," yet even he acknowledged that the transformation from the apartheid political order to a nonracial one was a radical transformation.[54] It was certainly a revolutionary constitutional change that maintained procedural continuity while decisively breaking with the past.

Instead of focusing on the process and the actors involved in it, we are interested in evaluating the implications of such a process for the concept of constituent power. Karol Edward Soltan, for example, suggested: "If constitution making proceeds in stages . . . we must abandon Sieyès's idea of the people as the constituent power. We build on what exists and on what we inherit from the past."[55] But Sieyès's revolutionary idea of constituent power need not be abandoned; in fact, our theory of constitutional revolution requires a better understanding of the complexities of constituent power. If the constitution-making process can take place in stages while maintaining legal continuity, does this necessarily mean that the South African constitution-making process effectively extinguished constituent power, turning it into a constituted power? Henk Botha, a South African constitutional scholar, raised the possibility that it did: "Constituent power was effectively reduced to constituted power, which had to comply not only with the procedural requirements entrenched in the interim Constitution, but also had to heed the 'solemn pact' represented by the constitutional Principles. The requirement of judicial certification of the constitutional text, which is unprecedented in the history of constitutionalism, contributed further to the weakening of popular sovereignty."[56]

Arguably, while allowing for a radical break with the past, this emphasis on legality and procedural continuity hindered the ability to make a more radical break with the past, since it enhanced the bargaining power of the white minority, created a presumption in favor of the validity of the status quo, and privileged particular interests and ideologies.[57] On the other hand, this new, ongoing process of constitution making and remaking is not confined to a single, historical constitutional moment of constitution making, but creates an opportunity for constituent power to assert itself at different times in the political life of the nation. As Botha wrote, "In the absence of a strict conceptual boundary between constitutional enactment and interpretation or between the founding and maintenance of the constitutional order, the possibility arises that sustained political engagement allied to legislative intervention or creative constitutional interpretation, may from time to time result in new constitutional beginnings."[58] This continuing space for new beginnings and contestations of the collective identity within the constitutional order seems to accord with the more deliberate, incremental changes produced by some constitutional revolutions.

Constitutional Revolution and the "Juridical Coup d'état"

The understanding that constituent power is able to manifest itself through formal constitutional procedures for a new constitution-making process or even through constitutional-amendment procedures seems acceptable, even to the theory of constituent power, since these two forms are part of the secondary constituent power—the instituted legal competence to create and revise constitutional norms. What if, however, a new beginning occurs through the exercise of purely constituted power, like a court?

Alec Stone Sweet defines "a fundamental transformation in the normative foundations of a legal system through the constitutional lawmaking of a court" as a "juridical coup d'état."[59] Stone Sweet is interested in the modification of a constitution through adjudication, such as judicial interpretation and application, resulting in constitutional law that alters—fundamentally—how the legal system operates, to the extent that it would have been rejected by the constitution's founders had it been placed on the negotiating table.[60] There are some important conceptual and terminological differences between Stone Sweet's idea of a "juridical coup d'état" and constitutional revolution as we define the term. We are unsure whether it is necessary to adopt an originalist approach and go back to the views and intentions of the framers in order to understand a revolutionary change by the judiciary, since our conceptualization of a revolution applies also when the constitution is understood to be a living instrument and the object of revolution is the constitution as it develops over time.[61] Moreover, whereas our use of the term "constitutional revolution" is normatively neutral, "coup d'état," as commonly understood, has a negative normative connotation.[62] Also, while our account of constitutional revolution refers to a paradigmatic displacement, however achieved, in the conceptual prism through which constitutionalism is experienced in a given polity, a coup d'état conceptually identifies a change of the ruling group with unchanged authority structures. Thus, the two terms are not conceptually identical. Finally, in contrast to Kelsen, for whom a coup d'état is a species of revolution, Stone Sweet's conceptualization of a coup d'état and our conceptualization of constitutional revolution are not revolutions in a Kelsenian sense.[63] What is decisive for Kelsen is the manner of constitutional change, while we focus on substance. Thus, constitutional revolutions or juridical coup d'états can occur without a break in the chain of legality. Consequently, the term "constitutional revolution" may be better suited to describing a change brought about by the judiciary that results in fundamentally altered structures of authority. Moreover, Stone Sweet's definition focuses solely on the judicial branch as the "agent" of this fundamental change, while our much broader formulation includes other "legal agents" such as ordinary legislators or constitutional amenders that—like the judiciary—are constituted organs with the authority to act under the constitution.[64] These organs too may bring about a fundamental change in the constitutional ordering—a constitutional revolution (or a juridical coup d'état, to use Stone Sweet's terminology).

Notwithstanding these differences, the underlying core understanding of a juridical coup d'état is in line with our understanding of a constitutional revolution through the courts. According to Stone Sweet, a juridical coup d'état proceeds through the exercise of powers that, as a matter of form but not substance, were properly delegated to the judicial authority by the basic norm. But the substance of the judicial decision might not have been authorized, or might even have been forbidden, by the substance of the prior basic norm. Accordingly, although not all "creative judicial law-making" results in a juridical coup, all juridical coups will likely be created by such creative judicial rulings.[65] Indeed, courts clearly participate in informal constitutional change, yet not every such constitutional change is revolutionary; a revolutionary constitutional change makes a paradigm shift in the basic principles or features of the constitutional order.[66]

Stone Sweet claimed that judges who instigate constitutional revolutions displace "constituent authority as regulators of constitutional development."[67] Moreover, because a juridical coup d'état fundamentally changes the *Grundnorm,* it is not easily defended as a deduction from the *Grundnorm* or with reference to pre-coup legal materials. Therefore, courts delivering such decisions base them on new theories of the constitution, and "a huge amount of doctrinal activity is devoted to defending the coup d'état, on functional and other normative grounds."[68]

This account seems to fit the constitutional revolution that took place in Israel through the actions of the Court. In the *Mizrahi Bank* case, in holding that the Knesset possesses constituent authority and may bind its legislative powers, the Supreme Court was placing itself as the final arbiter of which group holds constituent authority. Justice Aharon Barak painstakingly devotes a huge amount of doctrinal activity to defending the Knesset's constituent authority, based on the theoretical and jurisprudential models of Kelsen, Hart, and Dworkin. Nevertheless, Barak's models present a plethora of challenges. Kelsen's basic norm is not a legal norm, since it is not created by another legal norm. The basic norm, for Kelsen, is metalegal; it is a hypothesis or a fiction.[69] To better determine whether the Knesset possesses constituent authority, one has to examine the basic norm of the State of Israel. But Kelsen's theory does not deal with the creation of the basic norm, and his theory cannot assist in providing an answer to the question who holds constituent authority, since, for him, it lies in the basic norm, which is external to the legal norm. The controversial claim by Justice Barak that "the basic norm for Israel . . . is that the Provisional Council of State is the supreme authority of the State of Israel" discloses nothing about the existence or absence of constituent authority by the current Knesset. It is possible to theorize a basic norm according to which the current Knesset possesses constituent authority, but it is likewise possible to theorize a basic norm according to which only the First Knesset held constituent authority, as Justice Cheshin claimed.[70]

In contrast with Kelsen, Hart claimed that the identification of legal norms is made in accordance with the "rule of recognition"; a legal norm is accepted as a normative standard if people conduct their behavior according to it.[71] The test of the rule of recognition is a positive, not a normative, one. So the question of the Knesset's constituent authority is empirical: Does a majority of the population acknowledge such an authority and its implications? Whereas Justice Barak dedicates many pages of his judgment to confirming—through analyses of the state's constitutional history, the Knesset's self-conception, the views of legal scholars, and case law—that a majority of the population acknowledges the Knesset's constituent authority, these were not all entirely convincing. Indeed, from a positivist perspective, the answer to the question whether the Knesset possesses constituent power cannot be found in legal theory, but only in political theory or a theory of the state.[72] Consider, then, Dworkin's normative theory, in which the law is the best interpretation of the legal history of the state. The best interpretation is that which presents the law and the community at their highest achievement of political morality.[73] Hence, the question of the Knesset's possession of constituent authority should be answered by seeking the best interpretation of Israel's legal history from the perspective of political morality. Barak's lines of reasoning are historical and rely on the "social and legal consciousness of the Israeli community."[74] They are not based on a conclusive political philosophy or a theory of the state regarding its purposes, the role of the government, and the essence of the constitution. Justice Cheshin's minority opinion raised several challenges to Justice Barak's recognition of constituent authority, which led Cheshin to conclude: "The Constituent Assembly—Was it you or was I dreaming? We respond: Forty-seven years ago, it was you, but today you are but a sweet dream."[75]

Besides the question of constituent authority, also open to interpretation were the questions how to solve a conflict between basic laws and ordinary legislation, and what was the Court's power to conduct judicial review. Although the Basic Laws of 1992 included explicit limitations on the legislative powers of the Knesset, they lacked a supremacy clause or an explicit provision governing their own status. A plausible interpretation is that the Basic Laws possess the status of an ordinary statute. Such an interpretation—which is compatible with the early understanding, following the Harari Resolution, that until the integration of the Basic Laws into a full constitution, their status is that of ordinary legislation—would have allowed the Knesset to violate any of the provisions of a Basic Law if it did so expressly, similar to a "notwithstanding" mechanism.[76] Ruth Gavison, one of the foremost critics of the majority opinion in the *Mizrahi Bank* case, thus claimed, "There is no precedent, anywhere in the world, wherein the court decides on the supremacy of basic laws, and confers to itself the power of judicial review of Knesset legislation, without the existence of a full constitutional document and without explicit provision."[77] Regardless of the correctness of the *Mizrahi Bank* judgment, it was a creative judicial decision that brought about a revolution in the constitutional order, conforming to Stone Sweet's characterization of a juridical coup d'état. It was "a fundamental transformation in the normative foundations of a legal system through the constitutional lawmaking of a court."[78]

As detailed, however, in chapter 6, the *Mizrahi Bank* judgment could not have been rendered without the enactment of the two Basic Laws on human rights. And the constitutional revolution could not have arrived without its judicial affirmation. Each required the other. It is not mistaken to claim that "the juridical coup is more aptly understood as part of a wider and multi-perspective frame of the analysis of constitutional transformations."[79] As in the *Mizrahi Bank* case, a judicial decision can trigger, support, or conclude an ongoing constitutional revolution. The constitutional revolution "leaves the legal order floating in limbo for some time," and it is not self-identifying: "It depends on other authorities whether the coup actually was successful," and "whether or not one may speak of a successful juridical coup can only be determined in retrospect."[80] Arguably, in the Israeli case, the revolution was "floating in limbo" between 1992, when the two Basic Laws on human rights were enacted, and 1995, when the Court provided a retrospective affirmation of the revolution. The fundamental transformation established by the Court was then accepted by other officials (in the Hartian sense), since the Knesset and the governmental departments accepted the judgment and followed the ruling. But as Stone Sweet pointed out, with its questionable, disputed legitimacy, "the likelihood that any juridical coup d'état will provoke doctrinal wars, big and small, is . . . high."[81] This was certainly the case with the *Mizrahi Bank* case and the constitutional revolution in Israel. A judicial decision holding that a constitution was given to the state without any broad public or political debate became a focus of profound and enduring doctrinal controversy over the legitimacy of the assertion by the Court of its judicial review authority. Along with other factors, this controversy has led to a counterrevolution. But apart from the legitimacy deficit, is there anything that a constitutional revolution through courts can teach us about constituent power?

Contesting Constituent Power and Constituted Power

Earlier in this chapter, we noted that when the constitution is replaced through constitutional mechanisms, the traditional distinction between constituent power and constituted power becomes blurred. The challenge is exacerbated when the organ bringing about the revolution of the constitutional order is not the amendment power, which is a special kind of power situated between primary constituent power and ordinary constituted powers, but a purely constituted organ, such as the judiciary. As noted, according to Sieyès's traditional distinction, constituent power is the power to create a constitution: a power external to the legal order and superior to constituted power. Constituted powers are powers that are created by the constitution—the legislature, the executive, and the judiciary—and limited by it; they are situated within the legal order and possess legal competences.

In previous chapters, we described instances of a revolutionary change in the legal order occurring without the use of extraconstitutional means and under the rule of law. It is exactly in this situation that the traditional distinction between constituent and constituted powers is called into question. How can a constituted organ possessing only a limited legal competence be the bearer of constituent power and bring about a constitutional revolution? Is it not the case that by assuming constituent power, the constituted organ has overstepped its mandate and acted ultra vires?

Constitutional revolutions contest the traditional understanding of the relationship between constituent power and constituted power and may lead to an alternative understanding of the theory of constituent power. Constitutional revolutions support Luigi Corrias's claim that "what the juridical coup shows is how constituent power and constituted power are much closer connected to each other than the dualistic model of Sieyès suggests."[82] Instead of a binary separation between the two, we argue that even a constituted organ can successfully exercise constituent power, yet this exercise runs along a spectrum of legitimacy.

"The birth of a new legal order," Corrias added, "cannot be justified without referring (to a minimal degree) to the authorities overthrown."[83] As shown in chapter 3, when constitutional revolutions are brought about by using constitutional amendments, the authority is obvious; it is the official constitutional mechanism permitting the constitution to be formally changed. Thus, when the Hungarian communist Parliament lawfully amended the 1949 Constitution to bring about a substantively new constitutional order, legal legitimacy was based on the old constitution. And in Japan, where, according to the new constitution, sovereignty resides with "the Japanese people" who "proclaim" and "establish" the constitution, it was actually the emperor who, according to the preface to the constitution, "sanctions and promulgates" the "amendments" to the Meiji Constitution. And in Israel, the *Mizrahi Bank* judgment was a radical transformation that claimed to be no more than an ordinary interpretation of the Basic Laws. What the Supreme Court claimed to be doing was acting completely within the established boundaries of the legal text of the Basic Laws. Or as Corrias noted, "The court can only be a constituent power while claiming to remain a constituted power."[84]

A court may claim that it remains a constituted power, but when engaged in the activities of a constitutional revolution, it turns itself into a constituent power. According to Theodor Schilling, "Sometimes a constituted power may make itself into a constituent power. Indeed, in engaging in a revolution, the court necessarily abandons its role as a constituted power under the pre-revolutionary constitution and recreates itself as a constituent power."[85] This, for Schilling, occurs only rarely in juridical revolutions. In the South African constitution-making process, through the certification cases, the Constitutional Court was perhaps actively exercising (or at the very least coexercising) constituent power by participating in the process. But in other cases, Schilling contended, the Court's contribution amounted to merely an interpretation or revision of the constitution, and since "such interpretations . . . do not touch the genotype of the constitution, the only thing they tell us about the relationship between constituent and constituted powers is that constitutions may develop in ways not foreseen by the constituent power and that this may be due to acts of constituted powers."[86] But what if this is precisely what a court does, modifying or destroying the genotype of the constitution? Are there limitations to the ability of courts to bring about constitutional revolutions?

Consider the judicial decision from Honduras with respect to presidential term limits. In this case, one of the basic principles in the Honduran Constitution of 1982 is the presidential term limit. Article 239 of the Constitution contains a prohibition on presidential reelection and stipulates that anyone who "violates" the no-reelection rule or who "proposes its reform" shall "cease immediately" to serve in a public post and be prohibited from serving in office for ten years. In addition, Article 374 declares that the no-reelection provision can under no circumstances be amended. Moreover, according to Article 42(5), citizenship may be lost by "inciting, promoting, or supporting the continuation or reelection" of the president.

In 2014, a group of fifteen congressional representatives belonging to the National Party challenged these constitutional rules regarding presidential reelection, and in early 2015 the former president of the National Party, Rafael Callejas, challenged Article 239 itself, claiming it should be inapplicable. According to the challenges, the prohibition on reelection infringed fundamental rights such as the right to be elected, the right to vote, and freedom of expression. In a unanimous judgment of April 22, 2015, the Constitutional Chamber of the Honduran Supreme Court held that the banning of reelection, the making of the reelection clause unamendable, and the loss of citizenship for promoting reelection were all unconstitutional and inapplicable.[87] The decision completely eradicated the rule on presidential term limits that had been at the core of the 1982 Constitution, allowing presidents to stay in office ad infinitum. The Honduran Court's decision brought about a constitutional revolution. And in this decision the Court was exercising a constituent power, not a constituted one.

As noted in chapter 2, a formal constitutional amendment that significantly alters the prevailing constitutional identity may often be regarded as unconstitutional for substantive reasons—making it an unconstitutional constitutional amendment. This is especially the case when the constitution—such as Article 79(3) of the German Basic Law—includes explicit unamendability by protecting certain fundamental principles from amendments, but occurs also in cases of implicit unamendability when courts, as in India, infer from the constitution implied limitations on the formally constitutional amendment power, in order to shield the constitutional identity. The rationale behind such unamendability is that certain constitutional amendments might be unconstitutional because they attempt to do more than merely amend the constitution: they attempt to change the constitutional identity, in effect replacing the constitution with a new one. Since such an act is reserved to the people in their constituent-power capacity, not to the more limited amendment authority, such an act may be regarded as ultra vires. As the German Federal Constitutional Court stated in the *Lisbon Treaty Case:* "From the perspective of the principle of democracy, the violation of the constitutional identity codified . . . in the Basic Law is at the same time an encroachment upon the constituent power of the people. In this respect the constituent power has not granted the representatives and bodies of the people a mandate to dispose of the identity of the constitution."[88]

Constitutions, however, change not only through formal amendments, but also, and in the majority of cases, through informal amendments brought about by judicial interpretation. Courts are constituted authorities. They are created by the constitution and inferior to the constituent power. As constituted organs, they are limited in their scope of action. Like other governmental bodies, courts must act within constitutional limits imposed on them. According to the theory of unamendability, the amendment power must remain within the constitutional limits provided by the constituent power. If the scope of the amendment power, which represents the instituted constituent power of the people and confers the ability to change other constituted organs such as the judiciary, legislature, and executive, is limited such that it cannot destroy the constitutional core and replace the constitution, all the more so are these limitations applicable to the court, which is an ordinary constituted organ and does not democratically represent the people.

Contemplating the limits of judicial activism, the question may be asked: "If the Constitution establishes some part of itself as being unchangeable, and this provision can be said to be addressed to both the legislature and the courts . . . does it also limit the power of the courts to change the meaning of that provision through interpretation? Does it require the judge to use a different and more restrictive method of interpretation than s/he would otherwise use?"[89] Ostensibly, it seems that if certain constitutional principles or provisions are considered unamendable, this logically means that courts cannot interpret them in a manner that modifies their core and thereby changes the constitutional identity. This does not mean that courts cannot interpret these provisions or principles. Courts retain the legal power to interpret and reinterpret constitutional provisions, even unamendable ones. What courts seemingly cannot do is change the essence of the core of the constitution and its basic principles, because such an action requires resorting to the constituent power. Therefore, certain informal constitutional changes by courts that—from a substantive perspective—replace the constitution with a new one can be considered a constitutional revolution through the courts or as an unconstitutional change by the courts.[90] Courts are constituted organs created by and owing their authority to the constitution. They do not have the competence to destroy the constitution or its basic principles, thereby replacing it with a new one. This is the role of constituent power. *Pouvoir judiciaire* is not *pouvoir constituant.*

Or is it? As we explained in previous chapters, a judicial decision, like the actions of other constituted organs, can in fact revolutionize the constitutional order. In Georg Jellinek's formulation of "the normative power of the factual" (freed from its original context), laws may be regarded as valid and recognized as effective by virtue of their existence.[91] A judicial decision that revolutionizes the constitutional order may be regarded prima facie as ultra vires (or as a juridical coup d'état). Yet when it succeeds, one may then say in retrospect that constituted power exercised constituent power. This presents us with a "relational" reading of "the normative power of the factual" and with a dialectical understanding of the relationship between constituent and constituted powers in the course of constitutional development and transformation.

"Who the People?"

Misgivings about a constitutional revolution brought about by a court, as happened in Honduras, derive from the view that it is the role of the people—not a court—to bring about such a fundamental change to the core of the constitution.[92] But can the people actually exercise their constituent power?

Returning to the South African constitution-making process: Botha criticized the argument that the people's constituent power was institutionalized, contending that there are no "self-present people capable of exercising constituent power without the need for mediation by law"; instead, he claims, the people's collective identity has a dynamic and fluid nature.[93] Botha's argument goes to the very core of the theory of constituent power: Is there a "people" who are holders of constituent power, and how can they exercise their authority?

The conundrum here is that "the people are the sovereign which cannot exercise their sovereignty," as Joseph de Maistre famously asserted. However, if the people are said to "exercise their sovereignty by means of their representatives," this "begins to make sense."[94] Indeed, Sieyès's conception of constituent power was attached to representation. For Sieyès, the "nation" is "a body of associates living under a *common* law, represented by the same *legislature*, etc."[95] Since "members of the association will have become too numerous and occupy too widely dispersed [a domain] to be easily able to exercise their common will themselves," there is a need for representation. This representation is extraordinary, because it is free and independent of any prior constitutional restrictions, forms, or procedures, and it should not be confused with the "ordinary representatives of a people," who possess only limited powers, confined to those granted to them by the positive constitution; these extraordinary representatives serve as "a surrogate for the Nation."[96] They do not necessarily "embody the constituent power," but they are the people's representative who interpret how constituent power is to be exercised.[97]

Carl Schmitt provided a different vision of the people's constituent power. Like Sieyès, Schmitt declared that although "the constitution does not establish itself," it "is valid because it derives from a constitution-making capacity . . . and is established by the will of this constitution-making power."[98] This constitution-making power, according to Schmitt, "is the political will, whose power or authority is capable of making the concrete, comprehensive decision over the type and form of its own political existence."[99] For Schmitt, the constitution is created through this act of political will and is composed of fundamental political decisions regarding the form of government, the state's structure, and society's highest principles and symbolic values, which represent "the core constitutional identity of a democratic political order."[100] Schmitt accepted Sieyès's distinction between constituent and constituted power, and conceived of constituent power as an "unmediated will" that can be expressed independently and cannot be regulated or restricted by positive legal procedures or process.[101] Any attempt to formalize it would be "akin to transforming fire into water."[102] By conceiving of constituent power as external to and above the constitution, and as never exhausted within the positive constitution, Schmitt rejected "juridical normativism."[103] Contrary to Sieyès, Schmitt rejected the theory of the representation of the people, deeming it antidemocratic: "The constitution-making will of the people cannot be represented without democracy transforming itself into an aristocracy."[104] Arato noted that this is the reason why "Schmitt considers it a fatal omission that . . . the [1791 French constituent] assembly did not consider it essential to have its constitutional product ratified in a popular referendum."[105] Schmitt's rejection of representation can be seen as his acknowledgment of democratic sovereignty.[106]

The idea that the people can directly express their will is manifested in some contemporary constitutional theories of popular sovereignty. As alluded to earlier, for Akhil Amar the people, who are the source of the constitution, delegate an amendment power to ordinary government, but without limiting themselves or replacing popular sovereignty. Consequently, the people, by a majority of voters, via a referendum or a special convention, retain their reserved and inalienable right to revise the constitution themselves, even outside the amendment process.[107] This conception of constituent power vests it in the "living members of the body politic." According to this conception, "the people" as a collective entity are similar to "the people" as the collection of persons of a certain polity who can manifest their will. Larry D. Kramer, for example, refers to the people as "an actual authority . . . not some abstract 'people.' "[108] A practical illustration of such an approach is the 1962 amendment to the French Constitution regarding the form of presidential elections, which was passed by a referendum initiated by President de Gaulle, in violation of the amendment procedure. When this "constitutional violation"—or "revolution," à la Kelsen—was challenged before the French Constitutional Council, it was held that the Council lacked competence to review laws passed by the people in a referendum, since they were a direct expression of national sovereignty.[109] The people allegedly expressed their popular sovereignty directly. Arguably, the election of a president who receives his legitimacy directly from the people contributed to the enduring French political stability.[110]

One problem raised by this conception is the circularity paradox of "the people" as the bearers of constituent power. The people who participated in the referendum and allegedly exercised constituent power—like others who take a part in constituent assemblies, and so on—were already constituted. Rules regarding who would be eligible to vote and participate in such an expression of the people's will were already established: thus, the famous paradox of constitutional democracy—"the constitution constitutes the people who in turn constitute the constitution."[111] And so, much like Botha, Hans Lindahl claimed that "there can be no gathering together of a multitude into a collective subject without acts that seize the initiative to include and exclude."[112]

A second problem is that such an act manifests merely the will of the majority—"we the majority," so to speak, not "we the people." But popular sovereignty is different from majority rule.[113] Simply put, the challenge is that the people cannot speak directly as a whole. Thus, for concrete constitutional practice, the idea of a people adopting a constitution or manifesting their constituent power in order to bring about revolutionary constitutional change does not seem to exist. Consequently, the very idea of a people acting in an identifiable, comprehensible, and unmediated way is often regarded as a kind of myth, a fiction.[114] As we saw in chapter 5, this critique of popular sovereignty as a mere fiction was at the heart of Rajeev Dhavan's evaluation of the Indian constitution-making process, which, although having been brought about by a Constituent Assembly, suffered from exclusions and representative deficiencies: "It was not," he maintained, "a 'We the people' Constitution. It was a 'We the rulers' Constitution."[115]

A contrasting theory of constituent power avoids the difficulties associated with a people's inability to speak as a whole. This theory vests constituent power not in the living people but rather in the imaginary collective or corporate body of society. This theory is based upon the medieval idea of the king's two bodies.[116] Its basic premise is that the king's body is split in two: private (human) and public (divine). While the private body is subject to decline and extinction, the public (corporate) body is perpetual. Scholars have adopted a modern version of this as the "People's Two Bodies." For Marcel Gauchet, within a democratic legal system one ought to distinguish between the "real" people, who can only express a momentary majoritarian will, and the "perpetual constituent people," who represent a mystical "trans-temporal" body, which embodies popular sovereignty and the will of which is superior to the majoritarian.[117] Like Gauchet, Jed Rubenfeld distinguished between the present people, who can only express their immediate current will, and the "generational people"—past, present, and future generations committed to a complex project of freedom and democracy over time.[118]

The main difficulty with this theory is that the "trans-temporal" or "generational" people can never express their will.[119] One possible solution to this difficulty lies in the role of constitutional moments such as revolutions. During normal times, the imaginary body of the people is absent and cannot directly express its will. But during significant moments, such as declarations of independence, revolutions, and referendums, this mythical body is rendered present by the group to which it belongs. It is in these exceptional, transformative moments that the transcendental power collapses into the present, traversing the polity's past, present, and future.[120] During such temporary, extraordinary times, the transcendent corporate body collapses into the immanent present, and popular sovereignty is manifested; the "sleeping sovereign" awakens.[121]

While this solution may explain revolutions and their effect on the image of society, it cannot explain constitutional revolutions that take place without a constitutional moment, that is, incrementally and through constituted organs. Constitutional revolutions force us to consider the exercise of constituent power in a less binary, more relational form. In these instances, a revolutionary change of the constitutional order takes place without a "temporary" collapse of the corporate body into the present and often, as in Israel and Hungary, without wide public or popular participation. It is here that the relational or reflexive account of constituent power becomes significant. According to this account, constituent power is vested in the people but not necessarily in the people as a multitude, because "constituent power exists only when that multitude can project itself not just as the expression of the many (a majority) but—in some senses at least—of the all (unity)," which requires an "intrinsic connection between the symbolic and the actual."[122] As Martin Loughlin argued, "Political power is generated through symbolic representation of foundation and constitution and is then applied through the action of government. Power thus resides neither in 'the people' nor in the constituted authorities; it exists in the relation established between constitutional imagination and governmental action."[123] Through these lenses, it becomes clearer how the people's constituent power may also be exercised through the acts of constituted organs and without a constitutional moment. There is always a relational arrangement between constituent and constituted powers.

Yet Loughlin acknowledged the role of force in constitutional revolutions: "Power is created through a symbolic act in which a multitude of people recognize themselves as forming a unity, a collective singular: we the people. That act cannot exist only in the realm of belief; it must also take effect in reality, and this will often involve the use of force."[124] Thus, this relational account of constituent power should not rule out a more direct, extralegal exercise of popular sovereignty. Constituent power does not collapse into constituted power. The former can be exercised outside the constitutional order or through constituted organs. The two are not mutually exclusive. Indeed, even those who regard as a myth the idea of "the people" as holder of constituent power must acknowledge that it is often direct action by "the people," as the real people of a multitude, which brings about a constitutional revolution, as the Arab Spring demonstrated.[125] As Nasser Abourahme points out with respect to the revolutionary process in Egypt: "Here is the constituent power of the sovereign body-politic of 'the people' in the flesh, as it were—no longer deferred to some representational body. . . . The generic notion of 'the people' will always be a fractal formation—it's measured neither in proportions nor size; it cannot be banalized as an issue of constituencies—'your millions versus ours.' What counts . . . is the 'fidelity to the event' that goes under the name of 'Tahrir.' "[126] When the people are mobilized in the public sphere, the "atomized individuals can transform themselves into collective actors."[127] Nonetheless, even such an account cannot provide a clear determination of who is "the people" of Egypt, as Zoran Oklopcic argued: "Is 'the people' the mass that presented itself in Tahrir Square on 1 July 2013, demanding the ousting of democratically elected President Morsi? Or the crowd that presented itself at Rabaa al-Adawiya Mosque on 14 August, forty-four days later, demanding his reinstatement?"[128] We are often confronted with conflicting attributions of constituent power. Also intriguing is the fact that even in the Egyptian scenario, spontaneous acts of force by the multitude were soon channeled into legal and constituted mechanisms; rupture and continuity coexisted.[129] The fall of President Mubarak was introduced in a declaration by the Supreme Council of the Armed Forces that suspended the 1971 Constitution but did not abrogate it. In fact, the Supreme Council sought only to amend the Constitution, a move much like the constitutional transformation described in chapter 3. For that purpose, a constitutional reform commission, chosen to propose constitutional amendments, was established. These amendments were then approved in a referendum. A later declaration by the Supreme Council eventually abrogated the Constitution, established an interim constitution, and called for elections to the parliament, which would then choose a constituent assembly. Interestingly, while the declaration set a deadline of six months for the constituent assembly to draft a constitution, the Supreme Council failed to set supraconstitutional principles that would bind the constitution-making process, as was successfully done in South Africa.

After the courts dissolved the constituent assembly, a second assembly was convened and managed to draft a constitution, which was later ratified in a referendum with little participation.[130] As pointed out in chapter 2, that Constitution did not survive.

The Arab Spring case has much to teach us about the nature of constituent power and its complicated relationship with constituted powers. In his study of revolutions in the Arab Spring, Nimer Sultany demonstrated how the distinction between constituent and constituted power is blurred, and how "constituent power is inexhaustible because the revolution is not reducible to an event and thus constitution-making fails to terminate constituent power." Also, "constituent power is not unfettered because the judiciary imposes constitutional continuity through unwritten constitutional principles, notwithstanding the revolutionary overthrow of the constitution. . . . Constituent power does not necessarily unfold unconstrained or produce 'rupture' . . . [and] limitations on popular will are not an expression of progressive dialectical evolution nor of a normatively acceptable affirmation of 'continuity' that maintains the democratic spirit."[131] Consistent with our argument in this book, Sultany claimed that "populist scholars assume more rupture than actually exists, and constitutionalist scholars misrepresent the effect of continuities."[132] A rigid distinction between constituent and constituted powers, Sultany correctly noted, may be analytically correct but misleading, since it is "not actual and practical."[133] Through our case studies of constitutional revolutions, we demonstrate precisely this complicated—nonbinary—relationship between constituent and constituted powers.

Whether considered mythical or actual, the construct "the people" carries real power for constitutional revolutions and their legitimacy. It "create[s] . . . pictures in our heads which make the structures of authority tolerable and understandable."[134] By telling ourselves a fictional story about "the people," we satisfy a "sort of psycho-legal need."[135] In this view, the idea of "the people" does not necessarily describe the mode of exercise of political authority, but rather its source. According to this conception, the people's constituent power should not be regarded as an "actual aggregate entity in the real world," but rather as "a concept that helps explain the normative basis for a constitution's claim to authority."[136]

Here, the mythical role of the people as holders of constituent power is of great importance both for the constitutional design of amendment procedures and for the legitimation of a constitutional revolution brought about through constituted organs. The Irish example is instructive in this respect.

The People as Amenders of the Constitution

Again, constituent power is identified, if only mythically or symbolically, with the idea of the people as authors of the constitution. Xenophon Contiades and Alkemene Fotiadou recently demonstrated how "formal amendment rules often attempt to furbish constitutional amendment with the symbolic force of the original exercise of the constituent power."[137] Indeed, constitutional-amendment processes that include the people's direct involvement through mechanisms such as referendums are attempts to imitate a constitutional moment in which the people's constituent power is incarnated. As Contiades and Fotiadou explained:

> The people are traditionally considered to have spoken during the exercise of the pouvoir constituant. Amending formulas may be described as replications of the constitutional moment where the pouvoir constituant was exercised, being attempted simulations of that primordial, constitution-making function. . . . This original constitution-making process is embellished with great symbolic force, the reproduction of which during every constitutional revision would be unfeasible. Yet, desire to somehow preserve the spirit of that moment is often apparent in constitutional arrangements that risk sacrificing practicality for symbolism.[138]

Through the formal mechanism of referendum, constitutional-amendment formulas aim to create an environment in which the people "awake," in a sense, to resume their role as constituent authors, and thereby increase the democratic legitimacy of the constitutional change. Here the myth of the people as holders of constituent power serves as the guiding narrative for constitutional design, even if only formally.[139] Indeed, an author-based theory of legitimacy considers constitutions to be "respect-worthy" in light of their makers, and the people are the most "legitimate" authors of democratic constitutions.

Thus, political necessities force a reliance on a "We the People" narrative. As Jawaharlal Nehru claimed with regard to the Indian constitution-making process, the power of independent India derived from the sovereign people, who could express their will in the Constituent Assembly. The fact that the revolutionary promise of independent India was only partially shared by the totality of the population—hence Nehru's reference to the "semi-revolutionary" people—did not detract from the reality that the Constitution's transformative purpose could succeed only if it could claim the legitimating mantle of popular sovereignty.

That is surely the case with constitution making, but also with other important constitutional changes. To be sure, when the people are involved in the amendment procedure, they act in their capacity as an instituted organ. Nonetheless, when the people are involved, they act as a "legitimation elevator" of the constitutional change.[140] For example, referendums and special assemblies carry a higher degree of "popular legitimacy" than ordinary legislatures.[141] A notable example is the exceedingly participatory South African constitution-making process, which enjoyed a high level of legitimacy.[142] Another interesting example is Ireland.

The Irish Constitution of 1937 is infused with the religious commitments of Catholic theology, especially concerning the protection of the family and the life of the unborn, which are in constant tension with certain precepts of liberal democracy and an increasingly secular citizenry.[143] Irish society has changed a great deal since 1937, and over the past several decades, Ireland experienced an incremental constitutional revolution, manifested in a fundamental change in its constitutional identity. Or as the Irish prime minister, Leo Varadkar, has pointed out, his country's "quiet revolution" was meant to establish "a modern constitution for a modern country."[144] This is mostly evident in some of the constitutional changes of recent years. In 2015, Irish citizens voted to constitutionalize the right to same-sex marriage, as recommended by the Convention on the Constitution, and in 2018 they voted to repeal the Eighth Amendment's strict prohibition on abortion and guarantee the right to legally obtain an abortion, two controversial issues opposed by the Catholic Church.

What is interesting about this revolutionary process is the involvement of the people, which occurred through a representative and deliberative citizens' assembly and direct popular vote in referendums. Ireland appears to have established a new model for allowing a legal approximation of the constituent power, one that grants constitutional revolution a necessary claim to popular sovereignty and thereby democratically legitimates a successful transformation in constitutional identity. For example, in 2016 a citizens' assembly of ninety-nine citizens, chaired by a Supreme Court justice, was convened. The citizens, representative of age, gender, social class, and region, were chosen randomly.[145] This inclusive assembly deliberated, considered public and expert comments, and live-streamed all its meetings to the public. Eventually, it voted to support the repeal of the Eighth Amendment, a recommendation that was then considered by a joint legislative committee representing the major parties of Ireland. The committee accepted the recommendation and put the repeal of the Eighth Amendment to a referendum, as required by the Constitution, in which it received the support of over 66 percent of voters.

The Irish model combined aspects of deliberative, inclusive, time-consuming, representative, and direct popular participation in an attempt to approximate the constituent power and thus confer the political and social legitimacy needed for such a revolutionary constitutional change to transpire and endure.[146] Indeed, the increased legitimacy of such a legal yet dramatic constitutional change is attributable to the process's approximation of the people's constituent power and its claim to truly express popular sovereignty.[147] As the leading student of constitutional referendums, Stephen Tierney, argued, "When referendums are used to make or recreate constitutions they can themselves take on a vital nation-building role. In light of these high stakes, from a civic republican perspective there . . . appears to be a prima facie case for direct popular engagement."[148] In fact, the case can be put even more strongly: "Citizen engagement, although of general importance in any political process, is all the more vital at the constitutional level and, in particular, in respect of fundamental constitutional decisions that implicate the very identity of a constitutional people."[149]

The successful process in Ireland and the increased legitimacy it received by claiming to express popular sovereignty, in contrast with the democratic legitimacy deficits of the constitutional revolutions in Hungary and Israel, demonstrate the importance of meaningful popular involvement in the progression of a constitutional revolution. This brings us back to the people.

The "dirty little secret" of contemporary jurisprudence, as Roberto Unger described it, is discomfort with democracy and fear of popular action.[150] But for some, such as Negri, the concept of constituent power belongs solely in the context of democratic theory.[151] The democratic understanding of constituent power challenges the discomfort that Unger describes, since it recognizes the ability of the people's constituent power to reemerge in "extraordinary moments, [when] politics opens up to make room for conscious popular participation and extra-institutional, spontaneous, collective intervention."[152] Democracy, according to Sheldon Wolin, is not a "form" but rather "an episodic moment" that dictates the constitution's substance, and is thus a representative moment in the nation's life.

Lior Barshack elaborated on the distinction between social structure and instances of communitas. During the latter, "the group is pervaded by constituent, seemingly boundless power and claims freedom from superimposed laws and constraints. Communitas is a lawless form of interaction: the normative system that structures everyday life is in the course of communitas suspended, challenged, and sometimes modified."[153] Resembling Barshack's notion of instances of "communitas," in these rare and episodic "moments of commonality . . . through public deliberations, collective power is used to promote or protect the well-being of the collectivity."[154] In these exceptional political moments, "power returns to 'the Community,' agency to 'the People,'" and the "political is remembered and recreated."[155]

If we believe that the source of political authority rests with the people and that "the ability to engage in constitutional change is a fundamental act of popular sovereignty," we need to find mechanisms that make it possible to bridge the gap between the "mythical people" and the "real people," that enable the people to exercise constituent power even in institutionalized form.[156] Therefore, recent scholarship has called for the development of democratic tools that will "return the epicenter of sovereignty to the people," especially in constitutional decisions.[157] Ali Riza Çoban, for example, argues that it is necessary to have legal arrangements that ensure a maximum level of democratic participation by the people during constitution making.[158] Indeed, the recent proliferation of referendums is an indicator of this broader trend toward engaging the people in constitutional matters.[159] Among current constitutions, more than 40 percent were publicly ratified by referendums and many others involved different forms of popular participation in the constitution-making process.[160] Today, popular participation is a distinctive feature of constitution making.[161] This is the case not only for constitution making but also for constitution amending. There has been a shift in modern constitutional design toward more inclusive and participatory mechanisms whereby the people can assume (or reassume) their constituent role and be actively involved in constitutional change, as the Irish and other examples demonstrate.[162] The people's involvement need not be limited to mere ratification via referendum: "The legitimacy and validity of the constitution requires not only popular ratification, but also real (or true) democratic involvement. A constitution made through ordinary parliaments and representatives is unacceptable."[163] This understanding does not reduce constituent power to mere acclamation—"soccer-stadium democracy"[164]—in the manner of Schmitt's conception of constituent power, according to which "the people's constitution-making will always express itself only in a fundamental yes or no."[165] Such a conception lacks any rational deliberation: "There is no discourse, no rational consideration, only irrational masses cheering or booing."[166] Process matters. In other words, for constitutional revolutions to manifest the people's will, popular participation is required before, throughout, and after the constitution-transforming process and cannot be limited solely to a yes or no vote in a referendum. It must be the expression of "we the people," not simply "oui, the people."[167]

Thus, for constituent power to approximately manifest the popular will, its exercise should incorporate actual, well-deliberated, and thoughtful free choice by society's members. It should be inclusive, participatory, time consuming, and deliberative. After all, the word "*constituere*," as Kalyvas reminds us, marks the act of founding together, jointly.[168] Important to this enterprise is the maintenance of freedoms: speech, fair elections, assembly, and association, the absence of which "spell[s] the death for the legal concept that is constituent power."[169] As the ultimate "juridification of politics," it would often be "the court that decides on whether constituent power has arrived."[170]

Constituent power is usually regarded as an a-legal power, existing outside the constitutional order and able to break constitutional bounds and rules in an attempt to create a new constitutional order. These are the concept's advantages but also its dangers. Hannah Arendt noted "the extraordinary ease with which the national will could be manipulated and imposed upon whenever someone was willing to take the burden or the glory of dictatorship upon himself," epitomized by Napoleon Bonaparte, "only the first in a long series of national statesmen who, to the applause of a whole nation, could declare: 'I am the *pouvoir constituant.*'"[171] Thus, for Arendt, the legacy of a radical constituent power is "a poisonous recipe for permanent revolution" by those who claim the absolute *pouvoir constituant* in the name of the people.[172]

As we have seen, however, constitutional revolutions that bring about paradigmatic displacement in the conceptual prism through which constitutionalism is experienced can occur without any mass mobilization of constitutional moments in an Ackermanian sense, and without any extralegal breaks, but instead occur incrementally under the existing constitutional framework. Constitutional revolutions can therefore teach us a great deal about the concept of constituent power.

Along with the two prevailing approaches, constitutional revolutions offer a third option for considering constituent power. For some, constituent power refers to the exercise of pure extralegal power that cannot be regularized by law. According to a counterapproach, since the people are never "self-present," constituent power can be exercised only under the law, through instituted mechanisms. But as the early revolutionary tradition, in addition to the more recent experience of the Arab Spring, demonstrates, constituent power can be exercised outside the law. Furthermore, constitutional revolutions reveal that constituent power can be exercised under the rule of law and through constituted organs. Focusing on the constitutional revolution thus necessitates a new kind of thinking about constituent power, including its complex relationship with constituted powers. Constituent power is external to the constitutional order and may be exercised extralegally. Yet such extralegality is not exclusive; constituent power may also be exercised legally through constituted organs.

What are the lessons of constitutional revolutions for constituent power? First, reducing constituent power to sheer power would be a mistake. As Ulrich Preuss explained, "Being directed at the creation of an order whose structure is, so to speak, anticipated in its actions, the constituent power ceases to be mere force."[173] Second, the exercise of constituent power, even if regarded as extralegal, necessitates a certain representational form; that is, the will that we attribute to "the people" ought to be revealed through some kind of representation. Therefore, to be exercised, constituent power must in some way act as an already-constituted power, since the constitution-making process necessitates a certain institutionalized framework through which the people can express their will.[174] Of course, the initiation or emergence of constituent power can be spontaneous and direct, like mass protests or popular revolutions, but the execution and formulation of the decisions of the constituent power require certain procedures and organization. Otherwise, constituent power would be left powerless and ineffective.[175] Consider, for example, the constitutional transformation of the Arab Spring, which began as spontaneous popular revolutions yet required democratic elections to constituent assemblies to consolidate the revolutions.[176]

To this, Hans Lindahl replies that "representation ensures that there is no direct access to the foundation of a collective in a pure present" and that "there is no way of definitely establishing whether an act taking place now is an act of constituent power or of constituted power; only retrospectively, and only inconclusively will it manifest itself as the one or the other."[177] Lindahl's claim highlights two crucial issues for the relationship between constituent power and constitutional revolutions. First, constitutional revolutions brought about by constituted organs, such as courts or legislatures, challenge the separation between constituent and constituted powers, since they allow constituted organs to exercise constituent power. Ultimately, "there can be no precise algorithm specifying the conditions for defining a people capable of exercising constituent authority," and the decision whether a constitutional norm was indeed a "true manifestation" of constituent power is made retrospectively.[178] As Tushnet notes,

> We can know that the constituent power has been exercised when a successful constitutional transformation has occurred. That is, identifying exercises of the constituent power is possible only in retrospect. . . . Sometimes ordinary constitutional processes can be used in the service of a revolutionary transformation. The reason, we can now see, is that in retrospect those processes should be understood as exercises of the constituent power itself, not an exercise of a delegated constituent power. . . . The amendment can be

taken to have worked a pro tanto constitutional revolution and therefore takes effect.[179]

And so when constituted organs successfully exercise constituent power, what results is a constitutional revolution. As argued in this chapter, legal-constitutional mechanisms such as constituent assemblies and referendums can aid the exercise of constituent power,[180] or at the very least its approximation, which points to an internal relation between constituent and constituted powers.[181] Such a complex, nonbinary understanding of constituent power, even under the rule of law, allows for constitutional revolutions through constitutional mechanisms while avoiding the risks of a "permanent revolution" in the Arendtian sense.[182]

A final and very important lesson is that to be successful and to endure, to become the very plenipotentiary imagination of the people's constituent power, constitutional revolutions should aim to include the people in a meaningfully inclusive, proactive, and deliberative way.[183] Regardless of how historically accurate the story we tell ourselves about "the people" as constitution makers, facilitating the process of popular participation in the authorship of their constitution enhances the legitimacy of a constitutional revolution.

8
Conclusion

IN 2009, THE HIGH COURT OF DELHI decided a case that very quickly came to be seen as emblematic of Indian constitutional identity, but whose overturning a few years later by a three-judge panel of the Supreme Court cast doubt on the stability of such a reading. In *Naz Foundation v. Government of NCT of Delhi,* the lower court declared unconstitutional a longstanding provision of the Indian Penal Code that had criminalized "unnatural" sexual acts between consenting adults in private—that is, homosexual conduct. The contested law had been drafted by Lord Macaulay in the nineteenth century, which allowed the justices to dismiss it as embodying a "Western concept," an alien intrusion into the subcontinent. Somewhat ironically, the High Court of Delhi fashioned a constitutional right of privacy largely out of materials appropriated from abroad, with copious references to American precedents. In doing so, the Indian jurists saw themselves as defending "a constitutional morality derived from constitutional values," and they embraced the teaching of B. R. Ambedkar, who had said at the Constituent Assembly: "It is perfectly possible to pervert the Constitution, without changing its form by merely changing its form of administration and to make it inconsistent and opposed to the spirit of the Constitution."[1] That they failed to elucidate the relevance of the many pages of their opinion devoted to other peoples' constitutions for maintaining the spirit of their constitution was regrettable (but not widely noticed).

Fortunately, others provided explanations. Sujit Choudhry, for example, persuasively argued that "the missing link between the comparative jurisprudence on same-sex rights and the basic premises of the Indian Constitution is the analogy between sexual orientation and untouchability."[2] He pointed out that the judgment's invocation of the ideals animating the adoption of the Indian Constitution, in particular the intention to advance a "social revolution," provided the broader context within which the criminalization of same-sex relations was assessed. The court explicitly appealed to Nehru's passionate devotion to the constitutional goal of inclusiveness. In addition, Choudhry revealed that what was not explicit in the text of the opinion—a specific reliance on the South African judiciary's linkage between discrimination based on caste and that related to sexual orientation—played an important role in the outcome of the case in India: "The idea of a constitution as a dynamic, evolving instrument of social change is arguably the principal influence of the Indian constitutional experience."[3] In this account, the Delhi High Court's ruling was an embodiment of the identity-marking commitment to "transformative constitutionalism." And so "*Naz Foundation* demonstrates that under the dialogical model, comparative materials can be used in a way that not only acknowledges, but also affirms, a distinct constitutional identity."[4]

Four years later, however, this affirmation was in effect challenged, even rejected, when the Supreme Court overturned the decision in *Naz Foundation*. The reversal was a major disappointment for those who had been encouraged by the lower court's ringing endorsement of a progressively inclusive political community, but also for anyone expecting to find in the opinion of the three-judge panel an engagement with the substantive arguments in the nullified judgment. The Court's ruling in *Koushal v. Naz Foundation* rested on two related arguments about judicial power: the sanctity of the "principle of presumption of constitutionality" and the impropriety of "extensively rel[ying] upon the judgments of other jurisdictions."[5]

These jurisprudential commitments were a direct repudiation of the idea that the Supreme Court is "an arm of the social revolution." Also manifest in the deference to Parliament as the source for legitimate expression of the indigenous will of the people is the presumption that determining the nation's constitutional identity is not to be achieved through the imposition of the judicial will. Thus, even if we assume that inclusiveness is one of the essentials of Indian constitutionalism and that an extensive documentary record supports such an assumption, the dynamic quality of identity and the dialogical process by which it emerges mean that the nature and boundaries of the inclusive constitutional ethos are embedded in a deep cultural matrix. From this milieu, counterpressures to the dominant creed exert a continuing though irregular force seeking a more favorable standing for a less inclusive identity reflective of vital strands within the nation's Hindu and Muslim traditions.

Taken together, then, the two decisions offer a window into the development of constitutional identity in India. The ruling by the Delhi High Court did not culminate in a definitive statement of identity, as was made clear by the Supreme Court's subsequent decision to transfer the struggle over same-sex rights from the judicial arena to the legislative. The episodic and untidy process of defining constitutional identity, with its thrusting and counter-thrusting in and out of courtrooms, proceeded in tandem with the evident disharmony between aspirations and behavior, and with the uncertainty that accompanies a progression whose end point is necessarily elusive.

Had this been the end of this narrative of sociolegal development, we would be left with very little to draw on in support of our reflections on constitutional revolution. But in September 2018 a five-member panel of the Indian Supreme Court revisited the provision of the Penal Code that criminalized homosexual conduct, unanimously striking it down: "The Indian Constitution is first and foremost a social document. The majority of its provisions are either directly aimed at furthering the goals of the social revolution or attempt to foster this revolution by establishing the conditions necessary for its achievement. . . . The Constitution of India recognises, protects and celebrates diversity. To stigmatise or to criminalise homosexuals only on account of their sexual orientation would be against the constitutional morality."[6]

Much of the commentary that followed this ruling, while highlighting its liberating implications for Indians who had lived under the shadow of the punitive statute, viewed what the Court had done as only a fairly modest step toward the achievement of full equality. Indian society remained very conservative in matters related to sex; decriminalization, therefore, should not inspire confidence in the imminent legalization of same-sex marriage. What could inspire confidence, however, is that the dialogical model that Choudhry saw at work in the *Naz* case, and that he correctly linked with the broader ambitions of India's transformative constitutionalism, was given a vigorous thrust forward by the Court's second reconsideration of the issue. In so doing, the justices made much more explicit the connection between sexual orientation and caste, and more generally, their connection with the revolutionary antisubordination commitments of the Constitution.

The revolutionary aspect is evident in the Court's invocation of Ambedkar's oft-used phrase "constitutional morality."[7] While the transition from colonial rule may have been legally sanctioned, for many of the newly independent state's founders, the radical restructuring of regime aspirations was the result of their handiwork. As the Supreme Court put it in the case at hand: "Constitutional morality at the time when the Constituent Assembly was set up was an alien notion."[8] Or as we have argued, the assembly's incorporation of this morality within the folds of its newly created governing document initiated a constitutional identity for the regime, which, as we saw in chapter 5, would require a "step by step" evolution to fulfill its revolutionary aspirations.

The justices made clear how the step taken in the immediate case was connected with the larger project of Indian constitutional identity.

> We must not forget that the founding fathers adopted an inclusive Constitution with provisions that not only allowed the State to undertake affirmative action to eradicate the systematic discrimination against the backward sections of the society and the expulsion and censure of the vulnerable communities by the so-called upper caste/sections of the society that existed on a massive scale prior to coming into existence of the Constituent Assembly. These were nothing but facets of the majoritarian social morality which were sought to be rectified by bringing into force the Constitution of India.[9]

As further explained in the Court's opinion, "the million dollar question as to why we adopted the Constitution" could be answered only if proper attention were directed to the radical ambitions of the framers: "Therefore, the purpose of having a Constitution is to transform the society for the better and this objective is the fundamental pillar of transformative constitutionalism." Their "ultimate goal" was "to make right the upheaval which existed in the Indian society before the adopting of the Constitution." Perhaps mindful of the conventional association of constitutions with preservative goals, Chief Justice Misra described the Constitution's aims as "almost revolutionary," although the qualifier was hardly warranted given the document's "aim of transforming a medieval, hierarchical society into a modern, egalitarian democracy."[10]

It is understandable why the language of revolution would lead a court to soften the impact of the word by attaching a modifier to its use. Achieving a revolution through law is not our accustomed way of thinking of how such change occurs. Still, how otherwise to depict the actions necessary for uprooting the entrenched inequalities and arbitrariness of an ancient feudal order? Consider, though, how in our account the concept of constitutional revolution can provide analytical clarity to this descriptive challenge. Thus, the judicial elimination of the criminal sanction against homosexual conduct in India is in itself a welcome development, not only for those who are the direct beneficiaries of decriminalization, but also for the many others whose sense of justice was offended by what had been done in the name of the law. Yet welcome as it might be, this occurrence is only an incremental change in the attainment of real equality in matters of sexuality; moreover, when placed within the broader context of social reconstruction, it appears even less consequential. But when this placement is inserted in the larger displacement in the way constitutionalism is experienced in the polity, its far-reaching—perhaps even revolutionary—implications come into focus.

Underscoring the incremental dimension of the change that often characterizes a constitutional revolution connects with another pivotal idea of this book, which is that disharmony, whether manifest in the incongruities lodged within a constitution or in the gap between inscribed commitments and external realities, is a critical element in comprehending the meaning of such revolutions. Understanding how it works requires serious engagement with sources from within the traditions of a polity that extend much further back in time than the specific occasions that are imbued with revolutionary significance. Thus, the Indian Constitution, as framed and amended, is permeated by a transformative ethos that establishes a radically egalitarian playing field on which a constitutional identity is to be constructed, but the document also expresses in more muted fashion an exclusivist voice with deep resonance in the history of the subcontinent. The interactive process intrinsic to a constitutional work in progress—as in our other cases as well—is the driving force behind the substantive transformation that is the hallmark of constitutional revolution. Perhaps most dramatically expressed in Israel, where the nation's founding document incorporates the dissonance that has accompanied the steady but halting movement from parliamentary to constitutional supremacy, the interaction of conflicting elements in a nation's historical narrative is at the core of a dynamic that often culminates in a reconstituting of the political order. And as the Hungarian story vividly demonstrates, these divergent strands can play out in a sequence of transformations that resonate with a more astronomical notion of revolution, one in which a newly ascendant constitutional identity assumes a decidedly ancestral look.

Final Thoughts

We began this book with some reflections on the American Declaration of Independence. Its revolutionary significance had both proximate and abiding implications, since it was both an argument for the political severance of the moment and a distillation of the principles that over time would constitute the new nation. As was quickly evident from the compromises of 1787, this latter meaning was contestable; so much so that decades later, John C. Calhoun could justify another severance—indeed another secession—as an appropriate response to policies that were "inconsistent with the character of the Constitution and the ends for which it was established."[11] While others, notably Lincoln, understood these ends differently, Calhoun was ironically pursuing the logic of the future president's First Inaugural, in which the people, "if they should grow weary of the existing government," could exercise "their REVOLUTIONARY right to dismember or overthrow it."

Lincoln, however, included an alternative path for a people no longer content with their prevailing state of affairs; they could "exercise their CONSTITUTIONAL right of amending it." By this, he was referring to "this country['s]" governing document, which his postwar successors in the

Republican Party succeeded in amending in order finally to render the Constitution consistent with their understanding of the nation's founding principles. The results could plausibly be described as revolutionary: "As in any revolution (including the American Revolution), some parts of the past endured, but the violent, permanent remaking of the country introduced a new, persistent set of arguments over voting rights, citizenship, federal power and the unrealized potential for a multiracial republic."[12] That it took a tragic and devastating war to determine which of the divergent versions of national-constitutional identity should predominate serves to clarify the revolutionary dimensions of this story, one that encapsulates the permutations of the constitutional revolution concept discussed in this book.

Lincoln was concerned with heading off the revolutionary act of secession intimated by Calhoun, but that was not the only antebellum revolutionary undertaking that troubled him. The Supreme Court's *Dred Scott* decision had struck him as a direct repudiation of the revolutionary principles in the Declaration of Independence. His response to that decision was in equal parts a denunciation of Chief Justice Taney's reasoning in the ruling and a condemnation of his political opponent, Stephen Douglas, for having aligned himself with it.

> I had thought the Declaration contemplated the progressive improvement in the condition of all men everywhere; but no, it merely "was adopted for the purpose of justifying the colonists in the eyes of the civilized world in withdrawing their allegiance from the British crown, and dissolving their connection with the mother country." Why, that object having been effected some eighty years ago, the Declaration is of no practical use now—mere rubbish—old wadding left to rot on the battle-field after the victory is won.[13]

By denuding the Declaration of its promise of equality, what Martin Luther King Jr. would later refer to as its "promissory note," the Court had, in effect, performed a counterrevolutionary act. The reply provided Douglas with the argument that he used repeatedly in his famous debates with Lincoln: in attacking the decision of the Court, Lincoln was counseling disobedience and undermining respect for the law. In his First Inaugural, the president famously addressed the charge:

> I do not forget the position assumed by some that constitutional questions are to be decided by the Supreme Court. . . . The candid citizen must confess that if the policy of the Government upon vital questions affecting the whole people is to be irrevocably fixed by decisions of the Supreme Court, the instant they are made in ordinary litigation between parties in personal actions the people will have ceased to be their own rulers, having to that extent practically resigned their Government into the hands of that eminent tribunal. Nor is there in this view any assault upon the court or the judges. It is a duty from which they may not shrink to decide cases properly brought before them, and it is no fault of theirs if others seek to turn their decisions to political purposes.[14]

Neither Lincoln's election, nor the firm position he took in questioning the finality of judicial decisions in which "the people will have ceased to be their own rulers," meant that the decision in *Dred Scott* denying people of African descent membership in the political community would be considered anything other than binding law. Through an act of judicial interpretation, a high court had proved itself capable, at least in the eyes of those who, like Lincoln, believed that the Constitution incorporated the Declaration's self-evident principle, of executing a constitutional revolution. The subsequent reversal of that judgment through the adoption of the Fourteenth Amendment was a prime example of Lincoln's other First Inaugural claim, that the people could exercise their constitutional right to amend the Constitution when it no longer comports with their thinking about what it must be held to mean. Whether the amended document is best understood as making amends, as King put it, for the "default on [the] promissory note" contained in the founding revolutionary promise, or as itself a "second American revolution," the achievement is a testament to the power of the extant legal process to effect what we have referred to as a paradigmatic shift in the way constitutionalism is experienced in a polity.

That shift represents the critical dynamic in our conceptualization of constitutional revolution. The followers of Calhoun succeeded in dismembering the Union and writing their own constitution, albeit one that largely resembled the document under which they had previously been governed. Still, it differed in several major ways from the U.S. Constitution, specifically in its express acknowledgment of slavery and in its declarations concerning the sovereignty of the states. Arguably, these material changes amounted in themselves to a transformation fundamental enough to satisfy our criterion for recognizing the occurrence of a constitutional revolution; although, in light of the accompanying dramatic rupture in political continuity, it might be easier to perceive the Confederate arrangement as revolutionary simply because it transpired outside the parameters of legality.[15] Thus, for a follower of Calhoun, who had always interpreted the 1787 Constitution as both proslavery and pro–state sovereignty, the two constitutions would not have represented a paradigm shift in orientation; yet the replacement of one by the other through the illegal act of secession would, as argued in chapter 2, qualify as a constitutional revolution by conventional thinking.

It has been our aim in this book to offer a wider conceptual perspective, one that would allow us to discern in the substantive transformation brought about by an amendment that led to a reordering in constitutional priorities, or a landmark judicial decision that left the constitutional landscape fundamentally reformed, a basis for affirming the reality of a constitutional revolution. The underlying concern here involves much more than semantics and the rhetorical satisfaction that accurate labeling can offer. Rather, it lies in the prospect that the revolution question will provoke productive debate and discussion about the events and activities that led to whatever constitutional modifications might have occurred. For Lincoln, *Dred Scott* was a judicial decision that, in its negation of primary regime principles, radically altered American constitutional identity. Others have disagreed, including contemporary scholars whose disdain for that ruling does not alter the fact that in their accounts the outcome in the case was not really radical at all, but sadly compatible with an enduring founding commitment of the polity.[16] Similarly, the question whether the Fourteenth Amendment put the course of American constitutional development on a new egalitarian trajectory is one that can and should be intensely contested. And if it did put it on such a course, how should we weigh the protracted, incremental, and uneven implementation of its goals in our substantive evaluation of the original amending changes?[17]

In each of the cases we examined, a plausible revolutionary scenario emerged from our application of the conceptual framework advanced in chapter 2. But accounting for them in this way requires openness to unconventional thinking about political occurrences for which the revolutionary designation is apposite. Such openness, however, does not demand an extravagant imaginary leap. Thus, if we look to domains outside the political, we are accustomed to certifying as revolutionary the type of change that is substantively groundbreaking despite its less than precipitous appearance. The Industrial Revolution, for example, was arguably no less revolutionary for taking an extended period of time to make the transition in the way things were produced, though even here orthodoxy can lead one to press the labeling pause button: "This period is appropriately labeled 'revolution,' for it thoroughly destroyed the old manner of doing things; yet the term is simultaneously inappropriate, for it connotes abrupt change. The changes that occurred . . ., occurred gradually."[18]

That historians still debate the dates marking the onset and completion of the revolution shows that the absence of a discernible and clearly articulated moment when the ways of the past were succeeded by something radically different underscores two main concerns in this book. First, the constitutionally transformative significance of a radical departure from previous experience ought not to be obscured by the nonexistence of an external source of rupture in continuity. And the protracted period that often attends the attainment—partial or full—of transformative objectives ought not to conceal their revolutionary significance. For historians of the Industrial Revolution, the assumptions that lead the constitutional theorist to be skeptical of these "ought nots" are noteworthy only for their obvious incongruence with the familiar connotation of the word "revolution." For constitutional theorists, however, these assumptions lie at the heart of the enterprise as traditionally practiced, encapsulated in the Kelsenian insistence on illegality as the sine qua non of revolutionary transformation.

What we have seen in the examples analyzed here provides us with both descriptive and normative perspectives on revolutionary transformation occurring in constitutional settings. The Hungarian, German, Indian, and Israeli cases are distinguishable in many ways; each, however, illustrates conceptually important aspects of what we refer to in this book as a constitutional revolution.

The constitutions in Germany and India were textual embodiments of a revolutionary break with the past, each establishing foundational principles upon which a distinctive constitutional identity could be realized. By emphasizing that a constitutional identity is something to be realized, we mean to counter the erroneous assumption that it exists simply by virtue of its literal incorporation in the boundaries of a text. Like Madison's concern in the *Federalist Papers* that written guarantees would not in themselves guarantee the protection of individual rights, that they were at best "parchment barriers," the act of including explicit constitutional language about identity in a document has at the moment of inclusion only aspirational significance.[19] Or as we maintain, it affirms a commitment and a direction; if the promise embodied in such language is actively pursued in a manner that over time renders the parchment constitutional identity a lived reality, then we can speak of a constitutional revolution.

Thus, as we have seen in India, the measured, "step by step" progression toward fulfillment of the reconstructive ambitions of the prevailing framers at the Constituent Assembly suggests an archetype for constitutional revolutions whose inception in a proclaimed assertion of the constituent power requires a protracted period of constitutional politics before the original expressive intent can in retrospect be viewed in plausibly revolutionary terms. The Directive Principles of State Policy conveyed the prevailing sense of a radical social ethos whose activation required a concerted mobilization of political resources, but the persistence of interests invested in the maintenance of existing social relations ensured that the constitution's transformational goals would only with difficulty be attained. What this means is that the existence of a constitutional revolution of this type is in principle contestable, with those declaring it a reality assuming a heavy evidentiary burden of proof.

The story in Germany was different in that the Basic Law's revolutionary commitment was manifest in the explicit entrenchment of the essentials critical to the new regime's rejection of the immediate past. This did not make the commitment any less aspirational, but it required of the nation's public institutions—with the Federal Constitutional Court playing the central role—unprecedented exertions of authority to demonstrate that the transition from tyrannical rule to constitutional governance was more than a mere parchment proclamation. With the Court's embrace, in the landmark *Southwest Case,* of the concept that it had the authority to invalidate a duly enacted constitutional amendment on the basis of its incompatibility with the newly formulated national constitutional identity, it effectively legitimated the constitutional revolution and signaled its resolute commitment to the defense of that identity: "Any constitutional provision must be interpreted in such a way that it is compatible with . . . [fundamental] principles and with the basic values of the framers of the constitution."[20] When, much later, the Court insisted on its right to defend these principles against any infringement by a supranational political entity, its determination to do so was tantamount to affirming that the earlier codification of the change in German constitutional identity had been unambiguously revolutionized. The Court could then constitute itself the principal bulwark against a counterrevolution.

Unlike the German and Indian experiences, the Hungarian and Israeli cases present constitutional revolutions that occurred without a constitutional moment corresponding to the framing of a formal written document blessed by the legitimating aura of the constituent power.

In Hungary, negotiations at a National Round Table for a peaceful transition ended the communist regime and gave birth to a new constitutional democracy. But in contrast with Kelsen's illegality criterion, this rejection of the former regime occurred within a formal reliance on legality for the transition to a new order. The revolutionary transformation was brought about within legal boundaries through formal constitutional amendments to the original 1949 communist Constitution. Notwithstanding this legal continuity, these amendments sought to revolutionize the constitutional order by creating a new system based on the rule of law, separation of powers, and rights protection. The Hungarian case thus presents a clear example of procedural legal continuity and substantive constitutional rupture. Since the new democratic regime derived its binding force from the old regime, it suffered from a legitimacy deficit, one exacerbated by the actions of a newly created Constitutional Court entrusted with vast review powers. This Court developed a theory of the "invisible constitution"—similar to the German holistic interpretation of the constitution in the *Southwest Case*—according to which the constitution was to be regarded as a unity of principles and rules. Yet the Hungarian Constitutional Court could not avert a counterrevolution. It failed to consolidate the liberal-democratic revolution within a new constitutional order that would define and entrench a clear national identity, and thereafter witnessed an incremental transformation from a liberal constitutional state to an illiberal one rooted in identity politics and Christian culture, attained through the use and abuse of the constitutional-amendment formula.

As in Hungary, the struggle over identity was central to the Israeli constitutional saga. The inability to agree on the core identity question—is the nation principally a Western democracy protecting universal values or a nation-state fulfilling the aspirations of the Jewish people?—led to postponement of the constitution-making process promised in the Declaration of Independence. A constituent moment, if there was one, passed without the creation of a constitution. In the absence of a formal constitution, protection of human rights fell to the Supreme Court, whose powers were constrained by the commitment to parliamentary sovereignty. The constitutional transformation that began with the enactment of the Basic Laws on human rights and that culminated with a landmark judicial decision demonstrated that a constitutional revolution's realization does not require a constitutional moment. Yet the manner in which this occurred raised profound questions about whether a liberal constitution could be created without an inclusive and conscious constitution-making process involving direct popular participation. The judicially driven revolution triggered counterrevolutionary forces that, as in Hungary, sought to derail the constitutional project. And so, the question whether a constituted organ arguably devoid of constituent authority could legitimately create a constitution continues to linger over the constitutional politics of Israel.

But not only in Israel. What emerges from our case studies of constitutional revolutions is that basic premises concerning the nature of constituent power—the generative power behind constitutional arrangements—need to be questioned. Thus, Emmanuel Joseph Sieyès's famous distinction between extraordinary constituent power and constituted powers appears more imprecise than most accounts in constitutional theory would have it. An ordinary constitutional process such as a formal amendment or a judicial interpretation can be used in the service of revolutionary transformation, and in such cases it is possible to appreciate that constituent power has been successfully exercised.

Still, that success does not guarantee a successful and enduring constitutional revolution. Although we have had it as our principal goal to provide conceptual clarity for that species of change that involves critical interruptions and departures in the workings of the constitutional order, we know that this analytical exercise has important normative implications. What Sanford Levinson referred to in an essay title as "The Continuing Specter of Popular Sovereignty . . . in an Age of Political Uncertainty" is never far from the descriptive matters discussed in these pages.[21] Just how critical the "We the People" narrative is to the fortunes of constitutional revolution has yet to be determined with the precision and care it requires. Our hope is that a foundation for such an inquiry is now in place.

NOTES

Unless otherwise noted, all translations are by the authors.

Chapter 1. Introduction

1. Roy Basler, ed., *The Collected Works of Abraham Lincoln* (New Brunswick, N.J.: Rutgers University Press, 1953), 2:405.
2. Ibid., 2:406.
3. Ibid.
4. John Quincy Adams, "American Principles," in Justin Buckley Dyer, ed., *American Soul: The Contested Legacy of the Declaration of Independence* (Lanham, Md.: Rowman and Littlefield, 2012), 31.
5. Ibid., 32.
6. See Peter C. Oliver, "Autochthonous Constitutions," in R. Grote, F. Lachenmann, and R. Wolfrum, eds., *Max Planck Encyclopedia of Comparative Constitutional Law* (Oxford: Oxford University Press, 2017); online, subscription required.
7. As noted by Andrew Arato, "The Indian assembly operated in a context of overall legal continuity. If there was a legal break at all, it was much more technical and much less significant than the illegalities of the American Federal Convention"; see Andrew Arato, *The Adventures of the Constituent Power: Beyond Revolutions?* (Cambridge: Cambridge University Press, 2017).
8. Shivprasad Swaminathan, "India's Benign Constitutional Revolution," *Hindu*, November 3, 2016. The author refers to an argument made by the British legal philosopher John Finnis, who noted that the framers of new Commonwealth constitutions took great care to do something illegal "so as to make up a revolution, however contrived." In Ireland, independence was granted under the Irish Free State Constitution Act of 1922, which was intentionally violated in 1937 when the Irish Parliament put the amended Constitution up for a referendum in

express violation of the stipulated procedures outlined in the earlier document. As Swaminathan points out, "It is widely accepted that this successfully severed the chain of validity with the Crown-in-Parliament and ensured an autochthonous Constitution."

9. Bhikhu Parekh, "The Constitution as a Statement of Indian Identity," in Rajeev Bhargava, ed., *Politics and Ethics of the Indian Constitution* (New Delhi: Oxford University Press, 2008), 46.
10. Swaminathan, "India's Benign Constitutional Revolution."
11. And so Jawaharlal Nehru could make "a claim of complete autochthony as well as a revolutionary declaration of sovereignty"; see Arato, *Adventures of the Constituent Power,* 298.
12. Peter Paczolay, "Constitutional Transition and Legal Continuity," *Connecticut Journal of International Law* 8 (1993): 563. Paczolay refers here to the ideas of Hans Kelsen, discussed in chapter 2.
13. Tarunabh Khaitan, "Directive Principles and the Expressive Accommodation of Ideological Dissenters," *International Journal of Constitutional Law* 389 (2018): 412–13. Khaitan's observation follows the teaching of Charles Lindblom and his view that "incrementalism in politics is not, in principle, slow moving . . . [and] is not necessarily, therefore, a tactic of conservatism" (quoted in ibid.).
14. Bruce Ackerman, *The Future of Liberal Revolution* (New Haven, Conn.: Yale University Press, 1992), 68.
15. Ibid., 65.
16. Cong. Globe, 39th Cong., 1st Sess. 2459 (1866).
17. See, for example, Michael W. McConnell, "The Fourteenth Amendment: A Second American Revolution or the Logical Culmination of the Tradition," *Loyola of Los Angeles Law Review* 25 (1992).
18. See, for example, Douglas H. Bryant, "Unorthodox and Paradox: Revisiting the Ratification of the Fourteenth Amendment," *Alabama Law Review* 53, no. 2 (2002).
19. Sanford Levinson, *Constitutional Faith* (Princeton, N.J.: Princeton University Press, 2011), 140.
20. László Sólyom, "Introduction to the Decisions of the Constitutional Court of the Republic of Hungary," in László Sólyom and Georg Brunner, eds., *Constitutional Judiciary in a New Democracy: The Hungarian Constitutional Court* (Ann Arbor: University of Michigan Press, 2000), 38.
21. Monika Polzin, "Constitutional Identity, Unconstitutional Amendments and the Idea of Constituent Power: The Development of the Doctrine of Constitutional Identity in German Constitutional Law," *International Journal of Constitutional Law* 14 (2016): 423.
22. Ibid., 424.
23. Parliamentary Debates V, vols. xii–xiii, pt. 11, 8820–22, May 16, 1951, in Subhash C. Kashyup, ed., *Jawaharlal Nehru and the Constitution* (New Delhi: Metropolitan Book Co., 1982), 147.

24. Arun K. Thiruvengadam, *The Constitution of India: A Contextual Analysis* (London: Bloomsbury, 2017), 2. Or as another Indian constitutional scholar has said, "Given the appalling living conditions of the majority of the people in the country, the framers understood the burden of the expectations they all carried, and instinctively knew that the new constitution had to be transformative if it had to have any durability or legitimacy" (Khaitan, "Directive Principles," 403).
25. Moshe Cohen-Eliya, "Israeli Case of a Transformative Constitutionalism," in Gideon Sapir, Daphna Barak-Erez, and Aharon Barak, eds., *Israeli Constitutional Law in the Making* (Oxford: Oxford University Press, 2013), 173, 174 (noting that "the Israeli case is . . . a unique instance of a transformative constitutionalism, in that the ambitious project is undertaken by the Supreme Court in the absence of a nationally defining moment and without legitimacy from the constitutional text").
26. Ruth Gavison, "The Constitutional Revolution: A Reality or a Self-Fulfilling Prophecy?," *Mishpatim* 28 (1997): 147 (Heb.).
27. United Bank HaMizrahi Ltd. v. Migdal, 49(4) P.D. 221, 475 (1995).
28. Hans Lindahl, "Constituent Power and the Constitution," in David Dyzenhaus and Malcolm Thorburn, eds., *Philosophical Foundations of Constitutional Law* (Oxford: Oxford University Press, 2016), 147.
29. Claude Klein, "Apropos Constituent Power: Some General Views in a Modern Context," in Antero Jyränki, ed., *National Constitutions in the Era of Integration* (The Hague: Kluwer International, 1999), 31.
30. Carl Joachim Friedrich, *Constitutional Government and Politics: Nature and Development* (New York: Harper & Brothers, 1937), 117.
31. Ulrich K. Preuss, "The Exercise of Constituent Power in Central and Eastern Europe," in Martin Loughlin and Neil Walker, eds., *The Paradox of Constitutionalism: Constituent Power and Constitutional Form* (Oxford: Oxford University Press, 2007), 211–22; Luc J. Wintgens, "Sovereignty and Representation," *Ratio Juris* 14, no. 3 (2001): 274.
32. A survey of 1978 revealed that more than half of the world's constitutions referred explicitly to the sovereignty of the people. See Hence van Maarseveen and Ger van der Tang, *Written Constitutions: A Computerized Comparative Study* (Dobbs Ferry, N.Y.: Oceana, 1978), 93. On how constitutions portray the people's sovereignty, see Denis J. Galligan, "The Sovereignty Deficit of Modern Constitutions," *Oxford Journal of Legal Studies* 33 (2013).
33. David S. Law, "Imposed Constitutions and Romantic Constitutions," in Richard Albert, Xenophon Contiades, and Alkmene Fotiadou, eds., *The Law and Legitimacy of Imposed Constitutions* (New York: Routledge, 2019), 34.
34. Basler, *Collected Works of Abraham Lincoln*, 2:401.
35. Ibid.

Chapter 2. Theorizing Constitutional Revolution

Epigraph: Bruce Ackerman, *The Future of Liberal Revolution* (New Haven, Conn.: Yale University Press, 1992), 1.

1. Christopher M. Kotowski, "Revolution," in Giovanni Sartori, ed., *Social Science Concepts: A Systematic Analysis* (Beverly Hills, Calif.: Sage, 1984), 405.
2. Crane Brinton, *The Anatomy of Revolution* (New York: Vintage, 1952), 26.
3. Ackerman, *Future of Liberal Revolution*, 47.
4. Bruce Ackerman, *We the People: Foundations* (Cambridge, Mass.: Harvard University Press, 1991), 19 (emphasis added).
5. Ibid., 206. Ackerman's disagreement with Arendt has to do with the latter's insistence that "once the 'social question' is placed on the political agenda, revolutionary politics inevitably degenerates into demagogy and dictatorship" (209). Thus, while applauding her emphasis on the political meaning of revolution, he criticizes her failure to appreciate the civic significance of social movements for the success of revolutions, particularly in the American case.
6. See Rivka Weill, "Evolution vs. Revolution: Dueling Models of Dualism," *American Journal of Comparative Law* 54 (2006): 432.
7. Ackerman, *Future of Liberal Revolution*, 65.
8. Weill, "Evolution vs. Revolution," 465.
9. As Jaroslav Krejci notes, "Both . . . understandings of revolution, the technical and the metaphorical one, have one important element in common, the change of the paradigm which has been the pivot of value orientation or criterion of truth for the phenomenon affected"; see Krejci, *Great Revolutions Compared: The Search for a Theory* (Brighton, U.K.: Wheatsheaf, 1983), 6.
10. Robert Dahl cautions that the prominence of revolution in the political vocabulary of a nation is a poor predictor of the degree of transformation one should expect to find: "Some of the most profound changes in the world take place in a quiet country like Denmark, where hardly anyone raises his voice and the rhetoric of revolution finds few admirers"; see Dahl, *After the Revolution? Authority in a Good Society* (New Haven, Conn.: Yale University Press, 1970), 3.
11. Alan Kuperman, e-mail to Gary Jacobsohn, January 20, 2013.
12. Giovanni Sartori, "Guidelines for Conceptual Analysis," in Sartori, *Social Science Concepts*, 26.
13. Or as Bruce Ackerman has suggested, "We might look for a concept [of revolution] capacious enough to encompass a broader family of phenomena" (*Future of Liberal Revolution*, 5).
14. Kotowski, "Revolution," 416.
15. Turkish Constitution as amended by Law No. 3272 of November 29, 1937.
16. Constitution of the Socialist Federal Republic of Yugoslavia (April 9, 1963).
17. Preamble, Constitution of Bulgaria, 1971.
18. Preamble, Constitution of the Czechoslovak Republic, 1948.
19. Constitution of Romania, Art. 1, sec. 3, 1991.
20. Preamble, Constitution of China as amended through 2004.
21. Fundamental Law of Cuba, as amended 1962.
22. Constitution of Vietnam, 1991.
23. Preamble, Interim Constitution of Nepal, 2007.
24. Preamble, Constitution of Panama, 1972.

25. Preamble, Constitution of the Islamic Republic of Iran, 1979.
26. Just as the idea of constitutional revolution may strike one as an oxymoron, so too does the notion of constitutional theocracy. For a very thoughtful analysis of the concept, see Ran Hirschl, *Constitutional Theocracy* (Cambridge, Mass.: Harvard University Press, 2010).
27. Put differently, what if the "achievements" of a revolution, or the principles that "inspired" a revolution, do not comport with threshold standards of constitutional governance, with what Lon Fuller famously referred to as "the inner morality of law"? See Fuller, *The Morality of Law* (New Haven, Conn.: Yale University Press, 1964), 41–44.
28. Hannah Arendt famously went one step further, not only worrying about constitutional legitimacy in such cases but also claiming that revolutions of this sort were really not revolutions at all: "Only . . . where the liberation from oppression aims at least at the constitution of freedom can we speak of revolution"; see Arendt, *On Revolution* (New York: Viking, 1963), 28. Or, as she wrote in a newly discovered essay, "Though many revolutions have ended in tyranny, it has also always been remembered that, in the words of Condorcet, 'The word "revolutionary" can be applied only to revolutions whose aim is freedom' "; see Arendt, "The Freedom to Be Free," *New England Review* 38 (2017): 58. So, for example, when the Preamble to the 1997 Eritrean Constitution refers to "the long and heroic revolutionary struggle for liberation," an Arendtian take would have it that the achievement of liberation by the Eritrean people qualifies as a revolutionary struggle only if it is an element in a larger collective effort to attain freedom. See, in this connection, Joshua Braver, "Revolutionary Reform in Venezuela: Electoral Rules and Historical Narratives in the Creation of the 1999 Constitution," in Richard Albert, Xenophon Contiades, and Alkmene Fotiadue, eds., *The Foundations and Traditions of Constitutional Amendment* (Oxford: Hart, 2017), 137. Borrowing from Bruce Ackerman, Braver argues that for Arendt, "revolutionary ruptures should be partial and not absolute" (143).
29. For example: " 'Nonviolent revolution' . . . is a contradiction in terms"; see Chalmers Johnson, *Revolutionary Change* (Boston: Little, Brown, 1966), 7. A notable exception to the position that violence is necessary was taken by Charles Tilly, who maintained that there could be "silent revolutions"; see Tilly, *From Mobilization to Revolution* (Reading, Mass.: Addison-Wesley, 1978), 195. More generally, a notable critique of "classical" studies of revolution is S. N. Eisenstadt, *Revolution and the Transformation of Societies: A Comparative Study of Civilizations* (New York: Free Press, 1978).
30. Arendt, *On Revolution,* chap. 4.
31. Thus, Chalmers Johnson wrote, "The radical changes that occurred in the United States during the New Deal . . . were . . . accomplished without resort to a revolution" (*Revolutionary Change,* 5). Bruce Ackerman offers a different interpretation: "I will consider a change from laissez-faire to a welfare state revolutionary—so long as it is achieved through self-conscious mass mobilization" (*Future of Liberal Revolution,* 6). As for the American Revolution, it may be understood as a constitutional

revolution in the sense that it was a struggle over the constitution. This argument has been made most effectively by the historian Jack P. Greene: "The revolution that occurred in North America during the last quarter of the eighteenth century was the unintended consequence of a dispute about law"; see Greene, *The Constitutional Origins of the American Revolution* (Cambridge: Cambridge University Press, 2011), 1.

32. The idea here is well captured by Hannah Arendt, who, in her classic work *On Revolution,* makes clear that the constitutionalizing of new governments is itself an unconstitutional act.

33. According to Michael Walzer, this trajectory has an ancient lineage, as seen in his invocation of biblical precedent to connect revolution and linearity: "The appeal of Exodus to generations of radicals lies in its linearity, in the idea of a promised end, in the purposiveness of the Israeli march. The movement across space is readily reconstructed as a movement from one political regime to another"; see Walzer, *Exodus and Revolution* (New York: Basic Books, 1984), 14.

34. Addressing the American case, Paul Kahn writes, "Law and revolution . . . are so tightly bound to each other in our political order that the investigation of either will trace its transformation into the other"; see Kahn, *The Cultural Study of Law: Reconstructing Legal Scholarship* (Chicago: University of Chicago Press, 1999), 120.

35. Hans Kelsen, "The Function of a Constitution," in Richard Tur and William Twining, eds., *Essays on Kelsen* (Oxford: Clarendon, 1986), 111.

36. Since the first historical constitution cannot derive its validity from an authorizing positive law, it rests on the presupposed "law-creating power" of the basic norm (*Grundnorm*), which is "not a positive norm, posited by a real act of will, but a norm presupposed in juristic thinking"; Kelsen, "The Function of a Constitution," 115. On Kelsen's *Grundnorm,* see, for example, Joseph Raz, "Kelsen's Theory of the Basic Norm," in Stanley L. Paulson and Bonnie Litschewski Paulson, eds., *Normativity and Norms: Critical Perspectives on Kelsenian Themes* (Oxford: Clarendon, 1998), 48.

37. Hans Kelsen, *General Theory of Law and State* (New Brunswick, N.J.: Transaction, 2006), 117. When the constitution changes in violation of the amendment rule, the validity of the new constitutional norm cannot rest on the chain of legality and requires the presupposition of a new *Grundnorm.* Thus, such a constitutional change may result in a change of the *Grundnorm* itself.

38. Ibid., 113.

39. Joel I. Colón-Ríos, "What Is a Constitutional Transition?," *National Journal of Constitutional Law* 37, no. 1 (2017): 44.

40. Kotowski, "Revolution," 409. See also Nader Sohrabi, *Revolution and Constitutionalism in the Ottoman Empire and Iran* (Cambridge: Cambridge University Press, 2011). According to Sohrabi, "The French Revolution assumed the status of the first constitutional revolution and the principal event of modern history" (16).

41. Another way of asking the question has to do with the totality (or lack thereof) of a given change. Thus, Chalmers Johnson distinguishes between "simple" and "total" revolutions. The first are usually aimed at "the normative codes governing

political and economic behavior, which are thought to be in need of change." In some cases, this can be done by promulgating or rewriting a constitution. The second are "aimed at supplanting the entire structure of values"; when successful, this change "alters the social system from one major archetype to another" (*Revolutionary Change,* 140, 139).

42. Barrington Moore, Jr., *Social Origins of Dictatorship and Democracy* (Boston: Beacon, 1966), 112.
43. Tilly, *From Mobilization to Revolution,* 193.
44. Arendt, *On Revolution,* 25. A recent application of Arendt's notion is found in Gábor Halmai, "Rights Revolution and Counter-Revolution: Democratic Backsliding and Human Rights in Hungary," in *Law and Ethics of Human Rights* (forthcoming, 2019; copy with the authors), arguing, contra to our approach, that Hungary has experienced only one constitutional revolution—that from communism to liberal democracy, while the second constitutional transformation, from a liberal to an illiberal order, cannot be labeled "revolutionary," since it does not represent a move from oppression to liberation, and should thus be labeled as a counterrevolution.
45. For Arendt, as Andreas Kalyvas points out, freedom in this context refers to "the capacity of a collectivity to lucidly institute new spheres of political participation, forms of self-government, and forums of public deliberation and contestation and thus to consciously shape and determine its political existence"; see Kalyvas, *Democracy and the Politics of the Extraordinary: Max Weber, Carl Schmitt, and Hannah Arendt* (Cambridge: Cambridge University Press, 2008), 202.
46. Cuba's Constitution seeks to "make possible the realization of the Revolution" (Fundamental Law of Cuba, as amended through 2004).
47. Jaroslav Krejci distinguishes these two examples under the heading of vertical and horizontal revolutions, the Cuban as illustrative of the first type, wherein an internally inspired societal restructuring results, and the American as representative of the second type, in which a dependent country secedes or frees itself from another country while experiencing important changes in governance (Krejci, *Great Revolutions Compared,* 6).
48. Ackerman, *We the People: Foundations,* 45.
49. Under this account, the Fourteenth Amendment would be an unconstitutional constitutional amendment, and the only question is whether the Supreme Court could invalidate it for that reason; see Gary Jeffrey Jacobsohn, *Constitutional Identity* (Cambridge, Mass.: Harvard University Press, 2010), chap. 2.
50. Michael W. McConnell, "The Fourteenth Amendment: A Second American Revolution or the Logical Culmination of the Tradition," *Loyola of Los Angeles Law Review* 25 (1991): 1160. According to McConnell, "When the Fourteenth Amendment was adopted, it can be said that the Constitution assumed its complete Madisonian form. . . . The most profound practical change wrought by the Fourteenth Amendment . . . was not a radical alteration in the theory of the Constitution, but the fulfillment of that theory" (1167). Needless to say, strong arguments are available on the other side, beginning with the observation that the Equal Protection

Clause constitutes a radical departure from the Constitution's textually explicit denial of such protection.

51. Hanna Lerner, *Making Constitutions in Deeply Divided Societies* (Cambridge: Cambridge University Press, 2011), 39.
52. Consider, for example, the following assessment of constitutional transformation in South America: "It matters less that their aspirations do not all come to fruition in the near term. Rome was not built in a day and neither will be the institutional landscape of the Andes. Constitutions almost by definition take time to take root"; see Zachary Elkins, "Constitutional [R]evolution in the Andes," in Rosalind Dixon and Tom Ginsburg, eds., *Comparative Law in Latin America* (Cheltenham, U.K.: Elgar, 2017), 16.
53. Kotowski, "Revolution," 425.
54. An increasing number of constitutions contain explicit provisions of unamendability in order to protect essential characteristics of the constitutional order or principles perceived, in light of historical circumstances, to be at great risk of repeal via the democratic process. Additionally, there has been a steadily increasing acceptance of the idea of implicit unamendability, namely, that certain principles lie beyond the reach of constitutional amenders. For details, see Yaniv Roznai, *Unconstitutional Constitutional Amendments: The Limits of Amendment Powers* (Oxford: Oxford University Press, 2017).
55. Ibid., 8.
56. Carl Schmitt, *Constitutional Theory* (1928), trans. Jeffrey Seitzer (Durham, N.C.: Duke University Press, 2008), 150.
57. Ibid. "A constitutional amendment that transforms a state resting on the monarchical principle into one ruled by the constitution-making power of the people is not at all constitutional" (ibid., 151).
58. Colón-Ríos, "What Is a Constitutional Transition?," 59. As we will see later, however, Schmitt's criteria for determining what counts as a substantive change of revolutionary significance were unusually demanding.
59. This was the early view of one observer of the Egyptian scene, who defined a constitutional revolution as an "instance of political reconstruction that follows a political revolution or regime change"; see Saïd Amir Arjomand, "Middle Eastern Constitutional and Ideological Revolutions and the Rise of Juristocracy," *Constellations* 19 (2012): 204. As Arjomand points out, "The Egyptian Revolution of January 25 . . . put the writing of a new constitution as the highest item on the agenda of political reconstruction" (209). Regarding that writing, an Egyptian legal reformer was quoted as saying: "If we keep the same institutions, it's going to be exactly like the first republic, without a new philosophy. The new republic should have the spirit of the revolution" (quoted in the *New York Times*, October 24, 2012, A9). See also Nathan J. Brown, "Egypt's Constitution Conundrum," *Foreign Affairs*, December 9, 2012, https://www.foreignaffairs.com/articles/egypt/2012-12-09/egypts-constitution-conundrum.
60. Antoni Abat i Ninet and Mark Tushnet, *The Arab Spring: An Essay on Revolution and Constitutionalism* (Cheltenham, U.K.: Elgar, 2015), 67.

61. Stephen Gardbaum, "Revolutionary Constitutionalism," *International Journal of Constitutional Law* 15, no. 1 (2017): 181.
62. It is difficult to disagree with the assessment of Abat i Ninet and Tushnet that "the time for . . . retrospective assessment of the events of the Arab Spring and thereafter rather clearly has not yet arrived" (*Arab Spring*, 10).
63. Hirschl, *Constitutional Theocracy*, 105.
64. A new constitution adopted in 2014 retained most provisions of its predecessor, including Article 2. However, it eliminated Article 219, thus weakening the prospects of greater religious sway over the meaning and direction of Egyptian constitutional development.
65. "As in the United States, the founding of new regimes in the Arab Spring post-revolutionary scenario will occur (if it does) in several stages" (Abat i Ninet and Tushnet, *Arab Spring*, 66). In January 2017, Egypt's Supreme Administrative Court delivered a judgment in which it held that after the "January 25/June 30" revolution, the ruler's "absolute sovereignty" was replaced by "popular sovereignty," and accordingly that the ruler is subordinated to the supremacy of the Constitution. This statement led Nimer Sultany to suggest that "although constitutional practice seems to revert back to pre–Arab Spring practice, some revolutionary principles survived the coup"; see Sultany, *Law and Revolution: Legitimacy and Constitutionalism After the Arab Spring* (Oxford: Oxford University Press, 2017), 251.
66. Lourens W. H. Ackermann, "The Legal Nature of the South African Constitutional Revolution," *New Zealand Law Review* (2004): 646.
67. Heinz Klug, *Constituting Democracy: Law, Globalism, and South Africa's Political Reconstruction* (Cambridge: Cambridge University Press, 2000), 115. See also Andrew Arato, who notes "the obvious fact that there was no classical revolution in South Africa"; see Arato, *The Adventures of the Constituent Power: Beyond Revolutions?* (Cambridge: Cambridge University Press, 2017), 255. Still, as he points out, "the transformation involved was as comprehensive and radical as in Central Europe, even if it did not involve the replacement of one type of economy by another" (255). Rather, the "replacement of the apartheid political order with its links to the Westminster model of parliamentary sovereignty, by a non-racial political order linked to constitutionalism was at least as radical as the establishment of constitutional democracies in Central Europe" (239).
68. DuPlessis v. DeKlerk, 3 SA 850 (1996), para. 126.
69. Kalyvas, *Democracy and the Politics of the Extraordinary*, 7.
70. In this regard, it is worth noting that in the course of the South African transition negotiations, the National Party's chief negotiator, Roelf Meyer, referred to the adoption of constitutionalism as a "paradigm shift," one that, among other things, led him to embrace the idea of a constitutional court with the power of judicial review; Meyer quoted in Samuel Issacharoff, *Fragile Democracies: Contested Power in the Era of Constitutional Courts* (New York: Cambridge University Press, 2015), 173.
71. Ackerman, *Future of Liberal Revolution*, 16.

72. Justice M. Cheshin in United Mizrahi Bank plc v. Migdal Cooperative Village, 49 (4) PD221 (1995), 540.
73. Aharon Barak, interview with Jacobsohn, New Haven, Conn., April 27, 2007. Not appreciating the revolutionary significance of what one is doing has also been discussed in the American context. Thus, Hannah Arendt wrote: "It was a passion for . . . political freedom, though not yet equated with a republican form of government, which inspired and prepared those to enact a revolution without fully knowing what they were doing" ("Freedom to Be Free," 60). Consider in this regard Robert McCloskey's discussion of the "constitutional revolution of 1937": "The Court's relationship to the American polity had undergone a fundamental change. Quite probably the judges themselves did not understand how great a withdrawal was portended by their about-face in 1937. But within a few years it would be plain to all that another constitutional era had ended and a new one had begun"; see McCloskey, *The American Supreme Court* (Chicago: University of Chicago Press, 1994), 119. Consider, too, Andrew Arato's discussion of Hungary: "In 1989 the population did not experience the process as any kind of revolution. Moreover, the main actors specifically avoided interpreting it in terms that evoked the traditions of revolution of 1848 and 1956"; see Arato, "Regime Change, Revolution and Legitimacy," in Gabor Attila Toth, ed., *Constitutions for a Disunited Nation: On Hungary's 2011 Fundamental Law* (Budapest: Central European Press, 2012), 48.
74. Vernon Bogdanor, "Constitutional Reform in Britain: The Quiet Revolution," *Annual Review of Political Science* 73 (2005): 90. It is worth noting that this is not foreclosed in Ackerman's account. Thus: "Not all big changes come through revolutions. Many, perhaps most, come through evolution" (Ackerman, *Future of Liberal Revolution*, 6). In our account, however, the constitutional import of such changes might well be considered revolutionary.
75. Weill, "Evolution vs. Revolution," 466.
76. Felicity Matthews, "Whose Mandate Is It Anyway? Brexit, the Constitution and the Contestation of Authority," *Political Quarterly* 88, no. 4 (2017): 609.
77. In a study focusing on the scope of transformation associated with changes in constitutional texts in South America, Zachary Elkins concludes, "The Bolivarian constitutions do indeed break from the past in what they provide substantively" ("Constitutional [R]evolution in the Andes," 16). Elkins explicitly distinguishes the constitutional text from the constitutional order, a distinction that should counsel caution in leaping to conclusions about the existence of a constitutional revolution.
78. Jack M. Balkin and Sanford Levinson, "Understanding the Constitutional Revolution," *Virginia Law Review* 87 (2001): 1094. "Constitutional revolutions always concern 'high politics'—the promotion of larger political principles and ideological goals" (1063). According to Robert Justin Lipkin, it is the change in the meaning of constitutional provisions that is the key criterion: "Indeterminate provisions invite revolutions"; see Lipkin, "The Anatomy of Constitutional Revolutions," *Nebraska Law Review* 68 (1989): 748. The legal historian G. Edward

White considers the legal changes wrought by the New Deal a constitutional revolution for the "altered epistemological sensibility" that was produced; see White, "The New Deal 'Constitutional Revolution' as a Crisis in Adaptivity," *Hastings Law Review* 48 (1996–97): 871.

79. It has, for example, been suggested that "the proper way to characterize the constitutional developments is as a 'Constitutional Evolution' rather than a 'Constitutional Revolution'"; see Yoseph M. Edrey, "The Israeli Constitutional Revolution/Evolution, Models of Constitutions, and a Lesson from Mistakes and Achievements," *American Journal of Comparative Law* 53, no. 1 (2005): 88.

80. "Constitutional practice is . . . unlike scientific practice in fundamental ways. Perhaps most obviously and importantly, unlike in science, a number of interpretive paradigms can coexist relatively peacefully in constitutional practice, and no one paradigm is likely to force the others out of business": Ian Bartrum, "Constitutional Value Judgments and Interpretive Theory," *Florida State Law Review* 40 (2013): 272.

81. For further elaboration, see Jacobsohn, *Constitutional Identity,* chap. 3.

82. Vicki C. Jackson, "What's in a Name? Reflections on Timing, Naming, and Constitution-Making," *William & Mary Law Review* 49, no. 4 (2008): 1280.

83. Greene, *Constitutional Origins,* xii. Consistent with an important thread in this chapter, Greene sees the contest over constitutional legitimacy between the metropolitan center and the colonials as one involving alternative conceptions of national identity (8).

84. What exactly constituted the revolutionary essence of the paradigmatic interpretive realignment that accompanied the "constitutional revolution" of 1937? The landmark cases of the New Deal Court such as *West Coast Hotel v. Parrish* (1937) and *Wickard v. Filburn* (1942) were doctrinally innovative in important ways, and they provided constitutional authorization for a future with more active and sustained state intervention in social and economic life; but also hard to ignore is that the jurisprudential underpinnings of these decisions reconnected with the foundational rulings of Chief Justice John Marshall in the early nineteenth century. Marshall represented one side of a divided political tradition whose alternative visions of the proper role of government have threaded their way through American constitutional development. Some scholars, including Balkin and Levinson, argue that the Court is currently at the center of another "paradigm shift" in constitutional law (Balkin and Levinson, "Understanding the Constitutional Revolution," 1051). If that turns out to be the case, the "revolution" that will be said to have occurred will resound with interpretive cadences from an earlier time, echoing the other side of the nation's bifurcated legacy.

85. For a good treatment of this matter, see Sylvia Brown Hamano, "Incomplete Revolutions and Not So Alien Transplants: The Japanese Constitution and Human Rights," *University of Pennsylvania Journal of Constitutional Law* 1 (1999); see also Ray A. Moore and Donald L. Robinson, *Partners for Democracy: Crafting the New Japanese State Under MacArthur* (New York: Oxford University Press, 2002). While acknowledging that there is much truth in the story of an "imposed"

constitution, they also find the depiction misleading. Thus, "It is one thing . . . to impose a constitutional text and quite another to establish constitutional democracy" (3). Similarly, David Law concludes that "it is a gross oversimplification, if not an outright mistake, to say that the [Japanese Constitution] was imposed"; see Law, "The Myth of the Imposed Constitution," in Denis Galligan and Mila Versteeg, eds., *The Social and Political Foundations of Constitutions* (Cambridge: Cambridge University Press, 2013), 241. Lawrence W. Beer understands both Japanese constitutional revolutions—of the nineteenth and twentieth centuries—as "assimilative reactions to Western Legal traditions"; see Beer, "Constitutional Revolution in Japanese Law, Society, and Politics," *Occasional Papers/Reprints Series in Contemporary Asian Studies* 5 (1982): 1.

86. Chaihark Hahm and Sung Ho Kim, "To Make 'We the People': Constitutional Founding in Japan and South Korea," *International Journal of Constitutional Law* 8 (2010): 826, 828. Andrew Arato makes a similar point: "Germany and Japan were constitutional regimes before the 1930s; what occurred after 1945 was first and foremost a restoration of those constitutional regimes"; see Arato, *Constitution Making Under Occupation: The Politics of Imposed Revolution in Iraq* (New York: Columbia University Press, 2009), 34.

87. Fakhreddin Azimi, *The Quest for Democracy in Iran: A Century of Struggle Against Authoritarian Rule* (Cambridge, Mass.: Harvard University Press, 2008), 2.

88. Ibid.

89. Similar observations have been made in reference to the post-1989 transitions in Europe. For example, "The revolution was not just an event of political discontinuity dismantling the communist system. It also reinstated cultural and political continuities and traditions suppressed or manipulated by the communist power": Jiří Přibáň, "Constitutional Symbolism and Political (Dis)continuity: Legal Rationality and Its Integrative Function in Post-Communist Transformations," in Adam Czarnota, Martin Krygier, and Wojciech Sadurski, eds., *Rethinking the Rule of Law After Communism* (Budapest: Central European University Press, 2005), 295, 309.

90. Nader Hashemi, "Religious Disputation and Democratic Constitutionalism: The Enduring Legacy of the Constitutional Revolution on the Struggle for Democracy in Iran," *Constellations* 17 (2010): 50; see also Janet Afary, *The Iranian Constitutional Revolution, 1906–1911: Grassroots Democracy, Social Democracy, and the Origins of Feminism* (New York: Columbia University Press, 1996), and Sohrabi, *Revolution and Constitutionalism.*

91. See Gary Jeffrey Jacobsohn, *The Wheel of Law: Indian Secularism in Comparative Constitutional Context* (Princeton, N.J.: Princeton University Press, 2003).

92. Alexis de Tocqueville, *Oeuvres Completes,* vol. 3, *Ecrits et Discours Politiques,* ed. J.-P. Mayer (Paris: Gallimard, 1962), 480.

93. *The Framing of India's Constitution: Select Documents* (New Delhi: Indian Institute of Public Administration, 1967), 2:265.

94. Jawaharlal Nehru was one of several members of the Constituent Assembly to invoke the name of Ashoka, the third king of the Mauryan Dynasty in the third

century B.C., a legendary figure particularly for those committed to the constitutional vision of secularism often articulated at the assembly. His inspirational meaning for many at the gathering is evident in what was to become the centerpiece of the Indian flag, the Ashokan wheel.

95. Paul W. Kahn, *The Cultural Study of Law: Reconstructing Legal Scholarship* (Chicago: University of Chicago Press, 1999), 48.
96. Arendt, *On Revolution,* 37.
97. Ibid., 19.
98. Ibid., 21.
99. Arno J. Mayer, *Dynamics of Counterrevolution in Europe, 1870–1956* (New York: Harper & Row, 1971), 47.
100. Arendt, *On Revolution,* 35.
101. Arendt, "Freedom to Be Free," 59.
102. Arendt, *On Revolution,* 38.
103. Also known as the Revolution of 1688, and sometimes inaccurately referred to as the "bloodless revolution," the Glorious Revolution resulted in the overthrow of James II by English Parliamentarians and the ascension of William III and Mary II, James's daughter. William led a Dutch fleet in a successful invasion of England—an invasion by invitation. The revolution produced permanent realignments in the political and religious spheres.
104. W. A. Speck, *Reluctant Revolutionaries: Englishmen and the Revolution of 1688* (Oxford: Oxford University Press, 1988), 1.
105. J. G. A. Pocock, "The Fourth English Civil War: Dissolution, Desertion, and Alternative Histories in the Glorious Revolution," in Lois G. Schwoerer, *The Revolution of 1688–1689: Changing Perspectives* (Cambridge: Cambridge University Press, 1992), 62.
106. Jacobsohn discusses this theory in *Constitutional Identity,* 95–100. The more radical view of the revolution was famously set forth by Richard Price, whose alternative understanding Burke challenged in his *Reflections on the Revolution in France.*
107. Speck, *Reluctant Revolutionaries,* 1.
108. Greene, *Constitutional Origins,* 48.
109. Lois G. Schwoerer, *The Declaration of Rights, 1689* (Baltimore: Johns Hopkins University Press, 1981), 291.
110. Pocock, "Fourth English Civil War," 54.
111. According to Lois Schwoerer, "The Declaration of Rights laid the foundations for genuine political and constitutional changes whose promise was fulfilled in the statutory formulation, the Bill of Rights. These two documents . . . undermine the notion that the Revolution of 1688–89 was nothing more than a palace coup" (*Declaration of Rights, 1689,* 282). She provides a specific breakdown of the articles in the Declaration that were truly radical in their constitutionally innovative features and those that can legitimately be perceived as restorations of known laws and statutes of England.
112. Speck, *Reluctant Revolutionaries,* 164.

113. Jennifer Carter, "The Revolution and the Constitution," in Geoffrey Holmes, ed., *Britain After the Glorious Revolution, 1689–1715* (New York: St. Martin's, 1969), 39–40.

114. Richard S. Kay has demonstrated how the Glorious Revolution involved the contradictory ideals of preserving the rule of law and simultaneously breaking certain fundamental rules of the English Constitution. This inherent contradiction allowed the revolutionaries who violated positive legal rules to use the rhetoric of maintaining fidelity to the Constitution and its underlying basic principles in order to justify their actions, thereby legalizing the revolution; see Kay, *The Glorious Revolution and the Continuity of Law* (Washington, D.C.: Catholic University of America Press, 2014).

115. Hanna Fenichal Pitkin, "The Idea of a Constitution," *Journal of Legal Education* 37 (1987): 169.

116. Claude Klein and András Sajó, "Constitution-Making: Process and Substance," in Michel Rosenfeld and András Sajó, eds., *Oxford Handbook in Comparative Constitutional Law* (Oxford: Oxford University Press, 2012), 426. According to the authors, "We may define a revolution in the legal sense as an amendment to the constitution, disregarding the rules of amendment. This was the case of the Articles of Confederation" (ibid.); see also Richard S. Kay, "The Illegality of the Constitution," *Constitutional Commentary* 4 (1987). A contrary view, that the Constitutional Convention was acting legally, is crafted in Akhil Reed Amar, "Popular Sovereignty and Constitutional Amendment," in Sanford Levinson, ed., *Responding to Imperfection: The Theory and Practice of Constitutional Amendment* (Princeton, N.J.: Princeton University Press, 1995), 89.

117. James Madison, *Federalist* 40, in *The Federalist*, ed. George W. Carey and James McClellan, Gideon Edition (1818; Indianapolis: Liberty Fund, 2001), 202 (emphasis in the original).

118. Ibid., 205, 203. In this regard, consider what another delegate to the convention, Oliver Ellsworth of Connecticut, had to say: "Because we have found defects in the confederation, must we therefore pull down the whole fabric, foundation and all, in order to erect a new building totally different from it without retaining any of its materials?"; quoted in Michael J. Klarman, *The Founders' Coup: The Making of the American Constitution* (Oxford: Oxford University Press, 2016), 144 (emphasis in the original).

119. Madison, *Federalist* 40, 203. A useful way of looking at the two documents—the Articles and the Constitution—is to view the movement of the first to the second as an eighteenth-century precursor of the two-stage paradigm of constitution making that emerged with considerable success in the late twentieth century. The model case is South Africa and the formal adoption of an interim constitution, providing an opportunity for constitutional learning that could be used to shape the second and final document. As Andrew Arato points out, the 1787 Constitution is a kind of second-stage product that, to use Madison's language, represented an improvement over the "inefficiency" of its predecessor. A similar understanding applies in France to the Constitution of the Fifth Republic in rela-

tion to that of the Fourth Republic; see Arato, *Constitution Making Under Occupation,* 71. There are important differences between the earlier and later experiences, particularly the fact that the modern two-stage paradigm does not involve a legal break between an old regime and a new one.

120. Madison, *Federalist* 40, 202.
121. Ibid., 247 (emphasis in the original).
122. Kalyvas, *Democracy and the Politics of the Extraordinary,* 227.
123. See Jacobsohn, *Constitutional Identity,* chap. 3.
124. See, in this regard, David J. Bodenheimer, *The Revolutionary Constitution* (Oxford: Oxford University Press, 2012), 24: "Much of the movement toward change was hidden by a conservative rhetoric that called for the restoration of the ancient constitution."
125. See the excellent collection of writings in Arthur J. Jacobson and Bernhard Schlink, eds., *Weimar: A Jurisprudence of Crisis* (Berkeley: University of California Press, 2002).
126. Carl Schmitt, "The Liberal Rule of Law," in ibid., 294. Schmitt's revolution denial is a highly contestable assertion traceable to what one scholar contends is a misreading of French revolutionary theory. In this misreading, Schmitt incorrectly argued that the popular-sovereignty principle incorporated in the *pouvoir constituant* was essentially unlimited in its power and hence not bound by the constraints of liberal constitutionalism; see William Scheurmann, "Revolutions and Constitutions: Hannah Arendt's Challenge to Carl Schmitt," *Canadian Journal of Law and Jurisprudence* 10 (1997): 145. Schmitt therefore was unimpressed by formal changes in the form of government, given that the same assumptions about the rule of law carried over through the constitutional changes of 1919. For others, the transformation in governmental form amounted to revolutionary change. Thus, the German scholar Michael Stolleis writes, "The revolutionary change in the form of government appeared to leave untouched the concept of law and the administrative and judicial apparatus that was applying to it"; see Stolleis, *A History of Public Law in Germany, 1914–1945* (Oxford: Oxford University Press, 2004), 66.
127. Schmitt, "Liberal Rule of Law," 295.
128. Gerard Hogan and Gerry Whyte, *J. M. Kelly: The Irish Constitution,* 4th ed. (Dublin: Lexis Nexis Butterworths, 2003), 51.
129. One could and perhaps should say that closure in the American case did not occur in a formal sense until the adoption of the post–Civil War amendments, nearly a century later. Analogously, we might cite the 1949 declaration of Ireland as a republic that was no longer a part of the Commonwealth, and the 1998 Good Friday Agreement aimed at ending the conflict in Northern Ireland, as subsequent landmarks toward achieving revolutionary closure in Ireland's constitutional narrative.
130. Leo Kohn, *The Constitution of the Irish Free State* (London: Allen & Unwin, 1932), 80.
131. Bill Kissane, *New Beginnings: Constitutionalism and Democracy in Modern Ireland* (Dublin: University College Dublin Press, 2011), 55. Similarly, Oran Doyle

wrote, "The 1937 Constitution was not a foundational event but rather a seminal event in the evolution of a constitutional order that had been gradually coming into existence since 1922"; see Doyle, *The Constitution of Ireland: A Contextual Analysis* (London: Hart, 2018), 26.

132. Kissane, *New Beginnings,* 62.
133. Kohn, *Constitution of the Irish Free State,* 80. Article 2 of the 1922 Constitution states: "All powers of government and all authority legislative, executive and judicial in Ireland are derived from the people of Ireland."
134. Arendt, *On Revolution,* 145.
135. Kissane, *New Beginnings,* 57.
136. Diarmuid Rossa Phelan, *Revolt or Revolution: The Constitutional Boundaries of the European Community* (Dublin: Round Hall Sweet & Maxwell, 1997), 358.
137. Ibid. Phelan supports his argument with rulings from the Irish Supreme Court. The key decision is the landmark *The State (Ryan) v. Lennon,* I. R. 170 (1935), in which Justice Fitzgibbon referred to the Constituent Assembly as "the mouthpiece of the people." The more familiar view is that espoused by Hogan and Whyte: "Opposition to the Treaty was central to the program of Mr. de Valera's party; and the posture of the Irish courts that led him, in 1937, to promote a fundamental break with the 1922 Constitution rather than merely amend it" (*J. M. Kelly,* 51).
138. The ambiguous status of the 1922 Constitution has been aptly described thus: "On the one hand, the legal origin of the constitution was not based exclusively on British sovereignty, since it was enacted by an Irish parliament, acting as a Constituent Assembly. Yet on the other hand it also did not represent an act of an Irish *pouvoir constituant* [constituent power], since its operation required the approval of the British Parliament" (Lerner, *Making Constitutions,* 174).
139. For example, the 1937 Constitution more than made up for the silence of its predecessor on the subject of the family. It stressed the centrality of the institution for Irish society and supported it with language steeped in Catholic natural law theology.
140. John A. Murphy, "The 1937 Constitution: Some Historical Reflections," in Patrick Twomey, ed., *Ireland's Evolving Constitution: Collected Essays* (Oxford: Hart, 1998), 27.
141. Quoted in Basil Chubb, *The Politics of the Irish Constitution* (Dublin: Institute of Public Administration, 1991), 27. De Valera's principal Catholic adviser, Father Edward Cahill, described the 1922 Constitution as "exotic, unnatural and quite foreign to the native tradition"; quoted in Sean Faughan, "The Jesuits and the Drafting of the Irish Constitution of 1937," *Irish Historical Studies* 26 (1988): 82. This surely was an exaggeration, though understandable in light of his goal of infusing the new document with a more obviously Christian animating spirit.
142. William E. Scheurman pointed out, "Schmitt's constitutional theory . . . haunts contemporary debates about the relationship between revolutionary politics and constitutional government"; see Scheurman, *Carl Schmitt: The End of Law* (Lanham, Md.: Rowman and Littlefield, 1999), 82. One way of understanding this is to find in Schmitt's theory a denial of revolutionary significance to any change

that results only in the transformation of the liberal constitutional experience. Or in our terms, by definition such transformations do not entail paradigmatic displacements of a magnitude justifying application of the revolutionary label.

143. Ackerman, *Future of Liberal Revolution,* 69.
144. Ackerman, *We the People: Foundations,* 204.
145. Quoted in Itamar Rabinovich and Jehuda Reinharz, eds., *Israel in the Middle East: Documents and Readings on Society, Politics and Foreign Relations, 1948–Present* (New York: Oxford University Press, 1984), 45.
146. As Ruth Gavison has observed, it is an "argument that would be inconceivable and clearly objectionable in almost any other country and it reveals one of the unique features of Israel"; see Gavison, "The Controversy over Israel's Bill of Rights," *Israel Yearbook on Human Rights* 15 (1985): 135.
147. Ackerman, *Future of Liberal Revolution,* 64.
148. See in this regard, Gary Jeffrey Jacobsohn, "A Lighter Touch: American Constitutional Principles in Comparative Perspective," in Karen Orren and John Compton, eds., *Cambridge Companion on the United States Constitution* (New York: Cambridge University Press, 2017).
149. Of course, the true completion of the revolution required much additional work. In a formal sense, though, the amendments represented the key moment in fulfilling, as Martin Luther King, Jr., famously said, "a promissory note to which every American was to fall heir."
150. Lerner, *Making Constitutions,* 194.
151. This applies not only to those revolutions we designate as constitutional. Thus, Jaroslav Krejci noted, "A revolution is a prolonged process lasting several decades rather than years, during which there are many shifts and changes in the supreme authority" (*Great Revolutions Compared,* 5).
152. Kissane, *New Beginnings,* 60.
153. Quoted in Lerner, *Making Constitutions,* 182.
154. See, in this regard, Jeffrey Tulis and Nicole Mellow, *Legacies of Loss* (Chicago: University of Chicago Press, 2017).

Chapter 3. Revolutionary Constitutional Amendments

Epigraph: Niccolò Machiavelli, *Discourses on Livy,* trans. Harvey C. Mansfield and Nathan Tarcov (Chicago: University of Chicago Press, 2009), 60.

1. For the text of the constitutional acts by Marshal Pétain, see H. J. Heneman, "Recent Governmental Reforms in France," *American Political Science Review* 35, no. 1 (1941).
2. Cited in Maximillian Koessler, "Vichy's Sham Constitutionality," *American Political Science Review* 39, no. 1 (1945): 91.
3. Machiavelli, *Discourses on Livy,* 74.
4. See, for example, Clinton L. Rossiter, *Constitutional Dictatorship; Crisis Government in the Modern Democracies* (Princeton, N.J.: Princeton University Press, 1948), 15–28.

5. As a lesson from this constitutional revolution under occupation, the French Constitution of 1946 states in Article 94: "In the case of occupation of all or part of the metropolitan territory by foreign forces, no procedure of amendment may be undertaken or continued." A similar prohibition is found in Article 89(4) of the 1958 Constitution.
6. Karl Loewenstein, "The Demise of the French Constitution of 1875," *American Political Science Review* 34 (1940): 871.
7. Ibid., 894.
8. Compare this with Istvan Pogany, "Constitution Making or Constitutional Transformation in Post-Communist Societies?," *Political Studies* 44, no. 3 (1996), according to which a "constitutional transformation involved not merely changes to the formal constitutional arrangements in a state but also, and crucially, a genuine transformation of the character and habitual mode of operation of a society's political and legal institution" (568).
9. Examples include the Dominican Republic's Constitutions in the Trujillo era and Afghanistan's 1990 Constitution, which is almost identical to the 1987 constitution; see Zachary Elkins, Tom Ginsburg, and James Melton, *The Endurance of National Constitutions* (Cambridge: Cambridge University Press, 2009), 55.
10. Richard Albert, "Constitutional Amendment and Dismemberment," *Yale Journal of International Law* 43 (2018): 1–3.
11. Ming-Sung Kuo, "Reconciling Constitutionalism with Power: Towards a Constitutional Nomos of Political Ordering," *Ration Juris* 23, no. 3 (2010): 398.
12. Tom Ginsburg, Zachary Elkins, and Justin Blount, "Does the Process of Constitution-Making Matter?," *Annual Review of Law and Social Science* 5 (2009), no. 5.
13. See Antoni Abat i Ninet and Mark Tushnet, *The Arab Spring: An Essay on Revolution and Constitutionalism* (Cheltenham, U.K.: Elgar, 2015); Nimer Sultany, *Law and Revolution: Legitimacy and Constitutionalism After the Arab Spring* (Oxford: Oxford University Press, 2017).
14. Elkins, Ginsburg, and Melton, *Endurance of National Constitutions*, 114–15.
15. Ibid., 129.
16. See, for example, Richard S. Kay, "The Illegality of the Constitution," *Constitutional Commentary* 4 (1987).
17. Claude Klein and András Sajó, "Constitution-Making: Process and Substance," in Michel Rosenfeld and András Sajó, eds., *The Oxford Handbook of Comparative Constitutional Law* (Oxford: Oxford University Press, 2012), 419, 426–28.
18. Albie Sachs, "South Africa's Unconstitutional Constitution: The Transition from Power to Lawful Power," *St. Louis University Law Journal* 41 (1996–97). For the certification cases, see *Re Certification of the Constitution of the Republic of South-Africa*, 1996(4) SALR 744 (CC); *Re Certification of the Amended Text of the Constitution of the Republic of South-Africa*, 1997(2) SALR 97 (CC).
19. Heinz Klug, *Constituting Democracy: Law, Globalism, and South Africa's Political Reconstruction* (Cambridge: Cambridge University Press, 2000), 154.
20. See, for example, Karol Edward Soltan, "Constitution Making at the Edges of Constitutional Order," *William and Mary Law Review* 49 (2007–8); Henk Botha,

"Instituting Public Freedom or Extinguishing Constituent Power? Reflections on South Africa's Constitution-Making Experiment," *South African Journal on Human Rights* 26 (2010).

21. See Emmanuel Joseph Sieyès, "What Is the Third Estate?," in *Political Writings* (Indianapolis: Hackett, 2003), 136; Carl Schmitt, *Constitutional Theory*, trans. Jeffrey Seitzer (Durham, N.C.: Duke University Press, 2008), 132.
22. See, for example, David Landau and Rosalind Dixon, "Constraining Constitutional Change," *Wake Forest Law Review* 50 (2015).
23. See, for example, Argentine Const., art. 30; Bulgarian Const., arts. 158–62; Nicaraguan Const., arts. 191–93; Swiss Const., arts. 138, 193. See Yaniv Roznai, "We the People, Oui, the People and the Collective Body: Perceptions of Constituent Power," in Gary J. Jacobsohn and Miguel Schor, eds., *Comparative Constitutional Theory* (Cheltenham, U.K.: Elgar, 2018), 295.
24. "Report on Constitutional Amendment," European Commission for Democracy Through Law (Venice Commission), Venice, December 11–12, 2009, 15, https://www.venice.coe.int/webforms/documents/default.aspx?pdffile=CDL-AD(2010)001-e.
25. Whereas between 1789 and 1944 only 17 percent of the world's constitutions included unamendable provisions, 27 percent of those enacted between 1945 and 1988 included such provisions, and of the constitutions enacted between 1989 and 2013, 53 percent included unamendable provisions. See Yaniv Roznai, *Unconstitutional Constitutional Amendments: The Limits of Amendment Powers* (Oxford: Oxford University Press, 2017), 20–21.
26. Elkins, Ginsburg, and Melton, *Endurance of National Constitutions*, 55.
27. Donald S. Lutz, "Toward a Theory of Constitutional Amendment," *American Political Science Review* 88, no. 2 (1994): 356.
28. The Austrian Constitution is multilayered and fragmented. Apart from the core constitutional document, other constitutional acts (or provisions) are found in ordinary statutes but carry constitutional rank. The Constitution also distinguishes between a revision and a total revision, which occurs when one of the basic principles of the Constitution is affected by an amendment; a different procedure is stipulated for each process; see Manfred Stelzer, "Constitutional Change in Austria," in Xenophon Contiades, ed., *Engineering Constitutional Change: A Comparative Perspective on Europe, Canada, and the USA* (London: Routledge, 2012), 7–34.
29. See Eivind Smith, "Old and Protected? On the 'Supra-Constitutional' Clause in the Constitution of Norway," *Israel Law Review* 44, no. 3 (2011).
30. Kris Deschouwer, "The Belgian Federation: A Labyrinth State," in John Loughlin, John Kincaid, and Wilfried Swenden, eds., *Routledge Handbook of Regionalism and Federalism* (Abingdon, U.K.: Routledge, 2013), 211.
31. Klein and Sajó, "Constitution-Making," 421.
32. For an insightful discussion of the 1980 Pinochet Constitution, see Daniel M. Brinks and Abby Blass, *The DNA of Constitutional Justice in Latin America: Politics, Governance, and Judicial Design* (Cambridge: Cambridge University Press, 2018).

33. On this transition, see Claudia Heiss and Patricio Navia, "You Win Some, You Lose Some: Constitutional Reforms in Chile's Transition to Democracy," *Latin American Politics and Society* 49, no. 3 (2007); Brian Loveman, "The Transition to Civilian Government in Chile, 1990–1994," in Paul W. Drake and Ivan Jaksić, eds., *The Struggle for Democracy in Chile* (Lincoln: University of Nebraska Press, 1995), 305.
34. Fredrik Uggla, "'For a Few Senators More'? Negotiating Constitutional Changes During Chile's Transition to Democracy," in William C. Smith, ed., *Latin American Democratic Transformations: Institutions, Actors, Processes* (Sussex, U.K.: Wiley & Sons, 2009), 171.
35. From the perspective of constitutional change, an interesting angle on the 1989 reform centers on the "rule of change" itself, since a constitutional loophole existed in the 1980 Constitution. The amendment rule required substantial quorums and the approval of certain amendments by two subsequent congresses. This provision made the constitution extremely rigid. But Chapter 14, which regulated the amendment process, could itself be amended with a legislative majority of 60 percent and presidential approval. During the negotiations, some of the parties believed that the incoming civilian administration might choose to use a double-amendment procedure: first amend Chapter 14 and then make whatever changes it wished. Accordingly, the regime regarded Chapter 14 as a risky loophole that had to be corrected. Thus, one of the features of the 1989 reform was simplification of the amendment procedure so as to eliminate the requirement of approval by consecutive congresses and to require qualified majorities of only 60 percent for passage of most constitutional provisions. The requirement of a two-thirds majority would be necessary to amend certain chapters (such as the ones regulating the armed forces, the national security council, the constitutional court, and the amendment process in Chapter 14); see ibid.
36. See, for example, Andrew Arato, "Revolution, Restoration, and Legitimization: Ideological Problems of the Transition from State Socialism," in Michael D. Kennedy, ed., *Envisioning Eastern Europe: Postcommunist Cultural Studies* (Ann Arbor: University of Michigan Press, 1994), 180, 189.
37. Jiunn-rong Yeh, "Constitutional Reform and Democratization in Taiwan, 1945–2002," in Peter C. Y. Chow, ed., *Taiwan's Modernization in Global Perspective* (Portsmouth, N.H.: Greenwood, 2002), 47, 54.
38. Ibid., 48. On this transition, see also Leng Chao-chuan and Lin Cheng-yi, "Political Change on Taiwan: Transition to Democracy?," *China Quarterly* 136 (1993).
39. Yeh, "Constitutional Reform and Democratization in Taiwan," 55–63. The amendments—like the U.S. example—were enacted at first as Additional Articles at the end of the Constitution rather than alterations of the original text. In the third round of amendments, all Additional Articles were added into the constitution.
40. Ibid., 65.
41. The idea that the creation of the new Japanese constitutional order was connected with the past is reflected in Article 10 of the Potsdam Declaration, according to which "the Japanese government shall remove all obstacles to the *revival and*

strengthening of democratic tendencies among the Japanese people" (emphasis added); see Dale M. Hellegers, *We, the Japanese People* (Stanford, Calif.: Stanford University Press, 2001), 1:120.

42. Chaihark Hahm and Sung Ho Kim, *Making We the People: Democratic Constitutional Founding in Postwar Japan and South Korea* (Cambridge: Cambridge University Press, 2015), 148; Koseki Shoichi, *The Birth of Japan's Postwar Constitution* (New York: Routledge, 2018).
43. Ray A. Moore and Donald L. Robinson, *Partners for Democracy: Crafting the New Japanese State Under MacArthur* (Oxford University Press, 2004), 152.
44. Katsutoshi Takami, "From Divine Legitimacy to the Myth of Consensus: The Emperor System and Popular Sovereignty," in Yoichi Higuchi, ed., *Five Decades of Constitutionalism in Japanese Society* (Tokyo: University of Tokyo Press, 2001), 9, 22–24; cited in Chaihark Hahm and Sung Ho Kim, "To Make 'We the People,'" *International Journal of Constitutional Law* 8 (2010): 827.
45. Hahm and Kim, "To Make 'We the People,'" 826.
46. Ibid., 825.
47. On the Otaka-Miyasawa debate, see Norikazu Kawagishi, "The Constitution of Japan: An Unfinished Revolution" (JSD diss., Yale Law School, 2003), 387–409, available at http://digitalcommons.law.yale.edu/ylsd/4; see also Yasuo Hasebe, "The August Revolution Thesis and the Making of the Constitution of Japan," *Rechtstheorie* 17 (1997).
48. Lawrence W. Beer, "Constitutional Revolution in Japanese Law, Society and Politics," *Modern Asian Studies* 16, no. 1 (1982). According to Beer, "Modern Japan has experienced two constitutional revolutions, one from the latter half of the nineteenth century until 1945, and the other since 1945. By 'constitutional revolution' is meant a long process in which a fundamental shift takes place in constitutional values diffused throughout society by means of law, administrative actions, judicial decisions, and education, both formal and informal" (33).
49. Takeshi Inoue, "The Constitution of Japan and Constitutional Reform," *Asia-Pacific Review* 23, no. 2 (2016).
50. For a review of the amendments to the Constitution, see Dae-Kyu Yoon, "Constitutional Amendment in Korea," *Korean Journal of Comparative Law* 16 (1988): 1–13.
51. Ibid., 5.
52. For an examination of the judicial process, the role of judges, and jurisprudence under authoritarian rule in South Korea, see Marie Seong-Hak Kim, "Travails of Judges: Courts and Constitutional Authoritarianism in South Korea," *American Journal of Comparative Law* 63 (2015).
53. On the political events and legal changes of 1987, see James M. West and Edward J. Baker, "The Constitutional Reforms in South Korea, 1987: Electoral Processes and Judicial Independence," *Harvard Human Rights Year Book* 1 (1988).
54. Yoon, "Constitutional Amendment in Korea," 11.
55. Amaya Alvez Marin, "Forcing Consensus: Challenges for Rights-Based Constitutionalism in Chile," in Colin Harvey and Alex Schwartz, eds., *Rights in Divided Societies* (Oxford: Hart, 2012), 249, 253.

56. Ibid., 159, citing Tomás Moulian, *Chile actual: Anatomia de un mito* (Santiago: LOM, 1997), 355; see also Juliano Zaiden Benvindo, "Preservationist Constitutional Change in Latin America: The Cases of Chile and Brazil," in Xenophon Contiades and Alkmene Fotiadou, eds., *The Routledge Handbook of Comparative Constitutional Change* (London: Routledge, 2020): "Though reaching democratic stability and a rather competitive political system, Chile will not fully redeem from its authoritarian legacy while the 1980 Constitution is still in force."
57. Georg Jellinek, "Constitutional Amendment and Constitutional Transformation" (1906), in Arthur J. Jacobson and Bernhard Schlink, eds., *Weimar: A Jurisprudence of Crisis* (Berkeley: University of California Press, 2000), 56–57.
58. Catherine Dupre and Jiunn-rong Yeh, "Constitutions and Legitimacy over Time," in Mark Tushnet, Thomas Fleiner, and Cheryl Saunders, eds., *Routledge Handbook of Constitutional Law* (Abingdon, U.K.: Routledge, 2013), 45, 53; Gabriel L. Negretto, "Replacing and Amending Constitutions: The Logic of Constitutional Change in Latin America," *Law & Society Review* 46, no. 4 (2012): 758.
59. Bruce Ackerman, *The Future of Liberal Revolution* (New Haven, Conn.: Yale University Press, 1992), 61.
60. See Mark F. Brzezinski, "Constitutional Heritage and Renewal: The Case of Poland," *Virginia Law Review* 77, no. 1 (1991): 103–10. One may argue that regardless of the content of the constitutional amendments, their mere enactment was meant to have an operative effect and was meant to be a manifestation of a revolution, marking a new era of constitutionalism.
61. For a historical account, see András Körösényi, *Government and Politics in Hungary* (Budapest: Central European University Press, 2000).
62. Rett W. Ludwikowski, *Constitution-Making in the Region of Former Soviet Dominance* (Durham, N.C.: Duke University Press, 1996), 31, citing William Sólyom-Fekete, "Hungary," in W. B. Simons, ed., *The Constitutions of the Communist World* (Berlin: Springer, 1980), 192.
63. See Bernadette Somody, "Raising the Standard? The Current Challenges in Human Rights Protection in Hungary," in Kyriaki Topidi and Alexander H. E. Morawa, eds., *A Constitutional Evolution in Central and Eastern Europe* (Farnham, U.K.: Ashgate, 2013), 211; Bennett Kovrig, "Hungary," in Teresa Rakowska-Harmstone, ed., *Communism in Eastern Europe* (Bloomington: Indiana University Press, 1984), 100.
64. The Communist Party had different names: the Hungarian Communist Party (MKP; 1944–48); the Hungarian Working People's Party (MDP, a merger between the former Hungarian Communist Party and the Social Democratic Party; 1948–56); and the Hungarian Socialist Workers' Party (MSZMP; 1957–89).
65. András Sajó, "The Difficulties of Socio-Legal Transition: Constitutional Efforts in Hungary," *University of New Brunswick Law Journal* 39 (1990).
66. Kovrig, "Hungary."
67. Laszlo Péter, *Hungary's Long Nineteenth Century: Constitutional and Democratic Traditions in a European Perspective; Collected Studies*, ed. Miklós Lojkóe (Leiden:

Brill, 2012), 174. On sham constitutions more generally, see David S. Law and Mila Versteeg, "Sham Constitutions," *California Law Review* 101 (2013).

68. István Kovács, "Constitutional Guarantees, Constitutional Law Council, Constitutional Court," *Acta Juridica et Politica* 39 (1990): 132.

69. Márta Dezső, *Constitutional Law in Hungary* (Netherlands: Kluwer Law International, 2010), 29.

70. For an overview of the first transformation, see Andrew Arato, "Constitution and Continuity in the East European Transitions—Part Two: The Hungarian Case," *Tilburg Foreign Law Review* 4 (1994); Gábor Halmai, "The Making of the Hungarian Constitution," in András Sajó, ed., *Out of and into Authoritarian Law* (The Hague: Kluwer Law International, 2002), 111; Halmai, "The Transformation of Hungarian Constitutional Law from 1985 to 2005," in András Jakab, Péter Takács, and Allan F. Tatham, eds., *The Transformation of the Hungarian Legal Order, 1985–2005* (Budapest: Kluwer, 2007), 1.

71. László Sólyom, "Revolution by Law: Peaceful Transition to Democracy in Hungary," *Yonsei Law Journal* 1 (2010): 1–5.

72. Arato claimed that roundtables that include relevant actors, by forcing them to compromise and reach agreements, may produce legitimacy; see, for example, Andrew Arato, "Conventions, Constituent Assemblies, and Round Tables: Models, Principles and Elements of Democratic Constitution-Making," *Global Constitutionalism* 1, no. 1 (2012).

73. The original text of Article 146 provided that "this Basic Law shall cease to apply on the day on which a constitution freely adopted by the German people takes effect." After reunification, this was revised to "this Basic Law, which since the achievement of the unity and freedom of Germany applies to the entire German people, shall cease to apply on the day on which a constitution freely adopted by the German people takes effect."

74. See Andrew Arato, *Post-Sovereign Constitution Making: Learning and Legitimacy* (Oxford: Oxford University Press, 2016), 104–6; for a focused analysis of the Hungarian case, see 161–222.

75. Dae Soon Kim, *The Transition to Democracy in Hungary: Árpád Göncz and the Post-Communist Hungarian Presidency* (Abingdon, U.K.: Routledge, 2013), 93–95; Gábor Halmai, "The Reform of Constitutional Law in Hungary After the Transition," 18 *Legal Studies* 188 (1998), 191. On referendums in Hungary, see Zoltán Pozsár-Szentmiklósy, "Direct Democracy in Hungary (1989–2016): From Popular Sovereignty to Popular Illusion," *Acta Universitatis Sapientiae* 6, no. 1 (2017).

76. The referendum was the result of a debate between two opposition parties—Fidesz and SZDSZ—on the one hand, and the state-socialist party, on the other, on how to elect the head of state. This question was of a purely political nature, since a reformist leader of the state-socialist party, Imre Pozsgay, was the most popular politician in the country at the time and therefore had a very good chance of being elected president in the case of a direct election.

77. Andrew Arato and Zoltán Miklósi, "Constitution Making and Transitional Politics in Hungary," in Laurel E. Miller, ed., *Framing the State in Times of Transition:*

Case Studies in Constitution Making (Washington, D.C.: U.S. Institute of Peace Press, 2010), 364: "The new constitution itself was not looked upon even by the new political elite—not to speak of the population in general—as of its own common making."

78. The supermajority requirement for certain legislative questions (the support of two-thirds of MPs present at the sitting of National Assembly) remained part of the constitutional system. For a detailed analysis, see Zoltán Pozsár-Szentmiklósy, "Supermajority in Parliamentary Systems: A Concept of Substantive Legislative Supermajority—Lessons from Hungary," *Acta Juridica Hungarica* 3 (2017).
79. Halmai, "Reform of Constitutional Law," 189.
80. András Sajó, "Reading the Invisible Constitution: Judicial Review in Hungary," *Oxford Journal of Legal Studies* 15 (1995): 254.
81. See András Jakab and Miklós Hollán, "Socialism's Legacy in Contemporary Law and Legal Scholarship: The Case of Hungary," *Journal of East European Law* 2–3 (2004).
82. András Sajó, "Preferred Generations: A Paradox of Restoration Constitutions," *Cardozo Law Review* 14 (1992–93): 854.
83. Bálint Ablonczy, *Conversations on the Fundamental Law of Hungary: Interviews with József Szájer, Hungarian Member of European Parliament, and Gergely Gulyás, Member of Parliament in Hungary*, trans. Zsolt Kozma ([Budapest]: Elektromédia, 2012), 26–27.
84. Initially, because of Parliament's lack of democratic legitimacy at the time of the Constitutional Court's creation, only five justices were elected to sit on the court. Five more justices were to be chosen by the newly elected Parliament in 1990. An additional five justices (for a total of fifteen) were to be elected in 1994 by the second democratically elected Parliament. But before this occurred, in 1994, the number of justices was determined to be eleven, and the Constitutional Court functioned in reality with nine to ten members during its first term; see Gábor Halmai, "The Constitutional Court," in Béla K. Király, ed., *Lawful Revolution in Hungary, 1989–1994* (New York: Columbia University Press, 1996), 243–44.
85. See, for example, Spencer Zifcak, "Hungary's Remarkable, Radical, Constitutional Court," *Journal of Constitutional Law in Eastern and Central Europe* 3 (1996); Kim Lane Scheppele, "Guardians of the Constitution: Constitutional Court Presidents and the Struggle for the Rule of Law in Post-Soviet Europe," *University of Pennsylvania Law Review* 154 (2006).
86. Nathan J. Brown and Julian G. Waller, "Constitutional Courts and Political Uncertainty: Constitutional Ruptures and the Rule of Judges," *International Journal of Constitutional Law* 14, no. 4 (2016): 824.
87. For the evolution of judicial review in Hungary, see, for example, Gábor Halmai, "Judicial Review in Hungary," *Tilburg Foreign Law Review* 2 (1993); Péter Paczolay, "Judicial Review of the Compensation Law in Hungary," *Michigan Journal of International Law* 13 (1992).
88. László Sólyom, "The Hungarian Constitutional Court and Social Change," *Yale Law Journal* 19 (1994): 224–25, 228–30; Gábor Halmai, "Establishing a State

Governed by the Rule of Law in Hungary," *Review of Central and East European Law* 22 (1996).

89. See Sajó, "Reading the Invisible Constitution"; Katalin Füzér, "The Invisible Constitution: The Construction of Constitutional Reality in Hungary," *International Journal of Sociology* 26, no. 4 (1996); Zoltán Szente, "The Interpretive Practice of the Hungarian Constitutional Court: A Critical View," *German Law Journal* 14, no. 8 (2013); see also László Sólyom, "The First Year of the Constitutional Court," *Acta Juridica Hungarica* 33 (1991); Catherine Dupré, *Importing the Law in Post-Communist Transitions: The Hungarian Constitutional Court and the Right to Human Dignity* (Oxford: Hart, 2003).

90. Judgment of October 31, 1990, Alkotmánybíróság [Constitutional Law Court], No. 23/1990 (X.31) AB (Hung.); see Tibor Horváth, "Abolition of Capital Punishment in Hungary," *Acta Juridica Hungarica* 33 (1991); Renáta Uitz, "Lessons from the Abolition of Capital Punishment in Hungary: A Fortuitous Constellation Amidst and Beyond Democratic Transition," *Acta Juridica Hungarica* 45 (2004).

91. Gábor Halmai, "A Coup Against Constitutional Democracy," in Mark A. Graber, Sanford Levinson, and Mark Tushnet, eds., *Constitutional Democracy in Crisis?* (Oxford: Oxford University Press, 2018), 243, 245.

92. See, for example, Kim Lane Scheppele, "The New Hungarian Constitutional Court," *Eastern Europe Constitutional Review* 8 (1999). This kind of judicial involvement has given rise to debate regarding whether it is advisable, given the special nature of the transition that Hungary experienced; see Ruti Teitel, "Transitional Jurisprudence: The Role of Law in Political Transformation," *Yale Law Journal* 106 (1997), which argues for strong involvement by a constitutional judiciary in times of transition; and Bojan Bugaric, "Courts as Policy-Makers: Lessons from Transition," *Harvard International Law Journal* 42 (2001), which argues for less intervention by a constitutional judiciary in structural issues of transition.

93. See, generally, Rett R. Ludwikowski, "Fundamental Constitutional Rights in the New Constitutions of Eastern and Central Europe," *Cardozo Journal of International and Comparative Law* 3 (1995), and, more particularly, András Jakab, "The Republic of Hungary," in Gisbert Flanz, Rüdiger Wolfrum, and Rainer Grote, eds., *Constitutions of the Countries of the World* (Oxford: Oxford University Press, 2008), 1, 15–22.

94. In the summer of 1995, the HCC struck down twenty-six provisions of an austerity package passed by the government as violations of the constitutional requirement of legal certainty, on the grounds that they conflicted with benefits and entitlements on which people relied. On the struggle between the Parliament and the Court over social rights, see Kim Lane Scheppele, "Democracy by Judiciary (Or Why Courts Can Sometimes Be More Democratic than Parliaments)," in Adam Czarnota, Martin Krygier, and Wojciech Sadurski, eds., *Rethinking the Rule of Law After Communism* (Budapest: Central European University Press, 2005), 25, 45–50.

95. 30/1992 (V. 26) CC Decision, CCD 1992, 167, 171–72, cited in Fruzsina Gárdos-Orosz, "The Underpinning and the Protection of Fundamental Rights Provided

by the Hungarian Constitution: Article 8 Paragraph (1)," *Acta Juridica Hungarica* 49 (2008): 406.

96. Ludwikowski, "Fundamental Constitutional Rights," 88, 144–45.
97. Arato and Miklósi, "Constitution Making and Transitional Politics," 350.
98. György Szoboszlai, "The Politics of Constitutional Amendment: Hungary's Lasting Transitory Constitution," in Mads Andenas, ed., *The Creation and Amendment of Constitutional Norms* (London: British Institute of International and Comparative Law, 2000), 174, 175.
99. Péter Paczolay, "Constitutional Transition and Legal Continuity," *Connecticut Journal of International Law* 8 (1993): 562.
100. See János Kis, "Between Reform and Revolution," *East European Politics and Societies* 12, no. 2 (1998).
101. Ibid., 377.
102. For a detailed study on lustration in postcommunist countries, see Peter Rožič, "Lustration and Democracy: The Politics of Transitional Justice in the Postcommunist World" (Ph.D. diss., Georgetown University, 2012).
103. Decision No. 11/1992 (III 5) AB. Constitutional Court Decision of 1992, p. 81, cited in Jiří Přibáň, *Legal Symbolism: On Law, Time, and European Identity* (Abingdon, U.K.: Routledge, 2016), 156. For an analysis of the continuity of law in Hungary, see also Ethan Klingsberg, "Judicial Review and Hungary's Transition from Communism to Democracy: The Constitutional Court, the Continuity of Law, and the Redefinition of Property Rights," *BYU Law Review* 41 (1992).
104. Decision No. 11/1992, p. 81.
105. Decision No. 11/1992, cited in Přibáň, *Legal Symbolism*, 156; see also Rožič, "Lustration and Democracy," 571.
106. Přibáň, *Legal Symbolism*, 156.
107. Ackerman, *Future of Liberal Revolution*, 71.
108. See, for example, András Jakab, "What Is Wrong with the Hungarian Legal System and How to Fix It," Max Planck Institute for Comparative Public Law and International Law Research Paper No. 2018-13 (July 13, 2018), available at SSRN, https://ssrn.com/abstract=3213378, which argues that "the crucial problem of institution-building in the 1989/90 constitutional system . . . was that issues of justice, of dealing with the past (i.e. the narrative) were swept under the carpet following a peculiar interpretation of the formal rules."
109. Constitutional Court of the Czech Republic, decision on the Law on the Illegality of and Resistance to the Communist Regime (December 21, 1993), cited in Mark S. Ellis, "Purging the Past: The Current State of Lustration Laws in the Former Communist Bloc," *Law and Contemporary Problems* 59, no. 4 (1996): 183.
110. Ibid., from the English-language version of the decision, which is available at Ústavní Soud, https://www.usoud.cz/en/decisions/19931221-pl-us-1993-lawlessness-1.
111. David Robertson, "A Problem of Their Own, Solutions of Their Own: CEE Jurisdictions and the Problems of Lustration and Retroactivity," in Wojciech Sadur-

ski, Adam Czarnota, and Martin Krygier, eds., *Spreading Democracy and the Rule of Law? The Impact of EU Enlargement for the Rule of Law, Democracy, and Constitutionalism in Post-Communist Legal Orders* (Dordrecht: Springer, 2006), 73, 83.

112. Andrew Arato, "Parliamentary Constitution Making in Hungary," *European Constitutional Review* 4 (1995): 45–46.

113. Sonja Priebus, "Hungary," in Anna Fruhstorfer and Michael Hein, eds., *Constitutional Politics in Central and Eastern Europe* (Berlin: Springer, 2016), 102.

114. László Sólyom, "The Rise and Decline of Constitutional Culture in Hungary," in Armin von Bogdandy and Pál Sonnevend, eds., *Constitutional Crisis in the European Constitutional Area: Theory, Law and Politics in Hungary and Romania* (Oxford: Hart, 2015), 18. For a general overview of this second transformation, see also Gábor Halmai, "The Unmaking of Hungarian Constitutionalism?," in Sajó, *Out of and into Authoritarian Law*, 257; Kriszta Kovács and Gábor Attila Tóth, "Hungary's Constitutional Transformation," *European Constitutional Law Review* 7 (2011).

115. Andrew Arato and Ertuğ Tombuş, "Learning from Success, Learning from Failure: South Africa, Hungary, Turkey, and Egypt," *Philosophy & Social Criticism* 39 (2013).

116. Andrew Arato, "Multi-Track Constitutionalism Beyond Carl Schmitt," *Constellations* 18 (2011): 324–51. See Article 24(5) of the Constitution: "The majority of four-fifth of the votes of the Members of Parliament is required to pass the parliamentary resolution on the detailed rules on the preparation of the new Constitution."

117. See Andrew Arato, "Elections, Coalitions and Constitutionalism in Hungary," *Eastern European Constitutional Review* 3 (1994): 29–31.

118. While the explanation of the amendment posited the sunset rule, the latter was not taken into the formal text of the amendment. Thus, peculiarly, despite the legislators' intention, the amended constitution did not contain any explicit sunset rule. But since parliamentary resolutions are in effect for specific legislative terms, a reasonable interpretation was that even without an explicit sunset clause, the provision would lose its validity in 1998, at the end of the term. In any case, to remove doubts regarding the provision's validity, it was formally repealed by a constitutional amendment adopted by a two-thirds majority on July 5, 2010. Arato claims that this repeal of the four-fifths rule of change by a two-thirds procedure was unconstitutional; see Arato, "Orbán's (Counter-)Revolution of the Voting Booth and How It Was Made Possible," *Verfassungsblog*, April 16, 2011, https://verfassungsblog.de/orbns-counter-revolution-voting-booth. One can question this argument, since if the provision had lost its validity in 1998, this explicit repeal was unnecessary.

119. Miklós Bánkuti, Gábor Halmai, and Kim Lane Scheppele, "From Separation of Powers to a Government without Checks: Hungary's Old and New Constitutions," in Gábor Attila Tóth, ed., *Constitution for a Disunited Nation* (Budapest: Central European University Press, 2012), 237, 254–55; see also Gábor Halmai, "Dismantling Constitutional Review in Hungary," *Rivista Di Diritti Comparati* 1/2019 (2019): 31.

120. In Verdict No. 184/2010 [X.28], the HCC declared Act 90 of 2010 (from August) to be unconstitutional and invalid based on the vagueness of the "immoral acquisition" criterion. The government reacted by enacting a wide bypassing law (Act 119 of 2010), stripping the court of the authority to review fiscal laws regarding budget and taxes, except in cases when specific human rights were infringed. The law was later deemed unconstitutional in accordance with the Fundamental Law of 2011; see Priebus, "Hungary," 116–17.

121. Priebus, "Hungary," 113, 118.

122. Ablofnczy, *Fundamental Law of Hungary,* 27.

123. Umut Korkut, *Liberalization Challenges in Hungary: Elitism, Progressivism, and Populism* (London: Palgrave Macmillan, 2015), 60.

124. Kim Lane Scheppele, "Guardians of the Constitution: Constitutional Court Presidents and the Struggle for the Rule of Law in Post-Soviet Europe," *University of Pennsylvania Law Review* 154 (2006).

125. András Jakab and Pál Sonnevend, "Continuity with Deficiencies: The New Basic Law of Hungary," *European Constitutional Law Review* 9 (2013).

126. For example, appointment to the HCC no longer requires input from the minority parties and is hence controlled by the government; the jurisdiction of the court has been limited; and the president of the court is no longer elected by fellow justices but by Parliament.

127. See, for example, Pál Sonnevend, András Jakab, and Lóránt Csink, "The Constitution as an Instrument of Everyday Party Politics: The Basic Law of Hungary," in von Bogdandy and Sonnevend, *Constitutional Crisis in the European Constitutional Area,* 33; Zoltán Fleck et al., "Opinion on the Fundamental Law of Hungary (Amicus Brief)," in Tóth, *Constitution for a Disunited Nation,* 455.

128. Gábor Halmai, "The Rise and Fall of Constitutionalism in Hungary," in Paul Blokker, ed., *Constitutional Acceleration Within the European Union and Beyond* (London: Routledge, 2018), 217, 219. The 2011 Fundamental Law was enacted on the basis of a constitutional provision providing Parliament with the authority to enact a constitution. Yet since the procedural requirement of the four-fifths majority had been abolished, this was done according to the ordinary two-thirds majority for amending the Constitution. The Fundamental Law explicitly refers back to the constitutional amendment procedure (Closing and Miscellaneous Provisions, No. 2): "2. Parliament shall pass the Fundamental Law according to Point a) of Paragraph (3) of Article 19 and to Paragraph (3) of Article 24 of Act XX of 1949." According to Article 19(3), the National Assembly would enact the Constitution of the Republic of Hungary, and Article 24(3) stated that to amend the Constitution, a two-thirds majority was needed.

129. Katalin Dobias, "The Role of Constitutional Identity in the Responses to the Terror Attacks in France and Refugee-Management Crisis in Hungary," *Annual Review of Constitution-Building Processes: 2015* (2016): 107.

130. See, for example, Johanna Fröhlich and Lóránt Csink, "Topics of Hungarian Constitutionalism," *Tijdschrift voor Constitutioneel Recht,* October 2012, 428;

Andrew Arato, "Regime Change, Revolution, and Legitimacy," in Tóth, *Constitution for a Disunited Nation,* 35, 48.

131. On January 4, 2013, the HCC invalidated certain provisions of the not-yet-promulgated Act on Electoral Procedure, holding that requiring registration for elections restricts the right to vote without constitutional justification; see Decision 1/2013. An English translation is available from the HCC, https://hunconcourt.hu/uploads/sites/3/2017/11/en_0001_2013.pdf.
132. Verdict No. 45/2012 [XII.29]. An English translation is available from the HCC, https://hunconcourt.hu/uploads/sites/3/2017/11/en_0045_2012.pdf.
133. On the impact of the Fourth Amendment on the system of checks and balances, see Kim Lane Scheppele, "Understanding Hungary's Constitutional Revolution," in von Bogdandy and Sonnevend, *Constitutional Crisis in the European Constitutional Area,* 111, 112–14.
134. Hungarian Constitutional Court, Decision 12/2013 (V. 24). See András Téglási, "The Struggle Between the Hungarian Parliament and the Constitutional Court from the 1989/1990 Political Transition up to the Present," in Tamara Ehs and Heinrich Neisser, eds., *Verfassungsgerichtsbarkeit und Demokratie: Europäische Parameter in Zeiten politischer Umbrüche?* (Vienna: Böhlau Verlag, 2017), 79, 85.
135. Minerva Mills Ltd. v. Union of India, A/I/R/ 1980 S.C. 1789, 1981. See a similar approach by the Supreme Court of Belize: British Caribbean Bank Ltd v. AG Belize (Claim No. 597 of 2011).
136. European Commission for Democracy Through Law (Venice Commission), Opinion on the Fourth Amendment of the Fundamental Law of Hungary (Opinion No. 720/2013, June 14, 2013). For an assessment of the role of the Venice Commission in constitutional change, see Maartje De Visser, "A Critical Assessment of the Role of the Venice Commission in Processes of Domestic Constitutional Reform," *American Journal of Comparative Law* 63, no. 4 (2015).
137. For an analysis of the Fourth and Fifth Amendments in light of the Venice Commission's criticism, see Imre Vörös, "The Constitutional Landscape After the Fourth and Fifth Amendments of Hungarian Fundamental Law," *Acta Juridica Hungarica* 55, no. 1 (2014): 1–20.
138. See Renáta Uitz, "Hungary's Attempt to Manage Threats of Terror Through a Constitutional Amendment," ConstitutionNet, April 28, 2016, http://www.constitutionnet.org/news/hungarys-attempt-manage-threats-terror-through-constitutional-amendment?utm_source=newsletter&utm_medium=email.
139. Decision 22/2016 (XII. 5.), AB on the Interpretation of Article E) (2) of the Fundamental Law (Const. Ct. Hung., November 30, 2016), para. 64; available in English at https://hunconcourt.hu/uploads/sites/3/2017/11/en_22_2016.pdf.
140. Ibid., para. 67.
141. Ibid., para. 94 of Judge Dr. István Stumpf's concurring opinion.
142. See Gábor Halmai, "Abuse of Constitutional Identity: The Hungarian Constitutional Court on Interpretation of Article E) (2) of the Fundamental Law," *Review of Central and East European Law* 43, no. 1 (2018): 23.

143. Kim Lane Scheppele, "Counter-constitutions: Narrating the Nation in Post-Soviet Hungary," paper presented at a colloquium of the Department of Political Science, George Washington University, Washington, D.C., April 2, 2004.
144. Ablonczy, *Fundamental Law of Hungary*, 26–27.
145. Renáta Uitz, "Can You Tell When an Illiberal Democracy Is in the Making?," *International Journal of Constitutional Law* 13 (2015): 280–81.
146. Gábor Halmai, "The European Parliament vs. the Hungarian Government," Jurist, September 20, 2018, https://www.jurist.org/commentary/2018/09/the-european-parliament-vs-the-hungarian-government/.
147. Office of the Prime Minister, Prime Minister Viktor Orbán's Speech at the 25th Bálványos Summer Free University and Student Camp, July 26, 2014, https://www.kormany.hu/en/the-prime-minister/the-prime-minister-s-speeches/prime-minister-viktor-orban-s-speech-at-the-25th-balvanyos-summer-free-university-and-student-camp. Later, Orbán started to use the term "Christian democracy" as a synonym of illiberal democracy; see Office of the Prime Minister, Prime Minister Viktor Orbán's Speech at the 29th Bálványos Summer Free University and Student Camp, July 28, 2018, www.miniszterelnok.hu/prime-minister-viktor-orbans-speech-at-the-29th-balvanyos-summer-open-university-and-student-camp/.
148. See David Landau, "Abusive Constitutionalism," *UC Davis Law Review* 47, no. 1 (2013).
149. Scheppele, "Democracy by Judiciary," 44.
150. See Stephen Gardbaum, "Are Strong Constitutional Courts Always a Good Thing for New Democracies?," *Columbia Journal of Transnational Law* 53 (2015).
151. Gerald N. Rosenberg, *The Hollow Hope: Can Courts Bring About Social Change?* (Chicago: University of Chicago Press, 2008), 426.
152. "It is a fraud on the constitution to respect its form while fighting its substance—or more exactly, it is the most interesting case of a fraud on the constitution": Georges Liet-Veaux, "La 'Fraude à la Constitution': Essai d'une Analyse Juridique des Révolutions Communitaires Récentes: Italie, Allemand, France," *Revue Du Droit et de Science Politique en France et à L'étranger* 59 (1943): 145.
153. Hans Kelsen, *Pure Theory of Law*, trans. Max Knight (Berkeley: University of California Press, 1967), 209.
154. J. M. Finnis, "Revolutions and Continuity of Law," in *Philosophy of Law: Collected Essays* (Oxford: Oxford University Press, 2011), 407, 415.
155. Stephen Michel and Ignacio N. Cofone, "Credible Commitment or Paternalism? The Case of Unamendability," in Richard Albert and Bertil Emrah Oder, eds., *An Unconstitutional Constitution? Unamendability in Constitutional Democracies* (Cham, Switzerland: Springer, 2018), 123. For example, Dian Shah demonstrates how constitutional amendments to the 1945 Indonesian Constitution have had a dramatic transformative influence and were imperative in the country's transition to a democracy. The decision to opt for formal amendments instead of a clean break with the previous authoritarian constitutional order allowed the government to avoid reopening specific contentious issues, in this case to avoid another debate about the secular or Islamic nature of the Indonesian constitutional

state; see Dian A. H. Shah, "Post-Soeharto Constitutional Amendment in Indonesia: Promises and Pitfalls," *Journal of Comparative Law* 14, no. 1 (2019): 56.

156. Uggla, "For a Few Senators More," 159, 164. See also Daniel M. Brinks and Abby Blass, *The DNA of Constitutional Justice in Latin America: Politics, Governance and Judicial Design* (Cambridge: Cambridge University Press, 2018).

157. Gabriel L. Negretto, "Constitution Making and Constitutionalism in Latin America: The Role of Procedural Rules," in Rosalind Dixon and Tom Ginsburg, eds., *Comparative Constitutional Law in Latin America* (Northampton, U.K.: Elgar, 2017), 17, 23–24.

158. For different types of legitimacy, see Richard H. Fallon, "Legitimacy and the Constitution," *Harvard Law Review* 118 (2005).

159. Andrew Arato, *Civil Society, Constitution, and Legitimacy* (Lanham, Md.: Rowman and Littlefield, 2000), 124–25; András Jakab, *European Constitutional Language* (Cambridge University Press, 2016), 159–60.

160. János Kis, "From the 1989 Constitution to the 2011 Fundamental Law," in Toth, *Constitution for a Disunited Nation*, 1, 20.

Chapter 4. Revolution, Counterrevolution, and the Question of German Constitutional Identity

Epigraph: *Aristotle's Politics*, trans. Benjamin Jowett (Oxford: Oxford University Press, 1916), 207.

1. Gerhard Casper, "The Karlsruhe Republic: Keynote Address at the State Ceremony Celebrating the 50th Anniversary of the Federal Constitutional Court," *German Law Journal* 2, no. 18 (2001), para. 2, https://germanlawjournal.com/wp-content/uploads/GLJ_Vol_02_No_18_Casper.pdf.

2. As Jens Woelk noted, "Hitler did not need to 'take power': instead of a *coup d'état* or a revolution, there was institutional continuity, at least in formal terms"; see Woelk, "Germany," in Dawn Oliver and Carlo Fusaro, eds., *How Constitutions Change: A Comparative Study* (Oxford: Hart, 2013), 144. Since what followed comported with constitutionalism in name only, terminological generosity is necessary in order to characterize Hitler's ascendance as a constitutional revolution. More important is how this history helps explain the Basic Law, which was, Woelk points out, intended to prevent "revolutions under the guise of legality" (ibid.). Such an understanding is consistent with our contention that for conceptualizing a constitutional revolution, it makes more sense to focus on substance than on process.

3. Casper, "Karlsruhe Republic."

4. This process may be understood as one manifestation of a point made in a German constitutional theorist's reflections on constitutional change: "[The constitutional state] is an aggregate of revolutionary and evolutionary processes"; see Peter Haberle, "The Constitutional State and Its Reform Requirements," *Ratio Juris* 13 (2000): 78. Another makes much the same point: "The constitution and the constitutional state based upon its very foundations have to be seen as the

historical results of revolutions and evolutions"; see Markus Kotzur, "Constitutional Amendments and Constitutional Changes in Germany," in Xenophon Contiades, ed., *Engineering Constitutional Change: A Comparative Perspective on Europe, Canada, and the USA* (London: Routledge, 2012), 141.

5. For an astute analysis of the development of constitutional identity in Germany, see Monika Polzin, "Constitutional Identity, Unconstitutional Amendments and the Idea of Constituent Power: The Development of the Doctrine of Constitutional Identity in German Constitutional Law," *International Journal of Constitutional Law* 14 (2016). Polzin traces the origins of the concept to the work of Carl Schmitt and Carl Bilfinger in 1928; they sought to justify implicit constitutional limits to the amendment power of the Weimar Constitution. Constitutional identity was not invoked in the drafting of the Basic Law and reemerged only after that document came into force.
6. *Southwest Case*, 1 BverfGE 14 (1951): "That a constitutional provision itself may be null and void, is not conceptually impossible just because it is a part of the constitution. There are constitutional provisions that are so fundamental and to such an extent an expression of a law that precedes even the constitution that they also bind the framer of the constitution, and other constitutional provisions that do not rank so high may be null and void, because they contravene those principles." *Privacy of Communications Case* (*Klass Case*, 30 BverfGE 1 [1970]): "The purpose of Article 79, paragraph 3, as a check on the legislator's amending the Constitution is to prevent the abolition of the substance or basis of the existing constitutional order, by formal legal means of amendment . . . and abuse of the Constitution to legalize a totalitarian regime."
7. Roberto Toniatti, "Sovereignty Lost, Constitutional Identity Gained," in Alejandro Saiz Arnaiz and Carina Alcoberro Llivina, eds., *National Constitutional Identity and European Integration* (Cambridge: Intersentia, 2013), 62.
8. Ibid., 67.
9. Here we should note one caveat. Stephen Gardbaum has written cogently on the concept of "revolutionary constitutionalism," which involves "using the constitution-making process to attempt to institutionalize and bring to a successful conclusion a political revolution": Gardbaum, "Revolutionary Constitutionalism," *International Journal of Constitutional Law* 15, no. 1 (2017): 173. He properly distinguishes his concept from the "neighboring term" "constitutional revolution," although our use of the latter idea is broad enough to incorporate his use of the related term.
10. One should add, with mixed success. See Zachary Elkins, Tom Ginsburg, and James Melton, *The Endurance of National Constitutions* (Cambridge: Cambridge University Press, 2009).
11. Article 24 is preceded by a replacement Article 23, which, according to its first provision, states: "The Federal Republic of Germany shall participate in the development of the European Union that is committed to democratic, social and federal principles, to the rule of law, and to the principle of subsidiarity, and that guarantees a level of protection of basic rights essentially comparable to that afforded by this Basic Law."

12. Ingolf Pernice, "The Treaty of Lisbon: Multilevel Constitutionalism in Action," *Columbia Journal of European Law* 15 (2009): 374; J. H. H. Weiler, "A Quiet Revolution: The European Court of Justice and Its Interlocutors," *Comparative Political Studies* 26 (1994).
13. Dieter Grimm, "Integration by Constitution," *International Journal of Constitutional Law* 3 (2005): 205.
14. Ibid.
15. Dieter Grimm, "Defending Sovereign Statehood Against Transforming the European Union into a State," *European Constitutional Law Review* 5 (2009): 355.
16. Dieter Grimm, "The Basic Law at 60: Identity and Change," *German Law Review* 11 (2010): 45.
17. Michel Rosenfeld is correct to see in the German model of constitutional identity a strong negation of the past and a commitment to endow the constitutional order with a new content. But we disagree with his comparison of German and American constitutional identities: "Constitutional identity . . . is much more central to national identity in the United States model than in the . . . German model. In short, in the German model, the constitution is supposed to provide the means for giving expression to an existing national identity." To the extent that in the United States the Constitution is importantly constitutive of the nation, Rosenfeld is correct, and in that sense it is also correct to highlight its centrality; yet to the extent that the new German constitutional order seeks to establish an "ethnocentric democracy," to see this effort as affirming an existing national identity may obscure its more radical intent; see Rosenfeld, "The European Treaty-Constitution and Constitutional Identity: A View from America," *International Journal of Constitutional Law* 3 (2005): 323.
18. Kotzur, "Constitutional Amendments and Constitutional Changes," 128.
19. For a different interpretation of the Court's posture toward the German past, see Michaela Hailbronner, "Rethinking the Rise of the German Constitutional Court: From Anti-Nazism to Value Formalism," *International Journal of Constitutional Law* 12 (2014).
20. As early as the 1960s, the Court of Justice of the European Communities ruled that European Economic Community law takes precedence over national law. In the landmark *Van Gend & Loos* case, it stated: "The Community [EEC] constitutes a new legal order of international law for the benefit of which the states have limited their sovereign rights": *Case C-26/62 Algemene Transport-en Expeditie Onderneming van Gend & Loos v. Nederlandse Administratie der Belastingen* (1963) ECR 1. The following year, the Court further stated: "By contrast with ordinary treaties, the EEC Treaty has created its own legal system which, on the entry into force of the Treaty, became an integral part of the legal systems of the Member States and which their courts are bound to apply": *Case C-6/64 Flaminio Costa v. E.N.E.L.* (1964) ECR 585. In 1967 the FCC acknowledged that the member states of the EEC transferred certain sovereign rights to the community; see BverfGE 22, 293, 296—*EG Verordnung*. Subsequent cases made clear that such transference could not extend to matters pertaining to German constitutional identity.

21. *Solange I Case,* BVerfG decision 2 BvR 52/71 of May 29, 1976, 37 BVerfGE 271, [1974] 2 CMLR 540. A year before, in the Indian case that is celebrated for having pursued the conceptual logic of this German legal thinking, one of the justices concluded, "The personality of the Constitution must remain unchanged": *Kesavananda Bharati v. State of Kerala* A SC 1461 (1973), 1624. From here, it is not a far cry to oppose constitutional change when it is viewed as a threat to the specific commitments one associates with the constitution's particular identity, as eventually transpired in India in connection with the intense struggle over the meaning of secularism. For an extended discussion of the German-Indian jurisprudential connection, see Gary Jeffrey Jacobsohn, *Constitutional Identity* (Cambridge, Mass.: Harvard University Press, 2010), 58–60.
22. *Solange I Case,* para. 6.
23. Donald P. Kommers and Russell A. Miller, *The Constitutional Jurisprudence of the Federal Republic of Germany,* 3rd ed. (Durham, N.C.: Duke University Press, 2012), 327.
24. Franz C. Mayer, "Rashomon in Karlsruhe: A Reflection on Democracy and Identity in the European Union," *International Journal of Constitutional Law* 9, nos. 3–4 (2011): 784.
25. Juliane Kokott, "Report on Germany," in Anne-Marie Slaughter, Alec Stone Sweet, and J. H. H. Weiler, eds., *The European Court and National Courts: Doctrine and Jurisprudence; Legal Change in Its Social Context* (Oxford: Hart, 1998), 90.
26. *Solange II Case,* 73 BVerfGE 339 (1986).
27. Jose Luis Martí, "Two Different Ideas of Constitutional Identity: Identity of the Constitution v. Identity of the People," in Saiz Arnaiz and Alcoberro Llivina, *National Constitutional Identity,* 20.
28. Consider James Madison's argument in *Federalist* 49. It was only in "a nation of philosophers" that a "reverence for the laws would be sufficiently inculcated by the voice of an enlightened reason"; see *The Federalist Papers,* ed. Clinton Rossiter (New York: Mentor, 1961), 314. Implicit in his calculation is the idea that a constitution, however reasonable and clear in its articulation of rules and principles, can succeed in translating word into deed (and thereby establish a discernible identity) only if fundamental continuity in basic law and actual constitutional practice are seen as two sides of the same coin.
29. Kommers and Miller, *Constitutional Jurisprudence of Germany,* 334.
30. *Maastricht Treaty Case,* 89 BVerfGE 155 (1993), at II.1a.
31. Ibid., at B.5.
32. Ibid., at II.3c.
33. Ibid. As Mattias Kumm noted, "The idea of subsidiarity is in the process of taking the place that the term 'sovereignty' has traditionally occupied in order to defend national communities against undue infringement of their capacity to govern themselves"; see Kumm, "Thick Constitutional Patriotism and Political Liberalism: On the Role and Structure of European Legal History," *German Law Journal* 6 (2005): 351. On the Court's protective stance regarding German sovereignty, see Bruno DeWitte, "Sovereignty and European Integration: The Weight of Legal

Tradition," in Slaughter, Sweet, and Weiler, *European Court and National Courts.* DeWitte pays close attention to the views of Justice Paul Kirchhof, who was the Second Senate's rapporteur in the *Maastricht Case*: "[Kirchhof] argues that the guarantee of *identity* of the German constitutional order must mean, at least, that the German Parliament is not allowed to *put an end to the German State* by transferring sovereignty to a newly created European federal state" (290).

34. This achievement is reflected in the title of Fritz Stern's illuminating memoir, *Five Germanys I Have Known* (2006).
35. Kokott, "Report on Germany," 111.
36. Ulrich K. Preuss, "Constitutional Powermaking for the New Polity: Some Deliberations on the Relations Between Constituent Power and the New Constitution," in Michel Rosenfeld, ed., *Constitution, Identity, Difference, and Legitimacy* (Durham, N.C.: Duke University Press, 204), 157.
37. For the best account in which it *is* appreciated, see Rogers Smith, *Civic Ideals: Conflicting Visions of Citizenship in U.S. History* (New Haven, Conn.: Yale University Press, 1997).
38. *Maastricht Treaty Case,* 89 BVerfGE 155 (1993), at II. B.5.
39. "The Basic Law is not a value-neutral document. Its section in basic rights establishes an objective order of values and this order strongly reinforces the effective power of basic rights. This value system, which centers upon the dignity of the human personality developing freely within the social community, must be looked upon as a fundamental constitutional decision affecting all spheres of law, both public and private. . . . Every provision of private law must be compatible with this system of values, and every such provision must be interpreted in its spirit": *Lüth Case,* 7BVerfGE 198 (1958). "Taken as whole," the Court said in the earlier *Southwest Case,* "a constitution reflects certain overarching principles": *Southwest State Case,* 1 BVerfGE 14 (1951), 32. Accordingly, the possibility that "a constitutional provision may itself be null and void" is predicated on the same conviction that led the Court in the *Luth Case* to align itself with an equally "un-American" approach to state action, namely, the belief in a coherent corpus of all-embracing principles whose objective standing requires nothing short of totality in relation to their enforcement. On this latter point, see Mattias Kumm, "Who Is Afraid of the Total Constitution? Constitutional Rights and the Constitutionalization of Private Law," *German Law Journal* 7 (2006): 350. For a comparison of the relative importance of American and German constitutional principles to national identity, see Gary Jeffrey Jacobsohn, "A Lighter Touch: American Constitutional Principles in Comparative Perspective," in Karen Orren and John Compton, eds., *Cambridge Companion on the United States Constitution* (New York: Cambridge University Press, 2018).
40. Abraham Lincoln, "First Inaugural Address, March 4, 1861," in Roy P. Basler, ed., *Collected Works of Abraham Lincoln* (New Brunswick, N.J.: Rutgers University Press, 1953), 4:269, digital production by University of Michigan Digital Library Production Services, 2001, https://quod.lib.umich.edu/l/lincoln/lincoln4/1:389?rgn=div1;view=fulltext.

41. See, for example, the entries in the special edition on the proposed European Constitution published in the *International Journal of Constitutional Law* in May 2005.
42. Pola Cebulak, "European Constitutional Identity 'Inside Out': Bringing European Jurisdiction Under One Roof," paper presented at the Advanced Issues of European Law Conference, Dubrovnik, Croatia, April 22–28, 2012, 22. On the federalism question and constitutional identity in Europe, see François-Xavier Millet, "National Constitutional Identity as a Safeguard of Federalism in Europe," in Loic Azoulai, Lena Boucon, and François-Xavier Millet, eds., *Deconstructing EU Federalism Through Competences,* European University Institute Working Papers, Law 2012/06, http://cadmus.eui.eu/bitstream/handle/1814/21298/LAW_2012_06_Rev2.pdf?sequence=3. Millet argues that a discourse of constitutional identity, traceable to the national-identity clause in the Maastricht Treaty, has emerged in Europe precisely to counteract the centralizing dynamic within the EU, against which other defenses of a more state-centered federalism are viewed as ineffective. In so doing, however, it balances unity with diversity.
43. Hauke Brunkhorst, "A Polity Without a State? European Constitutionalism Between Evolution and Revolution," in Eric Oddver Erikson, John Eric Fossum, and Augustin Jose Menendez, eds., *Developing a Constitution for Europe* (London: Routledge, 2004), 89.
44. "The powers of the European Parliament were progressively enhanced in successive revisions of the Treaties constituting the European Union, not least in the last such revision, the Treaty of Lisbon, which itself was but the famous European Constitution repackaged differently": J. H. H. Weiler, "The Crumbling of European Democracy," in Mark A. Graber, Sanford Levinson, and Mark Tushnet, eds., *Constitutional Democracy in Crisis?* (Oxford: Oxford University Press, 2018), 629.
45. Alfred Grosser, "The Federal Constitutional Court's *Lisbon* Case: Germany's 'Sonderweg'; An Outsider's Perspective," *German Law Review* 10 (2009): 1263.
46. As was pointed out in a moderately critical account of the *Lisbon* decision, "There is probably no other judgment in the history of the Karlsruhe Court in which the argument is so much at odds with the actual result"; see Christoph Schonberger, "*Lisbon* in Karlsruhe: Maastricht's Epigones at Sea," *German Law Review* 10 (2009): 1201.
47. Lars Vinx, "The Incoherence of Strong Popular Sovereignty," *International Journal of Constitutional Law* 11, no. 1 (2013): 124.
48. Daniel Halberstam and Christoph Möllers, "The German Constitutional Court Says 'Ja zu Deutschland!,'" *German Law Journal* 10 (2009): 13.
49. Schonberger, "*Lisbon* in Karlsruhe," 1207.
50. Jo Eric Khushal Murkens, "We Want Our Identity Back: The Revival of National Sovereignty in the German Federal Constitutional Court's Decision on the Lisbon Treaty," *Public Law* 2010, no. 3 (2010): 540.
51. Roland Bieber, "An Association of Sovereign States," *European Constitutional Law Review* 5 (2009): 397.

52. Pernice, "Treaty of Lisbon," 351. Or as Pietro Faraguna has noted, "What the German Federal Constitutional Court recognizes as constitutional identity . . . consists precisely of the same principles protected by the foundational principles of the EU"; see Faraguna, "Constitutional Identity in the EU: A Shield or a Sword," *German Law Journal* 18 (2017): 1639.
53. The complainants had argued that the act approving the treaty violated the Basic Law by infringing "the principle of democracy . . . in two respects: by the competences of the German *Bundestag* being undermined on the one hand and by a lack of democratic legitimation of the European Union on the other hand"; see *Lisbon Treaty Case,* 123 BVerfGE 267 (2009), para. 100.
54. Ibid., para. 274.
55. Ibid., para. 103.
56. Ibid., para. 298.
57. "In Germany, participation must, at the national level, comply with the requirements under Article 23.1 of the Basic Law. The Extending Act does not comply with these requirements in so far as the *Bundestag* and the *Bundesrat* have not yet been accorded sufficient rights of participation in European lawmaking and treaty amendment procedures" (ibid., para. 409).
58. See, for example, Jeffrey K. Staton and Georg Vanberg, "The Value of Vagueness: Delegation, Defiance, and Judicial Opinions," *American Journal of Political Science* 52, no. 3 (2008): 505: "The desire to craft consensus among a group of justices with diverse preferences may require opinion writers to sacrifice clarity."
59. "According to inside rumours, fierce battles were fought within the Court. The unanimous adoption of the judgment may possibly be explained as the result of a compromise": Christian Tomuschat, "The Defense of National Identity by the German Constitutional Court," in Saiz Arnaiz and Alcoberro Llivina, *National Constitutional Identity,* 214.
60. For more discussion, see Kommers and Miller, *Constitutional Jurisprudence of Germany,* 351.
61. Diarmuid Rossa Phelan, *Revolt or Revolution: The Constitutional Boundaries of the European Community* (Dublin: Round Hall Sweet & Maxwell, 1997), 355. "A seminal example of an essential element of constitutional identity defined through a specific constitutional provision is the Irish constitutional commitment to the protection of the right of the unborn": Faraguna, "Constitutional Identity in the EU," 1635. Since passage of the 2018 referendum removing this provision from the Constitution, this example is now one of historical interest only.
62. *Lisbon Treaty Case,* 123 BVerfGE 267 (2009), para. 218 (emphasis added).
63. Armin von Bogdandy and Stephan Schill, "Overcoming Absolute Primacy: Respect for National Identity Under the Lisbon Treaty," *Common Market Law Review* 48 (2011): 1419.
64. Monica Claes, "National Identity: Trump Card or Up for Negotiation?," in Saiz Arnaiz and Alcoberro Llivina, *National Constitutional Identity,* 111.

65. *Lisbon Treaty Case,* 123 BVerfGE 267 (2009), para. 218. One should note that the assertion that the Basic Law was created out of an exertion of the German people's constituent power is a highly contested point.
66. Ibid., para. 216.
67. Ibid., para. 340.
68. As Daniel Augenstein comments, "Supra-nationalism should not be understood in terms of a constitutional moment of rupture but as a continuous process of constitutional transformation that partly disentangles the state from the nation yet retains elements of the old national order"; see Augenstein, The Contested Polity: Europe's Constitutional Identity Between Religious and Secular Values," University of Edinburgh School of Law, Working Paper no. 2009/13 (2009), http://papers.ssrn.com/sol3/papers.cfm?abstract_id=1371524.
69. In Ackerman's "dualist democracy" formulation, major constitutional transformation occurs along the higher lawmaking track, culminating in a "constitutional moment" that embodies the power of a popular movement to effect fundamental change in constitutional direction. In contrast, the ordinary politics that occurs on the second track—the lower lawmaking system—has a preservative function, and one will not find examples of constitutional revolution along it; see, for example, Bruce A. Ackerman, *We the People: Foundations* (Cambridge, Mass.: Harvard University Press, 1991).
70. Interestingly, it was not just the Nazi rise to power that provided historical lessons. In her account of the "slow revolution," Margaret Barber Crosby writes of an earlier, much less well-known constitutional transformation: "The year 1896 marked a watershed in German history, because liberals achieved the legal revolution they had sought over the long course of the nineteenth century. . . . The old order was slowly declining behind a mass of *burgerliche* law. It was this that made Germany's revolutionary moment"; see Margaret Barber Crosby, *The Making of a German Constitution: A Slow Revolution* (Oxford: Berg, 2008), 212.
71. Brunkhorst, "Polity Without a State," 93.
72. Woelk, "Germany," 161.
73. During the Parliamentary Council deliberations leading to the adoption of the Basic Law, the counterrevolutionary implications of the eternity provisions were discussed by several participants. Thomas Dehler, a Free Democrat, "underlined the importance of such an eternity clause as pursuing the crucial aim of preventing revolutionaries from relying on the constitution to justify their revolution"; see Polzin, "Constitutional Identity, Unconstitutional Amendments," 423. As Polzin points out, not everyone agreed with him.
74. Kokott, "Report on Germany," 103.
75. *Lisbon Treaty Case,* para. 235.
76. Christopher M. Kotowski, "Revolution," in Giovanni Sartori, ed., *Social Science Concepts: A Systematic Analysis* (Beverly Hills, Calif.: Sage, 1984), 416.
77. *Lisbon Treaty Case,* para. 217. This would appear to be a response to the following claim made in oral argument: "According to the Basic Law, those entitled to vote have the right by a decision 'freely adopted to decide on the change of identity of

the Federal Republic of Germany that would be effected by its becoming a constituent state of a European federal state, and the concomitant replacement of the Basic Law. . . .' Article 146 of the Basic Law confirms the pre-constitutional right to give oneself a constitution from which constitutional authority emanates and by which it is bound. . . . It is the constituent authority alone, and not the constitutional authority emanating from the constitution, which is entitled to release the state constituted by the Basic law" (para. 179). One implication of the *Lisbon* judgment is that it produced a new interpretation of Article 146, namely, that it offers a legal basis for the German people to abolish the values protected by Article 79, paragraph 3. There is disagreement over this: others argue that such a legal right to abolish those values does not exist, that they are protected per se and can be eliminated only by an illegitimate process outside the law itself. (Our thanks to Monika Polzin for suggesting this to us.)

78. The paradoxical aspect can be seen in scholarly accounts of the *Lisbon* case. For example, one commentator writes, "In the Court's view, democracy essentially requires unrestricted external sovereignty in that any infringement of external sovereignty would infringe upon the constituent power of the people"; see Vinx, "Incoherence of Strong Popular Sovereignty," 116. Yet given the Court's ambivalence about the immunity of the original constituent power from a subsequent radical alteration that would violate universal principles of justice, it seems odd that there would be a strong appeal to sovereignty as a way of defending an idea—democracy—that is premised on these principles.
79. Bieber, "Association of Sovereign States," 399. As has also been pointed out, in the evolution of European integration, the idea of subsidiarity has been used in place of the traditional concept of sovereignty; see Kumm, "Thick Constitutional Patriotism," 351.
80. *Lisbon Treaty Case,* para. 211.
81. In advocating for a "democracy oriented" understanding of human dignity, Christoph Möllers calls attention to the deep tension in the Court's opinion: "Human dignity as the epitome of individuality and as the epitome of a democratic constitutional community poses a fundamental contradiction that no possible understanding of human dignity in the Basic Law can avoid"; see Möllers, "Democracy and Human Dignity: Limits of a Moralized Conception of Rights in German Constitutional Law," *Israel Law Review* 42 (2009): 426.
82. As Joseph Weiler noted, "We consider the integrity of our *national* constitutional orders not simply as a matter that is important to the good functioning of government and an orderly distribution of political power, but also as one of moral commitment and identity"; see Weiler, "Human Rights, Constitutionalism, and Integration: Iconography and Fetishism," in Erikson, Fossum, and Jose Menendez, *Developing a Constitution for Europe,* 62. Consider, too, Lars Vinx's critique of the Court's decision: "[A] democratic constitutional theory ought not to be based on a notion of strong popular sovereignty, and the claim that strong popular sovereignty is essential to democracy ought to be rejected"; see Vinx, "Incoherence of Strong Popular Sovereignty," 102. One can agree with Vinx's critique of the

Court's seeming embrace of strong popular sovereignty without having to embrace his further point that in doing so, it has essentially adopted a Schmittian view of the special status of prepolitical identity in German constitutional theory. Thus, whatever may be its consistency with such a view, the Court's position can just as easily be reconciled with a common, though flawed, understanding of constitutional democracy that can be found in places where Schmitt's theorizing is essentially irrelevant; see Walter F. Murphy, *Constitutional Democracy: Creating and Maintaining a Just Political Order* (Baltimore: Johns Hopkins University Press, 2007).

83. Mayer, "Rashomon in Karlsruhe," 785.
84. This they have done in several notable instances. Consider in this regard the rulings on the treaty in the Czech, Polish, and French courts.
85. Schonberger, "*Lisbon* in Karlsruhe," 1216.
86. Von Bogdandy and Schill, "Overcoming Absolute Primacy," 1419, 1452. Stated even more strongly, national courts and the judiciary of the EU have an obligation "to enter negotiations over national and constitutional identity"; see Claes, "National Identity," 123.
87. Toniatti, "Sovereignty Lost, Constitutional Identity Gained," 67.
88. Pernice, "Treaty of Lisbon," 353.
89. Toniatti, "Sovereignty Lost, Constitutional Identity Gained," 67.
90. Mayer, "*Rashomon* in Karlsruhe," 785. The mutability of constitutional identity is a concept well entrenched in the literature of constitutional patriotism. As Jan-Werner Müller writes, "Identity was not to be understood in static . . . terms—it was constituted precisely by a continuous civic self-interrogation and open argument about the past, and not least, the purging of problematic continuities with that past. In short, it was understood as a *process*"; see Müller, *Constitutional Patriotism* (Princeton, N.J.: Princeton University Press, 2007), 34. See also Kumm, "Thick Constitutional Patriotism," 353: "The idea of constitutional patriotism . . . provides a basic focal point for a plurality of identities that can challenge, complement and enrich one another."
91. *OMT Reference Case,* 2 BvRfGE 134 (2014), para. 103. In this case, the Court concluded that a constituent element of constitutional identity would be violated if Parliament were required to renounce budgetary autonomy in order to conform to requirements of EU law. As pointed out by one commentator, "Article 4(2) TEU and national constitutional identity as a limit of EU law can only work in a genuine spirit of co-operation. As far as the Court's OMT reference is concerned, one wonders whether the motivation for raising the issue was not exactly the opposite"; see Franz C. Mayer, "Rebels Without a Cause? A Critical Analysis of the German Constitutional Court's OMT Reference," *German Law Journal* 15 (2014): 133.
92. Charles Taylor, *The Ethics of Authenticity* (Cambridge, Mass.: Harvard University Press, 1991), 48.
93. Tomuschat, "Defense of National Identity," 219. Tomuschat points out in this connection that in the year after the *Lisbon* decision, the Court moved closer to his

own view in the important *Honeywell* case. In that judgment, it adopted a more conciliatory tone toward Europe, possibly in reaction to the negative response engendered by the previous ruling. Tomuschat finds it significant that the text of the opinion omits any reference to sovereignty, and that the Court expressed a greater openness to legal coordination with Europe (216). But any conclusion that the Court had abandoned the role it adopted for itself in *Lisbon* must be considered premature in light of its controversial decision in 2014 in the *OMT Reference Case.*

94. Mayer, "Rebels Without a Cause," 143. One should note that these sovereign interests doubtless include the Court's interest in not being overruled by a European court.

95. Ibid., 144.

96. In the *OMT Reference Case,* the advocate-general responded to the FCC's claim of a right to exercise identity review over EU acts by invoking the congruence argument: "[A] clearly understood open attitude to EU law should in the medium and long term give rise, as a principle, to basic convergence between the constitutional identity of the Union and that of each of the member states"; quoted in Monica Claes and Jan-Herman Reestrum, "The Protection of National Constitutional Identity and the Limits of European Integration at the Occasion of the *Gauweiler Case," German Law Journal* 16 (2015): 920.

97. This works both ways. "The European Union . . . exist[s] only to the extent that sovereignty is not akin to its very definition. Against this background, the new narrative of constitutional identity embodies a paradigmatic shift that admirably matches with what the EU is meant to be about: ensuring peace through law and trade, not politics": Millet, "National Constitutional Identity," 63. Millet elaborates: "On the one side, sovereignty still tends to be associated with absolute power, primacy of politics over law, of the collective over the individual. On the other side, constitutional identity carries opposite values: limitation of power, reign of law, primacy of the individual over the group" (62).

98. *Thompson v. Oklahoma,* 487 U.S. 815, 868n4 (1988).

99. Sujit Choudhry, "Migration as a New Metaphor in Comparative Constitutional Law," in Sujit Choudhry, ed., *The Migration of Constitutional Ideas* (Cambridge: Cambridge University Press, 2006), 1, 24–25.

100. For a detailed discussion, see Jacobsohn, *Constitutional Identity,* 187–202.

101. Phelan, *Revolt or Revolution,* 355.

102. In accordance with a ruling by the Irish Supreme Court, all major changes in EU treaties require a constitutional amendment, and in accordance with the Constitution, an amendment must obtain approval by referendum; see Maria Cahill, "Ireland's Constitutional Amendability and Europe's Constitutional Ambition: The Lisbon Referendum in Context," *German Law Journal* 9 (2008).

103. The protocol respecting the right to life was actually a clarification that reaffirmed a commitment set in 1992 in the Maastricht Treaty. Ireland received additional opt-outs in the Lisbon Treaty, as did other countries.

104. Ernils Larsson, "Abortion, Human Rights and the 2008 Irish Referendum on the Lisbon Treaty," http://www.euij-waseda.jp/common/pdf/WP_E.Larsson.pdf.
105. Ibid.
106. The 2009 concessions in Ireland are worth considering in connection with an important decision of the European Court of Human Rights rendered one year later. In *ABC v. Ireland,* the Court considered whether Irish laws that imposed severe restrictions on a woman's right to obtain an abortion violated mandates of the European Convention on Human Rights. The ECtHR largely upheld the official Irish position, ruling that while the restrictions clearly fell within the scope of Article 8 of the convention, they also fell within the "margin of appreciation" that must be extended to laws embodying the strong moral beliefs of the Irish people. The doctrinal reference was to the well-known formulation of the Strasbourg Court, according to which the tribunal will defer to a contracting party in order to accommodate a state's particular circumstances when the precise terms of the convention have not been satisfied. In effect, as we shall see, the doctrine applies in much the same way as does the identity clause in the law of the European Union, an acknowledgment in both instances that a comprehensive legal order should respect the principled essentials of its constituent parts.
107. Pietro Faraguna, "Taking Constitutional Identity Away from the Courts," *Brooklyn Journal of International Law* 41, no. 2 (2016): 525–54.
108. Case C-159/90, Society for the Protection of Unborn Children Ireland Ltd. v. Stephen Grogan and Others, 1991 E.C.R. 4685; see ibid., 553: "This judicial saga pushed Ireland to negotiate a permanent protocol to protect its constitutional protection of the right to life of the unborn."
109. A full accounting of this culmination would include developments occurring completely within Ireland, highlighting a social order whose transformation had outpaced the commitments of its fundamental law. Here the narrowing involved the gap between the constitutional text and the facts on the ground, which, if left unattended, had threatened to pose a crisis in constitutional legitimacy.
110. Möllers, "Democracy and Human Dignity," 432.
111. Maarten Stremler, "The Constitution as an Objective Order of Values," *Kutafin University Law Review* 4, no. 2 (2017).
112. Hanna Fenichal Pitkin, "The Idea of a Constitution," *Journal of Legal Education* 37 (1987): 169.
113. Bruce Ackerman, "Three Paths to Constitutionalism—and the Crisis of the European Union," *British Journal of Political Science* 45, no. 4 (2015): 3.
114. Ibid., 2.
115. Ibid., 5.
116. Ibid., 7.
117. Ibid.
118. Ernst Benda, "The Protection of Human Dignity (Article 1 of the Basic Law)," *SMU Law Review* 53 (2000): 448.
119. Hailbronner, "Rise of the German Constitutional Court," 632.

120. Ibid., 631.

121. Dieter Grimm, "Dignity in a Legal Context: Dignity as an Absolute Right," in Christopher McCrudden, ed., *Understanding Human Dignity* (Oxford: Oxford University Press, 2013), 385. Or as has been eloquently stated, "Nazism still legitimizes the guarantee of human dignity today by the abominable, vivid barbarism of its negation": Matthias Mahlmann, "The Basic Law at 60: Human Dignity and the Culture of Republicanism," *German Law Journal* 11 (2010): 10. And as viewed from abroad by the former president of the Israeli Supreme Court, Aharon Barak: "The supreme status of the constitution reflects Germany's rejection of its Nazi past and the severe violations of human dignity that characterized it. It places human dignity, which the Nazis desecrated, at the topmost rung of their ladder of values"; see Barak, *Human Dignity: The Constitutional Value and the Constitutional Right* (Cambridge: Cambridge University Press, 2015), 230.

122. Grimm, "Dignity in a Legal Context," 384. The FCC has said: "Neither original history nor the ideas and intentions of the framers are of decisive importance in interpreting particular provisions of the Basic Law": *Life Imprisonment Case,* 45 BVerfGE 187 (1977).

123. Catherine Dupré, "Constructing the Meaning of Human Dignity: Four Questions," in McCrudden, *Understanding Human Dignity,* 119.

124. Hailbronner, "Rise of the German Constitutional Court," 635. Hailbronner acknowledged that the Court over time embraced this role, developing the concept of an objective order of values in part as a response to the twin evils of Nazism and communism. A similar acknowledgment appears in Ackerman's account, in which the Court eventually projects itself into a guardian role as protector of fundamental rights and Enlightenment values; see Ackerman, "Three Paths to Constitutionalism," 7.

125. The Indian Court's aggressive pursuit of these goals under the rubric of "basic structure" has a clear connection with the actions of the German Court. In a 2006 case on reservations in public employment, the Indian Court observed: "Overarching and informing of these rights and values [under the basic structure doctrine] is the principle of human dignity under the German basic law. Similarly, secularism is the principle which is the overarching principle of several rights and values under the Indian Constitution. . . . The theory of basic structure is based on the concept of constitutional identity. The basic structure jurisprudence is a pre-occupation with constitutional identity"; see *M. Nagaraj & Others v. Union of India & Others,* AIR 2007 SC 71 (2006), Standards of Review of Constitutional Amendments section, para. 7.

126. Hailbronner, "Rise of the German Constitutional Court," 635.

127. *M. Nagaraj & Others v. Union of India & Others,* AIR 2007 SC 71 (2006), Standards of Review of Constitutional Amendments section, para. 10.

128. Hailbronner, "Rise of the German Constitutional Court," 631.

129. Mohit Sharma, "Constitution and Its Amendability: Indian Context," *Journal on Contemporary Issues of Law* 3, no. 7 (2017): 6, http://jcil.lsyndicate.com/wp-content/uploads/2017/08/Mohit-Sharma.pdf.

130. If the subject under consideration is dignity and sovereignty, the German Court is hardly the worst offender in its treatment of constitutional issues related thereto. The U.S. Supreme Court's Eleventh Amendment jurisprudence cannot be matched for its flawed reasoning. Thus, in defending the doctrine of sovereign immunity, the Court writes of dignity as if it were a property of political entities rather than individuals: "The preeminent purpose of state sovereign immunity is to accord States the dignity that is consistent with their status as sovereign entities" (*Federal Maritime Commission v. South Carolina State Ports Authority*, 535 U.S. 743 [2002], 760). As pointed out by Justice David Souter in a dissent in an earlier decision, this is a strange argument for a court in a constitutional democracy to make: "The Court assumes . . . that . . . 'dignity' is a quality easily translated from the person of the King to the participatory abstraction of a republican state. The thoroughly anomalous character of this appeal to dignity is obvious from a reading of Blackstone's description of royal dignity, which he sets out as premise of his discussion of sovereignty" (*Alden v. Maine*, 527 U.S. 706 [1999], 802).

131. Michael Rosen, *Dignity* (Cambridge, Mass.: Harvard University Press, 2012), 8.

132. Samuel Moyn, "The Secret History of Constitutional Dignity," in McCrudden, *Understanding Human Dignity*, 109.

133. Ibid., 96, 108.

134. Mahlmann, "Basic Law at 60," 11.

135. Möllers, "Democracy and Human Dignity," 425.

136. James Q. Whitman, "On Nazi 'Honour' and the New European Dignity," in Christian Jourges and Navraj Singh Gholeigh, eds., *Darker Legacies of Law in Europe: The Shadow of National Socialism and Fascism over Europe and Its Legal Traditions* (Oxford: Hart, 2003), 245. In this regard, David Fraser has provocatively argued against the view that "events in Germany between 1933 and 1945 constituted a radical break with the history, traditions and practices of European and German history"; see Fraser, *Law After Auschwitz: Towards a Jurisprudence of the Holocaust* (Durham, N.C.: Carolina Academic Press, 2005), 25. Whether or not one subscribes to his argument, his case against the "thesis of discontinuity of the Hitler period" (27), which claims that "the period 1933 to 1945 was indeed a revolutionary rupture with all that preceded it" (29), supports one of the central claims of this book, namely, that a constitutional revolution can occur with seeming continuity, that incremental constitutional actions rather than violent usurpation can bring about change of such substantial import as to be considered revolutionary.

137. At the height of the crisis, a Serbian official said, "What we expect from the EU is to tell us what the form of good behavior is. Is it what Germany is doing, where refugees are welcomed with medicine and food? Or is it where they are welcomed with fences, police and tear gas?" (*New York Times*, September 18, 2015, A9). And consider this rejoinder from the German foreign minister to his Czech counterpart's assertion of the primacy of national sovereignty in connection with policies toward migrants: "We can, as Europe, say that we will shut all

borders, and not let anyone else in." But in doing so, "we would betray our values" (*New York Times,* September 12, 2015, A9). The idea, then, that there has been convergence within the European community on the practical implications of a continent-wide commitment to human dignity can only be described as illusory.

138. Such an exercise occurred when the FCC in 2015 applied its identity review to justify its refusal to implement a European Arrest Warrant (EAW), which, according to the Court, would have violated an individual's human dignity as guaranteed under Articles 79.3 and 1.1. 2BvR 2735/14 (2015).
139. *Life Imprisonment Case,* at 229.
140. Pitkin, "Idea of a Constitution," 169.
141. Schmid quoted in Möllers, "Democracy and Human Dignity," 420.
142. Ibid., 431. The term "scope of conflict" was formulated by the American political scientist E. E. Schattschneider in his classic work *The Semi-Sovereign People: A Realist's View of Democracy in America.* As he argued, "The most important strategy of politics is concerned with the scope of conflict"; see Schattschneider, *The Semi-Sovereign People: A Realist's View of Democracy in America* (Hinsdale, Ill.: Dryden, 1960), 3. In Schattschneider's account, the privatizing and socializing of conflict in the United States is correlated with specific biases; thus, expanding the area of political contestation is associated with greater protection of individual rights and a commitment to equality. In principle, however, this directional bias, while characterizing much of the American experience, could play out differently elsewhere. As Schattschneider pointed out: "There is nothing intrinsically good or bad about any given scope of conflict" (17).
143. Schattschneider, *Semi-Sovereign People,* 3.
144. Ibid., 11.
145. *Lisbon Case,* para. 228.
146. Casper, "Karlsruhe Republic," para. 14.
147. Ibid., para. 15.

Chapter 5. India's Dynamic Constitution

Epigraph: John Stuart Mill, "Coleridge," in *Dissertations and Discussions: Political, Philosophical, and Historical* (London: Parker and Son, 1859), 1:423.

1. Parliamentary Debates V, vols. xii–xiii, pt. 11, 8820–22, May 16, 1951, in Subhash C. Kashyup, ed., *Jawaharlal Nehru and the Constitution* (New Delhi: Metropolitan Book Co., 1982), 147.
2. *Constituent Assembly Debates,* September 10, 1949 (Lok Sabha Secretariat, 1986), 9:1195; cited in Surya Deva, "Saving Clauses," in Sujit Choudhry, Madhav Khosla, and Pratap Bhanu Mehta, eds., *The Oxford Handbook of the Indian Constitution* (New Delhi: Oxford University Press, 2016), 641.
3. Granville Austin, *Working a Democratic Constitution: A History of the Indian Experience* (New Delhi: Oxford University Press, 1999), 69. Austin emphasizes that "the social revolutionary strand was put at the top of the national agenda by the

Constituent Assembly" (71). And as noted by an Indian constitutional scholar, "The incorporation into the Indian Constitution of two disparate components, that is, social revolutionary objectives as contained in the Preamble and the Directive Principles of State Policy and Fundamental Rights, was bound to introduce certain incompatibilities in the working of the Constitution"; see Ramashramy Roy, *Democracy in India: Form and Substance* (New Delhi: Shipra, 2005), 156.

4. The German constitutional theorist Dietrich Conrad was the key figure in transferring the German understanding to the Indian subcontinent. His work was cited by Indian justices in several of the cases concerning amendment provisions found unconstitutional by the Supreme Court.
5. Justice Chandrachud in *Minerva Mills, Ltd. v. Union of India*, AIR 1980 SC 1789, 1798.
6. *Kesavananda Bharati v. State of Kerala*, A SC 1461 (1973), at 1860.
7. Madhav Khosla, *The Indian Constitution* (New Delhi: Oxford University Press, 2012), 159. This perhaps explains its influence in Europe, especially for the justices on the German Court. Thus, it has been rightly pointed out that "the increasing preoccupation of European constitutional courts with 'constitutional identity' seems to mimic the basic structure doctrine [in India] insofar as it protects fundamental features of the material content of the national constitution"; see Maria Cahill, "The Ever Closer Remoteness of the Peoples of Europe? Limits on the Power of Amendment and National Constituent Power," *Cambridge Law Journal* 75, no. 2 (2016), 254.
8. Parliamentary Debates V, vols. xii–xiii, pt. 11, 8820–22, May 16, 1951, in Kashyup, *Jawaharlal Nehru and the Constitution*, 147.
9. This is consistent with Pratap Bhanu Mehta's contention that "the constitution was a radical idea, without itself containing guarantees that the social transformation it promised would come about"; see Mehta, *The Burden of Democracy* (New Delhi: Penguin, 2003), 56.
10. Sanjay G. Reddy, "A Rising Tide of Demands: India's Public Institutions and the Democratic Revolution," in Divesh Kapur and Pratap Bhanu Mehta, eds., *Public Institutions in India: Performance and Design* (New Delhi: Oxford University Press India, 2005), 457.
11. Andras Sajo, "Constitution Without the Constitutional Moment: A View from the New Member States," *International Journal of Constitutional Law* 2 (2004): 243.
12. As Cheryl Saunders notes, "People now expect actually to be involved in the constitution making process and not just symbolically associated with it"; see Saunders, "Constitution Making in the 21st Century," *International Review of Law* 4 (2012): 2. Specifically, "since at least World War II [public] participation in constitutional design has become more direct and has penetrated more deeply (or at least earlier) in the process": see Tom Ginsburg, Zachary Elkins, and Justin Blount, "Does the Process of Constitution-Making Matter?," *Annual Review of Law and Social Science* 5 (2009): 207.
13. Kashyup, *Jawaharlal Nehru and the Constitution*, 76.

14. Ibid., 26 (emphasis added).
15. Sarbani Sen, *The Constitution of India: Popular Sovereignty and Democratic Transformations* (New Delhi: Oxford University Press, 2007), 165.
16. Ibid., 26.
17. Ibid., 38.
18. Uday Mehta, "Indian Constitutionalism: Crisis, Unity, and History," in Choudhry, Khosla, and Mehta, *Oxford Handbook of the Indian Constitution*, 48.
19. Granville Austin, *The Indian Constitution: Cornerstone of a Nation* (New Delhi: Oxford University Press, 1966), xvii. There were, Austin allows, many other goals, but "transcendent among them was that of social revolution" (ibid.). As Ramashray Roy writes, "The one continuing theme . . . was the demolition of the old and antiquated structure of the Hindu society and reconstructing on its remains the grand edifice of new modern India with entirely a new institutional structure and procedures that would reflect an *idée directrice* entirely different from the one that prevailed earlier" (Roy, *Democracy in India*, 107).
20. Austin, *Working a Democratic Constitution*, 71.
21. Rajeev Dhavan, "Sarbani Sen, Popular Sovereignty, and Democratic Transformation: The Constitution of India," *Indian Journal of Constitutional Law* 2 (2008): 208.
22. Edmund S. Morgan, *Inventing the People: The Rise of Popular Sovereignty in England and America* (New York: Norton, 1988), 13. "The idea of an elected convention that would express enduring popular will in fundamental constitutions superior to government was a viable way of making popular creation and limitation of government believable. It was fictional, for it ascribed to one set of elected representatives meeting in convention a more popular character, and consequently a greater authority, than every subsequent set of representatives meeting as a legislature. But it was not too fictional to be believed and not so literal as to endanger the effectiveness of government" (91). In Andrew Arato's account, "fiction" was the appropriate nomenclature for "the claim that the Constituent Assembly was the people of India as stated by the Preamble of the 1950 Constitution"; see Arato, *The Adventures of the Constituent Power: Beyond Revolutions?* (Cambridge: Cambridge University Press, 2017), 300. For a denial that popular sovereignty was a "fiction" in relation to the framing of the Indian Constitution, that it was rather "one of the cardinal concepts of the constitutional edifice in India," see K. P. Krishna Shetty, *Fundamental Rights and Socio-economic Justice in the Indian Constitution* (Allahabad: Chaitanya, 1969), 9.
23. Dhavan, "Sen, Popular Sovereignty, and Democratic Transformation," 208. Elsewhere, Dhavan appears less wedded to this assessment and more amenable to a nuanced understanding: "The need for a radical social and economic transformation was accepted, but the Constitution manifested this goal in a much more circumspect way"; see Dhavan, "Republic of India: The Constitution as the Situs of Struggle; India's Constitution Forty Years On," in Lawrence W. Beer, ed., *Constitutional Systems in Late Twentieth Century Asia* (Seattle: University of Washington Press, 1992), 413.

24. Dhavan, "Sen, Popular Sovereignty, and Democratic Transformation," 219.
25. *Constituent Assembly Debates,* vol. 12, November 25, 1949, 979.
26. Presidential Address to the Indian National Congress, Lucknow, April 12, 1936.
27. Kashyup, *Jawaharlal Nehru and the Constitution,* 65.
28. Quoted in B. R. Sharma, *Socio-Economic Justice Under Indian Constitution* (New Delhi: Deep & Deep, 1984), 70.
29. Valerian Rodrigues, ed., *The Essential Writings of B. R. Ambedkar* (New Delhi: Oxford University Press, 2002), 485.
30. Chaihark Hahm and Sung Ho Kim, *Making We the People: Democratic Constitutional Founding in Postwar Japan and South Korea* (Cambridge: Cambridge University Press, 2015), 15, 16.
31. Ibid., 45.
32. Ibid., 279.
33. Sen's argument that "the constitution was an embodiment of the fundamental fact that sovereign power must reside only in the people" hardly distinguishes the Indian document from what has been claimed for most, perhaps all, constitutions in the modern era (Sen, *Constitution of India,* 159). What is more fundamentally distinctive is the dominant substantive vision that emanated from a major faction of the people.
34. Hahm and Kim, *Making We the People,* 57.
35. Chief Justice Charles Evans Hughes, "Speech Before the Elmira Chamber of Commerce," May 3, 1907, in *Addresses of Charles Evans Hughes, 1906–1916,* 2nd ed. (New York: Putnam's Sons, 1916), 185.
36. Austin, *Indian Constitution,* 80. As Upendra Baxi pointed out to one of the authors (Jacobsohn), there is something quaint about coupling courts, which are theaters of state adjudicatory power, with a revolutionary mission. The point is well taken, although Austin's use of the metaphor is, in Baxi's judgment, a fair representation of what many framers intended.
37. V. R. Krishna Iyer, "Towards an Indian Jurisprudence of Social Action and Public Interest Litigation," in Indra Deva, ed., *Sociology of Law* (New Delhi: Oxford University Press, 2005), 297.
38. Nick Robinson, "Expanding Judiciaries: India and the Rise of the Good Governance Court," *Washington University Global Studies Law Review* 8 (2009): 4.
39. Rajeev Dhavan captures Nehru's attitude toward the judiciary well: "Nehru's . . . model of governance sought to use 'law' as an instrument of social change. As long as the judiciary behaved itself, nothing more needed to be said. The judiciary was an extra, to be respected for what it was; and, perforce, to be feared if it got out of hand"; see Dhavan, "Judges and Indian Democracy: The Lesser Evil?," in Francine R. Frankel, Zoya Hasan, Rajeev Bhargava, and Balveer Arora, eds., *Transforming India: Social and Political Dynamics of Democracy* (New Delhi: Oxford University Press, 2000), 321.
40. Sanjay G. Reddy, "A Rising Tide of Demands: India's Public Institutions and the Democratic Revolution," in Kapur and Mehta, *Public Institutions in India,* 457.

41. Robinson, "Expanding Judiciaries," 5. In the same vein, Marc Galanter wrote, "Independence and nationhood are an epochal event in Indian civilization which makes possible a controlled transformation of central social and cultural arrangements"; see Galanter, *Competing Equalities: Law and the Backward Classes in India* (Berkeley: University of California Press, 1984), 562.
42. Quoted in Austin, *Working a Democratic Constitution,* 88.
43. Parliamentary Debates V, vols. xii–xiii, pt. 11, 8820–22, May 16, 1951; in Kashyup, *Jawaharlal Nehru and the Constitution,* 157.
44. "The Directive Principles of State Policy represent a dynamic move towards a certain objective. The Fundamental Rights represent something static, to preserve certain rights which exist" (ibid.).
45. Quoted in Sharma, *Socio-Economic Justice,* 94.
46. For many commentators, the courts should also be directed by these principles. For example: "It is difficult to say that the judiciary could ignore with impunity the directives of the ultimate sovereign": Shetty, *Fundamental Rights and Socio-economic Justice,* 85.
47. Tarunabh Khaitan, "Directive Principles and the Expressive Accommodation of Ideological Dissenters," *International Journal of Constitutional Law* 16, no. 2 (2018): 406. Khaitan demonstrates that the directive principles should also be understood as a device through which the consent of three dissenting factions—socialists, Gandhians, and cultural nationalists—could be secured for the draft constitution. Importantly, those principles directed toward social transformation produced only negligible disagreement.
48. Sudesh Kumar Sharma, *Directive Principles and Fundamental Rights: Relationship and Policy Perspectives* (New Delhi: Deep & Deep, 1990), 5. Or as a justice of the Supreme Court, K. Hegde, described them: "The purpose of the Directive Principles is to fix certain social and economic goals for immediate attainment by bringing about a non-violent revolution. Through such social revolution the Constitution seeks to fulfill the needs of the common man and to change the structure of society"; quoted in Roy, *Democracy in India,* 91. The debates in the Constituent Assembly made clear that attaining these objectives immediately was not the expectation of the framers. Rather, it was widely held that the nonviolent constitutional revolution would bring them about gradually.
49. In essence, Parliament was raising a question that would be revisited in the years ahead, albeit in order to elicit a different response: "If there are certain basic features of the Constitution beyond the purview of the amendment power, why should the judiciary be the sole judge in determining the contours of those features?"; see Surya Deva, "Saving Clauses: The Ninth Amendment and Articles 31A-C," in Choudhry, Khosla, and Mehta, *Oxford Handbook of the Indian Constitution,* 636.
50. Ibid., 642.
51. Austin, *Working a Democratic Constitution,* 97.
52. *Shankari Prasad Singh Deo v. Union of India* AIR 1951 SC 458 (1952). Thus the word "law" in Article 13 (giving the Court the power to rule laws invalid that were

in derogation of fundamental rights) did not, according to the Court, include constitutional amendments. Thirteen years later, the Court reaffirmed this interpretation (although not unanimously, as before) in *Sajjan Singh v. State of Rajasthan* AIR 1965 SC 845.

53. Robinson, "Expanding Judiciaries," 31. The government's argument in the case revealed that it saw the Court's possible declaration of a power to overturn an amendment as anything but conservative: "If the amending power is restricted by implied limitations, the Constitution itself might be destroyed by revolution. Indeed [the amending power] is a safety valve and an alternative for a violent change by revolution"; quoted in Austin, *Working a Democratic Constitution,* 199.
54. *Golak Nath v. State of Punjab,* AIR 1967 SC 1643 (n27) [38].
55. Indeed, it has been called "one of the more significant and globally acknowledged constitutional decisions of [the twentieth] century"; see Dhavan, "Judges and Indian Democracy," 315.
56. Upendra Baxi, *Courage, Craft and Contention: The Indian Supreme Court in the Eighties* (Bombay: Tripathi Private, 1985), 65. And as another leading authority on the Indian Constitution noted, "The *Kesavananda Bharati* decision was doubtless an attempt by the Supreme Court to rewrite the Constitution. Such limitations on the constituent power were unheard of till then"; see S. P. Sathe, *Judicial Activism in India: Transgressing Borders and Enforcing Limits* (New Delhi: Oxford University Press, 2002), 70. Sathe may be correct about the Court's ambition, but given the Court's key argument that the amending power is only derivative of the original constituent power, his further claim about limitations is questionable. Still, he was correct in observing that *Kesavananda* "was a revolutionary decision and belied all assumptions held till then" (8).
57. P. P. Rao, "The Constitution, Parliament and the Judiciary," in Pram Chopra, ed., *The Supreme Court Versus the Constitution: A Challenge to Federalism* (New Delhi: Sage, 2006), 73.
58. Dietrich Conrad, "Constituent Power, Amendment and Basic Structure of the Constitution: A Critical Reconsideration," *Delhi Law Review* 6–7 (1977–78): 13.
59. Ibid., 14.
60. Dawn Oliver and Carlo Fusaro, "Towards a Theory of Constitutional Change," in Dawn Oliver and Carlo Fusaro, eds., *How Constitutions Change: A Comparative Study* (Oxford: Hart, 2013), 405, 418.
61. Bhikhu Parekh, "The Constitution as a Statement of Indian Identity," in Rajeev Bhargava, ed., *Politics and Ethics of the Indian Constitution* (New Delhi: Oxford University Press, 2008), 46.
62. Madhav Khosla, "Constitutional Amendment," in Choudhry, Khosla, and Mehta, *Oxford Handbook of the Indian Constitution,* 248; Sathe, *Judicial Activism in India,* 78.
63. Robinson, "Expanding Judiciaries," 41. See also Pratap Bhanu Mehta: "Even the *Kesavananda* decision, while designed to protect the right of the courts to nullify constitutional amendments, was intended to provide greater justiciability to the

Directive Principles of State Policy than to protect Fundamental Rights as was the intent in *Golak Nath.* Almost all of the Supreme Court's celebrated 'activist' decisions . . . stemmed from a concern for equality rather than civil liberties": Pratap Bhanu Mehta, "India's Judiciary: The Promise of Uncertainty," in Kapur and Mehta, *Public Institutions in India,* 165.

64. As has been noted, the basic structure doctrine "should be seen as an attempt to identify the moral philosophy on which the Constitution is based" (Rao, "Constitution, Parliament and the Judiciary," 98). To be in a position to articulate the specific content of this moral philosophy is assuredly a more than symbolic undertaking, but doing so in a context where the invocation will have a direct effect on governmental policies ultimately matters more.
65. See especially Gerald N. Rosenberg, *The Hollow Hope: Can Courts Bring About Social Change?* (Chicago: University of Chicago Press, 1991).
66. Robinson, "Expanding Judiciaries," 34. We agree with Robinson, which is to say that we do not adhere to the alternative interpretive view that, following Ackerman, posits the existence of subsequent "constitutional moments" that brought about "dynamic changes in India's constitutional framework"; see Manoj Mate, "State Constitutions and the Basic Structure Doctrine," *Columbia Human Rights Law Review* 45 (2014): 486. *Kesavananda* and *Minerva Mills* were important moments in India's constitutional development not because they "brought about . . . a major shift in constitutional structure" (ibid.), but because they accelerated progress toward achieving the goals of the founding moment's incipient constitutional displacement.
67. Justice Chandrachud in *Minerva Mills, Ltd. v. Union of India,* AIR 1980 SC 1789, 1798. In *Waman Rao v. Union of India* 2 SCC 362 (1981), the companion case to *Minerva Mills,* the Court, in addition to upholding the basic structure doctrine, held that all post-*Kesavananda* amendments, including those placed in the Ninth Schedule, were reviewable by the judiciary. In a later case, *I. R. Coelho,* 7 SCC 7 (1999), the Court reaffirmed this holding, essentially completing the reversal of the jurisprudence of the 1950s.
68. *Minerva Mills,* at Principles of Constitutionality section, para. 2.
69. For analysis of the militancy-acquiescent distinction in constitutional experience, see Gary J. Jacobsohn, "The Sounds of Silence: Militant and Acquiescent Constitutionalism," in M. Richard Zinman, ed., *The Supreme Court and the Idea of Constitutionalism* (Philadelphia: University of Pennsylvania Press, 2009).
70. The most explicit recognition of this constitutional acknowledgment appears in Article 25: "(1) Subject to public order, morality and health and to the other provisions of this Part, all persons are equally entitled to freedom of conscience and the right freely to profess, practice and propagate religion. (2) Nothing in this article shall affect the operation of any existing law—(a) regulating or restricting any economic, financial, political or other secular activity which may be associated with religious practice; (b) providing for social welfare and reform or the throwing open of Hindu religious institutions of a public character to all classes and sections of Hindus."

71. A. M. Ahmadi, "The Constitution: Its Tryst with Destiny; Flawed or Fulfilled?," address delivered at the conference "Fifty Years of Indian Republic," Toronto, April 1, 2000.
72. Baxi, *Courage, Craft and Contention*, 65.
73. In the case of India's constitutional framers, the prevailing social structure, while deeply rooted in centuries of religious and cultural practice, was contestable, in accordance with sources from within the Indian tradition that are also a part of its prescriptive constitution. History revealed disharmony within established traditions and between the dominant strand and the society. "One of the remarkable developments of the present age," wrote Nehru shortly before independence, "has been the rediscovery of the past and of the nation"; see Jawaharlal Nehru, *The Discovery of India* (1946; rept., Oxford: Oxford University Press, 1997), 515. Nehru was one of several delegates at the Constituent Assembly to invoke the name of Ashoka, whose famous edicts have endured as a source of moral and ethical reflection for more than a millennium. Used both as an emulative model for behavior toward society's destitute and as a basis for criticizing the Hindu nationalist rejection of Indian nationhood as rooted in a composite culture, the Ashokan example shows how continuity in the construction of a constitutional identity can draw on alternative (and even dissenting) sources within one tradition, and then reconstitute them to serve at times as a reproach to other strands (and their societal manifestations) within the same tradition.
74. *S. R. Bommai v. Union of India* (1994), 3 SCC, at 65.
75. K. Suryaprasad, *Article 356 of the Constitution of India: Promise and Performance* (New Delhi: Konishka, 2001), 246. Also true, however, is that consistent with misgivings expressed by delegates to the Constituent Assembly, the provision has often been implemented for inappropriate reasons. Since 1950 there have been more than one hundred occasions when the President's Rule has been invoked under Article 356; a substantial majority of them were inspired by partisan calculations, namely, to advance the interests of the party in power in New Delhi. Such a record suggests that the original justification for including Article 356 powers—that they would be used only in the case of a serious interruption in the workings of the democratic process—was in fact wildly unrealistic. It also suggests that the corruption of emergency power was not an extraordinary occurrence, a conclusion whose ominous implications extend well beyond the parameters of any given government dismissal. Thus, the politicization of the process through which distant officials can effectively overturn a local electoral verdict of the people represents a serious threat to the maintenance of democratic institutions. The official analysis of how the President's Rule has been experienced is to be found in the *Sarkaria Report*, which recommended that Article 356 be used only in extreme cases. Its findings and recommendations were relied upon extensively in the opinions in *Bommai*.
76. *Constituent Assembly Debates*, 1949, 175. In the preceding sentence, Ambedkar said: "[I] would like to draw . . . attention to the article in the American Constitution, where the duty of the United States is definitely expressed to be to maintain the republican form of the Constitution."

77. *S. R. Bommai v. Union of India*, 3 SC 1 (1994), 237. As S. P. Sathe rightly pointed out, *Bommai* represented "a warning to the Hindu right and organizations that entertained the idea of a majoritarian Hindu state that any move in that direction towards constitutional amendment would be considered a violation of the basic structure of the Constitution" (*Judicial Activism in India*, 98). It was the successes of the Hindu right in electoral politics at the state level that led to the Court cases in *Bommai*.
78. *Luther v. Borden*, 48 U.S. 1 (1849), 47.
79. This becomes very clear when considering the struggle over slavery. To many abolitionists in the United States, the denial of self-government that was at the core of slavery amounted to a failure to secure republicanism in those states supporting that institution; but the same logic that would likely have kept the Supreme Court from reaching the merits of any federal intervention under Article IV in the end restrained the hand of the politicians from creating the predicate for such a case; see William Wiecek, *The Guarantee Clause of the U.S. Constitution* (Ithaca, N.Y.: Cornell University Press, 1972). John C. Calhoun's view would in all likelihood have carried the day: "The President would be obliged to support any extant legitimate regime" (135).
80. Quoted in Baxi, *Courage, Craft and Contention*, 91.
81. Sathe, *Judicial Activism in India*, 97.
82. *S. R. Bommai v. Union of India*, at 143.
83. Sathe, *Judicial Activism in India*, 176.
84. Ibid., 177.
85. *S. R. Bommai v. Union of India*, at 233.
86. Ibid., at 170.
87. Ibid., at 232. The "preamble is a key to understanding the relevant provisions of the Constitution" (236).
88. Ibid., at 234.
89. Ibid., at 220.
90. Quoted in Durga Das Basu, *Introduction to the Constitution of India*, 18th ed. (New Delhi: Prentice-Hall of India, 1998), 142.
91. *S. R. Bommai v. Union of India*, at 298.
92. In contrast, U.S. lawmaking institutions are not constitutionally directed to pursue particular social and political ends. They might have been so structured had the logic of the original draft of the Declaration of Independence prevailed, in which government was instituted to "secure . . . ends." But as Morton White has demonstrated, the replacement of "ends" with "rights" entailed only the obligation to guard rights already enjoyed by the people rather than to attain ends not yet in their possession; see Morton White, *The Philosophy of the American Revolution* (New York: Oxford University Press, 1978), 249. Without a specific constitutional mandate to direct the policy-making process, the reluctance of the judiciary to encroach on the prerogatives of the political branches is therefore understandable.

93. The new procedure—embodied in the National Judicial Appointments Act of 2014 and the Ninety-Ninth Amendment to the Constitution—was intended to replace the arrangement that had vested the selection of judges in a collegium of top-tier judges.
94. *Supreme Court Advocates-on-Record Association v. Union of India* (2015). Said Justice Kurian Joseph, "If the alignment of tectonic plates on distribution of powers is disturbed, it will quake the Constitution" (as quoted in the *New York Times*, October 16, 2015).
95. *Indian Medical Association v. Union of India*, 7 SCC 179 (2011), para. 146.
96. The new provision was inserted in response to a Supreme Court ruling that invalidated a state's reservation of seats for specific caste groups in state educational institutions. The Court in *State of Madras v. Champakam Dorairajan*, AIR 1951 SC 226, did not find persuasive the state's reliance on Article 46 to justify its reservations policy. It is worth noting that the First Amendment was adopted by the same members of the interim Parliament who drafted the Constitution.
97. Galanter, *Competing Equalities*, 381, 364.
98. As stated by Justice William Rehnquist in connection with the Due Process Clause of the Fourteenth Amendment: "Its purpose was to protect the people from the State, not to ensure that the State protected them from each other. The Framers were content to leave the extent of governmental obligation in the latter area to the democratic political processes"; in *DeShaney v. Winnebago County Department of Social Services*, 489 U.S. 189, 196 (1989).
99. Stephen Gardbaum, "Horizontal Effect," in Choudhry, Khosla, and Mehta, *Oxford Handbook of the Indian Constitution*, 602.
100. Shetty, *Fundamental Rights and Socio-economic Justice*, 157.
101. *P. A. Inamdar & Others v. State of Maharashtra & Others*, 8 SCC 139 (2005).
102. Galanter, *Competing Equalities*, 562.
103. *Indian Medical Association v. Union of India*, para. 2
104. The preamble of the Delhi Act stated: "An Act to provide for prohibition of capitation fee, regulation of Admission, fixation of non-exploitative fee, allotment of seats to Scheduled Castes, Scheduled Tribes and other socially and economically backward classes and other measures to ensure equity and excellence in professional education in the National Capital Territory of Delhi and for matters connected therewith or incidental thereto."
105. The Delhi government had granted an exemption from the 2007 law, which permitted the college to implement its admissions policy, but the Court found this exemption invalid as a violation of the purpose of the law.
106. *Indian Medical Association v. Union of India*, para. 73.
107. Ibid., paras. 105, 88.
108. Ibid., para. 108.
109. Ibid., para. 97.
110. Ibid., para. 87.

111. Ibid., para. 88. The overarching-principles concept had been articulated a few years earlier in another important reservations case amply cited by the Court; see *M. Nagaraj & Others v. Union of India & Others,* AIR 2007 SC 71 (2006).
112. *Indian Medical Association v. Union of India,* para. 86.
113. "The object of fundamental rights is to foster the social revolution by creating a society egalitarian to the extent that all citizens are to be equally free from coercion or restriction by the State" (ibid., para. 79). This statement comes from a major basic-structure case, *I. R. Coelho v. State of Tamil Nadu,* AIR 2007, SC 861 (2007).
114. *Indian Medical Association v. Union of India,* para. 79.
115. Ibid., para. 88.
116. Ibid., para. 89.
117. Plutarch, *The Lives of the Noble Grecians and Romans,* trans. John Dryden (New York: Modern Library, 1977), 14. The example continues to be a focal point of debate among philosophers of identity to this day; see, for example, Brian Smart, "How to Reidentify the Ship of Theseus," *Analysis* 32 (1972), and Francis W. Dauer, "How Not to Reidentify the Parthenon," *Analysis* 33 (1972).
118. *Indian Medical Association v. Union of India,* para. 90.
119. Ibid., paras. 91, 100.
120. Ibid., para. 91.
121. Ibid.
122. Ibid., para. 99.
123. Iyer, "Towards an Indian Jurisprudence," 308.
124. Such a stride can be walked back. But as Nick Robinson has observed, "Even when the Court's decisions have little immediate impact, the Court frequently fosters a political space in which its orders can eventually be implemented or other policy changes can occur" ("Expanding Judiciaries," 55).
125. *Indian Medical Association v. Union of India,* para. 122.
126. Ibid., para. 108.
127. Ibid., para. 146.
128. Plutarch, *Noble Grecians and Romans,* 24.
129. Nehru, *Discovery of India,* 156–57.
130. Shiva Rao, *Constituent Assembly Debates,* 501.
131. Ibid., 504.
132. James Madison, *Federalist* 48, in *The Federalist,* ed. George W. Carey and James McClellan, Gideon Edition (1818; Indianapolis: Liberty Fund, 2001), 256.
133. Lloyd and Suzanne Rudolph point out, "There was broad social and political consensus [at the Constituent Assembly] on the view that the only way India could dispense socio-economic justice to its people was not just through planned development, but by an effective transformation of Indian society"; see Lloyd I. Rudolph and Suzanne Hoeber Rudolph, *Explaining Indian Democracy* (New Delhi: Oxford University Press, 2008), 2:34. Much later in the same volume, they write, "Since 1947, Indian society has experienced a social revolution with

massive political consequences" (323). One can disagree with their ultimate assessment, but theirs is an example of the sequential analysis that is called for in reaching judgments about transformational constitutional revolutions.

134. Michael Walzer, *The Paradox of Liberation: Secular Revolutions and Religious Counterrevolutions* (New Haven, Conn.: Yale University Press, 2015), 132.
135. Galanter, *Competing Equalities*, 380.
136. Ran Hirschl, *Comparative Matters: The Renaissance of Comparative Constitutional Law* (Oxford: Oxford University Press, 2016), 174.
137. Ibid.
138. Nehru, November 25, 1948, quoted in Kashyup. *Jawaharlal Nehru and the Constitution*, 88.

Chapter 6. Constitutional Revolution Through Adjudication

Epigraph: CA 6821/93 United Mizrahi Bank v. Migdal Cooperative Village [1995] 49(4) P.D. 221, para. 66 to Justice Mishael Cheshin's opinion.

1. Rudolf Smend, "Constitution and Constitutional Law," in Arthur J. Jacobson and Bernhard Schlink, eds., *Weimar: A Jurisprudence of Crisis* (Berkeley: University of California Press, 2002), 213, 248.
2. See, for example, David A. Strauss, "The Irrelevance of Constitutional Amendments," *Harvard Law Review* 114 (2000–2001).
3. Richard Albert, "How Unwritten Constitutional Norms Change Written Constitutions," *Dublin University Law Journal* 38 (2015): 288–89; Jonathan L. Marshfield, "Courts and Informal Constitutional Change in the States," *New England Law Review* 53, no. 3 (2018): 453.
4. Dieter Grimm, "Constitutional Adjudication and Constitutional Interpretation: Between Law and Politics," *NUJS [National University of Juridical Sciences, Kolkata] Law Review* 4 (2011): 27.
5. See, for example, Sanford Levinson, "How Many Times Has the United States Constitution Been Amended? (A) < 26; (B) 26; (C) 27; (D) > 27; Accounting for Constitutional Change," in Sanford Levinson, ed., *Responding to Imperfection: The Theory and Practice of Constitutional Amendment* (Princeton, N.J.: Princeton University Press, 1995), 13, 33.
6. *Lochner v. New York*, 198 U.S. 45 (1905). See, for example, D. G. Stephenson, Jr., "The Supreme Court and Constitutional Change: Lochner v. New York Revisited," *Villanova Law Review* 21 (1976): 219.
7. Quoted in J. W. Peltason, *Corwin and Peltason's Understanding the Constitution*, 14th ed. (Fort Worth, Tex.: Harcourt Brace College, 1997), 191 (quoting Wilson).
8. República de Honduras Constitution (1982). Article 239 of the Constitution contains a prohibition on presidential reelection and also stipulates that anyone who "violates" the no-reelection rule or who "proposes its reform" shall "cease immediately" in their public posts and be prohibited from serving in office for ten years. In addition, Article 374 declares that the no-reelection provision can under no circumstances be amended. Moreover, according to Article 42(5), citizenship

may be lost by "inciting, promoting, or supporting the continuation or reelection" of the president.

9. Corte Suprema de Justicia, F-165, Decision of Apr. 22, 2015 (Constitutional Chamber, Supreme Court).
10. Richard Albert, "Constitutional Amendment and Dismemberment," *Yale Journal of International Law* 43 (2018): 68.
11. Jawaharlal Nehru to the Indian Constituent Assembly, New Delhi, August 14, 1947; cited in Bidyut Chakrabart, *Indian Politics and Society Since Independence: Events, Processes and Ideology* (New York: Routledge, 2008), 1.
12. CA 6821/93 United Mizrahi Bank Ltd. v. Migdal Cooperative Village [1995] 49(4) P.D. 221, para. 9 to Justice Cheshin's Judgment.
13. Ibid.
14. This change is visible in Amnon Rubinstein's seminal book *The Constitutional Law of the State of Israel* (with Barak Medina, 2 vols., 6th ed. [Jerusalem: Schocken, 2005]). In its third edition, published in 1980, the book opens with the constitutional order's basic principles, the first and fundamental principle being "Parliamentary Sovereignty." In the fifth edition, published in 1996, the principle appears only in chapter 11 and begins with a statement that the principle of the Knesset's sovereignty is not unlimited.
15. Bruce Ackerman, *The Future of Liberal Revolution* (New Haven, Conn.: Yale University Press, 1992), 27.
16. Ibid., 50.
17. Ibid., 65.
18. Ran Hirschl, "Constitutional Courts vs. Religious Fundamentalism: Three Middle Eastern Tales," *Texas Law Review* 82 (2004): 1858.
19. Peter H. Russell, *Constitutional Odyssey: Can Canadians Become Sovereign People?* 2nd ed. (Toronto: University of Toronto Press, 1993), 106; see also Jon Elster, "Forces and Mechanisms in the Constitution Making Process," *Duke Law Journal* 45, no. 2 (1995): 370.
20. A/RES/181(II), on Future government of Palestine, November 29, 1947, Part I.B. sec. 10.
21. The Declaration of the Establishment of the State of Israel, May 15, 1948.
22. On the election campaign, conducted amid the battles of the War of Independence, see Meir Chazan, "Israel Goes to the Polls: The Road to Elections for the Constituent Assembly, 1948–1949," *Israel Studies Review* 31, no. 2 (2016): 81–84.
23. Transition Law to the Constituent Assembly (1949), sec. 1: "The Provisional Council State will remain in office until the Constituent Assembly of the State of Israel convenes; with the convention of a Constituent Assembly, the Provisional Council State will dissolve and cease to exist"; cited in Gideon Sapir, "Constitutional Revolutions: Israel as a Case-Study," *International Journal of Law in Context* 5, no. 4 (2009): 358.
24. It appears that this name change was not understood as affecting the powers of the First Knesset in a manner that would cause it to lose its constituent authority;

see Ruth Gavison, "The Controversy over Israel's Bill of Rights," *Israel Yearbook on Human Rights* 15 (1985): 116n3.

25. Mark Tushnet, "Book Review: The Universal and the Particular in Constitutional Law: An Israeli Case Study," *Columbia Law Review* 100 (2000); Gary Jeffrey Jacobsohn, *Apple of Gold: Constitutionalism in Israel and the United States* (Princeton, N.J.: Princeton University Press, 1993), 3–18.
26. See Philippa Strum, "The Road Not Taken: Constitutional Non-Decision Making in 1948–1950 and Its Impact on Civil Liberties in the Israeli Political Culture," in S. Ilan Troen and Noah Lucas, eds., *Israel: The First Decade of Independence* (Albany: State University of New York Press, 1995), 83.
27. Joshua Segev, "Who Needs a Constitution? In Defense of the Non-Decision Constitution-Making Tactic in Israel," *Albany Law Review* 70, no. 2 (2007): 416–17.
28. Nir Kedar, "Ben-Gurion's Opposition to a Written Constitution," *Journal of Modern Jewish Studies* 12, no. 1 (2013): 1–16; Gavison, "Controversy over Israel's Bill of Rights," 113.
29. Jacobsohn, *Apple of Gold,* 101; Amos Shapira, "Why Israel Has No Constitution, But Should, and Likely Will, Have One," *St. Louis University Law Journal* 37 (1993): 285.
30. This allegation was expressed by Menachem Begin during the First Knesset's debates: "If the Constituent Assembly legislates a constitution, then the government will not be free to do as it likes"; cited in Jacobsohn, *Apple of Gold,* 110. Some scholars attributed Ben-Gurion's opposition to a constitution to his fear that a constitutional system would establish a strong judiciary; see Strum, "Road Not Taken," 92–93. Indeed, Ben-Gurion argued that judicial review was in tension with democracy and might even lead to injustice, citing U.S. Supreme Court examples; see Segev, "Who Needs a Constitution," 423.
31. Ilan Peleg, "Israel's Constitutional Order and Kulturkampf: The Role of Ben-Gurion," *Israel Studies* 3 (1998): 236.
32. Segev, "Who Needs a Constitution?," 416–18.
33. Harari Resolution, adopted June 13, 1950: "The First Knesset charges the Constitution, Legislative and Judicial Committee [of the Knesset] with the duty to prepare a draft Constitution for the State. The Constitution will be comprised of several Chapters, and each of the said Chapters shall in itself constitute a Basic Law. Each of the several chapters shall be brought before the Knesset as soon as the said Committee completes its work and all Chapters (already adopted) shall form the State's Constitution"; cited in Eliahu Likhovski, "Can the Knesset Adopt a Constitution That Will Be the Supreme Law of the Land?," *Israel Law Review* 4 (1969): 63. See also Z. Sigal and A. S. Rehany, "The Promised Constitution of the Promised Land: The Israeli Constitutional Experience," *Denning Law Journal* 12, no. 2 (1997): 67. For historical background, see Orit Rozin, "Forming a Collective Identity: The Debate over the Proposed Constitution, 1948–1950," *Journal of Israel History* 26 (2007).
34. Amnon Rubinstein, "Israel's Piecemeal Constitution," *Scripta Hierosolymitana* 16 (1967); Hanna Lerner, *Making Constitutions in Deeply Divided Societies* (Cam-

bridge: Cambridge University Press, 2011), 51–108; Adam Shinar, "Accidental Constitutionalism: The Political Foundations and Implications of Israeli Constitution-Making," in Dennis Galligan and Mila Versteeg, eds., *The Social and Political Foundations of Constitutions* (New York: Cambridge University Press, 2013), 207; Gideon Sapir, *The Israeli Constitution: From Evolution to Revolution* (Oxford: Oxford University Press, 2018), 11–31.

35. See Rosalind Dixon and Tom Ginsburg, "Deciding Not to Decide: Deferral in Constitutional Design," *International Journal of Constitutional Law* 9, nos. 3–4 (2011).

36. The Second Knesset (Transition) Law, 1951, sec. 5 and 10; see Claude Klein, "A New Era in Israel's Constitutional Law," *Israel Law Review* 6 (1971): 380.

37. For example, Melville B. Nimmer, "The Uses of Judicial Review in Israel's Quest for a Constitution," *Columbia Law Review* 70 (1970): 1239–40.

38. The Basic Laws enacted from the Harari Resolution to the early 1990s are the following: Basic Law: The Knesset (1958); Basic Law: Israel Lands (1960); Basic Law: The President of the State (1964); Basic Law: The Government (1968) (replaced 1992, 2001); Basic Law: The State Economy (1975); Basic Law: The Military (1976); Basic Law: Jerusalem, Capital of Israel (1980); Basic Law: The Judiciary (1984); Basic Law: The State Comptroller (1988).

39. Benjamin Akzin, "The Place of the Constitution in the Modern State," *Israel Law Review* 2 (1967): 14n14.

40. On the flexibility of not having a rigid constitution, see, for example, Lord Diplock, "On the Unwritten Constitution," *Israel Law Review* 9 (1974).

41. See, for example, Amos Shapira, "Judicial Review Without a Constitution: The Israeli Paradox," *Temple Law Quarterly* 56 (1983): 410, 429.

42. See Likhovski, "Can the Knesset Adopt a Constitution," 61, 63–64. The commitment to proceed to a formal constitution chapter by chapter was also questioned in the literature. Right after the Harari Resolution, the Knesset enacted the Law of Equal Rights for Women and the Law of Return, the latter guaranteeing the right of all Jews to become Israeli citizens. Although both laws carry a "constitutional law" character, they were not labeled "basic laws," which for some cast doubts on the "sincerity" of the Harari Resolution; see Gideon Sapir, "Constitutional Revolutions," 360; Ruth Gavison, "The Constitutional Revolution: A Description of Reality or a Self-Fulfilling Prophecy?," *Mishpatim* 28 (1997) (Heb.).

43. See, for example, e.g. HCJ 148/73, Kaniel v. Minister of Justice, 27(1) PD 794 (1973); CA 107/73, Negev v. State of Israel, 28(1) PD 640 (1974); HCJ 60/77, Ressler v. Chairman of Knesset Elections Committee, 31(2) PD 556 (1977).

44. CA 228/63 Ezuz v. Azar 17(1) PD 2541, 2547 (1963). See also Batzul v. Minister of the Interior 19(1) P.D. 337, 349 (1963): "The Knesset is supreme in the enactment of laws. The Knesset is free to choose the subject matter of its laws and to determine their contents. Every law or part of law which is enacted by the Knesset must be enforced. . . . After a law has been enacted by the Knesset and published in the Official Gazette, we must bow before it and not doubt its provisions, instructions and directives." See Eliahu Likhovski, "The Courts and the Legislative

Supremacy of the Knesset," *Israel Law Review* 3 (1968). For the classic notion of British parliamentary sovereignty, see A. V. Dicey, *Introduction to the Study of the Law of the Constitution,* 10th ed., ed. E. C. S. Wade (London: Macmillan, 1961).

45. Amnon Rubinstein, *The Constitutional Law of the State of Israel* (Tel Aviv: Schocken, 1969), 170 (Heb.).
46. Claude Klein, "The Constituent Authority in Israel," *Mishpatim* 2 (1970–71): 56 (Heb.).
47. HCJ 98/69, Bergman v. Minister of Finance [1969] 23(I) PD 693. For an English translation of the decision with brief comments by Peter Elman, Claude Klein, and Benjamin Akzin, see "Judicial Review of Statute," *Israel Law Review* 4 (1969): 559–78.
48. Claude Klein, "New Era in Israel's Constitutional Law." For different theories of the Bergman decision, see Rivka Weill, "Reconciling Parliamentary Sovereignty and Judicial Review: On the Theoretical and Historical Origins of the Israeli Legislative Override Power," *Hastings Constitutional Law Quarterly* 39, no. 2 (2011): 478–85.
49. *Bergman,* at 696. In his academic writings, Landau repeatedly emphasized that in *Bergman,* the court avoided deciding the major foundational questions brought before it regarding the legal status of the Basic Laws, but merely enforced formal procedural requirements as stipulated in the Basic Law; see, for example, Landau, "A Constitution as Supreme Law to Israel?," *Hapraklit* 27 (1971) (Heb.), and Landau, "Book Review—Eliahu S. Likhovski: Israel's Parliament—The Law of the Knesset," *Mishpatim* 4 (1972–73) (Heb.), claiming that the author overemphasized the importance of the *Bergman* case.
50. Aharon A. Bergman, "The Supremacy of the Knesset," *Israel Law Review* 6 (1971): 118.
51. Meir Shamgar, "On the Written Constitution," *Israel Law Review* 9 (1974): 474: "Bergman did not pretend to be an Israeli Marbury v. Madison but after it, the idea of further development of judicial review of legislation could not be regarded as entirely unexpected."
52. Nimmer, "Uses of Judicial Review," 1218. For an opposing view, see Robert A. Burt, "Inventing Judicial Review: Israel and America," *Cardozo Law Review* 10 (1989): 2015: "Bergman is actually the least important basis for the Israeli Supreme Court's contemporary claims for increased judicial authority."
53. Shapira, "Judicial Review Without a Constitution," 568.
54. See HCJ 246/81 Derech Eretz Association v. Broadcasting Authority [1981] 35(4) IsrSC 1; HCJ 141/82 Rubinstein v. Knesset Speaker [1983] 37(3) IsrSC 141; HCJ 142/89 La'or Movement v. Knesset Speaker [1990] IsrSC 44(3) 259.
55. See John Ferejon, "Judicial Power: Getting It and Keeping It," in Diana Kapiszewski, Gordon Silverstein, and Robert A. Kagan, eds., *Consequential Courts: Judicial Roles in Global Perspective* (Cambridge: Cambridge University Press, 2013), 349, 353, describing a "Marbury Moment" as a moment when "a high court asserts new jurisdiction or claims powers to control elected officials but does so in a subtle or strategic way that makes it hard for politicians to reject it."

56. See, for example, Eliahu S. Likhovski, *Israeli Parliament: The Law of the Knesset* (Oxford: Clarendon, 1971), 78: "One method of demonstrating the legislative supremacy of the Knesset is to follow Dicey and show that it can make and unmake any law and that no restrictions on its power to do so exist . . . even after the decision in the Bergman case, the Knesset is competent to legislate upon (a) all matters in the manner provided by its legislation process and (b) that apparently the validity of the legislation so passed, cannot be questioned in any court but (c) the Knesset can be bound by special procedural requirements of the legislative process laid down by its predecessors." See also Michael Sheftler, "Thoughts on Constitutional Problems," *Hapraklit* 26 (1971): 8–9 (Heb.).
57. See Shapira, "Judicial Review Without a Constitution"; Baruch Bracha, "The Protection of Human Rights in Israel," *Israel Yearbook on Human Rights* 12 (1982): 110; Asher Maoz, "Defending Civil Liberties Without a Constitution: The Israeli Experience," *Melbourne University Law Review* 16 (1988); Zeev Segal, "A Constitution Without a Constitution: The Israeli Experience and the American Impact," *Capital University Law Review* 21 (1992).
58. See, for example, HCJ 73/53 Kol Ha'am Ltd. v. The Minister of Interior [1953] IsrSC 7 871, regarding freedom of expression; Al-Karbutli v. Minister of Defense, [1948] 2 P.D. 5, regarding personal liberty; Peretz v. Local Council of Kfar Shmaryahu [1962] 16 P.D. 2101, 2116, regarding freedom of religion.
59. See HCJ 1/49 Bejerano v. The Minister of Police [1949] IsrSC 2, 80; HCJ 337/81 Miterani v. The Minister of Transportation [1983] IsrSC 37(3) 337, concerning freedom of occupation.
60. Gary Jeffrey Jacobsohn, "After the Revolution," *Israel Law Review* 34 (2000): 141.
61. See, for example, Jeffrey M. Albert, "Constitutional Adjudication Without a Constitution: The Case of Israel," *Harvard Law Review* 82 (1969); Amos Shapira, "The Status of Fundamental Individual Rights in the Absence of a Written Constitution," *Israel Law Review* 9 (1974).
62. See CA 450/70 Rogozinski v. The State of Israel (1971) 26(1) PD 129, 135. The case concerned a Jewish couple that had asked to marry in a civil ceremony and not according to Jewish law, as required by a 1953 law that provided for Jewish weddings to be conducted by rabbinical tribunals. The couple argued that the law infringed freedom from religion, a fundamental right recognized in the Declaration of Establishment. But the Supreme Court did not accept the claim, holding that the explicit laws of the Knesset prevailed over individual rights.
63. Shamgar, "On the Written Constitution"; Marina O. Lowy, "Restructuring a Democracy: An Analysis of the New Proposed Constitution for Israel," *Cornell International Law Journal* 22 (1989): 115.
64. See, for example, Draft Bill Basic Law: Human and Civil Rights, 1973, HH 448; Draft Bill Basic Law: Bill of Rights, 1983, HH 111. See Gideon Sapir, Daphne Barak-Erez, and Aharon Barak, "Introduction: Israeli Constitutional Law at the Crossroads," in Sapir, Barak-Erez, and Barak, eds., *Israeli Constitutional Law in the Making* (Oxford: Hart, 2013), 2.

65. The proposal passed the preliminary reading by an impressive majority of 53–19, with 4 abstentions; see Amnon Rubinstein, "The Story of the Basic Laws," *IDC Law Review* 13 (2012): 84 (Heb.).
66. Judith Karp, "Basic Law: Dignity and Liberty; A Biography of Power Struggles," *Mishpat Umimshal* 1 (1993) (Heb.).
67. Rubinstein, "Story of the Basic Laws," 88.
68. The Basic Law: Human Dignity and Liberty, sec. 10. On saving clauses, see Rivka Weill, "Bills of Rights with Strings Attached: Protecting the Past from Judicial Review," in Rosalind Dixon, Geoffrey Sigalet, and Grégoire Webber, eds., *Constitutional Dialogue: Rights, Democracy, Institutions* (New York: Cambridge University Press, 2019), https://ssrn.com/abstract=3050656.
69. Sec. 8 of Basic Law: Human Dignity and Liberty; sec. 4 of Basic Law: Freedom of Occupation.
70. Sec. 11 of Basic Law: Human Dignity and Liberty; sec. 5 of Basic Law: Freedom of Occupation.
71. Ariel L. Bendor, "Is It a Duck? On the Israeli Written Constitution," *Yale Israel Journal* 6 (2005): 56.
72. See Claude Klein, "Basic Law: Human Dignity and Freedom; A First Normative Assessment," *Hamishpat* 1 (1993): 124–25 (Heb.).
73. Claude Klein, "The Quiet Constitutional Revolution," *Maariv*, March 27, 1992 (Heb.).
74. Klein, "Basic Law: Human Dignity and Freedom." Years earlier, Klein laid down his theory of the Knesset's constituent authority to enact constitutional norms that bind itself; see Claude Klein, "Constituent Authority in Israel"; Klein, "Is There a Need for an Amending Power Theory?," *Israel Law Review* 12 (1978). On Klein's work, see Barak Medina, "Introduction," *Israel Law Review* 39 (2006): 5–9.
75. Amnon Rubinstein, "A Big Constitution Arrives," *Haaretz*, April 3, 1992 (Heb.).
76. David Kretzmer, "The New Basic Laws on Human Rights: A Mini-Revolution in Israeli Constitutional Law," *Israel Law Review* 26 (1992): 240–42.
77. Aharon Barak, "A Constitutional Revolution: Israel's Basic Laws," *Constitutional Forum* 4 (1993): 84.
78. Bruce Ackerman, *We the People: Foundations* (Cambridge, Mass.: Harvard University Press, 1991).
79. Basic Law: Human Dignity and Liberty passed its first reading 40–12, with 1 abstention, and its second and third readings 32–21, with 1 abstention. Basic Law: Freedom of Occupation passed its first reading 22–15, and its second and third readings 23–0; see Rubinstein, "Story of the Basic Laws," 94.
80. Rubinstein notes that since the votes on the basic laws on human rights took place many years after the historical moment of the state's establishment, the majorities by which they passed were impressive (ibid., 79).
81. Amnon Rubinstein, "The Knesset and Basic Laws on Human Rights," *Mishpat Umimshal* 5 (2000): 349 (Heb.).
82. Sapir, "Constitutional Revolutions," 364; Gavison, "Constitutional Revolution," 21.

83. Daphne Barak-Erez, "From an Unwritten to a Written Constitution: The Israeli Challenge in American Perspective," *Columbia Human Rights Law Review* 26 (1995): 321–22.
84. The Constitution for Israel movement originated in a draft constitution proposed by a group of professors from Tel-Aviv University led by Uriel Reichman. On this draft, see Lowy, "Restructuring a Democracy"; on the movement more generally, see Guy Bechor, *Constitution to Israel: A Story of a Fight* (Or Yehuda: Sifriyat Ma'ariv, 1996) (Heb.).
85. Barak-Erez, "Unwritten to a Written Constitution," 351–52.
86. See Rivka Weill, "Hybrid Constitutionalism: The Israeli Case for Judicial Review and Why We Should Care," *Berkeley Journal of International Law* 30 (2012): 375n119. Indeed, the movement managed to make the transition from a pure model of parliamentary democracy to a hybrid model calling for direct election of the prime minister, in an attempt to strengthen the standing of the government. This transformation, as reflected in Basic Law: The Government (1992), failed, and in 2001 the Knesset returned to the parliamentary model when it enacted Basic Law: The Government (2001).
87. Sapir, "Constitutional Revolutions," 364; see also Menachem Mautner, "Protection of Liberal Rights Amidst a 'War of Cultures' (Kulturkampf) Between Secular and Religious Groups," *Israel Yearbook on Human Rights* 48 (2018): 137: "Constitutions are usually viewed as embodiments of national unity; in dozens of countries of the world, 'Constitution Day,' a national holiday, is annually celebrated to note the people's achievement in adopting their State's constitution; and in many countries the moment of the constitution's signing is expressed in iconic paintings and statues. Needless to say, none of that exists in Israel."
88. Ran Hirschl, *Towards Juristocracy: The Origins and Consequences of the New Constitutionalism* (Cambridge, Mass.: Harvard University Press, 2004), 24, 50.
89. Aharon Barak, "Human Rights in Israel," *Israel Law Review* 39 (2006): 17.
90. On the *United Mizrahi Bank* case, see Suzie Navot, "Mizrahi Bank Case (Isr)," *Max Planck Encyclopedia of Comparative Constitutional Law* (online; subscription required).
91. See Claude Klein, "Basic Laws, Constituent Power and Judicial Review of Statutes in Israel: Bank Hamizrahi United v. Kfar Chitufi Migdal and Others," *European Public Law* 2, no. 2 (1996).
92. *Mizrahi Bank,* para. 5 to Justice Cheshin's Judgment.
93. Ruth Gavison, "Constitutional Revolution?," in Antonio Gambaro and Alfredo Rabello, eds., *Towards a New European Ius Commune* (Jerusalem: Sacher Institute, 1999), 517. Three of nine judges accepted President Barak's approach concerning the "dual crown" and the Knesset's constituent theory (Justices Levine, Zamir, and Maza); President Shamgar recognized parliament's absolute sovereignty; and three judges (Tal, Goldberg, and Bach) did not choose between Barak's and Shamgar's theories. This division led Rivka Weill to claim that there was no majority opinion for any of the theories; see Weill, "United Mizrahi Bank's Twentieth Anniversary: On the Piquant Story of the Hybrid Israeli Constitution," *Tel-Aviv University Law Review* 38 (2016): 513n50 (Heb.).

94. *Mizrahi Bank*, para. 32 to President Shamgar's Judgment. For Shamgar's theory, see also Meir Shamgar, "On the Knesset's Authorities in the Constitutional Area," *Mishpatim* 26 (1995) (Heb.).
95. *Mizrahi Bank*, para. 21 to President Shamgar's Judgment.
96. In Justice Cheshin's judgment, he mentions precisely this paradox; see ibid., para. 77.
97. Ibid., paras. 35, 66.
98. Eli Zalzberger, "The Knesset's Constituent Authority: Two Side Remarks to Obiter, or Invitation to Re-open the Debate," *Mishpat Umimshal* 3 (1996): 687–89 (Heb.).
99. This thesis finds its roots in the prior writings of some constitutional scholars, notably Claude Klein from the early 1970s; see Klein, "Constituent Authority in Israel"; Klein, "Need for an Amending Power Theory," 203.
100. *Mizrahi Bank*, para. 5 to President Barak's Judgment.
101. Hans Kelsen, *Pure Theory of Law*, trans. Max Knight (Berkeley: University of California Press, 1967), 193.
102. *Mizrahi Bank*, para. 6 to President Barak's Judgment.
103. H. L. A. Hart, *The Concept of Law*, 2nd ed. (Oxford: Clarendon, 1994), 100.
104. *Mizrahi Bank*, para. 7 to President Barak's Judgment.
105. Ibid., para. 8 to President Barak's Judgment, referring to Ronald Dworkin, *Law's Empire* (Cambridge, Mass.: Harvard University Press, 1986), and Dworkin, *A Bill of Rights for Britain* (London: Chatto & Windus, 1990).
106. *Mizrahi Bank*, para. 8 to President Barak's Judgment.
107. Ibid., para. 54.
108. Ibid., para. 59.
109. Ibid., para. 64.
110. Ibid., para. 65.
111. *Marbury v. Madison*, 5 U.S. 137 (1803). For elaboration, see Yoram Rabin and Arnon Gutfeld, "Marbury v. Madison and Its Impact on the Israeli Constitutional Law," *University of Miami International and Comparative Law Review* 15 (2007); Gutfeld and Rabin, "The Judicial Review Controversy: Marbury v. Madison and Its Manifestations in the Israel Constitutional Revolution," *Israel Yearbook on Human Rights* 45 (2015).
112. *Mizrahi Bank*, para. 78 to President Barak's Judgment.
113. Ibid., para. 79.
114. Ibid.
115. Alexander Hamilton, *Federalist* 78, in *The Federalist*, ed. George W. Carey and James McClellan, Gideon Edition (1818; Indianapolis: Liberty Fund, 2001), 404.
116. Quoted in Thomas C. Grey, "Origins of the Unwritten Constitution: Fundamental Law in American Revolutionary Thought," *Stanford Law Review* 30 (1978): 843.
117. Ibid., 869.
118. See Joshua Segev, "Was It a Dream or Reality: Justice Cheshin on the Knesset Constituent Authority," *Netanya Academic College Law Review* 6 (2008) (Heb.).

119. *Mizrahi Bank*, para. 9 to Justice Cheshin's Judgment.
120. Ibid., para. 10.
121. Ibid., para. 34: "The people had chosen the constituent assembly ex lege to compose its constitution, and the Constituent Assembly thus had its roots in the people, from which it directly derived its authority. From this we learn that it was the real constituent assembly, the one and only one that had the authority to give the people a constitution for which purpose it had been chosen by the people. This could not be said of the other Knessets that followed the First Knesset."
122. Ibid., paras. 27–28; see also paras. 23–26. To this, President Barak replied, "The principle of transfer or agency, according to which an agent is not a principal[,] does not apply here. The Knesset was given the power to enact a constitution by means of the basic norm and according to the basic understanding of the Israeli community. This power was given to every Knesset. The First Knesset did not pass powers to the Second Knesset, just as the Twelfth Knesset did not pass legislative power to the Thirteenth Knesset. A later Knesset is not the agent of an earlier Knesset. The Knesset is the central organ of the State, and according to our constitutional structure it is endowed with both constituent and legislative authority" (*Mizrahi Bank*, para. 43 to President Barak's Judgment).
123. *Mizrahi Bank*, para. 32 to Justice Cheshin's Judgment.
124. Ibid., paras. 37–44, 48–57.
125. Ibid., para. 63.
126. Ibid., para. 13.
127. See Ariel Bendor, "Entrenchment and Constitution: Bergman Decision and the Constitutional Discourse in Israel," *Mishpatim* 31 (2001): 824n12 (Heb.).
128. HCJ 1715/97 Israel Inv. Managers Association v. Minister of Finance, 51(5) PD 367, 417 [1997] (Isr.).
129. Justice Cheshin also agreed, without any additions, with a majority opinion in a case in which the Supreme Court invalidated the constitutionality of a provision in the Military Justice Law, 1955, which allowed the detention of a solider for up to ninety-six hours before bringing him before a judge. See HCJ 6055/95 Tzemach v. Minister of Defense 53(5) PD 241 (1999).
130. Mishael Cheshin, "Responses," *Netanya Academic College Law Review* 6 (2007): 503–4 (Heb.).
131. Ibid., 504.
132. *Mizrahi Bank*, para. 63 to Justice Cheshin's Judgment.
133. HCJ 212/03 Herut—The National Jewish Movement v. Chairman of the Central Elections Committee for the Sixteenth Knesset [2003] 57(1) PD 750, para. 4 to President Barak's Judgment.
134. Amnon Reichman, "That Is Not How to Construct a Constitution," *Orech Adin* 35 (2002) (Heb.); Ariel Bendor, "Four Constitutional Revolutions?," *Mishpat Umimshal* 6 (2003) (Heb.).
135. See, for example, Hillel Sommer, "From Childhood to Maturity: Outstanding Issues in Implementation of the Constitutional Revolution," *IDC Law Review* 1 (2004): 63 (Heb.).

136. See, for example, HCJ 1384/98 Avni v. Prime Minister [1998] 52(5) PD 206, concerning Basic Law: The Government; HCJ 212/03 Herut and HCJ 3511/02 Negev Coexistence Forum v. Ministry of Infrastructure [2003] IsrSC 57(2) 102, concerning Basic Law: The Judiciary.

137. HCJ 3434/96 Hoffnung v. Knesset Speaker [1996] IsrSC 50(3) 57, 70, 75.

138. EA 92/03 Mofaz v. Chairman of the Central Elections Committee for the Sixteenth Knesset [2003] IsrSC 57(3) 793; see Avigdor Klagsbald, "A Contradiction to a Basic Law," *Hapraklit* 48 (2006) (Heb.).

139. Aharon Barak, "On Constitutional Implications and Constitutional Structure," in David Dyzenhaus and Malcolm Thorburn, eds., *Philosophical Foundations of Constitutional Law* (Oxford: Oxford University Press, 2016), 53, 64; Aharon Barak, "Implied (Judicial) Limitation Clause," in Aharon Barak et al., eds., *Eliahu Mazza Book* (Tel Aviv: Nevo, 2015), 77 (Heb.).

140. See Hillel Sommer, "The Non-Enumerated Rights: On the Scope of the Constitutional Revolution," *Mishpatim* 28, nos. 1–2 (1997) (Heb.).

141. See Aharon Barak, *Human Dignity: The Constitutional Value and the Constitutional Right* (Cambridge: Cambridge University Press, 2015), 156–70.

142. See HCJ 7015/02 Ajuri v. The IDF Commander [2002] IsrSC 56(6) 352; HCJ 2006/97 Janimat v. The Central Commander [1997] IsrSC 51(2) 65 (1).

143. HCJ 5432/03 SHIN for Equal Representation of Women v. The Board for Cable and Satellite Broadcasting [2004] IsrSC 58(3) 65; HCJ 721/94 EL-AL Israel Airlines v. Danielowitz [1994] IsrSC 48(5) 749; HCJ 4541/94 Miller v. The Minister of Defense [1995] IsrSC 49(4) 94.

144. CA 105/92 Re'em Engineer Contractors v. Nazareth-Ilit Municipality [1993] IsrSC 57(5) 19; PPA 4463/94 Golan v. The Prison Services [1996] IsrSC 52(5) 826; see Dalia Dorner, "Does Israel Have a Constitution?," *St. Louis University Law Journal* 43 (1999): 1331.

145. See HCJ 7715, 1554/95 Shoharie Gilat v. The Minister of Education and Culture [1996] IsrSC 50(3) 2; LCA 4905/98 Gamzu v. Yeshayahu [2001] IsrSC 55(3) 360; HCJ 2599/00 Yated v. The Ministry of Education [2002] IsrSC 56(5) 834; HCJ 5578/02 Manor v. Minister of Finance [2004] 59(1) PD 729; HCJ 366/03 Commitment to Peace and Social Justice Society v. Minister of Finance [2005] (2) IsrLR 335; HCJ 10662/04 Hassan v. National Insurance Institute [2012]. See also Aharon Barak, "Forward," in Yoram Rabin and Yuval Shany, eds., *Economic, Social and Cultural Rights in Israel* (Tel-Aviv: Ramot, 2005) (Heb.); Yoram Rabin and Yuval Shany, "The Israeli Unfinished Constitutional Revolution: Has the Time Come for Protecting Economic and Social Rights?," *Israel Law Review* 37 (2003–4).

146. See HCJ 6427/02 Movement for Government Quality in Israel v. The Knesset [2006] 61(1) PD 619, regarding equality; HCJ 10203/03 The National Census LtD v. Attorney General [2008] 62(4) PD 715, regarding political expression.

147. Suzie Navot, *The Constitution of Israel: A Contextual Analysis* (Oxford: Hart, 2014), 235. Following the expansive interpretation of Basic Law: Human Dignity, the Knesset refrained from constituting new Basic Laws on human rights. This

was clearly manifested by one of the leaders of the religious parties, Knesset Member Arie Deri, who claimed that "even if the Knesset should decide to add the Ten Commandments to the constitution, we would still oppose that because they would still be subject to the Supreme Court's interpretation" (cited in ibid., 42).

148. Yoseph M. Edrey, "The Israeli Constitutional Revolution/Evolution, Models of Constitutions, and a Lesson from Mistakes and Achievements," *American Journal of Comparative Law* 53, no. 1 (2005).

149. *Mizrahi Bank*, paras. 1–2 to Justice Zamir's Judgment. Justice Cheshin did not agree with this view: "I agree that the Bergman ruling was a milestone in the Supreme Court's rulings. This was the first time that the Court struck down Knesset legislation, and in so doing the Court recognized the justiciability of the procedure and the Court's authority to nullify Knesset legislation. However, in terms of overall constitutional doctrine, I think that the ruling can be understood as being required by the 'internal' authority of the Knesset, in other words, it is derived from the Knesset's authority to limit its authority, and to entrench a law against a majority of less than 61 Knesset members" (*Mizrahi Bank*, para. 95 to Justice Cheshin's Judgment). For a similar view, see Patricia J. Woods, "The Ideational Foundations of Israel's 'Constitutional Revolution,'" *Political Research Quarterly* 62, no. 4 (2009): "Did Israel experience a constitutional revolution beginning in 1992 with the passage of these two new Basic Laws? No. I argue that Israel has experienced a constitutional revolution, but it was a slow process that began at least as early as the 1969 Bergman case" (811).

150. See, for example, David Kretzmer, "The Path to Judicial Review in Human Rights Cases: From Bergman and Kol Ha'am to Mizrahi Bank," *Mishpatim* 28 (1997): 373 (Heb.); Yoav Dotan, "Constitution to Israel? The Constitutional Dialogue After 'The Constitutional Revolution,'" *Mishpatim* 28 (1997): 172–76 (Heb.).

151. Weill, "Reconciling Parliamentary Sovereignty and Judicial Review," 460.

152. Charles-Louis de Secondat, baron de Montesquieu, *De l'Esprit des Lois* (Amsterdam, 1749), bk. 11, chap. 6, 140.

153. Aharon Barak, "The Constitutional Revolution: 12th Anniversary," *IDC Law Review* 1 (2004): 16.

154. Uriel Lin, introduction to Moshe Nisim, ed., *The Basic Laws of the State of Israel* (Ashkelon, Israel: Sapir Institute, 2003), 4; cited in Barak, "Constitutional Revolution," 17.

155. Barak, "Constitutional Revolution," 18–19.

156. Jacobsohn, "After the Revolution," 140.

157. Frank I. Michelman, "Israel's 'Constitutional Revolution': A Thought from Political Liberalism," *Theoretical Inquiries in Law* 19 (2018): 748.

158. Judicial activism "assumes that the judiciary has a key role in shaping legal policy"; see Ariel L. Bendor, "The Relevance of the Judicial Activism vs. Judicial Restraint Discourse," *Tulsa Law Review* 47 (2011).

159. Moshe Landau in "A Debate: The Mizrahi Bank Case—After Three Years," *Hamishpat* 5 (2000): 254 (Heb.); see also Landau, "Giving a Constitution to Israel Using Judicial Ruling," *Mishpat Umimshal* 3 (1996) (Heb.).
160. *Mizrahi Bank,* paras. 133–35 to Justice Cheshin's Judgment. In 2000, one of us wrote, "It is surely premature to render definitive judgment concerning the type or magnitude of the change associated with the 1992 additions to the Basic Laws. . . . How enduring this development is, and how prominent among other as yet undeclared commitments it turns out to be is anybody's guess" (Jacobsohn, "After the Revolution," 143–44).
161. Barak, "Human Rights in Israel," 34.
162. Guy Lurie, "Invalidating Legislation: Is Israel an Anomaly?," Israel Democracy Institute, April 26, 2018, https://en.idi.org.il/articles/23372.
163. Aharon Barak, "The Constitutionalization of the Israeli Legal System as a Result of the Basic Laws and Its Effect on Procedural and Substantive Criminal Law," *Israel Law Review* 31 (1997).
164. Rubinstein, "Knesset and Basic Laws"; Yaniv Roznai, "The Basic Laws on Human Rights and the Legislative Process in the Knesset: You've Got to Practice What You Preach?," "Law and Man: Festschrift for Amnon Rubinstein," special issue, *IDC Law Review* 14 (2012) (Heb.).
165. Michelman, "Israel's 'Constitutional Revolution,'" 748–49.
166. See, for example, Menachem Hofnung, "The Unintended Consequences of the Unplanned Legislative Reform: Constitutional Politics in Israel," *American Journal of Comparative Law* 44 (1996): 597–99; Dotan, "Constitution to Israel," 190–200.
167. On some reasons why the Basic Laws have not been repealed, see Ori Aronson, "Why Hasn't the Knesset Repealed Basic Law: Human Dignity and Liberty? On the Status Quo as Counter-Majoritarian Difficulty," *Tel Aviv University Law Review* 37 (2016) (Heb.).
168. See, for example, Nuno Garoupa and Tom Ginsburg, *Judicial Reputation: A Comparative Theory* (Chicago: University of Chicago Press, 2015), 171, which mentions that the judicial opinions of former Israeli Supreme Court chief justice Aharon Barak were "frequently analyzed and borrowed abroad."
169. For domestic criticism, see, for example, Ruth Gavison, "The Role of Courts in Rifted Democracies," *Israel Law Review* 33 (1999): "The Supreme Court and the President of the Supreme Court enjoy great acclaim and respect within Israel and abroad, but have recently come under attack from a variety of sources." For international criticism, see, for example, Richard A. Posner, "Enlightened Despot," *New Republic,* April 23, 2007, https://newrepublic.com/article/60919/enlightened-despot; Robert Bork, "Barak's Rule," *Azure* 27 (2007), http://azure.org.il/include/print.php?id=34. For analyses, see Barak Medina, "Four Myths of Judicial Review: A Response to Richard Posner's Critique of Aharon Barak's Judicial Activism," https://ssrn.com/abstract=992972; Hillel Sommer, "Richard Posner on Aharon Barak: Things You See from There, Are Not Seen from Here," *Hapraklit* 49 (2000) (Heb.).

170. See Menachem Mautner, *Law and the Culture of Israel* (Oxford: Oxford University Press, 2011), ix.

171. See Ruth Gavison, Mordechai Kremnitzer, and Yoav Dotan, *Judicial Activism, for and Against: The Role of the High Court of Justice in Israeli Society* (Jerusalem: Magnes, 2000) (Heb.); Amnon Reichman, "Judicial Constitution Making in a Divided Society: The Israeli Case," in Kapiszewski, Silverstein, and Kagan, *Consequential Courts,* 233, 245–58.

172. Yoav Dotan, *Lawyering for the Rule of Law: Government Lawyers and the Rise of Judicial Power in Israel* (Cambridge: Cambridge University Press, 2014), 49.

173. Wojciech Sadurski, "Constitutional Courts in Transition Processes: Legitimacy and Democratization," Sydney Law School Legal Studies, Research Paper No. 11/53 (2011), 4.

174. Mautner, *Law and the Culture of Israel,* 110; see also Hirschl, *Towards Juristocracy,* 214; Ran Hirschl, "The Socio-Political Origins of Israel's Juristocracy," *Constellations* 16, no. 3 (2009); Ran Hirschl, "Israel's 'Constitutional Revolution': The Legal Interpretation of Entrenched Civil Liberties in an Emerging Neo-Liberal Economic Order," *American Journal of Comparative Law* 46, no. 3 (1998).

175. Jacobsohn, "After the Revolution," 148.

176. Stephen Gardbaum, "Are Strong Constitutional Courts Always a Good Thing for New Democracies?," *Columbia Journal of Transnational Law* 53 (2015): 320: "Where it is actively exercised, the power of judicial review can and has triggered political backlashes against the judiciary that threatens to reduce or eliminate its independence, a clearly counterproductive development and one that courts often have few powers or means to resist."

177. Garoupa and Ginsburg, *Judicial Reputation,* 117.

178. Mark Tushnet outlined the kinds of backlash seen after heroic judges (such as Barak) leave the scene: "The first-generation court exercises constitutional review aggressively, and in doing so it sets itself against important political actors who retain power even as the heroic court fades from the scene; that generates a backlash against aggressive constitutional review. . . . Backlash takes several forms: through restrictions on the constitutional court's jurisdiction, as in Hungary . . . through changes in methods of judicial selection, as has been tried in Israel"; see Tushnet, "After the Heroes Have Left the Scene: Temporality in the Study of Constitutional Court Judges," in Christine Landfried, ed., *Judicial Power: How Constitutional Courts Affect Political Transformations* (Cambridge: Cambridge University Press, 2019), 292, 297.

179. See Nadiv Mordechay and Yaniv Roznai, "A Jewish and (Towards Hybrid) Democratic State? Constitutional Retrogression in Israel," *Maryland Law Review* 77, no. 1 (2017); Roznai, "Israel: A Crisis of Liberal Democracy?," in Mark A. Graber, Sanford Levinson, and Mark Tushnet, eds., *Constitutional Democracy in Crisis?* (Oxford: Oxford University Press, 2018), chap. 21. This process began with the appointment of Professor Daniel Friedmann, a strong opponent of the constitutional revolution, as minister of justice, a role in which Friedmann attempted to curtail the powers of the court; see Doron Navot and Yoav Peled, "Towards a

Constitutional Counter-Revolution in Israel?," *Constellations* 16 (2009). On Friedmann's approach to the court's judicial activism, see Daniel Friedmann, *The Purse and the Sword,* trans. Haim Watzman (Oxford: Oxford University Press, 2016).

180. Mautner, "Protection of Liberal Rights," 146.
181. "Justice Minister, Chief Justice and A-G Clash Publicly over Court Authority," *Times of Israel,* December 21, 2017, https://www.timesofisrael.com/justice-minister-chief-justice-and-a-g-clash-publicly-over-court-authority.
182. Revital Hovel, "Justice Minister Slams Israel's Top Court, Says It Disregards Zionism and Upholding Jewish Majority," *Haaretz,* August 29, 2017, https://www.haaretz.com/israel-news/1.809617.
183. Arie Perliger and Ami Pedahzur, "The Radical Right in Israel," in Jens Rydgren, ed., *The Oxford Handbook of the Radical Right* (New York: Oxford University Press, 2018), 667, 672–75.
184. In that respect, the Basic Law not only may affect the Arab or Palestinian citizens of Israel, who comprise about 20 percent of the population, but also—as Eyal Benvenisti and Doreen Lustig suggest—may be contextualized "within the crumbling Israeli-Palestinian peace process and the growing prospects of a one-state-solution, which poses a serious legitimacy problem for one people that rules over another. For the proponents of this Basic Law it offers a legitimating principle for the subordination of another people with which they hope the majority of the Jewish voters would identify"; see Benvenisti and Lustig, " 'We the Jewish People': A Deep Look into Israel's New Law," Just Security, July 24, 2018, https://www.justsecurity.org/59632/israel-nationality-jewish-state-law.
185. See Suzie Navot, "A New Chapter in Israel's 'Constitution': Israel as the Nation State of the Jewish People," *Verfassungsblog,* July 27, 2018, https://verfassungsblog.de/a-new-chapter-in-israels-constitution-israel-as-the-nation-state-of-the-jewish-people/.
186. See Yoram Hazony, "The Current Crisis in Israel's Constitution," in Simon Rabinovitch, ed., *Defining Israel: The Jewish State, Democracy, and the Law* (Cincinnati: Hebrew Union College Press, 2018), 145, 154: "The disappearance of Jewish national self-determination from the court's list of the legitimate aims of Israeli policy is what stands behind the present crisis of Israel's constitution. It is what stands behind the need for a Basic Law reaffirming Israel as the national state of the Jewish people."
187. Mautner, "Protection of Liberal Rights," 22.
188. Petition for an Order Nisi, Adalah, the Legal Center for Arab Minority Rights in Israel and Others v. The Knesset and Attorney General, HCJ 5866/18, 53.
189. Ibid., at 8.
190. Suzie Navot and Yaniv Roznai, "From Supra-Constitutional Principles to the Misuse of Constituent Power in Israel," *European Journal of Law Reform* 21, no. 3 (2019).
191. Revital Hovel and Noa Shpigel, "Israel's Justice Minister Warns of 'An Earthquake' If Top Court Kills Nation-State Law," *Haaretz,* August 5, 2018, https://

www.haaretz.com/israel-news/premium-justice-minister-warns-of-earthquake-if-court-kills-nation-state-law-1.6343122.

192. Suzie Navot, "The Constitutional Dialogue: A Debate Through Institutional Mechanisms," *Mishpatim Online* (2018) (Heb.).
193. Mautner, "Protection of Liberal Rights," 143.
194. Ibid., 129.
195. The Israeli constitutional order thus became unique for applying American-style judicial review to primary legislation, yet its constitutional laws are enacted through ordinary legislative procedures, in the British style; see Weill, "Hybrid Constitutionalism."
196. Navot, *Constitution of Israel*, 10.
197. *Mizrahi Bank*, para. 52 to President Barak's Judgment.
198. Barak, "Constitutionalization of the Israeli Legal System," 5.
199. Mautner, "Protection of Liberal Rights," 144.
200. Dan Avnon, "The Israeli Basic Laws' (Potentially) Fatal Flaw," *Israel Law Review* 32 (1998): 543.
201. Aharon Barak, "The Constitutional Revolution: Protected Human Rights," *Mishpat Umimshal* 1 (1992–93) (Heb.).

Chapter 7. Constitutional Revolutions and Constituent Power

Epigraph: Carl J. Friedrich, "Militant Government and Dictatorship," *Annals of the American Academy of Political and Social Science* 267 (1950): 4.

1. Hannah Arendt, *On Revolution* (New York: Penguin, 1965), 21.
2. Martin Loughlin, "On Constituent Power," in Michael Dowdle and Michael Wilkinson, eds., *Constitutionalism Beyond Liberalism* (Cambridge: Cambridge University Press, 2017), 151.
3. Daniel Lee, *Popular Sovereignty in Early Modern Constitutional Thought* (Oxford: Oxford University Press, 2016), 142–43; Martin Loughlin, "Constituent Power Subverted: From English Constitutional Argument to British Constitutional Practice," in Martin Loughlin and Neil Walker, eds., *The Paradox of Constitutionalism: Constituent Power and Constitutional Form* (Oxford: Oxford University Press, 2007), 28.
4. Claude Klein, "A propos Constituent Power: Some General Views in a Modern Context," in Antero Jyränki, ed., *National Constitutions in the Era of Integration* (The Hague: Kluwer International, 1999), 31. On later development of the concept in France, see Lucia Rubinelli, "Taming Sovereignty: Constituent Power in Nineteenth-Century French Political Thought," *History of European Ideas* 44, no. 1 (2018).
5. See, for example, Joel Colón-Ríos, "Rousseau: Theorist of Constituent Power," *Oxford Journal of Legal Studies* 36, no. 4 (2016).
6. Lucia Rubinelli, "How to Think Beyond Sovereignty: On Sieyès and Constituent Power," *European Journal of Political Theory* 18, no. 1 (2016).
7. Emmanuel Joseph Sieyès, *Préliminaires de la Constitution: Reconnaissance et exposition raisonnée des droits de l'homme et du citoyen, Lu les 20 et 21 juillet, 1789, au Comité de Constitution* (Baudoin, 1789), 19.

8. Emmanuel Joseph Sieyès, *What Is the Third Estate?* (1789), trans. Michael Sonenscher, in *Political Writings* (Indianapolis: Hackett, 2003), 136; see Timothy Murphy, "Constituent/Constituted Power," in John Protevi, ed., *Edinburgh Dictionary of Continental Philosophy* (Edinburgh: Edinburgh University Press, 2006), 105.
9. Sieyès, *What Is the Third Estate?,* 134–37.
10. Egon Zweig, *Die Lehre vom Pouvoir Constituant* (Tübingen: Siebeck, 1909), 116–17, 135–37, cited in Mark Vishniak, "Justification of Power in Democracy," *Political Science Quarterly* 60, no. 3 (1945): 361.
11. See Maria Cahill, "Ever Closer Remoteness of the Peoples of Europe? Limits on the Power of Amendment and National Constituent Power," *Cambridge Law Journal* 75, no. 2 (2016). As Lior Barshack writes, it is through the separation of powers that constituent power, "the sacred communal body," is expelled to "the corporate, absent realm"; see Barshack, "Notes on the Clerical Body of the Law," *Cardozo Law Review* 24, no. 3 (2003): 1161.
12. Bronislaw Baczko, "The Social Contract of the French: Sieyès and Rousseau," *Journal of Modern History* 60 (1988).
13. For a contextualization of Sieyès's doctrine, see Thomaz Pereira, "Constituting the Amendment Power: A Framework for Comparative Amendment Law," in Richard Albert, Xenophon Contiades, and Alkmene Fotiadou, eds., *The Foundations and Traditions of Constitutional Amendment* (Oxford: Hart, 2017), 105.
14. Julien Oudot, *Conscience et science du devoir: Introduction à une explication nouvelle du Code Napoléon* (Paris: Durand, 1856), 2:397–98.
15. Sieyès, "What Is the Third Estate," 136.
16. Georges Burdeau, *Traité de science politique,* 3rd ed. (Paris: LGDJ, 1983), 173.
17. Sieyès, "What Is the Third Estate," 136–37.
18. Matt Whitt, "The Paradox of Sovereignty: Authority, Constitution, and Political Boundaries" (Ph.D. diss., Vanderbilt University, 2010), 159–60.
19. Antonio Negri, *Insurgencies: Constituent Power and the Modern State* (Minneapolis: University of Minnesota Press, 1999), 15.
20. Ibid., 3, 10–11, 333. It is precisely because of the concept's radical and nonlegal elements that Illan rua Wall suggested that human rights should be conceived in terms of constituent power; see Wall, *Human Rights and Constituent Power: Without Model or Warranty* (Abingdon, U.K.: Routledge, 2012).
21. See Renato Cristi, "The Metaphysics of Constituent Power: Schmitt and the Genesis of Chile's 1980 Constitution," *Cardozo Law Review* 21 (1999–2000): 1763–75; William Partlett, "The Dangers of Popular Constitution-Making," *Brooklyn Journal of International Law* 38 (2012): 42; David Landau, "Constitution-Making Gone Wrong," *Alabama Law Review* 64, no. 5 (2013).
22. Although he admitted that "it would be frightening if every legislature had the right to make alterations to the constitution"; see Louis-Marie Prudhomme, *Révolutions de Paris, dédiées à la nation et au district des Petits-Augustins: Avec gravures et cartes des departemens du Royaume de France* (1790), 3:23.
23. Raymond Carré de Malberg, *Contribution à la Théorie Générale de l'Etat,* 2 vols. (1922; rept., Paris: CNRS, 1962), 2:489–500.

24. See William Partlett, "The American Tradition of Constituent Power," *International Journal of Constitutional Law* 15, no. 4 (2017).
25. See, for example, Richard S. Kay, "The Illegality of the Constitution," *Constitutional Commentary* 4 (1987).
26. James Wilson, *Commentaries on the Constitution of the United States of America* (London: Debrett, J. Johnson, and J. S. Jordan, 1792), 38–39.
27. See Jason Frank, " 'Unauthorized Propositions': 'The Federalist Papers' and Constituent Power," *Diacritics* 37, nos. 2–3 (2007).
28. Stephen M. Griffin, "Constituent Power and Constitutional Change in American Constitutionalism," in Loughlin and Walker, *Paradox of Constitutionalism*, 49, 66.
29. Robert Roswell Palmer, *The Age of the Democratic Revolution: The Challenge* (Princeton, N.J.: Princeton University Press, 1959), 215. This is what Gordon Wood termed the "institutionalization of revolution"; see Wood, *The Creation of the American Republic, 1776–1787* (Chapel Hill: University of North Carolina Press, 1969), 614.
30. Akhil R. Amar, "Philadelphia Revisited: Amending the Constitution Outside Article V," *University of Chicago Law Review* 55 (1988): 1054–58; Amar, "The Consent of the Governed: Constitutional Amendment Outside Article V," *Columbia Law Review* 94 (1994): 457–500; Amar, "Popular Sovereignty and Constitutional Amendment," in Sanford Levinson, ed., *Responding to Imperfection: The Theory and Practice of Constitutional Amendment* (Princeton, N.J.: Princeton University Press, 1995), 89, 89–101.
31. Olivier Beaud, *La Puissance de l'état* (Paris: PUF, 1994), 310–19.
32. Yaniv Roznai, *Unconstitutional Constitutional Amendments: The Limits of Amendment Powers* (Oxford: Oxford University Press, 2017), chap. 4.
33. Carl J. Friedrich, *Constitutional Government and Politics: Nature and Development* (New York: Harper & Brothers, 1937), 117.
34. Martin Loughlin, "Reflections on the Idea of Public Law," in Emilios A. Christodoulidis and Stephen Tierney, eds., *Public Law and Politics: The Scope and Limits of Constitutionalism* (Aldershot, U.K.: Ashgate, 2008), 47, 64.
35. See Richard Tuck, *The Sleeping Sovereign: The Invention of Modern Democracy* (Cambridge: Cambridge University Press, 2016).
36. Riccardo Guastini, "On the Theory of Legal Sources," *Ratio Juris* 20, no. 2 (2007): 305: "In no legal system can constituent power—which is not to be confused with the power of constitutional amendment—be regarded as an institutionalized source: otherwise, it would not be 'constituent' but 'constituted.' "
37. Andreas Kalyvas, "Popular Sovereignty, Democracy, and the Constituent Power," *Constellations* 12, no. 2 (2005): 228.
38. Justice Chandrachud in *Minerva Mills, Ltd. v. Union of India*, AIR 1980 SC 1789, 1798.
39. Madhav Khosla, *The Indian Constitution* (New Delhi: Oxford University Press, 2012), 159.
40. Lech Garlicki and Zofia A. Garlicka Sowers, "Unconstitutional Constitutional Amendments," *Vienna Journal on International Constitutional Law* 12, no. 3 (2018): 312.

41. Jeffrey A. Lenowitz, "Why Ratification? Questioning the Unexamined Constitution-Making Procedure" (Ph.D. diss., Columbia University, 2013), 87.
42. Friedrich, *Constitutional Government and Politics,* 118.
43. Richard S. Kay, "Constituent Authority," *American Journal of Comparative Law* 59 (2011): 735.
44. Mark Tushnet, "Constitution-Making: An Introduction," *Texas Law Review* 91 (2012–13): 2006.
45. David Landau and Rosalind Dixon, "Constraining Constitutional Change," *Wake Forest Law Review* 50 (2015).
46. Kostas Chryssogonos, "Popular Involvement in Constitution-Making," *Revue européenne de droit public* 20, no. 4 (2008).
47. Mark Tushnet, "Peasants with Pitchforks, and Toilers with Twitter: Constitutional Revolutions and the Constituent Power," *International Journal of Constitutional Law* 13, no. 3 (2015): 649.
48. Carl Schmitt, *Constitutional Theory,* trans. Jeffrey Seitzer (Durham, N.C.: Duke University Press, 2008), 132; see also Marco Goldoni and Christopher McCorkindale, "Why We (Still) Need a Revolution," *German Law Journal* 114, no. 12 (2013): 2214–15.
49. Kay, "Constituent Authority," 727–28.
50. Kemal Gözler, *Pouvoir Constituant* (Bursa, Turkey: Ekin Yayınevi, 1999), 39–44.
51. Kalyvas, "Popular Sovereignty, Democracy, and Constituent Power," 232–33.
52. See Andrew Arato, *Post-Sovereign Constitution Making* (Oxford: Oxford University Press, 2016).
53. See Heinz Klug, *Constituting Democracy: Law, Globalism, and South Africa's Political Reconstruction* (New York: Cambridge University Press, 2000), 175–76.
54. Andrew Arato, *The Adventures of the Constituent Power: Beyond Revolutions?* (Cambridge: Cambridge University Press, 2017), 239. For an elaboration of the constitution-making process in South Africa, see 233–56.
55. Karol Edward Soltan, "Constitution Making at the Edges of Constitutional Order," *William & Mary Law Review* 49 (2007–8): 1419.
56. Henk Botha, "Instituting Public Freedom or Extinguishing Constituent Power? Reflections on South Africa's Constitution-Making Experiment," *South African Journal on Human Rights* 26 (2010).
57. Ibid., 71–72.
58. Ibid., 70–71.
59. Alec Stone Sweet, "The Juridical Coup d'État and the Problem of Authority," *German Law Journal* 8, no. 10 (2007): 915.
60. Ibid., 916.
61. In addition to the difficulty of inferring the likelihood of rejection if the framers had been confronted with the question; see Neil Walker, "Juridical Transformation as Process: A Comment on Stone Sweet," *German Law Journal* 8, no. 10 (2007): 930.

62. See Wojciech Sadurski, "Juridical Coups d'État—All over the Place: Comment on 'The Juridical Coup d'État and the Problem of Authority' by Alec Stone Sweet," *German Law Journal* 8, no. 10 (2007): 936.
63. Theodor Schilling, "Alec Stone Sweet's 'Juridical Coup d'État' Revisited: Coups d'État, Revolutions, Grenzorgane, and Constituent Power," *German Law Journal* 13, no. 3 (2012): 292; see Hans Kelsen, *General Theory of Law and State* (New Brunswick, N.J.: Transaction, 2006), 117.
64. Gianluigi Palombella, "Constitutional Transformations vs. 'Juridical' Coups d'État: A Comment on Stone Sweet," *German Law Journal* 8, no. 10 (2007).
65. Stone Sweet, "Juridical Coup d'État," 916–17. The *Lüth* case, BVerfGE 7, 198 (1958), mentioned in chapter 4, which held that "constitutional values" permeate "all spheres of law," including private law, may be an instance of such a juridical coup d'état, according to Stone Sweet (ibid., 918–22).
66. Jonathan L. Marshfield, "Courts and Informal Constitutional Change in the States," *New England Law Review* 51, no. 3 (2017); Richard S. Kay, "Formal and Informal Amendment of the United States Constitution," *American Journal of Comparative Law* 66 (2018).
67. Alec Stone Sweet, "Response to Gianluigi Palombella, Wojciech Sadurski, and Neil Walker," *German Law Journal* 8, no. 10 (2007): 952.
68. Stone Sweet, "Juridical Coup d'État," 927; see also Stone Sweet, "Response," 951.
69. Hans Kelsen, *Pure Theory of Law*, trans. Max Knight (Berkeley: University of California Press, 1967), 200: "If we ask for the reason of the validity of the historically first constitution, then the answer can only be (if we leave aside God or 'nature') that the validity of the constitution—the assumption that it is a binding norm—must be presupposed."
70. See Eli Zalzberger, "The Knesset's Constituent Authority: Two Side Remarks to Obiter, or Invitation to Re-open the Debate," *Mishpat Umimshal* 3 (1996): 690 (Heb.).
71. H. L. A. Hart, *The Concept of Law*, 2nd ed. (Oxford: Clarendon, 1994), 97–108.
72. See generally Martin Loughlin, "The Concept of Constituent Power," *European Journal of Political Theory* 13 (2014): 221–23.
73. Ronald Dworkin, *Law's Empire* (Cambridge, Mass.: Harvard University Press, 1986), 255.
74. Zalzberger, "Knesset's Constituent Authority," 691.
75. CA 6821/93 United Mizrahi Bank Ltd. v. Migdal Cooperative Village [1995] 49(4) P.D. 221, para. 63 of Justice Cheshin's Judgment.
76. Mizrahi Bank, para. 124 of Justice Cheshin's Judgment.
77. Ruth Gavison, "The Constitutional Revolution: A Description of Reality or a Self-Fulfilling Prophecy?," *Mishpatim* 28 (1997): 28 (Heb.).
78. Stone Sweet, "Juridical Coup d'État," 915.
79. Palombella, "Constitutional Transformations vs. 'Juridical' Coups d'État," 945.
80. Luigi Corrias, "The Legal Theory of the Juridical Coup: Constituent Power Now," *German Law Journal* 12, no. 8 (2011): 1554, 1566.
81. Stone Sweet, "Juridical Coup d'État," 917.

82. Corrias, "Legal Theory of the Juridical Coup," 1569.
83. Ibid., 1566.
84. Ibid., 1567.
85. Schilling, "Stone Sweet's 'Juridical Coup,'" 309.
86. Ibid.
87. Corte Suprema de Justicia, F-165, poderjudicial.gob.hn/Documents/FalloSCONS23042015.pdf (Span.); for an analysis, see David Landau, Rosalind Dixon, and Yaniv Roznai, "From an Unconstitutional Constitutional Amendment to an Unconstitutional Constitution? Lessons from Honduras," *Global Constitutionalism* 8, no. 1 (2019); David Landau, "Presidential Term Limits in Latin America: A Critical Analysis of the Migration of the Unconstitutional Constitutional Amendment Doctrine," *Law & Ethics of Human Rights* 12, no. 2 (2018): 239–43.
88. Lisbon Treaty Case, 123 BVerfGE 267 (2009), para. 218.
89. Radim Dragomaca, "Constitutional Amendments and the Limits of Judicial Activism: The Case of the Czech Republic," in Willem Witteveen and Maartje De-Visser, eds., *The Jurisprudence of Aharon Barak: Views from Europe* (Nijmegen, Netherlands: Wolf Legal, 2011), 198.
90. See Yaniv Roznai, "Unconstitutional Constitutional Change by Courts," *New England Law Review* 51, no. 3 (2018).
91. Georg Jellinek, *Allgemeine Staatslehre,* 3rd ed. (1928; rept., Bad Homburg: Hermann Gentner Verlag, 1960), 339.
92. Richard Albert, "Constitutional Amendment and Dismemberment," *Yale Journal of International Law* 43, no. 1 (2018): 68–69.
93. Botha, "Public Freedom or Constituent Power," 81–82.
94. Joseph de Maistre, "Study on Sovereignty" (1794–95), in *The Generative Principle of Political Constitutions: Studies on Sovereignty, Religion, and Enlightenment* (New Brunswick, N.J.: Macmillan, 1965), 93.
95. Sieyès, "What Is the Third Estate," 97.
96. Ibid., 134, 139; see Martin Loughlin, "Representation and Constitutional Theory," in Carol Harlow, Paul P. Craig, and Richard Rawlings, eds., *Law and Administration in Europe: Essays in Honour of Carol Harlow* (Oxford: Oxford University Press, 2003), 47, 58.
97. Albert Soboul, "Some Problems of the Revolutionary State, 1789–1796," *Past & Present* 65 (1974): 54; see Alexander Somek, *Individualism: An Essay on the Authority of the European Union* (Oxford: Oxford University Press, 2008), 28n54.
98. Schmitt, *Constitutional Theory,* 64, 76.
99. Ibid., 125.
100. Ibid., 76–77.
101. Ibid., 126–32.
102. William E. Scheuerman, *Carl Schmitt: The End of Law* (Lanham, Md.: Rowman and Littlefield, 1999), 71.
103. Ibid., 152; see Renato Cristi, "Carl Schmitt on Sovereignty and Constituent Power," *Canadian Journal of Law and Jurisprudence* 10 (1997): 198.

104. Schmitt, *Constitutional Theory*, 128; see generally Duncan Kelly, "Carl Schmitt's Political Theory of Representation," *Journal of the History of Ideas* 65, no. 1 (2004).
105. Andrew Arato, "Forms of Constitution Making and Theories of Democracy," *Cardozo Law Review* 17 (1995–96): 203.
106. Anne Norton, "Pentecost: Democratic Sovereignty in Carl Schmitt," *Constellations* 18, no. 3 (2011); Andreas Kalyvas, "Carl Schmitt and the Three Moments of Democracy," *Cardozo Law Review* 21 (1999–2000): 1536–37.
107. See, for example, Amar, "Philadelphia Revisited."
108. Larry D. Kramer, *The People Themselves: Popular Constitutionalism and Judicial Review* (New York: Oxford University Press, 2004), 253.
109. See CC Decision No. 62-20 DC, November 6, 1962; see also Denis Baranger, "The Language of Eternity: Constitutional Review of the Amending Power in France (Or the Absence Thereof)," *Israel Law Review* 44, no. 3 (2011): 392–94; Jean Philippe Derosier, "The French People's Role in Amending the Constitution," in Albert, Contiades, and Fotiadou, *The Foundations and Traditions of Constitutional Amendment*, chap. 16.
110. Lucien Jaume, "Constituent Power in France: The Revolution and Its Consequences," in Loughlin and Walker, *Paradox of Constitutionalism*, 79.
111. Duncan Ivison, "Pluralism and the Hobbesian Logic of Negative Constitutionalism," *Political Studies* 67 (1999): 84; see also Kevin Olson, "Paradoxes of Constitutional Democracy," *American Journal of Political Science* 51, no. 2 (2007), and Pasquale Pasquino, "The Un-constituent Power of the People: Article 138 of the Italian Constitution and Popular Referendum," special issue, *Italian Law Journal*, 2017:143: "From a legal vantage point, the people are always a constituted organ: a list of names (the citizens-voters) and a set of rules (voting or other legal authorizing rules, to begin with) to produce a collective will that cannot exist without rules written by someone who legally and materially preexists the 'people.'"
112. Hans Lindahl, *Fault Lines of Globalization: Legal Order and the Politics of A-Legality* (Oxford: Oxford University Press, 2013), 216.
113. See Henry Paul Monaghan, "We the People[s], Original Understanding, and Constitutional Amendment," *Columbia Law Review* 96 (1996): 165–66.
114. Edmund S. Morgan, *Inventing the People: The Rise of Popular Sovereignty in England and America* (New York: Norton, 1988), 14, 58.
115. Rajeev Dhavan, "Sarbani Sen, Popular Sovereignty, and Democratic Transformation: The Constitution of India," *Indian Journal of Constitutional Law* 2 (2008): 208. Again, it is one thing to claim that a certain process of speaking on behalf of the people was not sufficiently inclusive; it is a different thing to completely negate the idea of the sovereign people as the driver of constituent power.
116. Ernst Kantorowicz, *The King's Two Bodies: A Study in Mediaeval Political Theology* (Princeton, N.J.: Princeton University Press, 1958).
117. Marcel Gauchet, *Révolution des pouvoirs: La souveraineté, le peuple et la représentation, 1789–1799* (Paris: Gallimard, 1995), 45–47.

118. Jed Rubenfeld, *Freedom and Time* (New Haven, Conn.: Yale University Press, 2001); Rubenfeld, "The Moment and the Millennium," *George Washington Law Review* 66 (1997–98): 1100.
119. Michel Troper, "The Logic of Justification of Judicial Review," *International Journal of Constitutional Law* 1, no. 1 (2003): 119–20.
120. Dieter Grimm, "Integration by Constitution," *International Journal of Constitutional Law* 3, nos. 2–3 (2005): 201. See also Paul W. Kahn, "Political Time: Sovereignty and the Transtemporal Community," *Cardozo Law Review* 28, no. 1 (2006): 266–71; Kahn, *Political Theology: Four New Chapters on the Concept of Sovereignty* (New York: Columbia University Press, 2011), 140; Lior Barshack, "Constituent Power as Body: Outline of a Constitutional Theology," *University of Toronto Law Journal* 56 (2006); Barshack, "Political Theology and the Authenticity of Modern Experience," *Jerusalem Review of Legal Studies* 5 (2012): 2–3, 13; Barshack, "Time and the Constitution," *International Journal of Constitutional Law* 7, no. 4 (2009): 554, 557; Barshack, "Clerical Body of the Law," 1164; Barshack, "The Subject of Ideals," *Cultural Values* 4, no. 1 (2000): 82.
121. Tuck, *Sleeping Sovereign*.
122. Loughlin, "Concept of Constituent Power," 229–32. Loughlin is building on Hans Lindahl's concept of "the people" as an imaginary collective body of the group that represents the consent of the real people. Conceived in these terms, the claim of "the people" to constitutional authorship is inevitably reflexive, the result of a retrospective self-attribution and self-identification, and a projection into the future; see Hans Lindahl, "Constituent Power and Reflexive Identity: Toward an Ontology of Collective Selfhood," in Loughlin and Walker, *Paradox of Constitutionalism*, 9, 19.
123. Loughlin, "Concept of Constituent Power," 231.
124. Ibid.
125. See Antoni Abat i Ninet and Mark Tushnet, *The Arab Spring: An Essay on Revolution and Constitutionalism* (Cheltenham, U.K.: Elgar, 2015), 64.
126. Nasser Abourahme, "Past the End, Not Yet at the Beginning: On the Revolutionary Disjuncture in Egypt," *City* 17, no. 4 (2013): 427.
127. Charles Tripp, *The Power and the People: Paths of Resistance in the Middle East* (Cambridge: Cambridge University Press, 2013), 133.
128. Zoran Oklopcic, *Beyond the People: Social Imaginary and Constituent Imagination* (Oxford: Oxford University Press, 2018), 135.
129. Nimer Sultany, *Law and Revolution: Legitimacy and Constitutionalism After the Arab Spring* (Oxford: Oxford University Press, 2017), 246–51.
130. Arato, *Adventures of the Constituent Power*, 347–49.
131. Sultany, *Law and Revolution*, 290.
132. Ibid., 290–91.
133. Ibid., 297.
134. Daniel T. Rodgers, *Contested Truths: Keywords in American Politics Since Independence* (Cambridge, Mass.: Harvard University Press, 1998), 5.
135. Barbara Darby, "Amending Authors and Constitutional Discourse," *Dalhousie Law Journal* 25 (2002): 221.

136. Tushnet, "Constitution-Making," 1987–88.
137. Xenophon Contiades and Alkmene Fotiadou, "The People as Amenders of the Constitution," in Xenophon Contiades and Alkmene Fotiadou, eds., *Participatory Constitutional Change: The People as Amenders of the Constitution* (Abingdon, U.K.: Routledge, 2017), 15.
138. Xenophon Contiades and Alkmene Fotiadou, "Models of Constitutional Change," in Xenophon Contiades, ed., *Engineering Constitutional Change: A Comparative Perspective on Europe, Canada, and the USA* (Abingdon, U.K.: Routledge, 2012), 417, 430.
139. See Andras Sajó, "Enthusiasm and Acquiescence in Constitution-Making," *Indian Journal of Constitutional Law* 3 (2009): 27.
140. Iris Marion Young, *Inclusion and Democracy* (Oxford: Oxford University Press, 2000), 5–6.
141. See, for example, David Butler and Austin Ranney, "Theory," in David Butler and Austin Ranney, eds., *Referendums Around the World: The Growing Use of Direct Democracy* (Washington, D.C.: AEI, 1994), 11, 17–21; Laurel E. Miller, "Designing Constitution-Making Processes: Lessons from the Past, Questions for the Future," in Laurel E. Miller and Louis Aucoin, eds., *Framing the State in Times of Transition: Case Studies in Constitution Making* (Washington, D.C.: U.S. Institute of Peace Press, 2010), 601, 612.
142. Heinz Klug, "Participating in the Design: Constitution-Making in South Africa," *Review of Constitutional Studies* 3 (1996).
143. On Irish constitutional-identity disharmony, see Gary J. Jacobsohn, *Constitutional Identity* (Cambridge, Mass.: Harvard University Press, 2010).
144. "Ireland Abortion Referendum: Quiet Revolution—Irish PM," *BBC*, May 26, 2018, https://www.bbc.com/news/av/world-europe-44264690/ireland-abortion-referendum-quiet-revolution-irish-pm.
145. On the Irish Constitutional Convention of 2012–14, which gave "ordinary" citizens, selected randomly, a leading role in constitutional change, see David M. Farrell, Clodagh Harris, and Jane Suiter, "Bringing People into the Heart of Constitutional Design: The Irish Constitutional Convention of 2012–14," in Contiades and Fotiadou, *Participatory Constitutional Change*, chap. 7.
146. Consider in this regard the following observation: "There is value in retaining a venerable Constitution which, though widely criticized, has a central place in Irish life. Rather than a constitutional revolution focused solely on promulgating a new constitutional text, what Ireland in 2017 needs is two-fold: first, a coherent package of reforms put to the Irish people, which addresses the anachronisms and deficiencies of the text and pursues real political reform; and second, a cultural revolution that sees Ireland shed its tolerance of impunity, of censorship, and of mediocre government"; see Tom Gerald Daly, "Unfinished Revolutions: Constitutional Pasts and Futures in Ireland and Mexico," *Journal of Institutional Studies* 4 (2018): 935.
147. For an elaboration of the process and its enhanced legitimacy, see Joseph Cozza, "Ireland's Quiet Revolution: Exploring the Role of Popular Sovereignty and

Constituent Power in Constitutional Transformation," paper submitted to the University of Texas at Austin (2018; copy with authors). Interestingly, it is also due to the people's participation in a referendum that the Irish Supreme Court has consistently held that the people are the creator of the Constitution and the supreme authority. Accordingly, constitutional amendments made by the people in a referendum that expresses their will become the fundamental and supreme law of the land; such an expression of the people's will is unlimited and cannot be reviewed or nullified by courts; see, for example, Aileen Kavanagh, "Unconstitutional Constitutional Amendments from Irish Free State to Irish Republic," in Eoin Carolan, ed., *The Constitution of Ireland: Perspectives and Prospects* (Dublin: Bloomsbury Professional, 2012), 331.

148. Stephen Tierney, *Constitutional Referendums: The Theory and Practice of Republican Deliberation* (Oxford: Oxford University Press, 2012), 15. The Irish experience of 2018 would appear to conform to Tierney's preference for "popular deliberation coexisting with elite deliberation, providing sites of interconnection and mutual reinforcement of deliberative decision-making, since referendums are always embedded within broader representative systems" (44).
149. Ibid., 186.
150. Roberto Mangabeira Unger, *What Should Legal Analysis Become?* (London: Verso, 1996), 72.
151. Negri, *Insurgencies,* 1.
152. Andreas Kalyvas, *Democracy and the Politics of the Extraordinary: Max Weber, Carl Schmitt, and Hannah Arendt* (Cambridge: Cambridge University Press, 2008), 7.
153. Lior Barshack, "Transformations of Kinship and the Acceleration of History Thesis," *Theoretical Inquiries in Law* 8, no. 1 (2007): 199.
154. Sheldon Wolin, "Fugitive Democracy," in Seyla Benhabib, ed., *Democracy and Difference: Contesting the Boundaries of the Political* (Princeton, N.J.: Princeton University Press, 1996), 31, 39.
155. Ibid., 41–43; see also Sheldon Wolin, *Politics and Vision* (Princeton, N.J.: Princeton University Press, 2004), 602–3.
156. Melissa Schwartzberg, *Democracy and Legal Change* (Cambridge: Cambridge University Press, 2009), 6.
157. Antoni Abad i Ninet, "From Popular Sovereignty to Constitutional Sovereignty?," Buffalo Legal Studies Research Paper No. 2011–007, April 10, 2010.
158. Ali Riza Coban, "The Continuity Problem of the Constituent Power," in Arno Scherzberg, ed., *Verfassungstheorie und Verfassungsgebung: Überlegungen anlässlich der Diskussion um eine Verfassungsreform in der Türkei* (Münster: LIT Verlag, 2012), 49, 56n13.
159. Stephen Tierney, "Whose Political Constitution? Citizens and Referendums," *German Law Journal* 14, no. 12 (2013): 2194.
160. See, for example, Justin Blount, "Participation in Constitutional Design," in Tom Ginsburg and Rosalind Dixon, eds., *Comparative Constitutional Law* (Northampton, Mass.: Elgar, 2011), 49; Zachary Elkins, Tom Ginsburg, and

Justin Blount, "The Citizen as Founder: Public Participation in Constitutional Approval," *Temple Law Review* 81 (2008); see also Mila Versteeg, "Unpopular Constitutionalism," *Indiana Law Journal* 89, no. 1 (2014): 10, noting that "today, 34% of all constitutions require ratification by popular referendum, while in 1950, only 7% did."

161. Cheryl Saunders, "Constitution Making in the 21st Century," *International Review of Law* 4 (2012).

162. See Contiades and Fotiadou, *Participatory Constitutional Change.*

163. Antoni Abat i Ninet, *Constitutional Violence: Legitimacy, Democracy and Human Rights* (Edinburgh: Edinburgh University Press, 2013), 14.

164. Stephen Holmes, *The Anatomy of Antiliberalism* (Cambridge, Mass.: Harvard University Press, 1996), 49.

165. Schmitt, *Constitutional Theory,* 128; see Scheuerman, *Carl Schmitt,* 71–72.

166. Christoph Burchard, "Carl Schmitt on Democracy and International Relations," *Leiden Journal of International Law* 19 (2006): 13; see also Jean L. Cohen, "Beyond Political Theology: Comment on Kalyvas on Carl Schmitt," *Cardozo Law Review* 21 (1999–2000): 1591.

167. One notable proponent of democratic constitutional change, Joel Colón-Ríos, argued that in order to acquire democratic legitimacy, fundamental constitutional changes, which are episodic by nature, should take place through the most participatory process possible, allowing citizens the opportunity to propose, deliberate, and decide on such changes. Constitutional regimes must leave a door open for the constituent power to reemerge separately from the ordinary amendment procedures, namely, through participatory mechanisms that facilitate the exercise of constituent power; see Colón-Ríos, "The Second Dimension of Democracy: The People and Their Constitution," *Baltic Journal of Law and Politics* 2, no. 2 (2009); Colón-Ríos, "Notes on Democracy and Constitution-Making," *New Zealand Journal of Public and International Law* 9, no. 1 (2011); Colón-Ríos, "The Counter-Majoritarian Difficulty and the Road Not Taken: Democratizing Amendment Rules," *Canadian Journal of Law and Jurisprudence* 25, no. 1 (2012). Together with Allan Hutchinson, Colón-Ríos contended that if democracy is about self-government, then fundamental constitutional rules should originate in an exercise of popular participatory self-legislation by the people, preferably through an elected constituent assembly, triggered by popular initiative—especially as regards changing the constitutional regime—and ratified by the people before coming into effect. In their account, constituent power should not be "muzzled and contained"; rather, it should allow popular agency to create and re-create constitutional regimes; see Allan C. Hutchinson and Joel Colón-Ríos, "Democracy and Constitutional Change," *Theoria* 58 (2011): 51–53.

168. Kalyvas, "Popular Sovereignty, Democracy, and Constituent Power," 235.

169. Shouvik Kumar Guha and Moiz Tundawala, "Constitution: Amended It Stands?," *NUJS Law Review* 1 (2008): 543.

170. Ming-Sung Kuo, "The Two Faces of Constituent Power," *Indian Journal of Constitutional and Administrative Law,* "The Forum," September 30, 2018, http://ijcal.in/the-two-faces-of-constituent-power.
171. Arendt, *On Revolution,* 163.
172. See William E. Scheuerman, "Revolutions and Constitutions: Hannah Arendt's Challenge to Carl Schmitt," *Canadian Journal of Law and Jurisprudence* 10 (1997): 151; Scheuerman, "Constitutionalism in an Age of Speed," *Constitutional Commentary* 19 (2002): 383.
173. Ulrich K. Preuss, *Constitutional Revolution: The Link Between Constitutionalism and Progress* (Amherst, Mass.: Prometheus, 1995), 4.
174. Martin Loughlin, *Foundations of Public Law* (Oxford: Oxford University Press, 2010), 227; Loughlin, *The Idea of Public Law* (Oxford: Oxford University Press, 2004), 113; Yasuo Hasebe, "On the Dispensability of the Concept of Constituent Power," *Indian Journal of Constitutional Law* 3 (2009): 41.
175. Joel Colón-Ríos, *Weak Constitutionalism: Democratic Legitimacy and the Question of Constituent Power* (London: Routledge, 2012), 87.
176. Abat i Ninet and Tushnet, *Arab Spring,* 66.
177. Hans Lindahl, "Possibility, Actuality, Rupture: Constituent Power and the Ontology of Change," *Constellations* 22, no. 2 (2015): 171.
178. Kay, "Constituent Authority," 742; Melissa Schwartzberg, "Should Progressive Constitutionalism Embrace Popular Constitutionalism?," *Ohio State Law Journal* 72, no. 6 (2011): 1303, 1314.
179. Tushnet, "Peasants with Pitchforks," 647.
180. Alexander Somek, "The Owl of Minerva: Constitutional Discourse Before Its Conclusion," *Modern Law Review* 71 (2008).
181. Miguel Vatter, "Legality and Resistance: Arendt and Negri on Constituent Power," in Timothy S. Murphy and Abdul-Karim Mustapha, eds., *The Philosophy of Antonio Negri: Revolution in Theory* (London: Pluto, 2007), 2:52, 66–67.
182. Mikael Spång, *Constituent Power and Constitutional Order: Above, Within, and Beside the Constitution* (Basingstoke, U.K.: Palgrave Macmillan, 2014), 45.
183. Oklopcic, *Beyond the People.*

Chapter 8. Conclusion

1. *Naz Foundation v. Government of NCT of Delhi* (2009), para. 79; *Constituent Assembly Debates,* November 4, 1948 (Lok Sabha Secretariat, 1986), 7:38.
2. Sujit Choudhry, "How to Do Comparative Constitutional Law in India: *Naz Foundation,* Same Sex Rights, and Dialogical Interpretation," in Sunil Khilnani, Vikram Raghavan, and Arun K. Thirunengadam, eds., *Comparative Constitutionalism in South Asia* (New Delhi: Oxford University Press, 2013), 78.
3. Ibid., 82.
4. Ibid., 48.
5. *Koushal v. Naz Foundation* (2013), paras. 26, 52.
6. *Nautej Singh Johar and Others v. Union of India* (2018), para. 80.

7. Menaka Guruswamy, one of the attorneys who argued the case before the Court, explained her reliance on constitutional morality as first posited by B. R. Ambedkar: "What is constitutional morality? It is all these cases that are anticipated and adjudicated by the Supreme Court. Constitutional values are a conceptual fabric—think of it as a highly expandable fabric that you wrap yourself around with each individual instance that you bring to the court. It an expansive concept like basic structure. It will be adjudicated and applied per case. Someone asked me a while ago in an academic setting, 'You rely on Ambedkar so much'—I talk about [his work], I've quoted him extensively when I write—'Why is that?' The reason is very simple: Ambedkar is timeless. I use his thoughts from the Constituent Assembly in an assortment of cases—LGBT rights, allegations of extrajudicial killings by security personnel, special police officer in Chhattisgarh"; see Arshu John, " 'The Beauty of the Constitution Is That It Compels Us to Unlearn Our Prejudices': Menaka Guruswamy Discusses the Section 377 Judgment," *Caravan: A Journal of Politics and Culture,* September 10, 2018, https://caravanmagazine.in/gender-sexuality/menaka-guruswamy-discusses-section-377-judgment.
8. *Nautej Singh Johar and Others v. Union of India,* para. 114.
9. Ibid., para. 123.
10. Ibid., para. 95.
11. John C. Calhoun, *Disquisition on Government: And, a Discourse on the Constitution and Government of the United States* (Charleston, S.C.: Steam Power-Press of Walker and James, 1851), 300.
12. Gregory P. Downs, "Why the Second American Revolution Deserves as Much Attention as the First," *Washington Post,* July 19, 2017.
13. Abraham Lincoln, "Speech on the Dred Scott Decision," June 26, 1857, in Lincoln, *Speeches and Writings, 1832–1858* (New York: Library of America, 1989), 400.
14. Abraham Lincoln, "First Inaugural Address," in Lincoln, *Speeches and Writings, 1859–1865* (New York: Library of America, 1989), 230–31.
15. Consider in this regard Paul Kahn's slightly different take on this: "Without a successful constitutional product, revolution is unsuccessful. Indeed, without a constitution, what looked like revolution was not really revolution at all. The states that joined the Confederacy did not have a revolution. Rather, they engaged in an illegal act of rebellion. We know this because their project of constitutional creation failed"; see Paul W. Kahn, *The Cultural Study of Law: Reconstructing Legal Scholarship* (Chicago: University of Chicago Press, 1999), 48.
16. See Mark A. Graber, *Dred Scott and the Problem of Constitutional Evil* (New York: Cambridge University Press, 2006).
17. The multifaceted settlement imposed by congressional Republicans on the South remains a source of intense scholarly disputation. It is hard to ignore the conclusion of a leading chronicler of the period: "The general verdict of historians is that Republicans failed to achieve their goals in Reconstruction"; see Michael Les Benedict, *Preserving the Constitution: Essays on Politics and the Constitution in the Reconstruction Era* (New York: Fordham University Press, 2006), 168. That conclusion seems sensible given the sorry state of racial justice in 1877, yet a longer view,

emphasizing "the enduring changes in the laws and Constitution that fundamentally altered federal-state relations and redefined the meaning of American citizenship," leads one to the safer assessment that "historians have yet to produce a coherent account of [Reconstruction]"; see Eric Foner, *Reconstruction: America's Unfinished Revolution, 1863–1877* (New York: Harper Perennial, 2014), xvii.

18. Joseph A. Montagna, "The Industrial Revolution," Yale–New Haven Teachers Institute, http://teachersinstitute.yale.edu/curriculum/units/1981/2/81.02.06.x.html.
19. "Will it be sufficient to mark, with precision, the boundaries of these departments, in the constitution of the government, and to trust to these parchment barriers against the encroaching spirit of power?": James Madison, *Federalist* 48, in *The Federalist*, ed. George W. Carey and James McClellan, Gideon Edition (1818; Indianapolis: Liberty Fund, 2001), 256.
20. *Southwest Case*, 1 BverfGE 14 (1951).
21. Sanford Levinson, "The Continuing Specter of Popular Sovereignty and National Self-Determination in an Age of Political Uncertainty," in Mark A. Graber, Sanford Levinson, and Mark Tushnet, eds., *Constitutional Democracy in Crisis?* (Oxford: Oxford University Press, 2018), 651.

INDEX